THE LONG ROAD
TO FREEDOM

ALSO BY WALTER LAQUEUR

Communism and Nationalism in the Middle East, 1956

The Soviet Union and the Middle East, 1959

Young Germany, 1962

Russia and Germany, 1966

The Road to War, 1967

Europe Since Hitler, 1970

A History of Zionism, 1972

Weimar, 1975

Guerrilla, 1976

Terrorism, 1977

The Missing Years, 1980

The Terrible Secret, 1981

The Fate of the Revolution, Revised and Updated, 1987

Walter Laqueur

THE LONG ROAD
TO FREEDOM

Russia and *Glasnost*

Charles Scribner's Sons

·

NEW YORK

Charles Scribner's Sons
Macmillan Publishing Company
866 Third Avenue, New York, NY 10022

Library of Congress Cataloging-in-Publication Data
Laqueur, Walter, 1921–
The long road to freedom: Russia and Glasnost/by Walter Laqueur.
p. cm.
ISBN 0-684-19030-3
1. Soviet Union—Politics and government—1982– 2. Soviet Union—
Intellectual life—20th century. 3. Soviet Union—Economic
conditions—1976– 4. Soviet Union—Social conditions—1970–
I. Title.
DK288.L37   1989   88-39263
947.085—dc19   CIP

Macmillan books are available at special discounts for bulk purchases
for sales promotions, premiums, fund-raising, or educational use.
For details, contact:

Special Sales Director
Macmillan Publishing Company
866 Third Avenue
New York, NY 10022

10 9 8 7 6 5 4 3 2 1

Designed by Jack Meserole

Printed in the United States of America

For Naomi

CONTENTS

PREFACE

This book deals with the new political style and the new mood which have emerged in the Soviet Union since Mikhail Gorbachev's appointment as the secretary general of the Communist Party. I am concerned also with the fascinating information that has come to light on Soviet society and culture, on the way the system is run and how its citizens feel, topics on which much more is now known as the result of the phenomenon called *glasnost*. After years of almost unrelieved boredom Moscow has become the most intriguing capital in the world. The Soviet Union is in a state of ferment, and the fact that it is impossible to say how long the age of revelations will last and how far it will go only adds to the excitement.

My starting point is nineteenth-century Russia, and I conclude with some speculations on developments likely to take place in the years to come. I have been interested in things Russian for a long time, and I found it difficult to refrain from occasional reflections on the course of Soviet history. The right place for such comment is, I believe, within a discussion of various aspects of *glasnost* and its results so far. The details which have emerged will keep the experts busy for years to come, and many specialized studies will have to be written or rewritten. But it is not too early to draw an interim balance sheet.

Is it possible to write about *glasnost* without dealing at the same time with its consequences, namely the political and economic changes that it brings? My answer is, very briefly, that while the revelations are an accomplished fact, *perestroika* is as yet largely a thing of the future. Nor do I believe that very startling changes are likely to take place in the foreseeable future. True, some Soviet leaders want to effect profound changes in the economic and social system but also by taking into account the "human factor." This, given the conditions in the Soviet Union, would amount to a cultural revolution. I am not aware of successful cultural revolutions except over a very long time or in the wake of a major disaster such as a war. There are a very few exceptions, such as the opening up of Japan under the Meiji dynasty. I do not think that the preconditions for such a revolution exist at present in the Soviet Union.

A great many revelations may as yet come, but I believe that, by and large, the further limits of *glasnost* have been reached. There could be a retreat; it seems to me unlikely that there will be significant progress beyond the parameters established by the Soviet leadership. This raises the question of whether *glasnost* can survive unless there will be substantial economic and social change. What is the use of openness unless the evils that have been correctly diagnosed are removed?

But some Soviet leaders believe that economic reforms can be achieved with only a minimum of political reform. Furthermore, Russian history shows that *glasnost* does not necessarily lead to radical political changes.

There is no more glaring, more biting document of *glasnost* in Russian literature than Gogol's comedy *The Revisor*. It is a devastating panorama of the corruption, mendacity, and servility in Russian society and of the dead hand of the bureaucracy. But censorship created no difficulties: when the play was first performed, in 1836, Tsar Nicholas I laughed long and loudly, and once he had given the sign, everyone else followed suit. Gogol was not persecuted but instead received a golden watch worth eight hundred rubles. And the state of affairs continued as before.

What is *glasnost*? I shall discourse further on the history of the concept, but to prevent misunderstandings a first comment may be called for. *Glasnost* came as a surprise to most observers of the Soviet Union, and there has been much admiration for those who have initiated a more truthful policy after many decades of official and unofficial mendacity. *Glasnost* means self-criticism; it implies that the ever-widening gap between words and deeds is admitted. Such an approach demands courage; it would undoubtedly be far easier and politically less risky to continue with the old habits. It is therefore not astonishing that there is obstinate resistance against *glasnost* inside the Soviet Union. Nor is its future assured in view of the many vested interests opposing it.

But *glasnost,* however intrinsically important, is an approach, a style; it is not the substance of Soviet politics. This has frequently been misunderstood in the West, especially with regard to foreign policy. Time and again it has been asked why the Soviet leadership continued or adopted a certain policy even though, as Western observers saw it, it contradicted *glasnost*. The short answer is that *glasnost per se* does not aim at basic, structural changes in the Soviet system and has nothing to do with the aims of Soviet foreign policy. It wants to make the system work better, more efficiently. There has been a certain amount of "new thinking" (another of the new key words) on foreign policy which may lead eventually to radical change. But this, in any case, is not *glasnost*.

For the Russian intelligentsia *glasnost* is a spiritual event of enormous importance, a breath of fresh air after decades of stifling censorship. (The very word "spiritual"—*dukhovny*—has had a re-naissance in recent years.) For many other Russians it is an impor-tant device to let off steam, to give vent to their frustrations. But the majority seem more interested in better housing and food supplies than in cultural freedom. There has been, I suspect, greater enthusiasm and also greater expectations with regard to *glasnost* in the West; the very word is used more often (and far more indiscriminately) here than in the East. This is not surprising; Russians know better than foreigners that there have been many false dawns in the history of their country. Misunderstandings concerning the character of *glasnost* and exaggerated expectations about its scope and prospects may lead to disappointment in the West once the element of novelty has worn off. *Glasnost* might be slowed down or halted, debates can be stopped, new revelations forbidden. And yet the impact of the words of truth on millions of people should not be belittled.

Glasnost has been an enormous step forward in comparison with the dismal state of affairs that prevailed before. But the coun-try has as yet a long way to go toward true political and cultural freedom.[1] One example which has nothing to do with either high politics or high culture should suffice. Moscow, as everyone knows, is the beloved capital of Russia. Its praises have been sung by every Russian poet since Pushkin, its manifest destiny stressed by Dostoyevski and many others. One would expect there to be a guidebook providing names and addresses of institutions and individuals as well as a workable map for such a great city, but this is not the case. There was such a guidebook *(Vsya Moskva)* around the turn of the century and there were such maps; ironically,

[1]A Soviet writer recently noted that "the word freedom almost disappeared from our dictionary" (Nikolai Popov, *Sovetskaia Kultura*, January 28, 1988).

they were published by an editor of the far right, A. S. Suvorin. These were substantial, well-produced volumes of fifteen hundred pages. They included names, addresses, telephone numbers, and detailed maps. After the revolution there was a similar, more modest work of reference which still gave some names and addresses: readers who wanted to dial Stalin's office were advised to use the number 1–72–69. This book ceased to appear in 1937. The only present work of reference is the Moscow telephone directory, which appears once every five years, is half the size of Suvorin's guide, and is not available in Moscow's hotels. The last issue appeared in the summer of 1987; it does not even give the address of the Presidium of the Supreme Soviet reception office though every Soviet citizen knows that it is located at the corner of Marx and Kalinin avenues. Many scientific institutes and factories are not listed at all, not to mention more sensitive offices, even though some of them through newspapers and billboards all over Moscow advertise their location. Nor is there a proper map listing the streets of Moscow, although, as a Soviet newspaper recently noted, this lack will not hinder foreign intelligence services who by means of aerial photography can watch not only buildings but the cars in the streets. However, it makes it extremely difficult for Muscovites to find their way to a street which they have not visited before.[2]

In short, a great deal of *glasnost* is still needed even in basic affairs of daily life, and I do not feel particularly optimistic with regard to the further progress of freedom in the Soviet Union at this time. The champions of *glasnost* have gone, I suspect, as far as they feel they can go for the time being. It is easier to be more hopeful with regard to the distant future. In ten or twenty years, with the rise of yet another generation, there could be a new initiative to take *glasnost* beyond its present limits.

Whatever the immediate political prospects for *glasnost,* there is no denying that the Soviet Union has become a far more interesting country than in the past. A leading Russian intellectual of the 1840s relates in his autobiography that he and his friends would hire a carriage to intercept the mail coach on its way from Smolensk. These young men were so fascinated with the philosophical discussions then proceeding in Berlin that they simply could not wait for the arrival of the most recent German periodicals carrying

---

[2]*Moskovskaia Pravda,* December 28, 1987; *Vsya Moskva,* Moscow, 1900; Karl Schloegel, *Moskau lesen,* Berlin, 1984, pp. 101–12. According to a recent Moscow newspaper report, even the telephone numbers of some kindergartens are still unlisted for security reasons.

essays by Schelling and other luminaries; they had to stage a philosophical holdup. Little did I expect that after the utter boredom
of decades I would come one day to await with similar impatience
the arrival of the most recent products of *glasnost* as I stood in line
in front of the kiosks of Soyuzpechat, which continued to have the
monopoly for the sale of the Soviet press. Such exciting periods
of intellectual ferment do not continue forever, but one ought to
be grateful while they last.

The story of *glasnost* is by and large the account of the revelations of shortcomings and failures in the recent history of the
Soviet Union. This must have come as a shock to those who accepted the announcements of the previous rulers of the country
according to which Soviet society was perfect, or, at the very least,
the most perfect in the world. A study of *glasnost* has, of necessity,
to put much of the emphasis on these negative revelations. But
there is yet another aspect of *glasnost* which should not be forgotten and which I hope to relate one day in another book. The
struggle for *glasnost* does not begin on the day when the green light
was given from above. It certainly received a great new momentum
in 1985, but if *glasnost* became an age of hope it was mainly owing
to the men and women, old and young, who had gone through a
hard school and were waging an uphill struggle against the forces
of inertia and darkness. Even after 1985 it was a battle fraught with
some danger; it is always more popular to spread pious lies than
the bitter, painful truth. The men and women in the front rank of
the struggle for *glasnost* have shown talent and valor uncommon in
any age and not that frequent in our days among the Western
intelligentsia. They personify what is great and noble in the tradition of Russian culture. Their contribution to the history of the
freedom of the human spirit is all the more admirable because the
odds against them were heavy and the outcome of their struggle
uncertain.

If it would still be the custom as it was a hundred years ago to have
an envoy for a book of this kind I would have wavered whether to
opt for Horace's *Semel emissum volat irrevocabile verbum* or for Vergil's
Carpent tua poma nepotes. The former, in rough translation, means
that once a word has been allowed to escape it can not be recalled,
the other "your descendants shall gather your fruits." Both seem
applicable to the *glasnost* phenomenon.

I am grateful for the help I received in my work from the Lynde and Harry Bradley Foundation, Milwaukee, and the Earhart Foundation, Ann Arbor, and I owe a debt of gratitude to Janusz Bugajski, my friend and associate at CSIS, Washington, D.C., as well as to my research assistants Jeanette Bezemer, Adriana Ercolano, Monika Michejda, Ilinca Popescu, and Alina Zyszkowski, whose enthusiasm was matched only by their competence.

Washington, D.C.
December 1988

THE LONG ROAD
TO FREEDOM

CHAPTER 1

A Monologue in Moscow

WHITHER RUSSIA? *Kamo gradeshi,* in the words of the Russian Church liturgy. The answer once seemed clear: it was one of the most predictable countries, but it is so no longer.

There is much to see in Moscow these days, more to talk about and, above all, to read. Russia is on the move again. Or is it just talk on the need to move? Soon after Stalin's death a short story was published, banned after publication, but now resurrected and frequently quoted. "Say openly what's wrong. The people will move mountains for a straight word."[1] But will they?

Whither the Soviet Union? The question has been asked for a long time and now more often than ever. In other parts of the world the fate of nations has been compared to a ship ("Sail on, O ship of State . . ."), but Russia is a giant land mass and the standard image for a long time has been the troika:

And you, my Russia, are you not speeding along like a troika which no one can overtake? Is not the road smoking beneath your wheels, the bridges thundering as you cross them and everything is left behind and the spectators struck by the portent, stopping to wonder whether you're not a thunderbolt launched from heaven? What unknown force lies hidden in your mysterious steeds? . . .

Whither are you speeding on, my Russia? Whither? Answer me! But no answer comes. For you are overtaking the whole world and one day you will force all nations, all empires, to stand aside and give you way. . . . (Gogol)

[1] Alexander Yashin, *Rychagi* [The levers], *Literaturnaia Moskva,* Vol. 2, 1956; reprinted in *Nedelia,* 20, 1987.

It is a wonderful parable, but how little does it correspond to reality. The road is no longer smoking under its wheels and the bridges are not thundering; few stop to wonder; the horses have been unharnessed and the *iamshik,* the coachman, is not to be seen. Perhaps he has gotten drunk again in a nearby tavern. True, the spectators have become accustomed to sudden spasms of hectic activity. With great fanfare the troika is racing forward only to retreat later on, to stop, or continue the race in a circle.

Gorbachev wrote in *Perestroika* that one of the mightiest powers in the world has risen up to replace the backward, semi-colonial and semi-feudal empire. Who would deny it? Enormous industrial complexes now exist, even though some are already a little out-dated. Virtually everyone is now literate, and the armed forces are strong and feared. But would this not have happened under *any* political regime slightly more dynamic than that of the Tsar? Russia was the world's strongest military power for a long time; in the 1750s the Russians conquered Berlin if they had and could have stayed there, and in 1814 they were, after all, in Paris. Russia's gross national product before the First World War was about one half that of America, and the same is still true today. The Far Eastern rickshas have sped ahead more quickly than the Russian troika. The faces of the people in the metro, the busses, and the restaurants do not radiate happiness. What is causing the sullen-ness and the discontent?

Recently I read the impressions of a British traveler:

Russia is a country with a disagreeable climate, an arid summer produc-ing uncertain harvests which sometimes result in starvation, an intoler-able long winter, a damp and unhealthy spring and a still more unhealthy autumn; a country in which there are next to no decent roads; where the provincial towns are overgrown villages, squalid, squatting, dismal, de-void of natural beauty and unredeemed by art; where the cost of living is high and the expense of life is out of proportion to the quality of goods supplied; where labor is dear, bad and slow; where the sanitary conditions in which the great mass of the population live are deplorable; where every kind of disease, including plague, are rampant; where medical aid and appliances are inadequate; where the poor people are backward and ignorant and the middle class slack and slovenly; and where progress is deliberately checked and impeded in every possible way; a country gov-erned by chance where all forms of administration are arbitrary, uncer-tain and dilatory; where all forms of business are cumbersome and bur-dened with red tape; where bribery is an indispensable factor in business and administrative life; a country burdened by a vast official population which is on the whole lazy, venal and incompetent; a country where political liberty and the elementary rights of citizenship do not exist; where even the programs of concerts are censored; where freedom of conscience is hampered; where everybody acts regardless of his neighbor; a country of extremes, of moral laxity and extravagant self-indulgence; looking upon all individuals' originality and distinction with suspicion; a people jealous of anything or anyone who emerges from the ranks and rises superior to the average; a people slavish to the dead level of mediocrity and the stereotyped bureaucratic pattern; a nation of ineffectual rebels. . . .[2]

These are harsh words, forgiven to a native son, never to a foreigner. The indictment was written before the revolution, and the author concluded in an optimistic vein, murmuring: "*Doux pays,* I admit all that and in spite of it Russia has for me an indescribable fascination. In spite of all that, I love the country and admire and respect the people."

This is the case for the defense. It rests on faith, on Tyutchev's *"v Rossii mozhno tolko verit."*[3] As Turgenev wrote Alexander Herzen when his friend engaged for a while in Slavophile dreams: "You are like a physician who has diagnosed a serious illness in a patient but who still insists that the patient will recover because he is a Russian or a Frenchman, or something else. . . ."

Was Herzen right? Or Turgenev? What country can be rationally understood? Foreigners have almost always seen either the best or the worst of Russia, and frequently their judgment has been wrong. Some have denied Russia all genius, original thought, any depth of thought and emotion. Victor Hehn lived among the Russians for forty years and spoke the language like a native. But he wrote that all Russians were congenital liars, that Pushkin was a poor man's Byron. He did not even like their lifeless skin and brutal faces. Russians, he wrote, lacked the gift of putting two and two together; no Russian, for instance, was able to become a railway engine driver.[4] Hehn would have been greatly surprised by the cosmonauts.

[2]Maurice Baring, *The Mainspring of Russia,* London, 1914, pp. 312 et seq. Baring (1873–1945) was a distinguished Oxford don, the translator of Russian poetry and prose, and editor of the *Oxford Book of Russian Verse.*
[3]The last line of a famous quatrain: "Russia cannot rationally be understood . . . one has to believe in Russia."
[4]Victor Hehn, *De moribus Ruthenorum,* Berlin, 1892. Hehn (1813–1890) was a Russian-born archivist and cultural historian who late in life moved to Germany.

Culture for Hehn was German culture, and the Russians could of course not compete with Kant and Hegel and Schelling. But neither did Russian culture produce Adolf Hitler. Russian history is sad and full of disasters. But there have been few other people speaking with equal ruthlessness about the wretchedness of Russian society, about the consequences of despotism, about the absence of spontaneity, the fact that everything was imposed from above. This critique began with Cha'adayev and Gogol, not with the Westerners. The authorities wanted to put Cha'adayev into a lunatic asylum for writing that Russia had given nothing to the world, that it had not added anything to the sum total of human ideas. Can one name a more relentless critic of the state of Russia than Herzen, he who predicted that if the despotism continued for another hundred years all the good qualities of the Russian people would be gone? Or Chekhov, who wrote that he did not know one honest man in his native Taganrog? Surely he exaggerated. Even Custine wrote, "Fundamentally they judge their country more harshly than I." They knew the worst about themselves, they did not need foreigners for this purpose. They know that "the main heritage of our accursed past was not at all capitalism (which never succeeded in developing in Russia) but serfdom *(krepostnichestvo)*. This is deeply buried in the hearts, souls and pores of people, and without understanding this, much in our national character cannot be understood."[5] One should therefore not belittle a movement—*glasnost*—which makes such painful introspection possible.

Glasnost has proved that the spirit of liberty is not dead in Russia. It has also shown that among its present-day advocates are men and women of integrity, cultural substance, and sophistication. Where did they come from? Whence their erudition, acumen, analytical power, emotional force? For those accustomed to the cultural sterility and the abysmally primitive level of the Stalin era and the Brezhnev age, the writings of these last years have certainly come as a great surprise. They have shown that underneath the barren surface a cultural tradition continued to exist in Russia and that its spokesmen have little to learn from the West. A thinking Russian, Herzen once wrote, is the most independent being on earth. One could add perhaps that because of his long suffering he is superior in some respects to the Western intelligentsia, less

[5]Georgi Kunitsyn, *Literaturnaia Rossia,* February 26, 1988.

likely to be preoccupied with fads and pseudo-problems, more aware of the essential issues of our time.

Foreigners have written harsh things about Russia and this has angered the Russians. But Russia *was* a backward country; what Fletcher, Herberstein, or Olearius wrote about Russian manners and customs in the sixteenth and seventeenth centuries about religion, secrecy, and absolute power was not much exaggerated. They were truthful observers.

But the foreigners were by no means all hostile. The German J. C. Kohl, not a philosopher but the author of guidebooks almost 150 years ago, was one of the first to write with affection about the *chorny narod,* the great mass of the unwashed. The men and women who appeared at first glance repulsive, dirty, and noisy were, he wrote in 1842, kind, courteous to one another, and not at all servile. Even the Russian rogues had a romantic integrity; even Russian cheating was done with adroitness and elegance. It was difficult to be angry with them.[6] Kohl noted that Russians consumed incredible quantities of alcohol but there were no Hogarthian scenes in Russia. And he reached the conclusion that the consequences of both despotism and alcohol were less depraving in Russia than elsewhere. He quoted Voltaire, who, at the age of eighty, wrote that if coffee was indeed a poison, it was a very slow one.

Russians are tough. What other people would have survived the Tartars, Tsarism, Stalinism, and countless other afflictions? Others might have suffocated but as Herzen wrote, reviewing Custine, "Our lungs are stronger." Is it not a sign of strength and honesty if they now talk openly about their weaknesses? We ought to keep things in perspective if we hear about the consequences of alcoholism and drugs and the decline of family ties. More than a hundred years ago Hehn predicted that in a few generations the Russian people would be decimated as the result of alcoholism. But it has not been decimated yet, and the social cost of alcoholism in America, more than a hundred billion dollars, is also not negligible.

One can think of other mitigating circumstances, but this is not of much comfort to the Soviet leaders who once believed in the superiority of their system. For decades they claimed and perhaps

[6]J. C. Kohl, *Russia,* London, 1842.

truly believed that the West was decadent and doomed; the presence of social evils in the West cannot serve as an excuse for Soviet failures. Seventy years after the revolution, a new kind of human being, *homo Sovieticus,* should have emerged, superior in every respect to the decadent West. Where is that new species? In 1950 the Soviets claimed to have formed it, and again in 1970, but just now it can nowhere be seen. I found an analysis, astute but painful, in one of the journals, and not even by one of the main advocates of *glasnost:* "Let us assume," writes Antonov,

that a prosperous Western businessman visits our country encountering almost 300 million human beings who have perfected their talents so that they have become like Pushkin, Glinka or Lomonossov. Human relations are based on consideration, mutual esteem and help, goodness and a competition in generosity rather than the chase of material goods. In such a case the outcome of the competition between the two systems would be obvious, and not a single shot need be fired. Nor would it be necessary to make an all-out effort to increase the output of goods in our economy. But this, alas, we never understood. Our attitude to culture—in the widest sense—was, that if we had it, well and good, but if there was no culture, one could also manage for the time being.[7]

Many of the early revolutionary dreams have faded. In a recent novel describing the life, thoughts, and emotions of the young enthusiasts building the Moscow metro in the 1930s, the following conversation takes place:

MARGARITA: Do you think we shall have Communism in ten years?
MITYA: *aged seventeen, but already head of a shock-workers brigade:* No, earlier, first in Moscow, then in the rest of the country. . . .[8]

These were the noble dreams, but human nature does not change in a few decades; perhaps it does not change at all. There has been no real cultural revolution and there is none in sight. There has been a tremendous gap between ambitions and realities: Russian radicals have dreamed of world revolution, and Russian conservatives have invoked the idea of a third Rome and quoted Dostoyevski on Russia's universal destiny. A great price has been paid for these dreams, and what has been achieved?

True, there was much promise; as Tyutchev said about his native country, "Alas, so much dirt and so much promise." Not only the believers in a Russian manifest destiny shared his view;

[7]M. Antonov, *Literaturnaia Rossia,* July 29, 1987.
[8]Serge Antonov, *Vaska . . . Yunost,* 1987, pp. 3–4.

Alexander Herzen, too, was a staunch believer in Russian largesse *(shirokaia natura)*. He always stressed the fact that in the Russian character there was something which united the best qualities of the French and the Germans. He firmly believed that Russia had the greatest democratic potential and the chance of a more brilliant future than other nations.

Whither Russia? Do we face a replay of the old controversy between Westerners and Slavophiles? Some Russian historians, including Plekhanov, the founding father of Russian Marxism, regarded all of Russian history in the light of this dispute. But today there is not much enthusiasm in Russia for the fellow Slavs, Poles, Czechs, Yugoslavs, and other ingrates. There has been a new search for roots, but it is limited to the Russian past and traditions. As for the "Westerners," there is an abiding interest in many things Western, but it is cultural and social rather than political. No one in his right mind proposes to transfer Western political doctrines and institutions to the Soviet Union. No one believes that parliamentary democracy could work in Russia in the foreseeable future.

Does it mean a return to autocracy, back to the princes of Kiev who invited a ruler from abroad? ("Our country is great and abundant but there is no order in it—come and rule over us!") Does it mean a revival of the nineteenth-century conservatives, preaching absolute trust in the Tsar, high priest and king at the same time, claiming that even the crimes of the rulers had to be suffered like a scourge sent by God? The recent defense of Stalin's crimes is in the same tradition; while regrettable and unforgivable, they have to be accepted because there was no alternative. Russia, it is argued, is not Europe, and perhaps it is unpromising ground for freedom and popular sovereignty.

Among other things, *glasnost* has given the Soviet reader for the first time the works of Karamzin, the earliest great Russian historian. He is still topical, describing how Ivan IV for amusement cut off the ear of one of his army commanders, who did not express indignation but thanked the Tsar for his charity: "Such was the Tsar, such were his people. Should we be more surprised at him or at them? If he excelled in torture, they excelled in patience."

Karamzin relates how Russia experienced the terror of autocrats, how she endured them with love for autocracy because she believed that God sends plagues and earthquakes and tyrants; how the sufferers were dying on the scaffolds with generous humility for their fatherland, for faith and loyalty without even a thought of mutiny.

The belief that God sends the plague and earthquakes has been eradicated, but tyrants are still given the benefit of the doubt. Basic instincts do not easily change; the Russians never respected and loved democracy as they respected and loved autocracy. As Ambassador Sukovski told the foreigners who came to Moscow and wondered about Ivan IV: "We are always devoted to our Tsars, kind or cruel." Perhaps they came to respect the cruel more than the kind. Democratization has been the slogan under Gorbachev but democracy does not work unless there are sufficient democrats, as the Germans found out to their detriment after 1918. The Russians have many sterling qualities but they are not strong on self-discipline and independent action. The idea of history as the unfolding story of freedom has not grown on Russian soil. Democracy is based on the willingness to compromise, on common sense and tolerance, of which there has been no surfeit in Russian history. As one of the thinkers of *glasnost,* an economist and novelist, recently wrote:

Sobriety, moderation, common sense were never popular in Russia; somehow or other our people are always in search of a holy idea and everything was subordinated to its pursuit: It was all or nothing. We need neither progress nor prosperity, not charity nor human conditions of life if they derive from the head rather than the heart. We rather burn together with some new Avakuum—for any fairy tale, for any hope if it originated with some holy fool, if it has to do with the next world rather than this.[9]

The Russian genius has not been in democratic politics; it may change, but not soon. Too much freedom makes many Russians feel uncomfortable; do we want them to feel that way?

Does the Soviet Union face another long period of authoritarian-bureaucratic rule based on some kind of nationalist-socialist ideology, with a minority of intellectuals valiantly (and ineffectually) raising the banner of freedom? The old Slavophiles were eccentrics, their ideas of Russia's past illusory and their hopes for its future wishful thinking. But their rejection of the West was based

[9]Nikolai Shmelyev, *Pashkov Dom, Novy Mir,* 6, 1987, p. 105. Avakuum, head of the sect of the Old Believers opposing church reforms, was burned with other heretics in 1682.

on profound knowledge; they knew their Schiller and German philosophy better than most Germans and some of them expressed themselves as well in French as in Russian. Who of their descendants would have the courage to say (as Cha'adayev did) that he has not "learned to love his fatherland with his eyes shut, forehead bowed and mouth closed"? Today's Russophiles do not know the West and most are not very eager to learn more about it. Westernism, as far as they are concerned, is rock music (which they detest) and a sinister, giant conspiracy against Russia and all things Russian. One detects a strong odor of *kvasni* patriotism, of Okhotny Ryad, of the ideas of the Black Hundred.[10]

Back in the last century Alexander Herzen noted that the "stifling atmosphere and dumbness of Russian life, curiously combined with its vitality and rumbustious character, provoke all sorts of crackpot outbursts in our midst." There are supporters of the extreme right in every country; America has them, Europe has them. It would be unnatural if such groups did not exist in Russia. It would be doubly unnatural if they did not appear now that the old ideology is disintegrating. In 1917, with the victory of Marxism, the triumph of Westernism over its opponents seemed to be total. For many years since, the pendulum has been swinging back. Internationalism is still invoked on occasion but it is no longer in fashion. It is too close to "cosmopolitanism," which is thought to be very sinful.

Most Slavophiles of the nineteenth century were not conservatives but knew that Russia's present condition was intolerable and a return to the past impossible. The Russophiles of our days are also aware that the old Russian village and all connected with it have gone forever and cannot be resurrected. Some of them have been merciless in describing the present state of Soviet life and manners. Much as they dislike the "aliens"—those of non-Russian birth—in the Soviet Union, they do not spare their own kin.

There is much *kvasni* patriotism, but there is also self-criticism. Without the Russian ecologists, mainly of the right, the systematic damage to the environment would have been greater. They were among the main advocates of the campaign against alcoholism; what they say about the decline of family ties and its consequences is not all wrong. Their views about rock music and pop culture are

[10]Kvasni: after the slightly alcoholic Russian drink, usually made of bread. Okhotny Ryad: formerly a street in Moscow, the meat market, known as the bulwark of the most reactionary petty bourgeois militants, sympathizers of the extreme right.

shared by critics in the West. They know more or less what kind of Russia—and Russians—they dislike: modernism, liberalism, big-city life, bureaucracy, Jews, a permissive society, and the omnipresent Freemasons. They have some vague ideas about a moral and cultural revival, but they don't know how to set about it. They are intolerant and incline toward hysteria, and hysteria in politics can be dangerous. The main dangers, as they see it, are the "sinister forces" inside Russia and abroad, practicing Russophobia? When Gorbachev visited Washington in December 1987, he was wined and dined like no Russian leader before him; "Moscow Nights" was sung in the White House, people wore "I love Gorby" T-shirts, and a Café Glasnost was opened. And just then the Russophiles uttered dire warnings about the deep, burning, all-consuming Russophobia of "our eternal enemy." Ridicule in Russia does not kill.

There are overexcited people in every society, and perhaps one should not take the political *obiter dicta* of writers of fiction too seriously. They have some influence but they do not make Soviet policy. This is a multinational empire, and the Russian nationalists with, perhaps, a few exceptions, have no wish to dismember it. And would it be progress if an independent Turkmenistan and Tadjikistan would arise? In any case, the bureaucracy will not let them. A high admission fee was paid to the exclusive club of the superpowers and they do not want to lose it just for the sake of ethnic purity.

An official doctrine is still needed, a set of beliefs to provide legitimacy to the regime. What is it going to be? Old style Marxism-Leninism has become a ritual and a bit of a laughingstock. In Aitmatov's *Plakha (The Execution Block)* there appears a party journalist, the "newspaper Kishi," who talks like an editorial from *Pravda.* He speaks incessantly about socialism and the party. But no one listens to him, people refer to him with a smile, he is the village idiot. True, some of the tenets of Marxism-Leninism have entered the bloodstream of the system, even if they are a little less every year, even if they look more and more like populism. Meanwhile the liberals have invoked Lenin for more than two decades whenever they wanted to smuggle in some dissenting idea: Lenin as the enemy of the bureaucracy and of *meshanstvo,* [11] Lenin as the

[11]Herzen first defined *meshanstvo* as a state of mind characterized by lack of creativity, lack of new ideas and ideals, narrow-mindedness, and the habit of uttering platitudes.

great pragmatist, Lenin as the advocate of freedom of speech and cultural freedom.

It is ideological warfare by proxy. When the conservatives attack Trotsky, they often mean Lenin and his generation with their radical ideas about two Russian cultures, one progressive, the other reactionary and to be rejected. If Lenin had had better judgment, he would never have collaborated with Trotsky, the anti-Russian cosmopolitan. Some even want to make Trotsky Stalin's evil genius, full of contempt for Russian traditions, providing Stalin with execrable ideas such as the collectivization of agriculture and the militarization of society. The extremists of the right also invoke the peril of Zionism. But what they really mean has nothing in common with Herzl and Weizmann, the Basel program and the state of Israel. Occasionally the cat is let out of the bag, as it was in Leningrad some time ago when one of them said, "Nothing can be changed in our country without giving up Marxism, that deeply Zionist doctrine. . . ."[12] Sophisticated speakers have put it more obscurely, but the intention is clear. One can have great fun by using Aesopian language: Under Tsarist censorship Lenin wrote on the situation in Japan, but his readers understood that he had Russia in mind. Now Lenin's ideas are given the same treatment.

Russian nationalism, pure and simple, cannot be the official doctrine of a multinational empire, and so the party leadership is stuck with Leninism at least for some time to come. Which means that a genertion is growing up (indeed, has grown up) which knows all the obligatory formulas and does not believe a word of them. They are going through a *Sinnkrise* like young generations in the West. But life goes on: There are some eighteen-odd million bosses in the Soviet Union, big bosses and small, who do not want to lose their jobs, who have a vested interest in the existence of the system. They will fight for its survival. They will think of something to provide legitimacy to the system.

Meanwhile, there are safety valves to let off steam; everyone is against the bureaucracy, open season has been declared on the bureaucrats—the harmless ones, to be sure, not those of the army, the party, or the police. This is an old habit used even by right-wing propaganda in Tsarist times. The bureaucracy, then as now,

[12]*Sovetskaia Kultura,* November 24, 1987. See also A. Kuzmin, *Nash Sovremennik,* 3, 1988, for references to the identification of Marxism and Zionism.

was figured as one of the main villains, preventing real communion between the Tsar and the people. But is it not a little risky to undermine belief in the servants of the state? As the Russian philosopher Kozma Prutkov put it, "Only in the service of the state will ye know the truth" (Aphorism 89).[13] One can put on the brakes if criticism should get out of hand. In addition, there is always that old acquaintance, the siege mentality: the bureaucrats agree with the dissidents of the right that the fatherland is in danger. The bureaucrats may not really believe it but it makes governing the country so much easier.

All this sounds very cynical, a far cry from the idealism of the old Russian intelligentsia whose struggle for freedom was an inspiration to the whole world. But this Russian intelligentsia disappeared from the face of the earth long ago. The flame of hope is still burning, but it flickers in the storm and it could be extinguished. The present upsurge may be followed by setbacks, and if a new Gogol were to arise, he would no longer invoke the image of a majestic troika rushing past awestruck pedestrians. He could well compare it with the procession in which the unfortunate participants have to retreat three steps after every four they have advanced. It is not the quickest way to make progress and it may not show striking results in our time. Our good wishes accompany the pilgrims.

Or perhaps it would be more appropriate to compare the gradual liberation from the burden of the past with the exodus from Egypt of the children of Israel. It is a precedent which has occurred to some present Soviet thinkers. The geographical distance between Egypt and Palestine is not great but it took Moses forty years to cross it and there might have been good reasons why a more rapid crossing would not have been indicated; on first impulse the wanderers in the wilderness might have turned down the Ten Commandments. Today, as more than a century ago, many freedom-loving Russians are praying:

> Lord, set your chosen followers free,
> Release them from their ancient bands,
> Entrust the flag of liberty
> At last, to Russian hands.[14]

[13]Prutkov, a satirical figure, the personification of the obedient, unquestioning bureaucrat, created by Count Aleksei Konstantinovich Tolstoi (1817–1875) and two of his cousins.
[14]Nikolai Nekrasov (1821–1877), "A Hymn." My gratitude goes to Esther Polyakovski Salaman, who many years ago translated this poem together with Francis Cornford.

However, freedom will not come as an act of God, not even of the general secretary, but only if a majority of the people want it and fight for it. And many Russians still believe, as a leading Slavophile once put it in an open letter to the Tsar, that the Russian people are not a people concerned with government, that they have no aspiration toward self-government, no desire for political rights, and not so much as a trace of lust for power.[15] It might be tempting to regard Russian history of the last 150 years as the story of liberty, but it would be far from historical truth. Today they have left serfdom behind but they are still in the wilderness, except in their noble dreams. They have seen too many false dawns but they have not abandoned hope.

[15]Konstantin Aksakov (1817–1860), "On the Internal State of Russia" (1855).

CHAPTER 2

_____

Stagnation

FTER DECADES of stagnation, Soviety society is in a
state of ferment. *Perestroika* and *glasnost, demokratisatsia*
and *uskorenie* have entered our political vocabulary just as
NEP and Sputnik did in past ages. Soviet politics have
again become interesting. Is it the second Russian revolution, as
some have proclaimed, or merely a short interval of little consequence, yet another false dawn of which there have been so many
in Russian history?

The drama began to unfold on the day in March 1985 when
Mikhail Sergeevich Gorbachev was elected first secretary of the
Communist Party of the Soviet Union. There are detailed, if not
entirely trustworthy, accounts of who voted for him, and who
against, and how the Central Committee staff was waiting with
bated breath until a messenger arrived and announced, as customary on such an occasion, *"Habemus Papam!"*; how some of those
present were overjoyed, and the others dejected because they had
put their money on the wrong horse; how Gromyko officially proposed Gorbachev as "a man of strong conviction and a sharp and
deep mind" when the Central Committee met on March 11. The
real decision had, of course, been taken by the ten members of the
Politburo well before.

Historians are never quite certain what period or event to take
as their starting point. Perhaps Brezhnev's death in November
1982, which opened the interregnum; or Khrushchev's overthrow
in October 1964; or Stalin's funeral in March 1953. A Soviet novelist describing the funeral and the state of deep shock which had

seized the masses noted the general belief that not a single man had passed away; rather, a whole historical period had come to an end. Yet at the same time there was the feeling that both the man and his heritage were still alive.[1] But novelists are no more reliable witnesses than other human beings; other eyewitnesses reported astonishing indifference among the masses and few, if any, manifestations of spontaneous mourning.[2]

But present-day Russia cannot be understood without Stalinism, and how to interpret Stalin without Lenin? Nor does Russian history begin in November 1917; in recent years it has become even more obvious than before how much of prerevolutionary Russia there is in the Soviet Union of today—thoughts, emotions, and basic attitudes. With all the violent upheavals there is no better proof than Russia that history is indeed a seamless web.

For several generations the Russian revolution and the Soviet system that evolved from it have been the central political events of this century. There was enormous interest in all things Soviet: Moscow became the Mecca of political pilgrims who returned with reports that they had seen the future—and that it worked. Many Russian books were translated and films were shown in the West, and there was great fascination with the planned economy at a time when capitalism seemed at the end of its tether. The Soviet Union seemed a giant social and cultural laboratory; all kinds of new ideas were discussed there and tried out—very much in contrast to the tired West, which seemed to have run out of initiative as well as ideas.

True, there were growing doubts as the Soviet Union turned inward in the 1930s, as most of the protagonists of the heroic period of the revolution were executed for crimes which strained the imagination of even the staunchest fellow travelers, as the Cult of the Leader assumed proportions unprecedented in the modern history of mankind. But then war came and Stalin was our ally against Hitler; in view of the enormous losses suffered by our Russian allies it would not only have been politically unwise but positively churlish to dwell at length on the shortcomings of the regime. The wartime alliance broke down and was followed in due course by the Cold War. But even in the years of tension there were not a few in the West who found mitigating circumstances

[1] P. Proskurin, *Imya Tvoe,* Kishinev, 1985, pp. 564, 575.
[2] See, for instance, R. Tucker, *The Soviet Political Mind,* New York, 1971, *passim.*

for Stalin, the house he had built, and the policies he pursued.

The main problem from the Soviet point of view in the post-Stalin era was not so much Russophobia—a phenomenon increasingly invoked in Moscow. There was little if any hatred; there was rather a steady decline of interest in things Russian. True, the Soviet Union was still a very important country about to become a superpower, and for this reason its declarations and actions were of great consequence to diplomats, generals, and chiefs of intelligence. But it had become stagnant and predictable. No new impulses emanated from Moscow; the period of cultural and social experimentation was long over.

Even foreign Communists no longer showed much interest. For Western Marxists Soviet ideology became something of an embarrassment and even in the Third World the Soviet Union was not much in demand except as an arms dealer and a political counterweight against the West. The Soviet Union, in brief, had become a conservative society. Western economists were of two minds as to what extent it had been a success or a failure, but hardly anyone thought of it as a model for the outside world except perhaps in the fields of space travel, chess, and athletics.

The fate of the Soviet revolution was different in some important respects from that of all others. Unlike the French revolution the Russian knew no Thermidor, no triumphant counterrevolution, no Napoleon. Neither was it able to develop and move forward; it became frozen, its ideology as well as its institutions ossified.

This perception of the Soviet Union as a stagnant society was by no means limited to hostile foreign observers; it reflected to a considerable extent the mood inside the country. Fewer and fewer Russians were reading new books and magazines. They still listened to the radio, and watched movies and television simply because no other entertainment existed. Mass culture drew its inspiration from the West, from jeans to rock music. In later years a member of the Politburo was to describe the boredom of the period as follows:

The administrative braking mechanism led to serious shortcomings within culture itself. Personal prejudice, unthinking bans and manifestation of cliquishness started to give Soviet people a certain distrust of anything offered in the form of spiritual sustenance. Print runs of newspapers and magazines fell. Audiences no longer went to the theater; this was covered up by the enforced distribution of tickets and subsidies. They did not go to the movies; this was covered up by machinations in reports. Many artistically mediocre or morally false works received high awards.[3]

The story of how Nikita Khrushchev emerged as the most powerful figure in the Soviet hierarchy within three years after Stalin's death has been told many times. He had been a member of the Politburo for more than ten years but was probably the least-known member of the leadership and for this reason the most underrated, a man of many contradictions: semi-educated yet of great native shrewdness, an old Bolshevik in the traditional mold yet an ardent reformer, an impulsive man who genuinely wanted to break with Stalinism, who clearly analyzed the crucial issues facing Soviet society at the time, but who was too much a child of the system to envisage and carry out lasting changes.

Yet with all his harebrained schemes Khrushchev has entered Soviet history as a liberating influence, and it was not an accident that having been turned into a nonperson during the Brezhnev era he was more fondly remembered under Gorbachev.

Khrushchev gave a strong impetus to de-Stalinization with his sensational speech at the Twentieth Congress (1956) and again at the Twenty-second, in the face of much opposition by the conservative old guard (the "antiparty group" of Molotov, Kaganovitch, and others). Many—but by no means all—of Stalin's Communist victims were rehabilitated, including all marshals and generals but only two or three marginal figures from among the accused in the Moscow show trials. Soviet and Communist Party history was rewritten in a more truthful way, but only a small part of the truth was revealed. Of these revelations, not a few were later retracted under Brezhnev. Khrushchev wanted to rehabilitate Bukharin and the "right-wing opposition" of the late 1920s but again retreated facing opposition. A commission was appointed under Khrushchev to investigate the circumstances of the murder in 1934 of Kirov, the second most important leader after Stalin at the time. There is reason to assume that Stalin was involved in this assassination but the findings of the commission were never made public. Stalin's coffin was removed from the Lenin mausoleum after the Twenty-second Party Congress, but Stalin's spirit was by no means

[3]N. A. Yakovlev, speech in Kaluga, *Sovetskaia Kultura,* July 21, 1987.

exorcised. Even Khrushchev proclaimed on many occasions over the years that Stalin had been a great leader and organizer who had enormous merits as far as the building of a socialist society was concerned. The changes which took place under Khrushchev can be summarized as follows:

1. Most, though not all, political prisoners were released and some of the nationalities exiled under Stalin to Central Asia were permitted to return. Not all regained their previous status as autonomous republics or regions.

2. Laws were introduced and promulgated which improved the legal position of urban workers, increased pensions and minimum wages, limited working hours, reformed social security, and discontinued the obligatory loans which Soviet citizens had to give to the state under Stalin.

3. Khrushchev's educational reforms gave preference to those who had already held a job in industry, agriculture, or some other field.

4. Khrushchev tried to combat embezzlement, bribe-taking, parasitism, and corruption, although these measures were applied in a haphazard and ineffective way; death sentences were carried out against offenders who were not well-connected. The new militia (the Druzhini) founded to help the police was either ineffective or, in some cases, terrorized the population.

5. Khrushchev initiated a great many economic reforms, but his main interest was in practical details; he had no overall concept, and the changes he introduced, even if positive, lacked cohesion and consistency. He spent about a third of his time on travels inside the Soviet Union and abroad. He got easily excited by innovations and new ideas and would rashly try to apply them even if they were not generally applicable. His impetuosity and exaggerated optimism led him to foolish predictions—e.g., the Soviet Union would catch up and overtake the most developed Western nations such as the United States in output and productivity within the next ten to fifteen years. These predictions were incorporated in the new party program—and this at a time when Japan and the EEC were making faster progress than the Soviet Union. There was a substantial upturn in the Soviet economy in 1958–59, but the momentum could not be sustained.

6. One of the major issues confronting Khrushchev (as his successors) was the dismal performance of agriculture. All kinds of grandiose schemes were introduced, including the development of virgin lands in Asia, the drastic reduction of the number of villages, and the introduction of new work methods. Only a few of these innovations proved effective. Khrushchev's concern with agriculture was so deep that shortly before his downfall he tried to reorganize the Communist

Party and the state apparatus into industrial and agricultural sectors. These ill-conceived measures were later discontinued.

7. Under Khrushchev the Communist Party regained its preponderant role vis-à-vis the state apparatus and the political police it had lost under Stalin. The old leaders were ousted one by one: the removal of the "antiparty group" was followed by the "resignation" of Bulganin (1958) and Voroshilov (1960) as well as the ouster of Marshal Zhukov, who had played a crucial role in bringing Khrushchev to power. At a decisive showdown in 1957 there had been a seven-to-four majority in the Politburo against Khrushchev. He responded by convoking the Central Committee in which he had majority support. Seven years later his enemies were to use similar tactics against him.

On the whole, norms of behavior became more civilized under Khrushchev. None of those ousted from the leadership were arrested, let alone executed. Beria was the exception, and the charges against him (that he had been a British spy) were in the best Stalinist tradition. But the purge of the KGB leadership took place a few weeks after Stalin's death before even a semblance of "socialist legality" had been restored. While Khrushchev's power was great, his rule was not remotely as absolute as Stalin's. The "collective leadership" lasted for about two years after Stalin's death: after that date Khrushchev, appointed first secretary of the party in September 1953, had fortified his position to such an extent—mainly through appointments of his own people in the apparatus of the Central Committee—that effective power, within the limits indicated, passed again into the hands of one man. Khrushchev was never deified in the way Stalin was, but following a deeply rooted Soviet tradition, no major speech was made, no article or book on a political or economic subject published, which did not invoke Khrushchev's authority.

After a promising beginning Khrushchev's cultural reforms came to a halt. His inconsistent policy, as in other fields, was a bitter disappointment to those who had hoped for a lasting and far-reaching thaw. The publication of novels such as Dudintsev's *Not by Bread Alone* and Ehrenburg's *Thaw* in the early years after Stalin's death had raised high expectations. But the reaction of party and government following the appearance (in Italy) of Pasternak's *Dr. Zhivago*, a basically unpolitical book, showed the narrow limits of cultural de-Stalinization. Pasternak was not permitted to accept the Nobel Prize but had instead to write a letter of recantation to *Pravda*, and a Politburo member suggested that this greatest living Soviet poet be deprived of his nationality. Many other writers, including "liberals" such as Fedin, Simonov, and Katayev, joined the attacks against Pasternak.

There was a second cultural thaw in the early 1960s in the wake of which Yevtushenko's *Babi Yar* and *Heirs of Stalin* were published, as well as Tvardovski's *Vasili Tyorkin,* and, above all, Solzhenitsyn's *One Day in the Life of Ivan Denisovich,* the first novel published in the Soviet Union dealing with life in the Gulag. Solzhenitsyn's novel had been passed by Khrushchev personally against the resistance of other party leaders who had demanded, at the very least, major cuts.

This second thaw constituted the high tide of de-Stalinization. It was followed, almost immediately, by official attacks against liberal writers and artists, whose work (it was argued) was of no use to the toiling masses. Khrushchev himself joined the campaign; he was not willing to tolerate even the mildest forms of avant-garde art and literature, a point of view that emerged during his famous visit to the Neizvestni exhibition in the Manege Hall ("painted with a donkey's tail . . . ").

The idea that writers, or intellectuals in general, should act as social critics, as the conscience of the nation, was totally unacceptable to the party leadership. As Khrushchev said in his speech at the Writers' Congress in May 1959, "If anyone is to reveal and lay bare faults and shortcomings, it is the party and the Central Committee." If the pseudo-science of Lysenko was refuted after year-long debates and against much resistance, this act was less in the spirit of free and unfettered scientific enquiry than an admission by pragmatists that Lysenkoism did not work and had done harm to Soviet agriculture.

Thus the impetus of de-Stalinization and liberalization had petered out well before Khrushchev was overthrown in the fall of 1964. If he did not fight more consistently for reforms the reasons were obvious. His own ideological and cultural interests were limited, and he was warned time and again by his advisers that too much cultural freedom constituted a major deviation from Marxism-Leninism and would trigger off negative, possibly dangerous political consequences. Nor should it be forgotten that support for such liberalization was limited to sections of the intelligentsia. The people at large were, as Pavel Litvinov once noted, as authoritarian as the rulers.

After Khrushchev had been overthrown, many accusations were hurled against his "subjectivism": that he had engaged constantly in huge, ill-prepared schemes, that he had frequently failed to consult his colleagues about important decisions but instead promoted members of his own family (such as Alexei Adzubei, his son-in-law), that his initiatives in foreign policy had been unsuccessful. The disarray in the world Communist camp and the break with China also occurred under his rule. There is some truth in these allegations but they are one-sided: in the final analysis Khrushchev, almost alone among Communist leaders, realized that Russia needed far-reaching changes to solve her political, economic, and social problems. While in theory supporting economic modernization, most other leaders opposed radical change. In his search for solutions Khrushchev antagonized and offended many of the top leaders as well as the medium and lower echelons of the bureaucracy. The redivision of the Soviet Union into 105 major units (Sovnarchozy) threatened the power of the district secretaries, and the whole *nomenklatura* suffered when tax-free additional salaries, most of them received for many years and regarded as God-given, were taken away.

The industrial workers were unhappy because, despite all the promises for a wonderful future, supplies were still highly unsatisfactory. There was discontent in the army because its budget had been cut and in the security services because their importance in the system had greatly diminished. Khrushchev made too many enemies and had few supporters.

But it is only fair to recall that, where Khrushchev failed, his successors were not more successful. This is true as much with regard to scientific-technological innovation as with agriculture. If Khrushchev failed to overcome the apathy of the work force by providing incentives, if the Soviet Union suffered some foreign political setbacks under his rule, if he failed to break the stifling influence of the bureaucracy, the same is true *a fortiori* with regard to Brezhnev and his allies. They tried to solve the grain problem by making both enormous investments in agriculture and massive purchases abroad and did not succeed in the end. They did not dare to confront the bureaucracy but, on the contrary, let it expand and gave it more power. Khrushchev did not lack courage: he thought (as Alec Nove has put it) that he could correct defects through the party machine and then correct the party machine itself. Instead the party machine got rid of him.[4]

Leonid Brezhnev, who had engineered the overthrow of his predecessor in 1964, remained in power up to the day of his death eighteen years later. He had belonged to the Central Committee and been an alternate member of the Politburo even under Stalin, having earned his spurs in the Ukraine and Moldavia. His subsequent career in Moscow was rapid, perhaps because he personified better than anyone else the qualities expected of a Communist leader of the post-Stalin era. He was not an old Bolshevik in the Spartan mold or a fanatic ideologist but an extrovert and a firm believer in the policy of live-and-let-live. He was an inveterate optimist and as he grew older he preferred not to be bothered with unpleasant facts.

He belonged to the generation which had lived through forced industrialization of the 1930s, the collectivization of agriculture, the mass purges, the war, and the difficult years of reconstruction—surely he deserved to enjoy the good things in life as conditions became easier in the 1960s and 1970s. There were no purges as under Stalin, no social and economic experiments as under Khrushchev. True, Kosygin, the second man in the Politburo, who also served as prime minister at the time, pressed for economic reform aiming at decentralization, greater incentives, tying wages to output and prices to demand. But Kosygin was a sourpuss and probably exaggerated (as Brezhnev saw it) the economic difficulties facing the country. Kosygin's initiative was quietly sabotaged by the bureaucracy, a fact which seems not to have caused sleepless nights to Brezhnev.

The Soviet system had its drawbacks, but somehow it did work and Brezhnev's device was "no experimentation." He firmly believed in the "stability of cadres," which is to say that leading Communists should be replaced only in case of gross disloyalty or incompetence. The fact that a district party secretary or the head of a factory showed only mediocre capacity was not enough to cause his demotion. Brezhnev reasoned, perhaps not without justification, that one never knew whether a change would not be for the worse.

The secretary general of the CPSU collected impressive cars—a

[4]In Martin McCauley, *Khrushchev and Khrushchevism,* London, 1987, p. 70.

Rolls-Royce, a Mercedes, a Lincoln Continental. He was a vain man but not an egoist. He also liked those around him to enjoy themselves. The *nomenklatura* never had it so good. Under his reign Soviet troops invaded Czechoslovakia and Afghanistan and the concept of the Brezhnev doctrine was born; but the heyday of détente also occurred in his time. All in all it was a period of almost unprecedented calm and, if one believed the official statistics, also an era of substantial, steady growth. The party and the KGB kept their secure position as pillars of the regime; the lot of the lower echelons of the party and state bureaucracy improved; new orders and awards were established such as the Order of October, of Friendship of Peoples, of Worker's Glory and others. Brezhnev helped himself to as many of them as feasible; in the end he had seven Orders of Lenin and was a hero of the Soviet Union four times over, not to count many other awards and distinctions. He also received the Lenin Prize for literature for his autobiography, a work of monumental insignificance which apparently was not even written by him.

But the masses also benefited to a certain extent—virtually every family received a television set and a refrigerator. There was some *panem* and a lot of circuses: the celebration of the fiftieth anniversary of the October revolution (1967), of Lenin's one-hundredth birthday (1974), and, above all, the Moscow Olympic Games. Some dissidents made unpleasant noises, and Stalin and his lackeys such as Zhdanov were partly rehabilitated. The cultural policy of the regime was markedly less liberal than Khrushchev's, which had not been a paragon of cultural freedom either. But not that many people cared about the fate of the editor of *Novy Mir* or of academician Sakharov. The fact that 107 million Russians were rehoused during the seventies was a matter of greater interest.

According to the official histories the two Brezhnev decades witnessed enormous progress in virtually every respect. In Krasnoyarsk the biggest electricity plant was built and the biggest gas pipeline was constructed, as was BAM, the Baikal-Amur railway line, 3,200 kilometers long, "the construction of the century." Thousands of new factories were completed during the decade; the GNP grew by 63 percent, productivity in industry by 56 percent. The Tiumen oil and natural gas fields were developed, the output of commodities of mass consumption almost doubled, and medical services were improved. A new constitution was adopted in 1977, and the media reported that not less than 140 million people had participated in the debates preceding it. According to these books it was an exciting period of heroic work of growing Communist consciousness, of the steady progress of Soviet political, economic, and military power.[5]

When Gorbachev was to criticize in later years the Brezhnev era as one of stagnation *(zastoi),* of poor leadership, the encouragement of servility, and the emasculation of critical discussion, his Politburo colleague Egor Ligachev noted that this was not how he remembered the 1970s. He had been district party secretary of Tomsk at the time and he recalled the upbeat mood of the period, the general enthusiasm which had prevailed in those years.

Ligachev could have recalled that the Brezhnev cult and the official optimism was *de rigueur* at the time, that not only unabashed flatterers such as Aliyev of Baku took part in it, but also future reformers and critics such as Andropov and Gorbachev. When Brezhnev's autobiography was published, Gorbachev praised it as a work of enormous ideological significance.[6] But why single out Gorbachev? A cursory look at contemporary Western comments shows a similar picture with regard to the journalists stationed in Moscow and also to academic Sovietology.

There were probably no foreigners who felt more at home in the Soviet Union than Klaus Mehnert and Alexander Werth; both had been born in Russia, one in Moscow, the other in Petersburg; their command of the language was perfect. Werth reported about the young Russians who thought that their country was the most wonderful in the world, and Mehnert noted that the successful Russian of today recalled the puritanism of the seventeenth century. According to Mehnert, another great asset of the regime was the dynamic energy of the Soviet people which every visitor became aware of as soon as he entered the country. Mehnert also noted the widespread belief among the Russians that technology was a panacea.

[5]I. B. Berchin, *Istoria SSSR: Sovietski Period,* Moscow, 1987, pp. 540 et seq.

[6]Among the eyewitness accounts of the late Brezhnev era and the transition period, Mark Frankland's The *Sixth Continent* should be singled out (London, 1987) as well as Richard Owens's *Comrade Chairman* (New York, 1986). From among the more theoretical works Timothy J. Colton's *The Dilemma of Reform in the Soviet Union* should be mentioned as well as Severyn Bialer's *The Soviet Paradox* (New York, 1986). The most convenient systematic surveys were provided by the annual volumes of the Bundesinstitut in Cologne, e.g., *Sowjet Union 1984/85,* etc.

One of the most respected American writers on the Soviet Union called the Brezhnev era a "high level of stability and governability"; all major groups of Soviet society had participated in the general improvement of living conditions, and by and large the Soviet regime had been able to deliver the goods and to satisfy people's expectations for higher standards of living. Another prolific Sovietologist wrote that to understand Brezhnev one had to regard him as a U.S. boss; he also had warm praise for the bureaucracy. It was quite wrong, he said, to believe that the bureaucracy ruled the Soviet Union and opposed any significant change. The author of a highly praised French textbook on the Soviet Union noted that the intelligentsia, which elsewhere stood for contention, was integrated into the Soviet system, not alienated from it. As for the population at large, essential needs such as security, education, health, and leisure appeared to be satisfied. Some British academics were greatly impressed by the lot of the Soviet worker under Brezhnev: there was greater unity between manual and nonmanual labor, between managers and workers, between the trade unions and the party than in the Western world. The same academics were impressed by the motivation of the young people in the Soviet Union—the trade unions provided an integrating mechanism giving "young people a sense of belonging."[7]

Viewed in the light of the revelations of the late 1980s such comments make curious reading. One can think of mitigating circumstances, especially with regard to the early Brezhnev period in which a certain optimism and the belief in the omnipotent power of technology were indeed widespread. Popular expectations at the time were not high and the essential needs (very modestly defined) were in fact satisfied.

Rereading some old articles of mine I came across the following, written in 1960 after a twelve-month absence from the Soviet capital:

Moscow in 1960 is a city of prosperity. Measured by Western standards it is a modest sort of prosperity. . . . But the Soviet citizen does not measure by Western standards; he only knows that he is better off than he was a year ago and that in 1961 he will be able to buy even more for his money. . . . In 1960 Khrushchev can claim with greater truth (than Stalin in 1935) that "they never had it so good"—as Macmillan did on

[7]David Lane and Felicity O'Dell, *The Soviet Industrial Worker*, Oxford, 1978, p. 144

the eve of the last British elections. After more than forty years of deprivations many believe the good life is just around the corner. Just now,
comparisons with the West are quite irrelevant; they may become important later on. Among Mr. Khrushchev's inexhaustible supply of old popular sayings there must be one to the effect that the appetite grows while
eating.[8]

Some writers, including Mehnert, saw certain danger signs and
seeds of weakness. Thus Basil Kerblay noted the dangers of apathy, inefficiency, double thinking, and double standards of behavior as well as problems with the nationalities. He correctly predicted that the future of Soviet society depended not only on
objective factors such as economic growth, social processes, and
the expansion of military might but also on the subjective assessments of the evolution made by individuals and groups.

Skeptical and even downright pessimistic views became more
frequent in the West toward the end of the Brezhnev era; the loss
of vigor and direction on the part of the Soviet leadership was no
longer a secret and became a cause of concern even to the most
sympathetic Western commentators.

From the revelations during the age of *glasnost* we know that
between 1979 and 1982 the Soviet economy virtually stood still,
that life expectancy declined and infant mortality rose, that alcohol
sales tripled, that the agricultural policy was a disaster, that working conditions became worse and queues longer, that the quality
of goods produced was often abysmal. The eleventh five-year plan
was not fulfilled and the standards of living of various strata of the
population actually deteriorated. But the worst thing (as Abel
Aganbegyan, one of the most prominent spokesmen of the Gorbachev era, put it) was not the lack of increase in production or the
failure of living standards to improve; it was the loss of morale
among people, the loss of interest in work, corruption and the
abuse of power of office.[9]

By the late 1970s the feeling was gaining ground that the system was not working well at all, that there was something radically
wrong and that a further deterioration seemed likely. As one observer put it, "The new Soviet man had turned pessimist."[10]

[8]"Return to Moscow," *New Republic*, October 3, 1960.
[9]Aganbegyan gave countless interviews; probably the most detailed appeared in *Ogonyok*,
29 and 30, 1987: *"Chelovek i Ekonomika."*
[10]John Bushnell, in Stephen F. Cohen, et al., eds., *The Soviet Union Since Stalin*, Bloomington,
1980.

Turns toward pessimism can be found in the annals of many nations, and it is never easy to point to the reasons which trigger off the changes in mood. Sometimes they have occurred after a military defeat or an economic crisis, but at other times they took place in deepest peace or without any obvious economic reason. What could have caused the change of mood in the Soviet Union and when exactly did it occur? According to Timothy Colton there was a feeling of euphoria when Brezhnev's seventieth birthday was celebrated in 1976, a feeling that great things had been achieved and that yet greater achievements were around the corner.[11] If so, the euphoria was certainly not universal; there was an undertone of deep pessimism well before in the writings of many Soviet novelists—on both the left and the right—especially among the village writers *(derevenshiki),* such as Abramov, Shukshin, and Rasputin, to mention only the most famous among them. The crop failure of 1975 should have been a last warning sign; a close observer noted that Soviet (economic) middle-class pessimism was, in fact, palpably felt well before the agricultural disaster,[12] whereas the working class, by and large, had never quite shared the optimism of the middle class because that had never shared the privileges and rewards of those who had been included in Stalin's "big deal."

Economic dissatisfaction certainly did play an important role in the growth of pessimism. Or perhaps it would be more accurate to point to the expectations for a better future which had been very high and which were not fulfilled. It had been promised under Khrushchev, after all, that in the very near future Soviet society would catch up with and overtake the West. As long as Soviet society was sealed off from outside information, Soviet citizens were not in a position to compare their own lot with the situation in the developed Western countries. But gradually information percolated which persuaded Soviet citizens that, far from catching up, their system was falling behind—and this at a time when consumerism, the possession of material goods for which the word *veshism* was coined, had become a central concern of Soviet society.

But there were other reasons for the growing pessimism which had little or nothing to do with the economic situation. Communism had envisaged not just a tremendous growth in industrial and

[11]Timothy J. Colton, *The Dilemma of Reform in the Soviet Union,* New York, 1986, p. 24.
[12]Bushnell, loc. cit.

agricultural output; it had promised the emergence of a new type of Soviet man. A new man and woman had indeed emerged, but there was no enthusiasm about the result. The agonizing question "What has become of us?" was asked by Vasili Shukshin, one of the most gifted of the younger writers (and producers and actors), and it was echoed throughout the Soviet Union. There was the general feeling that not only had the quality of life deteriorated but also the relationship among human beings. Elementary human solidarity seemed on the way out, as did compassion; people seemed no longer to care about one another. Culturally the seventies were a desert; all that mattered was money and, of course, connections with the right people. As an anonymous Soviet author wrote, there was no reason to fear an attack from the outside. What enemy would take the risk of an attack if he could be reasonably sure that in another decade or two, half of the country would be paralyzed in an alcoholic stupor and unable to defend themselves?

Brezhnev and his colleagues were not entirely unaware of the growing malaise facing the country, such as the incompetence of the central planners, the shortages of metal and fuel, the disasters in agriculture, the do-nothing attitude of officials in high places and low who never fulfilled plans, falsified statistics, and merely paid lip service to instructions from above. In two speeches in 1978 and 1979 he cajoled and threatened the bureaucracy and, as usual, everyone agreed with him and promised to mend his ways. Again, as customary, nothing happened. At the same time nepotism and corruption spread. The district and regional secretaries of the party ruled the country like nineteenth-century viceroys and so did the first secretaries of the Central Asian and Caucasian republics; when Brezhnev or other leading members of the Politburo came to visit them, there would be a royal welcome with red carpets, impressive ceremonies, and many presents. The local leaders would report tremendous achievements in all fields, industry, agriculture, social services— much of it pure fantasy, most grossly exaggerated. In various places Mafia-like organizations spread which, in collaboration with the local administration, more or less officially collected protection money.

These were not entirely new practices; corruption, nepotism, and arbitrary rule by the bureaucracy had characterized Russia under the Tsars, after all. True, new records were established in the 1970s, but even these might have been accepted had there been the feeling that the leadership was in strong hands, that the people in the Kremlin were men of vigor as well as of vision and a sense of direction. But the average age of Politburo members in 1980 was seventy, and there was not much evidence of either wisdom or vigor. Their public appearances became less frequent, their speeches shorter and more tired. It was embarrassing to watch tottering old men being helped to their seats on state occasions.

"Developed socialism," the official definition of the late Brezhnev era, became a synonym for senility on the top and apathy among the masses. For years the feeling was spreading that something ought to be done to invigorate the leadership. But the impatient younger people were in no position to do so. The system had developed in such a way that nothing could be done until nature took its course—which happened to be the case on November 10, 1982, when Brezhnev died. As usual, the announcement was delayed—this had been the practice frequently under the Tsars from Ivan IV onward, as well as in the case of Lenin and Stalin. Certain habits seem to persist in Russia quite irrespective of political systems.

In the summer of 1982 Yuri Andropov had left the KGB, which he headed for fifteen years, to become a secretary of the Central Committee, clearly in preparation to succeed the ailing Brezhnev who, by that time, no longer took an active part in the leadership. It would have been against established rules and made a bad impression if the head of the secret police had become the central figure in the Kremlin without a more neutral, transitional assignment.

Andropov looked like a professional man, a lawyer, perhaps, or a physician going on in years, dignified and slightly world-weary. He had acquired, for reasons not entirely clear, the reputation of an intellectual (he wore glasses) and a closet liberal—admittedly more outside the Soviet Union than in Russia. He was a reasonably well-educated man, certainly in comparison with most of his colleagues in the Politburo, even though one would look in vain in his speeches and articles for interesting new ideas, literary allusions, elegance of style, or depth of analysis. Perhaps he had these qualities, but if so, he knew well to hide them. The characteristics which made his rise to high office possible were those of a seasoned *apparatchik* and competent administrator rather than an original thinker and creative innovator.

During the last two years of Brezhnev's life a number of scandals occurred—or rather became public—affecting members of his close family. There is reason to assume that the KGB, then still under Andropov, helped to spread the rumors so as to undermine the position of the secretary general and his supporters among the leadership. When Andropov in his eulogy for Brezhnev on Red Square talked about the heavy loss to the party, nay to all mankind, of the glorious son of the fatherland, the ardent Marxist-Leninist, the outstanding leader of the Communist Party and the Soviet state, the most eminent leader of the world Communist movement and workers, there was little if any conviction behind it; it was the usual case of *de mortuis nil nisi bunkum.* [13]

Like the other leaders of the party Andropov lived sheltered from the harsh realities of Soviet life; neither he nor his wife had to queue in front of the shops, nor was he dependent on the services provided by the Soviet health service for ordinary mortals. But owing to his job he was in a unique position to know the real state of the Union, not the one reported in speeches on state occasions and in *Pravda* editorials. Over the years the KGB must have supplied him with a steady stream of information, not only about the White House and American military preparedness but also about the Soviet economy, social conditions, and the mood of the people—the growing corruption, apathy, and cynicism on the home front.

Yet during the fourteen months he was to stay in power, hardly any change for the better could be registered in domestic affairs; in foreign affairs, on which he should have been especially well-informed, there was actually a deterioration in the situation. Soviet policy showed no initiative except some truculent gestures which led to self-isolation. It is not difficult to think of mitigating circumstances. Andropov was approaching old age when he was elected and, in any case, fourteen months hardly gave sufficient time to effect far-reaching reforms. In the beginning of this period he was preoccupied with consolidating his position by ousting some of the dead wood, meaning the old Brezhnevites, and bringing in his own people. Once his base of power had been strengthened his health

[13] Y. V. Andropov, *Izbrannie Rechi i Stati,* Moscow, 1983, p. 207.

deteriorated to such an extent that he could no longer take an active part in the daily conduct of the affairs of state.

It could well be that Andropov saw the need for reform; but history judges results, not good intentions. The people he picked, such as Aliev from Azerbaidjan and Romanov from Leningrad, were far from outstanding; his speeches were cautious, almost timid, and while he freely admitted that in some respects the state of affairs was unsatisfactory, there was no sense of particular urgency in them, no demand for immediate and far-reaching change. The changes he did introduce were of no great consequence, such as the publication of short official statements after the weekly Politburo meetings. Before his last disease, "limited industrial experiments" were announced; but there had been such experiments all along in Soviet history and no one took this very seriously.

He appeared as a strict disciplinarian: there were systematic police raids in Moscow and other cities to harass black- and gray-marketers and to find out whether people were visiting bathhouses or dentists during working hours. This practice was so unpopular that it had to be discontinued after a while. Measures against corruption were tightened and also against dissidents. He called for the intensification of ideological warfare and on a few occasions he was shown on television mixing with workers in a Moscow factory and other ordinary people. But he lacked the common touch; there was nothing natural, spontaneous and easy in these appearances, and thus they did not contribute either to his stature or the feeling that a new era had dawned in the Soviet Union. It was a period of quarter measures, of decisions adopted but not carried out and thus not essentially different from the late Brezhnev era.

Andropov was perhaps the first Soviet leader to admit that he had no ready answers to all problems; this referred above all to the economy. His advisers told him that agriculture was in a shocking state, that the supply of goods of mass consumption was insufficient, that new incentives were needed and that *uravnilovka* (egalitarian wages) had gone too far. And so, on a few occasions, and despite the fact that he had no special interest or experience in economics, he made suggestions which, while not novel in any way, were sensible and were later on picked up and continued by Gorbachev—specifically, the need for a new system of management and central planning.

He even hinted on occasion that it might be desirable to take the public more into the confidence of the party leadership ("to speak with people seriously, frankly and not avoiding difficult subjects"). In his last major speech, addressing the Central Committee in June 1983, the word was first mentioned which was later to be invoked so often: *glasnost.* He said that there was the possibility of further democratizing the process of decisions concerning great questions of state and public life. But he made it immediately clear that he referred above all to accountability on the part of unions, women, and youth organizations. He said that it would surely help to bring the activity of party and state closer to the needs and interests of the people, which was not the same as consulting the population *before* certain important decisions were taken.[14]

Andropov died on February 9, 1984, after his aides had announced many times that he would soon recover and return to work, just as it had been the custom during Lenin's last year of life. He was succeeded by Chernenko, a singularly unfortunate choice. A native of Siberia who had met Brezhnev in Moldavia in 1950 and attached himself to this rising star, he became his confidant and *chef de cabinet.* He was quite unknown to the Soviet public. After his first appearances in public with the cruel TV cameras and microphones focusing on him, the embarrassment became acute. Here was another leader who had no *gravitas,* exuded no charisma, stumbled through his speeches, showed no sign of dynamism, of creativity, who seemed only half-alive, a figurehead (and an ill-chosen one at that) rather than a forceful leader. There were the usual comments by foreign statesmen and their sidekicks who had seen him for a few minutes in the Kremlin: Chernenko, they said, was a practical man, authoritative, gracious, refreshingly free of polemics. But his appearances belied these diplomatic comments: he seemed to be refreshingly free of anything.

He was, in brief, a nonentity. The ridicule was perhaps a little unfair. If he had no education worth mentioning, the same was true of Khrushchev. Nor could it be claimed that Brezhnev or Andropov had been orators in the tradition of Demosthenes. If he had not served in the army during the war but merely in the border police (a fact now held against him), the same was true for most

[14]Andropov, loc. cit., p. 291.

members of the Politburo. He was in many ways a typical *apparatchik* of the higher echelons, who in his prime would probably have acquitted himself as a competent organization man. Russia has much of the time been ruled by elderly people. The revolution had brought a change in this respect, but only for a while. In Tsarist Russia, Stolypin had been almost the only dignitary who had reached a position of paramount influence before he was fifty. Most others had been dignified gentlemen with gray or no hair rather than bundles of nervous energy.

Chernenko's misfortune was that he came to power when he was long past his prime, always breathless, beset by various diseases such as emphysema, and when, on the other hand, there was growing disenchantment and impatience among the Soviet people who had watched within the last few years two leaders go through a process of sad physical and intellectual decline, who craved a leader who was strong and intelligent enough to tackle at long last the growing problems facing their country. Chernenko was a sad disappointment to the people at large and became the butt of many cruel jokes. The embarrassment of the people who were actually running the country, the apparatus of the Central Committee, was, if possible, even more acute. These were men in their forties and fifties, on the whole of a higher intellectual caliber and greater sophistication, who understood only too well that they now faced more wasted years. For while state and party, army and KGB would continue to function under their supervision, they were not in a position to effect major change. All the important decisions which had been postponed for ten years or longer again had to be deferred.

If the new leader was so obviously a nonentity, who had been responsible for his election in the first place? He was a stopgap candidate; one of the younger members of the Politburo such as Gorbachev or Romanov or perhaps even the seventy-year-old Grishin would have been a more obvious choice. But the Politburo was split between the old Brezhnevites (such as Chernenko) and the followers of the late Andropov; and the "younger" members were also at loggerheads. Romanov and Grishin well understood that the appointment of Gorbachev would mean the end of their careers and vice versa.

Chernenko personified the maintenance of the status quo and for this reason he had the support of the old Brezhnevites afraid of losing their jobs. Furthermore, many bureaucrats feared the inevitable shake-up which would follow the appointment of a new and more vigorous leader; the underworld was relieved, because of the harassment by the security organs while Andropov had been in power.

There were few personal or political changes under Chernenko except for the ouster or demotion of a few Andropov followers and the fact that Molotov, the old Stalinist, was reinstated in the party. On his seventy-fourth birthday Chernenko got his fourth Order of Lenin. The Russian nationalists who had been bothered by Andropov's excessive Leninism felt relieved because they thought that the Siberian Chernenko was one of their own. It is impossible to know whether this was a correct assumption, for during the year when the new secretary general was in office he did not carry out his functions most of the time; he rested in the Crimea or was hospitalized near Moscow. There was the usual pretense that he was still running the country and in September 1984 he made, in fact, a few public appearances when he addressed the Soviet writers' union and gave them the usual good advice to stay closer to the people, to carry out the instructions of the party and so on.

For much of this time Gorbachev presided over the meetings of the leading party and state organs, and on occasion he was even referred to as our "second general secretary"—an office which did not constitutionally exist. Gorbachev enjoyed the backing of two of the main kingmakers in the Politburo, Gromyko the veteran foreign-policy minister, and Ustinov, who had for many years presided over the mighty defense industries. But he was not yet home and dry; Ustinov, another septuagenarian, died in December 1984, and the Romanov-Grishin coalition tried everything it could to block Gorbachev's promotion. But Grishin had not been a success as Moscow party secretary, whereas Romanov's lifestyle as the Leningrad satrap had been on various occasions, at home and abroad, unbecoming of an old Bolshevik.

And so, following a last tug of war, Gorbachev emerged as the most likely successor in the weeks before Chernenko's death in March 1985. He was elected, apparently by a narrow margin, and gave the usual eulogy to the Central Committee praising his predecessor as an outstanding leader of the Communist Party and the Soviet state. But it was a refreshingly short eulogy of two or three minutes which singled out Chernenko's insistence on "collective leadership" (the "apple of his eye"), an apparent attempt by Gorbachev to put his rivals at ease. Having made this kudo to his late predecessor he went on for the next half hour to elaborate on the main issues confronting, as he saw it, the party leadership—a decisive turn in the economy, *uskorenie,* democratization, and, once again, *glasnost.* [15]

[15]Gorbachev, *Izbrannie Rechi,* Moscow 1987, Vol. 2, pp. 129–30.

CHAPTER 3

The Rise of Gorbachev

U P TO HIS APPOINTMENT as general secretary of the party in 1985, the biography of Gorbachev reads like the model story of a young Communist who never made a wrong move. He was born in 1931 in Privolnoye, a village near Stavropol in the Northern Caucasus, a third-generation Communist. His grandfather had been a party member; his father was an economist and local party official. Young Gorbachev lived through the German occupation of his native region. After the war he continued his schooling and also worked for a while as a combine-harvester operator. At an astonishingly young age he received the Order of the Red Banner (for services in labor). At nineteen he went to study law in Moscow, where he met Raissa, his future wife.

From the beginning a lucky star seems to have been shining over his career. It was not easy in those years for a village boy to enter the most prestigious Russian university. Having been a member of the Komsomol, the Communist youth organization, he joined the party by the time he was twenty. His subsequent career was rapid: first secretary of the regional Communist youth organization, secretary of the regional party propaganda department, second secretary of the District Committee in 1968, first secretary two years later and at the same time member of the party Central Committee. Stavropol district is one of the most important agricultural regions and traditionally a good jumping board for yet higher office. Both Suslov, the party ideologist of the sixties and seventies, and Andropov had worked there. In between Gorbachev had earned a second academic degree, this time in the field of agricul-

ture. The secretary of a district committee is something like a
viceroy but Gorbachev's eyes were clearly set to get even higher
office. In 1978 he was appointed a secretary of the Central Committee of the party—which meant transfer to Moscow. In 1979 he
became a candidate member of the Politburo, the year after a full
member, the youngest at the time. In his early years in Moscow he
did not figure prominently on the political scene and few Western
Sovietologists rated his chances very high before 1983.[1]

It is probably not of great consequence to establish in retrospect
his main sponsors at the time; the Soviet system rests on *chefstvo,*
which is a modern version of the feudal principle of *nul homme sans
seigneur.* He had struck some of the key figures in the Kremlin as one
of the most capable leaders of the younger generation, a reliable and popular executive. If he had any specific political views, he
kept them to himself. His first years in the Politburo were no doubt
the most difficult. Being the most junior member he was given the
least popular assignment, namely agriculture—and this at a time
when Soviet agriculture was in a state of deep crisis: despite enormous investments, there were few returns.[2] An assignment of this
kind was high-risk, almost an invitation to disaster, and it is a sign
of Gorbachev's adroitness to have survived politically.

He was saved by the death of Brezhnev, who, in retrospect,
became the scapegoat (not without reason) for the failure of the
"food program" of the late 1970s; Andropov, Brezhnev's successor, liked Gorbachev and had singled him out for promotion. He
began to travel abroad; more important, he took an active part in
the appointment of new cadres. Furthermore, the harvest of 1983
was better than in previous years, and as new members joined the
Politburo Gorbachev could free himself from the burdensome appointment which could have ruined his career.

---

[1]Severyn Bialer (*Stalin's Successors,* Cambridge, 1980) mentioned his name just once. Jerry
Hough thought he was one of five possible candidates to inherit Brezhnev's mantle, but he
rated Romanov higher (*Soviet Leadership in Transition,* Washington, D.C., 1980). Archie
Brown picked him as a winner: "He has attracted little or no attention as a possible
successor to Brezhnev, yet he is in a number of respects the most obvious choice" (A. Brown
and Michael Kaser, eds., *Soviet Policy for the 1980s,* Bloomington, 1982). It is only fair to note
that Brown wrote two years after Bialer and Hough. Writing in 1983, Hough also opted for
Gorbachev who, he said, had a 90 percent chance to be elected as a successor. But such
prescience was weakened by the admission that the "political meaning of Gorbachev's rise
is not totally clear," which was one way of saying that it was not clear at all (*Problems of
Communism,* January–February 1983).
[2]The experts later established that for every ruble invested in agriculture, the state got only
half a ruble in return, and later on there was a further decline in this respect.

By the time Andropov died Gorbachev was widely regarded as the second man in the Politburo and his position was strong enough to survive the Brezhnevite revival under Chernenko. While the Brezhnevites did not, of course, regard him as one of their own, they did not consider him an active enemy either. Moreover, there was always a certain reluctance to demote a Politburo member unless he appeared to be a real danger. Thus Gorbachev succeeded not just in maintaining but in fortifying his position until, with the help of powerful allies, he was made the new general secretary after Chernenko's death.[3]

What new ideas did Gorbachev bring to his task? What were his priorities? There were some indications even in his first speeches, but they were not yet very marked. He maintained that the country had achieved major successes in all spheres of public life, and that it was justly proud. Soviet society (he said) had resolved the major social problems; since 1950 the national income had risen tenfold, per-capita income had increased fivefold: "Our successes are indisputable and commonly recognized."[4] So far there was not much difference between the standard speeches and articles of the Brezhnev period, a listing in a vein of self-congratulation of the achievements and victories gained. But Gorbachev did not stop there; there was a "but"—and it became longer, more detailed, and more emphatic as time went by. In the speech of April 1985 he said that alongside the successes there were unfavorable trends during the last few years and quite a few difficulties had arisen: "We have to put an end to waste, to change the sluggish pace of progress of science and technology in most industries. We have to improve management"—and so on.

In his report to the Central Committee of June 1985 he said, "Our domestic needs primarily dictate the need for accelerating our social and economic development. . . . the party and all the people will have to overcome the negative trends and sharply change things for the better." He became quite specific: the ministries of mechanical engineering, of livestock, and of farming and

---

[3]At the nineteenth party conference, three years later, Ligachev, Gorbachev, main antagonist, declared that the decisions taken in March 1985 could have been completely different and that Gorbachev was elected only thanks to the "firm stand taken by Chebrikov, Solomontsev, Gromyko, and a large group of party district secretaries." *Pravda,* July 1, 1988.
[4]Report to the Central Committee on April 23, 1985; speech in the Kremlin Palace on the occasion of the fortieth anniversary of the victory in World War II; report to the Central Committee on June 11, 1985, on accelerating scientific and technological progress; Gorbachev, *Izbrannie Rechi i Stati;* Vol. 2, pp. 152 et seq., pp. 186 et seq., pp. 251 et seq.

building materials were singled out for blame and also certain republics and districts. They wanted more funds while insisting that the planning targets should be reduced. Gorbachev complained about red tape in Chelyabinsk and slow development in Krasnoyarsk, about inefficiency in Lvov, about nonintegrated projects, mismanagement, insufficient modernization, and parasitic attitudes.

The Twenty-seventh Party Congress (February 1986) was a further milestone in his career. Gorbachev noted that there were still "many organizations" that did not feel the need for drastic reform; the habit to speak vaguely was deeply engrained, as was the fear of revealing the real state of affairs: "We shall not be able to move a single step forward if we do not learn to work in a new way, do not put an end to inertia and conservatism in any of their forms." He spoke of the need to combat window dressing, sluggishness, formalism, indifference, the habit of letting good things get bogged down in empty and endless discussions, departmentalism, localism, excessive paper work, and other bureaucratic practices. There was a seemingly endless list of aberrations, and Gorbachev complained as early as June 1986 about the presence of those who had opted for a wait-and-see approach or simply did not believe that the economic and political turnabout planned by the new leadership could be successful. Words were substitutes for deeds; as in the olden days no action was taken in response to criticism. "Restructuring becomes a mere illusion": everything is all right in words, but there is no real change.[5]

Most of these complaints had been made before, but seldom if ever in such a concentrated way. The rhetoric became progressively more emphatic. In February 1986, in an interview with *Humanité,* the French Communist newspaper, Gorbachev had been asked whether a new revolution was under way. He answered, "Certainly not," and added that it would be more correct to say that the progress of the cause of Bolshevism initiated seventy years earlier was now given an additional boost. In fact, the very word "reform" had not been used by him prior to the Twenty-seventh Congress, and some of his colleagues did not use it even after that date. Yet in the following months there was increasingly talk among the Gorbachev camp about radical, sweeping reform, and eventually the word "revolution" was used both

[5]Political report to the Twenty-seventh Congress, February 25, 1986; report at the Central Committee Plenary Meeting, June 16, 1986; Mikhail Gorbachev, *Selected Speeches and Articles,* Moscow, 1987, pp. 439, 466–67, 530–33.

as a noun and as an adjective (as in "revolutionary changes").

In *Perestroika: New Thinking for Our Country,* Gorbachev wrote that "perestroika" was a revolution. It had proved more difficult than we at first imagined, he said, and we had to reassess many things. "Revolution requires the demolition of all that is obsolete, stagnant and hinders fast progress. Without demolition, you cannot clear the site for new construction. . . ."

What caused the rising urgency in the appeals that measures should be taken to reinvigorate the Soviet economy, to get the country going again? It was not just the native impatience of the new general secretary, though this, too, might have played a certain role. Perhaps it came because Gorbachev, who had known previously only in general terms that the economy was not in good shape, now realized the full extent of the calamity. His experts told him that stagnation had set in even before the late 1970s, that between 1976 and 1980 only Britain among all industrialized nations had shown a slower growth rate, that between 1981 and 1985 there was a further decline in Soviet growth, that the last five-year plan had not been fulfilled, that in 1984 the Soviet growth rate was less than 1.5 percent—i.e., less than the increase in population—and that in early 1985 when Gorbachev was made general secretary, production failed to increase altogether; there might have been, in fact, an actual decline.[6]

Gorbachev, who had taken a special interest in economics during his years in Moscow, realized that unless he succeeded in getting the economy to move again, economic decline would affect all aspects of Soviet life. It would cause shortages of supplies, including some of the basic ones, a deterioration in the social services, and a weakening of the Soviet armed forces. Above all, there was the danger that the decline would continue and that, failing to carry out major investment and modernization, the Soviet Union would fall further behind in the years to come. If this was not an "acute crisis," a term Soviet leaders would use only with the greatest reluctance, the situation was certainly fraught with grave dangers.

Certain measures could be taken with relative ease without touching the roots of the system: one could impose stricter labor discipline, threaten the bureaucrats with loss of jobs or privileges

[6]CIA and DIA: *Gorbachev's Modernization Program. A Status Report,* March 19, 1987. Submitted to the subcommittee on National Security Economics of the Joint Economic Committee, Congress of the United States. (CIA estimates of the Soviet economy in the years prior to 1985 had been on occasion too optimistic.)

if they failed to deliver, older party secretaries and managers could be replaced by younger and more dynamic ones. This kind of approach had been used many times from Stalin's days on; it usually worked for a little while, acting as a minor palliative. Gorbachev's single major innovation during his first year in office was the anti-alcohol campaign introduced merely a month after his appointment. The idea was, of course, not new; there had been some halfhearted campaigns in the fifties and sixties, but never with so much fanfare and emphasis. This had the double advantage of being supported by Politburo members like Ligachev, who had demanded a campaign of this sort for a long time, and of embarrassing some of Gorbachev's rivals in the Politburo, such as Romanov, a notorious drinker, who were bound to be hurt.

During 1985 and early 1986 the main changes that did take place were in the constitution of the leading bodies of the party. Romanov was ousted from the Politburo in July 1985 and Grishin a few months later. Gromyko remained but became chairman of the Presidium of the Supreme Soviet; he was replaced as foreign minister by Shevardnadze, a Georgian police chief and party leader. Tikhonov, one of the oldest members of the Politburo, was replaced by Nikolai Ryzhkov. Baibakov, the perennial head of Gosplan, went out; Nikolai Talizin was appointed in his place. Others from among Gorbachev's supporters who joined the Politburo were Yakovlev and Eltsin, the new Moscow party secretary. Some of the oldtimers were still too influential to be replaced, such as Sherbitski of the Ukraine, or could be removed only at great political risk: this was the case with Kunaev of Kazakhstan, whose ouster later on triggered the Alma Ata riots.

Thirty-nine of the 101 members of the Council of Ministers were replaced, fourteen of the twenty-three heads of the departments of the Central Committee, forty-seven of the 150-odd key local party secretaries throughout the Soviet Union. The Central Committee elected at the Twenty-seventh Party Congress (March 1986) had some 30 percent new full members; most key figures in the media and leading institutes were replaced but few, if any, in the KGB and not many in the army. But many of these changes were due to old age rather than a different political orientation. Most of the new appointees did not owe their promotion to personal or political ties to the Gorbachev camp. Even at the end of two years of his rule, the new party general secretary could not count on a majority in the leading party bodies. Thus the Central

Committee plenum, which took place in January 1987, had to be postponed three times because Gorbachev could not be certain of its support for his policies. When at long last it was convened, he had to be satisfied with a compromise.

On all previous occasions, from Stalin to Brezhnev, the secretary general had first consolidated his power base and only then tried to push through his policies. Gorbachev was a man in a hurry who advocated change even before he was certain of support. He could count only on the secretariat of the Central Committee—an important lever in Soviet decision making but not the only one. He could remove local party leaders but he could not deprive them of their seat in the Central Committee—only the party congress had this right. The number of people who had been demoted, the anti-Gorbachev faction inside the Central Committee, was steadily growing.

Gorbachev knew better, of course, than to frighten off the majority of the leading party workers by extreme statements. His general record during the first year was one of reticence. A semi-independent Moscow observer, Zhores Medvedev, summarized Gorbachev's record during the first year as follows: "The changes in domestic policy were merely cosmetic. Policies were better presented, the style was more modern but there was little new in the contents."[7]

Gorbachev's report at the Twenty-seventh Party Congress, which had been expected with great hope by the party of reformers, was an anticlimax, just as eighteen months later his speech on the occasion of the seventieth anniversary of the October revolution disappointed his well-wishers after it had been assumed for many months that it would be a turning point in Soviet history—or at least in Soviet historiography.

Gorbachev's personal *uskorenie* (acceleration) occurred during the second half of 1986 and in particular during the first months of 1987, reaching its culmination with the Central Committee meeting of June 1987.

What were Gorbachev's basic ideas, which he could not fully express during his first year in office? Some of his frustration was expressed in his speech to the Central Committee in January 1987. He complained that the theoretical concepts of socialism had remained essentially on the level of the 1930s and 1940s, that the

[7]Zh. Medvedev, *Gorbachev*, New York, 1986, p. 208.

causes of such stagnation went back far into the past to the age of Stalinism (not mentioned by name) when authoritarian evaluations and opinions had become unquestionable truths and when vigorous debates and creative ideas had disappeared. The Stalinist ideas and practices, the very organization of society, had been elevated to dogma. There seemed a "braking process" at work, a concept widely discussed in the months that followed.

It was a denouncement of conservatism and an appeal to modernize Soviet society—within the framework of enlightened Marxism-Leninism. This meant less bureaucracy, central planning, and coercion in the economic sphere, more reliance on private initiative and incentive, greater honesty in public life, greater mobilization of the masses in the drive for improving Soviet Society. It was not a program thought out consistently and in great detail (though his economic advisers had fairly clear ideas) but rather a vague longing, an attempt to rekindle the enthusiasm of the early 1920s, which appeared in retrospect to have been the golden period of Soviet history. There was much talk about the NEP—the liberalization of the Soviet economy during the last years of Lenin's life. While the historical NEP was, of course, a thing of the past, there was much toying with the idea of again giving some greater freedom to personal initiative.

Gorbachev had no wish to deviate in any essential aspect from the canons of Leninism; he wanted, as he frequently put it, more rather than less socialism. He was a man of the *apparat,* who had no wish to undermine one-party rule or indeed to modify radically the political and social system which had evolved over seventy years. As one foreign observer put it, the Gorbachev generation was the Brezhnev generation with smarter suits, more up-to-date technology, and smoother public relations.[8] One could have also added: with higher education, more dynamic and impatient in approach. When they said "democracy" they meant a more enlightened dictatorship. They wanted to cure the malaise which prevented further growth and development; hence the constant attacks against bureaucracy, corruption, waste, and lack of initiative.

It must have been clear to Gorbachev and those supporting him that even minor reforms would cause strong resistance. Gorbachev's analysis of the state of Soviet economy and society was by no means fully shared by all his colleagues. Some may have be-

[8]Richard Owen, *Comrade Chairman,* New York, 1987, p. 230.

lieved in their innermost heart that whereas certain reforms were perhaps desirable, it was unlikely that they would ever succeed. One article widely discussed at the time asked, "Whose pies are more succulent?" The author argued that capitalism had apparently higher production efficiency which Communism could not match. But Communism had social values and social justice, and the fact that production efficiency was not as high in the Soviet Union as in bourgeois countries was not so terrible in the last resort. In any case, one had to opt either for free enterprise with its abundance of commodities or for Soviet-style rigidly centralized leadership. There was no third way, just as one could not be a little bit pregnant.

Others thought that it was pointless to engage in apocalyptic rhetoric about the horrible consequences of stagnation. For even if these predictions were correct (which in their view was by no means certain), such warnings were bound to undermine the faith of the masses in the cause of Communism and the competence of their leadership.

Gorbachev's economic spokesmen such as Aganbegyan claimed that considerable successes had been achieved even in 1986 and 1987: some 20 percent more houses had been built than in the years before, and agricultural production had grown by 5 percent in 1986, as much as the total increase during the last five-year plan. Life expectancy had gone up by two years following the restrictions imposed on the sale of alcohol. Others would argue that if such progress had been made following the imposition of sterner discipline, why engage in dangerous social and economic experiments?

These circles were particularly apprehensive about the possible effects of *glasnost* and democratization. Every Soviet leader, including Stalin, had paid lip service to the accountability of the leaders to the masses, to "democratic centralism" as the basic principle, and to Bolshevik self-criticism. But this was little more than a ritual; underlying their style of leadership was the firm belief that the Soviet people (and the party) needed a strong hand, that excessive democratization would lead to chaos, to the undermining of the official doctrine and leadership, and the penetration of all kinds of "alien" influences.

In short, there was the fear, nay the certain belief, that the country would either become ungovernable, or that the liberal reforms would get out of hand and lead to far-reaching, undesirable transformations. These fears were by no means groundless, for those who wanted to reevaluate the collectivization of agriculture under Stalin in the late 1920s would most likely end up criticizing the present system of Soviet agriculture. Those who demanded that de-Stalinization be pursued would eventually demand that the actions of the army and the KGB should also be subjected to *glasnost* and perhaps even demand a revision of the privileges of the *nomenklatura,* as some misguided writers in *Pravda* had done in 1986. In brief, even those who acknowledged the need for certain economic and social reforms did not believe that these should be carried out in an atmosphere of *glasnost* and democratization but as changes have usually been carried out in Russia—by order from above.

Gorbachev had first used the word *glasnost* in an article he had written for a literary magazine in 1974.[9] He had used the term occasionally on some subsequent occasions, but probably not more than some other Soviet leaders. He had mentioned it in his speech in the electoral campaign to the Supreme Soviet (February 1984) and again as an "inalienable part of social life" in a speech to the Central Committee (December 1984). After he had become secretary general he told the party district secretaries (October 1985) that the party ought to be healthy—hence the need for broad *glasnost.* Again, in his interview with *Humanité,* he pointed to the danger that deeds might diverge from words in Soviet political life; to prevent this, "we fight with the weapon of criticism, we fight with the weapon of *glasnost* and criticism."[10]

It seems to have been clear to Gorbachev from the beginning that institutional changes would not suffice to get the country moving again; attention had to be given to the "human factor." This meant above all imposing stricter discipline, stamping out corruption and indifference. But it also meant the active participation of the masses, which is to say some kind of democratization, some electoral reform, and *glasnost.*

Gorbachev's frustration during his first year of office must have driven him toward greater emphasis on spiritual, political, cultural, and moral regeneration, the realization that *perestroika* would not work but for something akin to a cultural revolution, within, of course, strict limits. Hence his appeal at the January 1987 plenum to "develop democratization, to involve people's energy and inter-

[9] *Don,* 2, 1974.
[10] Gorbachev, *Sochineniia,* Vol. 2, p. 95; Vol. 3, p. 159.

est in all the processes of our lives. This is the most important thing, the main point of everything, comrades."[11] Thus 1987 became the year of *glasnost* but it also rallied the forces opposed to it.

The leadership was far from unanimous about the reforms suggested by Gorbachev and especially the ways he suggested for carrying them out. There was also considerable resistance among the people. This had been anticipated by Tatyana Zaslavskaia, one of the chief ideologists of *perestroika,* well before it was under way. There were, as she saw it, whole classes and sections of the population which had a vested interest in the maintenance of the *status quo.* There were some fifteen or twenty million bosses, big, medium, and small, and their family members in the Soviet Union who would either lose their jobs or some of their power, status, and privileges as the result of reforms. They were associated with the giant ministries in Moscow and the Gosplan, as well as the cadres in the field. At the very least, their life and work would become much more complicated, what with the newfangled ideas about self-financing, greater incentives, and wage and price differentials. The old system, under which only numbers counted and where payment was made according to whether the plan was fulfilled, not whether the products were needed by anyone, or were of sufficient quality to be used, had much to recommend itself in their eyes; in any case, they had grown up with this system and knew no other. But the proposed reforms were also not liked by the many who derived all or part of their income—frequently the bigger part—from Russia's second economy: if the shortages disappeared they would lose their function in society. The reforms were resented by many workers who firmly believed—as the director of a factory wrote to *Pravda*—that the worse the management, the worse the general performance of a factory, the more a worker was likely to earn: he would get additional wages for overtime and free days to work *nalevo*—that is to say, in the second economy.

Under Brezhnev's system of live-and-let-live whole regions and sectors of the population had escaped the control of the center: while it was claimed that the Soviet Union had a planned economy, it had in fact only the pretence, or the illusion, of one. This was true, in particular in the Central Asian and Caucasian republics and also in wide regions of the R.S.F.S.R.: as long as the secretary of the district committee would report that the plan had been

[11]*Pravda,* July 15, 1987.

fulfilled and that all instructions from the Center were unquestioningly obeyed, no one was to bother them and ask for detailed accounting. Many Western experts reached the conclusion that the working class had begun to escape the control of the party leadership.[12] A place of work of sorts was assured to everyone and prices were relatively stable. Why should they support higher prices following the withdrawal of state subsidies for bread, milk, meat, rents, and other goods and services; why make a greater effort so as to increase productivity? Lastly, the organs of political control and repression, the policemen, censors, and informers: they, too, had no desire to see their numbers and status reduced or, at best, to feel frustrated because their freedom of action would be limited. Thus the forces opposing substantive reforms were many and powerful.

Those who supported *perestroika* were relatively few: many, though by no means all, intellectuals; and some idealists, young and old, who took their Communism seriously and who shared Gorbachev's conviction that a regeneration of the system was long overdue. They were mainly limited to the big cities; according to many reports *perestroika* never reached the more distant parts of the Union. True, the intellectuals had key positions in the media, above all the all-important television, whose programs reached the last village. But it was one thing to listen to the fine discussions on the TV screen, and another, more painful, to accept a reduction in one's living standards. For there could be no doubt that temporarily, at least, a broad section of the society would suffer from the reforms, and no one could predict for certain what effects they would have in the longer run.[13]

[12]A. Becker, et al., "Twenty-seventh Congress of the Communist Party of the Soviet Union," *Report from the Airlie House Conference,* December 1966, p. 4.

[13]On Gorbachev's strategy during the first two years of his incumbency, see Thane Gustafson and Dawn Mann, "Gorbachev's First Year: Building Power and Authority," *Problems of Communism,* May–June 1986; Jerry F. Hough, "Gorbachev Consolidating Power," *Problems of Communism,* July–August 1987; Thane Gustafson and Dawn Mann, "Gorbachev's Next Gamble," *Problems of Communism,* July–August 1987; Severyn Bialer and Joan Afferica, "The Genesis of Gorbachev's World," *Foreign Affairs,* 3, 1985; Thane Gustafson, "The Crisis of the Soviet System of Power and Mikhail Gorbachev's Political Strategy," *East West Forum,* April 1987; Timothy J. Colton, *The Dilemma of Reform in the Soviet Union,* New York, 1986, pp. 82–106; and research papers by Elizabeth Teague, Philip Hanson, and others issued by Radio Liberty Research during 1986 and 1987.

CHAPTER 4

Glasnost and Stalin's Ghost

THE WHOLE COUNTRY is now debating Stalin": thus a Soviet writer in June 1988.[1] True, a great many people, including perhaps a majority in the party leadership, were arguing that the debate should never have taken place. It was undermining the authority of the party, and it was spreading confusion and uncertainty. It culminated in the decision to cancel end-of-term history tests in Soviet schools in 1988.[2] But the very passion with which the opponents were making their case was showing that they, too, were deeply enmeshed in the Stalin debate whatever their ideological preferences. As Marx had written in the introduction to one of his most famous books, the tradition of all dead generations was weighing like a nightmare on those now alive. Since there had never been a serious attempt to confront the Stalinist past, the issue squarely became one of the crucial features of *glasnost.*

The Meaning of *Glasnost*

According to Smirnitski's Russian-English dictionary *glasnost* is a synonym for publicity, to give publicity; according to Dal's prerevolutionary classic dictionary it means "being generally

[1]Genrikh Volkov, *Sovetskaia Kultura,* June 7, 1988.
[2]*Izvestiia* (June 10, 1988) commented as follows: "Huge, immeasurable is the guilt of those who deluded generation after generation, poisoning their minds and souls with their lies. . . . Canceling the examinations was the only sober and honorable decision." True enough, but why single out the historians who, after all, had only behaved like everyone else?

known"; a *glasni sud* is a public trial. It also meant in Tsarist Russia to be a member of a city council. It is the opposite of secrecy. Yet *glasnost* has a specific meaning which is not rendered by the word "publicity." In fact, the precise meaning cannot be conveyed in a few words in the English language. This need not, however, unduly bother us since, as we shall presently see, *glasnost* has been interpreted in various ways by different people in the Soviet Union. And equally often it has been misunderstood in the West.

The concept of *glasnost* in Russia has a long and honorable history but the roots of its negation go back even further. Describing the main features of Russian political life in the sixteenth century, a leading historian has drawn attention to a "practice of hermetic silence later known as *neglasnost,*" or as contemporary intelligence officials would say, the "need-to-know principle": those who needed to know, knew, and the others were kept in ignorance.[3]

As a Russian bureaucracy developed in the eighteenth and nineteenth centuries the phrase "This document is not subject to *glasnost*" (*Ne podlezhit glasnosti* or, more often, *Ne podlezhit ogle-sheniyu*) became standard. On the other hand, *glasnost* became one of the main demands of the radicals, above all of Alexander Herzen.

As far as I can ascertain Herzen used the term first when he decided not to return from a long trip to Western Europe. In one of the classics of Russian political literature, "From the Other Shore" ("Farewell," datelined Paris, March 1, 1849), he explained his decision to his friends in Moscow: "The struggle here, in Western Europe, is public despite the bloodshed and the tears. Woe to the vanquished—but they are not defeated before they had their word. . . . Where the free word has not been killed, the cause is not yet lost. Because of this open struggle, because of free speech, and *glasnost,* I remain here. For this I shall give everything. I paid much for this decision. . . ."[4]

The demand for *glasnost* figures prominently in all the early issues of *Kolokol (The Bell),* the only free Russian periodical at the time published by Herzen in London. "Where there is no *glasnost,*"

[3]Edward L. Keenan, "Muscovite Political Folkways," *Russian Review,* 1986, p. 145.
[4]"*S togo berega,*" "*Proshaite,*" March 1, 1849. *Polnoe Sobranie Sochinenia,* 22 vols. M. Lemke, ed., Petrograd, 1917–25, Vol. 5, pp. 386–91.

Herzen wrote, "and no legal right but only the charity of the Tsar, public opinion has no influence; the intrigues of the anteroom and the alcove prevail." Or, a few weeks later: "Whoever opposes *glasnost,* whoever is against the liberation of the peasants—he is an enemy of the people, he is our enemy."⁵ In the twelfth issue of *Kolokol* there was an article with the title "The Benefits of *Glasnost,* " and again a little later *glasnost* was listed as one of the main demands of the Russian opposition: "Open the lockgates of censorship and then you'll know what the people really think, what it hurts and torments, the evildoings of the police and the courts. Close down the third department!"⁶ Other contemporary writers mentioned *glasnost* but not that often. Chernyshevski, another radical, even opposed the slogan; he suspected that the government could use pseudo-*glasnost* to trick the people.⁷

We find the word *glasnost* mentioned forty times in Lenin's works, most notably in the article in *Pravda* (September 20, 1918) in which he suggested that *glasnost* in the press should serve as a tool for the mobilization and education of the toiling masses. Stalin was no believer in *glasnost;* his whole style of ruling was based on the principle of *neglasnost,* but the old term was nevertheless mentioned from time to time—for instance, by Leonid Brezhnev in Stalin's last year.⁸ Lip service to *glasnost* was never entirely discontinued.

Later on, the concept was revived in the writings of Sakharov and other dissidents. When Solzhenitsyn was excluded from the Soviet writers' union in 1969 he wrote in an open letter: "*Glasnost,* that is the first condition of health in all societies. He who does not wish this openness for his fatherland does not want to purify it of its diseases, but only to drive them inwards, there to fester."⁹

Under Brezhnev the old Stalinist words for criticism and self-criticism were far more frequently used than *glasnost,* but there were still references to it from time to time—for instance, in paragraph 9 of the new Soviet Constitution of 1977, which mentions "increasing *glasnost.* "

There was no change in the transition period after Brezhnev,

⁵*Kolokol,* December 1, 1857; *ibid.,* January 1, 1858.
⁶*Kolokol,* July 1, 1858. The "third department" was the political police in Tsarist Russia.
⁷For other examples of nineteenth-century use of the word, see the Appendix.
⁸L. I. Brezhnev in *Bolshevik,* September 17, 1952, pp. 50–70.
⁹Michael Scammel, *Solzhenitsyn,* New York, 1984, p. 676.

and the silence imposed on the Soviet media after Chernobyl indicated that no fundamental change had taken place. True, the Twenty-seventh Party Congress witnessed a certain relaxation of controls, but this had been a traditional ritual and was not taken too seriously at the time. However, the congress stimulated, as Vera Tolz has put it, the drive for *glasnost;* the media continued to break various tabus by mentioning drug abuse, the decline in the health system, and the general moral decay in Soviet society.[10]

The decision of the Politburo in August 1986 to halt the work on the diversion of the Siberian rivers into Central Asia was also a sign of the times: while the public stand taken against it by leading writers and other public figures was not the only factor which influenced the decision, it certainly contributed greatly to it. Instead of fading away, *glasnost* gathered momentum during the second half of 1986 and reached its climax in 1987. Issues were now discussed in public which had been forbidden for fifty years and longer, and there was both the demand for even more *glasnost* and expressions of concern that freedom had gone too far and was undermining the authority of state and party. The Soviet media, whose boredom had been proverbial, became interesting, and Soviet commentators (and especially the foreign experts among them) rightly noted that events *inside* the Soviet Union were now far more important than developments abroad. They were right.

Gorbachev defined *glasnost* as follows: "The new atmosphere is perhaps most vividly manifested in *glasnost.* We want more openness about public affairs in every sphere of life. Truth is the main thing. Lenin said: More light! Let the party know everything. As never before, we need no dark corners where mold can reappear. . . ."[11] Later on he added some observations about the duties of the press: "It should unite and mobilize people rather than disuniting them and generate offense and a lack of confidence."

These were sterling sentiments, but as Engels used to say, the proof of the pudding was in the eating. What if the truth was painful and divisive? What if it caused offense and lack of confi-

[10]V. Tolz, "A Chronological Review of Gorbachev's Campaign for *Glasnost,*" Radio Liberty, Report 66, 1987.
[11]M. Gorbachev, *Perestroika*, New York, 1987, p. 75. If Lenin said "more light," he no doubt took it for granted that all educated Russians of his generation would know from which great poet he had borrowed the saying.

dence? Was truth more important, or unity and confidence? Gorbachev and his colleagues were to face the dilemma soon.

The history of the concept of *perestroika* is much shorter and less impressive than the pedigree of *glasnost*. It was originally used in the field of building, but it appeared in the political language more often in a slightly different form (*pereustroistvo*) before 1917; it was used by historians and in the pamphlets of the extreme right. The far left at the time was in favor of revolution; the liberals advocated reforms, and the extreme right called for the rebuilding (or restructuring) of Russian society.

Perestroika became a favorite word in the early Stalin period; we find many references to it in newspaper articles about agriculture, transport, and literature.[12] In general, it meant some form of reorganization; in the cultural field it usually implied something akin to *Gleichschaltung*, the elimination of "alien" elements. Thus, to give but one example, an article about *perestroika* in the field of education published in 1952 stressed the need to accept Pavlovian methods all along the line.[13] In the 1980s it was by and large a synonym for change and reform. Since the word "reform" was potentially more controversial, *perestroika* prevailed.

The Burden of the Past

The difficulties of accepting true *glasnost* were nowhere more obvious than in the field of history. For many decades the leadership of the CPSU had found it impossible to come to terms with its own past. Not to put too fine a point on it, the writing of Soviet history under Stalin "wasn't history, it was prostitution. People knew exactly what had happened, but wrote something completely different."[14] This had changed somewhat since Stalin, but not very much. As Professor Afanasiev wrote, "As far as coming to terms with Stalinism is concerned we are still living under Stalinism even though we are saying that we are living in a great time."[15]

Gorbachev was clearly of two minds as to whether the discussion about the past should be reopened. In June 1986 he told a

[12]For instance, see references to *perestroika* in transport policy in *Pravda,* May 8, 1930.
[13]A. A. Smirnov in *Sovetskaia Pedagogika,* 8, 1952.
[14]Mikhail Shatrov, interview with *NRC Rotterdam Handelsblad,* October 31, 1987; FBIS-Sov-87-217, November 10, 1987.
[15]Interview with Austrian Radio domestic service, November 5, 1987; FBIS-Sov-87-215, November 6, 1987.

group of leading writers that one of the aspects still off-limits to *glasnost* was the Soviet past: "If we start to deal with the past, we'll dissipate all our energy. It would be like hitting the people over the head. We'll have to go forward. Eventually we'll sort out the past and put everything in its place. But right now we have to put our energy forward."[16] He put it perhaps a little clumsily, but his intention was clear. Everyone, or almost everyone, agreed that the books on Soviet history did not present the full truth—to put it in the most charitable way. But it was clearly more urgent to tackle present-day problems than quarrel about the rightful place of Bukharin and Trotsky in Soviet history. And it was also doubtful whether the country had the inner strength to cope with two major assignments, tackling the future *and* the past, at one and the same time.

Gorbachev was no cynic, but some of his colleagues probably were. They could argue with some justification that a postponement of the historical debate by ten or twenty years had much to recommend itself. Such a debate was bound to stir up many passions and to produce a great deal of dirty linen. At some future date it would no longer be a burning contemporary issue. In fact, it might no longer be of much interest to anyone but the professional historians. Even in 1987 some young people were bored by anti-Stalinist movies such as *Pokayanie (Repentance);* twenty years hence such a reaction would be even more common. Other opponents of applying *glasnost* to the past offered no less weighty reasons: any opening of this Pandora's box was bound to lead to a heavy concentration on the negative features in Soviet history, which would appear—inaccurately, they argued—as a chain of disasters. They could have added that even if this negative view of Russian history was true, it was not acceptable to patriots, who needed not only ideals to look forward to but also great achievements in the past to draw inspiration from. The wholesale destruction of the mythology of great achievements which had been constructed over many decades was irresponsible and politically dangerous.

Arguments of this kind concerning the sacred lies about the past have been heard at different times in many countries, and it is easy to see their political relevance. But at the same time it

[16]"Gorbachev Meets Soviet Writers," Samizdat account, Radio Liberty, 399/86, October 23, 1986.

seemed impossible to keep the past out altogether from the new mood of *glasnost,* as the seventieth anniversary of the October revolution approached and more than usual attention was given in the media to the events surrounding the year 1917.

By February 1987 Gorbachev seems to have reached the conclusion that the historians, too, needed some *glasnost.* In a speech to leading representatives of the Soviet mass media he said, "There should be no forgotten names or blanks either in history or literature." And again: "Those who made the revolution must not be pushed in the background. . . . It is immoral to forget or pass over in silence large periods in the life of our people." Gorbachev's moral qualms were not shared by most of his Politburo colleagues, whose interest in the importance of history was less pronounced, or who saw more clearly than he did the dangers of opening the sluice gates of historical truth.

De-Stalinization in the Soviet Union had begun almost immediately after Stalin's death. The "purge" which had begun during the last months of the life of the dictator was discontinued, and some of the surviving victims (for instance, the "physicians-poisoners") were released. The public, posthumous rehabilitation of Stalin's victims of the 1930s and 1940s was given formal sanction in Khrushchev's famous speech to the Twentieth Party Congress in 1956; on March 24, 1956, *Pravda* exposed the personality cult and made it known that many honest citizens and members of the Communist Party had been repressed without justification. There were further revelations in the subsequent years, and the issue again figured prominently at the Twenty-second Party Congress (October 1961).

However, after Khrushchev's fall in 1964 articles against the "personality cult" and the terror ceased to appear. According to the Brezhnev party line de-Stalinization had been carried too far; the "personality cult" had received too much attention at the expense of other aspects of building up socialism. In any case, the nature of Communism, Soviet rule, and society had not been affected by these temporary aberrations. Some persons had been rehabilitated who did not deserve it—for instance, Fyodor Raskolnikov, one of the heroes of Petrograd in 1917 who defected to France in 1938, facing a recall to Moscow and certain death.[17]

---

[17]Albert P. van Goudoever, *The Limits of Destalinization in the Soviet Union,* London, 1986, p. 131.

Raskolnikov was "dehabilitated," i.e., became again a villain in 1969, and some others suffered a similar fate—fortunately, for them, posthumously. Virtually the only rehabilitations which took place after 1965 concerned some veteran members of the secret police (Cheka and GPU). Whereas all the marshals, admirals, generals, and colonels of the Red Army had been rehabilitated under Khrushchev, the flower of the GPU which had also perished (twenty thousand, according to official figures) had fared less well, mainly, no doubt, because many of them had been instrumental in the "repression" of Soviet citizens, including their own colleagues. But as Andropov was rebuilding the KGB in the late 1960s, he needed at least a few "honest Chekists" from the 1920s and 1930s to establish some continuity. And since the heads of the GPU after 1930 (Yagoda, Yeshov, and Beria) were clearly beyond redemption, the KGB historians were looking for some less controversial figures, which they found without difficulty.

This, in broad outline, remained the state of affairs up to 1985. Stalin's crimes were belittled in the history books; on the other hand his great merits in peace and war were frequently mentioned in the press, in books, and in movies; his hundredth birthday (December 1979) was duly commemorated. Thus for twenty years after Khrushchev's fall some of the modest concessions to historical truth were again unmade or whittled down. And it is important to stress that even at the height of the de-Stalinization campaign it had been the custom to use euphemisms—"repression" stood for murder, "cult of the personality" for totally arbitrary rule and glorification of a leader without precedence in modern history. Many of Stalin's victims were rehabilitated only in a legal sense; they were found not guilty of the charges that had been brought against them at the time—such as of having poisoned wells in the Ukraine on behalf of the Gestapo, or the British or Japanese secret services. But they were not rehabilitated politically: Stalin and his henchmen had been right in removing them from positions of influence, but it had been wrong to bring fantastic charges against them and to execute them. Brezhnev and his colleagues were great believers in letting bygones be bygones; unlike some Shakespearean heroes their nights were not interrupted by the appearance of ghosts from the past.

A Soviet historian trying to write the history of his country faced insurmountable difficulties. He could not write about the 1930s, for, all other considerations apart, access to the archives was minimal. But he could not write about the postwar period either, again because there was no access to the sources and because of Khrushchev, who had become a nonperson. The ideal history book was one which mentioned no names; in a television interview in December 1987 Andrei Voznezenski drew attention to such a book which had just been published. It managed not to mention either Khrushchev or Brezhnev and there was hardly anything about Stalin either. Instead of writing about substance, many historians engaged in methodology: whether recent Soviet history should be subdivided into three, four, or more periods; whether the NEP ended in 1926 or 1927 or 1928. This was called "debates on periodization"; it was a relatively harmless pursuit and, of course, totally unproductive.

The call for *glasnost* made little impression on Soviet historians during 1985 and 1986. There were no major changes in the professional literature; Soviet historians either thought that there was no need for revaluations or, more likely, having no clear lead from the party authorities (but accustomed to being told what to do), they preferred to wait and see.

In the meantime, however, the initiative of confronting the past was taken up by playwrights, filmmakers, novelists, and journalists. Their works, to single out but some of the best known, include the plays of Mikhail Shatrov, such as *Brest Peace Treaty* and *Further—and Further;* movies such as *Pokayanie (Repentance)* and *Risk;* historical novels such as Rybakov's *Children of the Arbat;* and also the works of Dudintsev (on Lysenko); Daniil Granin (on the fate of Timofeev-Rezovski, another Soviet scientist); Vasili Belov and Boris Mozhaev (on the effects of the collectivization of agriculture); the poems of Tvardovski and Anna Akhmatova in honor of Stalin's victims; and countless articles in journals such as *Ogonyok* restoring some reputations and besmirching others without having received the permission of the authorities to do so.[18]

Increasingly, the historians faced a totally unprecedented situation: there were two (or even more) versions on topics such as the revolutions of 1917, collectivization, industrialization, the purges and Stalin's role in the Second World War—in other words, all the

[18]Thus Raskolnikov was again rehabilitated in 1987 whereas Trapeznikov, his accuser of 1966, was denounced. There were many favorable articles and references to the accused in the Bukharin trial of 1938 but also to some who had never been brought to trial, such as Bubnov (*Sovetskaia Kultura*, March 8, 1988).

important issues in the history of their country. Worse yet, there were some voices from within the profession claiming that the state of Soviet historiography was exceedingly bad. A member of the Estonian Academy of Sciences wrote in *Izvestiia* that no other social science discipline had undergone so many deformations. He compared Soviet historians with arithmeticians who knew the solution from the beginning and worked their way back. Historiography was lagging behind literature in dealing with the past, and the textbooks did not even dare to mention the names of those who had once been the main leaders of party and state.[19]

Yuri Afanasiev, head of the state institute of historical archives, said in a series of articles and interviews that the origins of Stalinism had not been analyzed nor had the extent of the damage been admitted. Very often the level of contemporary Soviet historiography was still that of the infamous "Short Course" of 1938 prepared on Stalin's personal instructions.[20]

Afanasiev's field of expertise, as his critics pointed out, was French history, but the military historian Alexander Samsonov belonged to the very top of the profession; he was a member of the Academy of Sciences. He, too, expressed great unhappiness about the state of Soviet historiography. He could not regard Stalin as a military leader of genius, as many of his colleagues did, in view of the lack of preparedness in June 1941, the decapitation of the Red Army in the years before, and various mistakes committed during the war.[21]

Other historians, too, expressed feelings of dismay about the state of affairs in their profession, noting that its credibility had been undermined.[22] But quite often these were quarrels within the family, inner-Leninist controversies: some professional historians had gone further in the early Khrushchev years in their attempts to reexamine the past. In 1987, in contrast, caution prevailed in the profession. When Pavel Volobuyev, a man of irreproachable Leninist convictions, uttered some mild criticism of the state of Soviet historical studies at a meeting of the Academy of Sciences in March 1987, he got virtually no support. As Professor Tikhvinski, the

[19]Polyakov, *Literaturnaia Gazetta,* July 29, 1987.
[20]*Sovetskaia Kultura,* March 21, 1987; *Moscow News,* 2, 1987; *Sovetskaia Estonia,* August 25, 1988.
[21]*Argumenty i Fakty,* 10, 1987.
[22]St. Tyutyukin, *Izvestiia,* April 3, 1987; Pavel Volobuyev, *Pravda,* March 27, 1987.

academic secretary of the history department of the Academy, put it, "We must not allow our historical science to be denigrated in its entirety under the guise of *perestroika.*" What he meant was that there should be as few revisions as possible and that there was no hurry in the first place; perhaps the party line would change again in the not-too-distant future.[23] As the major organ of the history profession noted in one of its periodical exercises in self-criticism, "Until recently historians have adopted a wait-and-see position." The passive resistance of many historians against *glasnost* led to criticism on the part of the Central Committee overseers.[24]

A group of high-level agricultural experts who had been arrested on Stalin's order in 1931 and accused of political conspiracy were rehabilitated in 1987 by the Supreme Court, and it was announced that their works would be published again. But they had not been party members, every one knew that they had not conspired, and some of the works of the most prominent of them such as Alexander Chayanov had in fact appeared in Moscow several years earlier.[25] The best-known abroad of this group was Nikolai Kondratiev of the "Kondratiev wave" fame. But his theory had been rejected in his homeland and his fame was therefore greater in America than in Russia. Their rehabilitation was not a major breakthrough nor was the fact that certain authors quoted Lenin's testament in which he had said some unfriendly things about Stalin. Lenin's testament had already been quoted under Khrushchev.

Thus in the early days of 1987 the situation on "the historical front" (as it would have been called in Stalin's days) was contradictory and confused. Soviet historians and interested laymen, of whom there were a great many, waited for a clear signal from their leaders, but they waited in vain. Ligachev, the second man in the Politburo at the time, made it known that he was against the practice of interpreting Soviet history as a chain of errors; while Stalin had frequently used the wrong methods, it was under him that the Soviet Union had emerged as one of the world's leading industrial powers. Gorbachev, too, seemed unwilling to join the campaign against Stalin. In an interview with *Humanité* he had told the

[23]Tikhvinski, in *Voprosy Istorii*, 3, 1986, and in *Novaia i noveishaia Istoria*, 2, 1987.
[24]V. Riabov, in *Voprosy Istorii KPSS.*, 3, 1987; "Perestroika i zadachi zhurnala Voprosy Istorii," *Voprosy Istorii*, 2, 1988.
[25]*Literaturnaia Gazetta*, 32, 1987.

French comrades that there was no such thing as Stalinism; it was a concept thought up by the enemies of Communism and used by them widely to discredit the Soviet Union and socialism.[26] Yet at the same time many Soviet writers, including Aitmatov, whom Gorbachev considered a friend, freely used the term "Stalinism" in a derogatory sense: "All of us are still under the influence of Stalinism, unable to think and act independently," said Aitmatov. Yet no one claimed that Aitmatov was an enemy of socialism and the Soviet Union. If so, who was to be believed?

Eventually Gorbachev modified his stand, perhaps under the influence of his advisers and friends. In a speech to the Central Committee in January 1987 he said that the causes of the present situation went back far into the past; and in July 1987, talking to key figures in the media, he declared that "we shall never be able to forgive and forget what happened in 1937–38." This theme reappeared in his speech commemorating the seventieth anniversary of the October revolution.

This was as far as Gorbachev was willing to go, but his followers expected more. Throughout 1987, right up to his speech in November, there had been high expectations that very soon the green light would be given for a wholesale rewriting of Soviet history; Bukharin, Zinoviev, Kamenev, perhaps even Trotsky, would be politically rehabilitated; a fairer approach would prevail vis-à-vis the Mensheviks and other left-wing opponents of the Bolsheviks. Some of these predictions appeared in interviews given by Soviet literary figures to Western journalists, and great was the disappointment when nothing quite so dramatic happened.

Why was it so difficult to make concessions to historical truth? Gorbachev, after all, must have felt closer in many respects to Bukharin's views than to Stalin's. And Bukharin had almost been rehabilitated thirty years earlier under Khrushchev.[27] The short answer is that this would have been possible only on the basis of a radical reassessment of Stalinism, and this still seemed very difficult for political reasons.

The leading anti-Stalin critics such as Afanasiev and Samsonov were clearly in a minority; Afanasiev was criticized by several col-

[26]Gorbachev, *Sochinenia*, Vol. 3, pp. 154 et seq.
[27]Essays taking a favorable view of Bukharin, the recollections of his widow, Larina, and some of his own articles were published in 1987 and 1988.

leagues for distorting facts and providing comforts to anti-Marxists.[28] Those who spoke out in Afanasiev's favor were usually men
and women from outside the profession. The leading historians,
the academicians and heads of institutes, preferred to stay out of
the debate. They knew from long experience that in their field
silence was golden. Samsonov, the military historian, came under
fire from the Stalinist novelist Stadiuk, according to whose own
recollections Stalin had been a great military leader. And in any
case was it not true that in his earlier works Samsonov had taken
a more favorable view of Stalin? It was indeed true, but not a
relevant argument, because Stadiuk knew perfectly well that in the
Brezhnev era such a line had been *de rigueur* for historians who
wanted to see their work published.

New revelations about the purges and trials came not from the
leading academicians but from journalists in the offices of *Ogonyok*
or young researchers like Dmitrii Yurasov, a twenty-two-year-old
student who had worked for some time in state and military archives. In a debate following a public meeting in Moscow he mentioned some interesting, hitherto unknown facts both about the
victims of the purges and the fate of the investigators and execu-
tioners.[29] The figure of twelve million inmates of the labor camps
at the time of Stalin's death appeared not in *Voprosy Istorii* but in
the Moscow Komsomol newspaper.

The active resistance on the part of many historians against
glasnost in their field brought about the intervention of the party
authorities; the dismissal of the editorial board of *Voprosy Istorii,* the
leading journal in the field, early in 1988 did not come as a total
surprise. The new editor-in-chief, A. A. Iskenderov, was expected
to make greater concessions to historical objectivity in contrast to
the mainly propagandistic role played by the profession in past
decades. But the new liberalism, as it soon appeared, was fairly

---

[28]*Moscow News,* April 10, 1987; *Sovetskaia Kultura,* July 4, 1987. Even as the historical
journals began to publish articles critical of Stalin and his system, the approach remained in many respects the same. Articles had to begin and end with quotations from
a Gorbachev speech or at the very least to invoke some recent party conference resolution. See, for instance, I. L. Mankova and Y. P. Sharapov, "Kult lichnosti i istoriko-par-
tiinaia nauka" (The Cult of the Individual and Party Historical Science), Voprosy istorii
KPSS, 5, 1988.

[29]*Russkaia Mysl,* May 29, 1987; *Moskovski Komsomolets,* February 22, 1988. The fact that
Yurasov was published in the official press by May 1988 showed that the pace of de-
Stalinization had quickened (*Sobesednik,* 22, 1988). Yurasov's remarkable career had begun
at the age of 14!; other laudatory articles appeared in *Neva* (10,1988) and *Sovetskaia Biblio-
grafia* (5, 1988).

narrow in scope among professional historians; there was no wish to go far beyond the limits of intellectual freedom that had been reached in the Khrushchev era.

A confrontation between leading historians and creative writers in Moscow in April 1988 still showed a great deal of self-satisfaction among members of the history profession. Those who agreed with Afanasiev that there had never been a country in which history had been falsified to such a degree were clearly a minority. As a colleague replied, ". . . after all, we *do* have a historical science. . . ." Many historians criticized the liberties allegedly taken by the writers of recent novels. But the novelists could still argue that their works were closer to historical truth than the writings of the professional historians, who, in the final analysis, had also been writers of fiction, albeit often unreadable fiction, with many footnotes and other trappings of a scientific approach.[30]

In principle, no one was opposed any longer to the rehabilitation of old Bolsheviks who had faithfully served the party and had been arbitrarily "repressed." Even Isaac Mints, a ninety-one-year-old member of the Academy, gave interviews in which he stated that "today we know far from all the names of the heroes of the past."[31] Mints, more perhaps than any other single figure, had played a central role in the falsification of Soviet historiography from Stalin's days on, and in the suppression that he now deplored. Mints's reformist zeal was thought by many insincere; it gave *glasnost* a bad name. But Mints had been more or less consistent over the years, and his motives may have been more complex than generally thought; he was at the end of his career and saw no need to adjust himself to yet another twist in the party line. He held no brief for Trotsky and the other deviationists from Stalin's line, to whose denigration he had devoted his whole life. But it had dawned on him in the late sixties and seventies that the liberals were not the only ones pressing for a revision of official historio-

[30]On the policy of the new editorial board of the journal, see *Voprosy Istorii*, 3, 1988. Details on the Moscow conference sponsored by the Academy of Science and the Union of Soviet writers in *Sovetskaia Kultura*, May 6, 1988, and *Voprosy Istorii*, 6, 1988.

[31]Tass, March 4, 1987; *Ogonyok*, February 1987; *Kommunist*, 12, 1987, pp. 66 et seq. Mints's statement was criticized by Soviet periodicals of the far right because his appeal would have led to the rehabilitation of Lenin's followers, many of whom were "Zionists." In fact, the accused in the first (Kameniev-Zinoviev) and the second (Radek-Piatakov) Moscow trials have been rehabilitated legally but not politically; the question of their standing in Soviet history has not been resolved. Their legal rehabilitation was made public in June 1988.

graphy. Quietly, almost imperceptibly, another revision was taking place initiated by right-wing nationalists, who in their novels and historical essays reached conclusions superficially similar to those Mints had preached for decades: they also hated Trotsky and all he stood for.

But their reasons were not the same. They hated Trotsky because he was a Communist, an internationalist, and a Jew. They said "Trotsky" and meant Lenin and the whole generation of old Bolsheviks. Mints was horrified to read in the 1970s new "revelations" according to which the March revolution of 1917 had not been carried out by the Bolsheviks, as he and his colleagues had claimed for many years, but that it was the result of a conspiracy of the Freemasons among the leadership of the bourgeois parties. He realized how far the glorification of Tsarist official nationalism had gone and as a result found himself in some sympathy with Afanasiev, who criticized the new apologists of Tsarism, who invoked the national destiny of the Russian people following in the footsteps of the extreme Slavophiles—and worse.[32]

The collectivization of agriculture in the late 1920s became yet another bone of contention; it was an issue of more than academic interest in view of the present plight of agriculture and the need for reforms. According to the official historiography, Stalin's policy of applying "extreme measures" (the "liquidation of the Kulaks as a class") had been by and large correct. Its basic outlines had been in the tradition of Lenin's thought, and its long-term consequences had been beneficial. The historians saw no reason to modify their views in 1986–7, except that the more liberal among them conceded that the cost in human lives had been high, that there had been excesses and serious shortcomings in carrying out collectivization. In brief, there were many "pluses" and "minuses," and there was a profound contradiction between the aim, which was good, and the means used to achieve it, which were not so good.[33] However, in the final analysis collectivization, according to both the old and new party line, was a success. Agricultural production was boosted and it enabled Stalin to mobilize material and manpower for the growth of industry.

But this official line had never been undisputed even under Brezhnev. Village writers too numerous to be mentioned here had published novels which conveyed a shattering picture of the coun-

[32]Afanasiev, *Sovetskaia Kultura*, March 21, 1987.
[33]*Sovetskaia Rossia*, October 11, 1987.

tryside during collectivization and ever after. These *derevenshiki* were anything but liberal intellectuals; they included orthodox Communists such as Mikhail Alexeev who had never deviated from the official ideology.[34] In 1986–87, as new books were published which had been suppressed before, even more depressing accounts emerged. As Vasili Bykov stated in an interview, the damage caused to peasant society during collectivization accounted for the enthusiasm with which the invading German armies were at first welcomed in 1941.[35]

Furthermore, such criticism came not only from the novelists; economists, too, argued that the long-term results of collectivization had been no more positive than the immediate consequences. There had been, in any case, other, more rational, alternatives of organizing agricultural production.

The role of Trotsky remained a crucial test facing the writers of Soviet history, second only to the role of his antagonist, Stalin. According to most contemporaries Trotsky was not a lovable man; he was arrogant, conceited, and not a team player. While more intelligent and more widely educated than most other Bolshevik leaders, his political judgment was frequently suspect and sometimes utterly wrong. He had originally been a Menshevik and had frequently quarreled with Lenin. He had been, as Lenin said after 1917, "with us but not of us."

Yet with all this he had joined Lenin in the summer of 1917, and Lenin had said that since then there had been no better Bolshevik than Comrade Trotsky. In carrying out the revolution and later in the civil war he had played a role equal to, and in some respects more decisive than, Lenin's. This was the judgment of all contemporaries from John Reed to Lunacharski. It was also the judgment of Stalin, who wrote on the occasion of the first anniversary of the revolution: "All the work of practical organization of the insurrection was conducted under the immediate leadership of the president of the Petrograd Soviet, Comrade Trotsky. It is possible to declare with certainty that the swift passing of the garrison to the side of the Soviet, and the bold execution of the work of the Military Revolutionary Committee, the party owes principally and above all to Comrade Trotsky."[36] Lenin, it will be remembered,

[34]Mikhail Alexeev, *Drakhuni*, published by *Nash Sovremenik* in 1981.
[35]*Literaturnaia Gazetta*, May 14, 1986.
[36]This Stalin quotation was used by Mikhail Shatrov in his play *Dalshe . . . Dalshe . . . Dalshe*, *Znamya* (January 1988). It was also featured in *Novy Mir* in November 1987. In the same

was at the time in hiding and could give advice from afar—but he could not actively intervene.

Subsequently, Trotsky had his differences with Lenin as had virtually all other Bolshevik leaders. But he continued to play a crucial role for several years, first as Foreign Commissar and subsequently as the founder of the Red Army who was in overall charge of its operations during the civil war. Trotsky was defeated in the struggle for power after Lenin's death. He headed the left-wing opposition inside the party, was excluded, exiled in 1927, and eventually killed in 1940 on Stalin's order.

The treatment of Trotsky is the litmus test of *glasnost* in Soviet historiography, precisely because for so many years he had been treated as the archvillain: he was Satan, Judas, Lucifer, the main traitor, the incarnation of all evil. One should have thought that almost half a century after his assassination it ought to have been possible to publish the truth about him. Since Trotskyism as a political movement had never constituted a real danger to Soviet power, what made a reexamination of Trotsky's role so difficult? True, he could now appear in some plays and novels—not as a collaborator with the Gestapo but merely as a doubtful character, a man who had never been a true Bolshevik, and who had almost always been wrong. This raised new questions. For if Trotsky had been both incompetent and unreliable, how to explain that the infallible Lenin had entrusted him with leading positions in party and state?

There were no more answers now to this question than there had been in the past. Some observers thought that there would be a rehabilitation of Trotsky and that it would be discovered that even this fallen angel had historical merits in the revolution and the civil war. But the campaign against him continued; it was said that deep in his heart he had always been an enemy, his activity had been very dangerous for the revolution, he had tried to sabotage the armed rising in Petrograd, he had engaged in personal intrigues, he had talked all day and left the truly important preparations for the Petrograd uprising to other comrades.

play Shatrov quoted Rosa Luxemburg's predictions about the Bolshevik revolution to which reference is made later on in the present chapter. Shatrov's violation of tabus annoyed some party leaders, for within a few days *Pravda* published an article criticizing his approach to history (January 10, 1988). This was followed by more attacks in the Soviet press; Shatrov's play was defended in an open letter written by a group of leading Soviet producers and actors in *Pravda* (February 29, 1988).

Long articles appeared in the Soviet press with such titles as "They Try to Embellish Little Judas," ridiculing the prediction by some foreign sources that Trotsky would be rehabilitated.[37]

Every creed needs its forces of light and darkness, and just as the medieval Church could not have detected certain merits in the Antichrist, Trotsky had to remain a villain: the belief was too deeply engrained. Any revision might have caused a schism; it would have undermined the faith of the believers, perhaps even given rise to the birth of a new religion. As Alexander Bovin, one of the leading liberals, put it: "Trotsky is an extreme example. He is too negative a personality in our history and in the consciousness of the people. They consider some of his actions, particularly the things he wrote abroad, to be treason. We can do nothing against it; we can give no explanations, but Trotsky is too hateful a person. Therefore this matter belongs to the last and most difficult phase in the process of revealing things."[38]

True, there were considerable differences of emphasis. Some historians continued to comment on Trotsky in a wholly negative way: Thus, if the Red Army had prevailed in the civil war, it had been despite, not because of, his leadership; if he had certain minor achievements to his credit, it was only because he had carried out Lenin's instructions. According to the same line of argument he had always been inclined toward adventurism; his inspiration had been petit-bourgeois, not that of a true revolutionary. Other historians, such as Volkogonov, Stalin's semi-official biographer, conceded that while Trotsky had been a negative phenomenon overall, he had not been an enemy of the revolution and of socialism while Lenin was alive; that he had been a talented organizer, publicist, and orator; and that he had a good under-

---

[37]*Sovetskaia Rossia,* September 27, 1987. There was, as so often, an anti-Semitic insinuation. Lenin had indeed called Trotsky "Judushka" in one of the pre-1914 polemics. But he referred to a personality in Saltikow-Shedrin's novel *The Golovievs*—not exactly an attractive figure, but a Russian country gentleman, not a Jewish traitor. The literary allusion would have been recognized by most readers in 1910; by 1987 this was no longer certain.

[38]*Magyar Hirlap,* November 6, 1987; in *FBIS,* November 17, 1987. It can be assumed that no one but a few censors ever had access to Trotsky's books and articles. The pretense of knowing remained, even under *glasnost.* Thus a literary critic named Pompeyev complained in *Sovetskaia Kultura,* November 10, 1987, that Rybakov (about whom more below) had been inaccurate in describing the events leading to Kirov's murder in 1934. How could Pompeyev have known without access to the secret police archives? The relevant files, it is reliably reported, were destroyed long ago. In 1988 some voices favored publishing Trotsky's writings (Afanasiev, *Literaturnaia Rossiia,* 24, 1988), and a few authors even went so far as to claim that Trotsky had certain merits during the revolution and the civil war. But this was bitterly contested by the right wing and ignored by the party leadership.

standing ("from within") of Stalin's motives and intentions. However, later on, Trotsky had involved the party in unnecessary internal debates, lost much of his erstwhile prestige, adopted positions
hostile to the Soviet Union and Marxism, and—a new accusation—
had contributed, albeit indirectly, to the victory of Stalinism.

The new element in *glasnost* was that different opinions could
be voiced on a great variety of topics, on Stalin and Trotsky as
much as on the prehistory of the Second World War, with some
historians arguing that Stalin's policy (the pact with Hitler) had
been the only possible one, while others maintained that there had
been alternatives.[39] But there were also obvious limits—for instance, with regard to Stalinism. It could be freely admitted that
Stalin had committed crimes; there was always Lenin to replace
him as the supreme authority, unsullied by any transgression. But
Stalin could not be entirely discarded by the party leadership without undermining the legitimacy of party and state. For this would
have brought about precisely a situation in which Soviet history
would have appeared in retrospect a chain of "arbitrary measures," failures and disasters from the middle 1920s to the middle
1980s. Furthermore, the problem extended beyond the Stalin era,
since the age of Khrushchev and Brezhnev had also been weighed
and found wanting.

There is yet another explanation: namely, the possibility that
the present generation of Soviet leaders knows little about the
historical facts of their party and country. The true facts have been
well hidden; no one but a few experts has had access to them for
more than fifty years. Today the sources are more readily accessible but leading politicians have more urgent preoccupations than
engaging in historical research. They may have received advice
from professional historians but these belong to the orthodox
school and have a vested interest in not revising Soviet history yet
another time; it would reflect badly on their lifetime work.

Thus many present-day Soviet leaders may genuinely believe
what they were taught when they were younger men, and this
probably reinforces their reluctance to reopen old and painful
debates. A radical reexamination of Stalinism, its origins and consequences, might cause great political damage. Why risk this, if it

[39]For an assessment of Trotsky in the old spirit, see N. Vasetski in *Argumenty i Fakty*, 34, 1988;
for a more detached, objective appraisal, see D. Volkogonov, *Pravda*, September 9, 1988.
Knizhnoe Obozrenie announced the publication of a selection of Trotsky's writings for 1989–
90.

is so much more important to look forward than to ponder the past? It is important to recall that the transition from Stalin to the present generation of Soviet leaders was gradual; there never was a fundamental break with the mentality and the institutions of the Stalin period, only a gradual development. Why not trust the healing power of time rather than engage in painful introspection?

Hence the need for a cautious approach to Stalinism, carefully weighing the alleged pluses and minuses. Stalin, as Gorbachev said in his commemorative speech of November 2, 1987, was an "extremely contradictory personality." He made an incontestable contribution to the struggle for Communism and he defended its gains. Under his leadership the heritage of Leninism was safeguarded in the ideological struggle against left-wing and right-wing deviationists; industrialization and the collectivization of agriculture were carried out in short order. Excesses were committed but in the final analysis consolidating socialism in the countryside was a transformation of fundamental importance. The personality cult was bad and so was the murder of many faithful Communists. But the Great Patriotic War was won in the end, and "a factor in the achievement of victory was the tremendous political will, purposefulness and persistence, and the ability to organize and discipline people in the war years by Joseph Stalin."[40]

This approach toward Stalin and his system, which prevailed under Gorbachev, was politically acceptable to the great majority of the leadership. It also shows that the roots of Stalinism are so deep, its consequences so strong, that the whole truth about it cannot be revealed publicly to this day.

That Stalin was a "contradictory personality" goes without saying; most people are. Some redeeming factors can perhaps be found even in Adolf Hitler: unemployment was eliminated under him, superhighways were built, and he was certainly a military leader of considerable daring and vision. True, his rule led to the total collapse of his country. Stalin, in contrast, was victorious. He emerged from the war as the strong and wise leader of a superpower; he only caused enormous political and moral harm to his cause. Perhaps the damage was not irreparable: from the ashes of the Nazi Reich a new democratic Germany has emerged. In Stalin's case the repair work will be harder and longer, precisely because the house he built was never quite dismantled. Hence the contra-

[40]*New York Times*, November 3, 1987.

dictions and the vacillations in the process of de-Stalinization; hence the initial resistance on Gorbachev's part, the new impetus given in 1987, the resistance shown in early 1988, and the quickening of the pace during the summer of that year.

Alternatives to Stalin?

Even leading Soviet experts still face great difficulties trying to come to terms with the Stalin phenomenon. Some of these difficulties are political, others psychological and self-inflicted. The case of Professor-General Volkogonov, the author of the first official (or semi-official) Stalin biography, is most instructive. Volkogonov refers to Stalin's crimes and madness, but this does not prevent him from accepting interpretations which are manifestly absurd. Thus he tries to explain the purges and the terror of the 1930s with reference to Trotskyite and Nazi acts of provocation.

Trotsky's book *The Revolution Betrayed* had appeared in 1936, and Volkogonov reveals for the first time that a Russian translation was prepared by the Soviet security organs and handed to Stalin toward the end of 1937. Because Trotsky mentioned in this book that he still had support in the party and the army, and because he repeatedly used the slogan "Down with Stalin," could it not be that Stalin decided to engage in the bloody massacres of the political and military leadership after reading it?

The theory, alas, does not fit the chronology. By the time the NKVD delivered the Trotsky translation to the Kremlin, most of the victims were already under arrest and many had been shot. But even if Trotsky had written his book earlier and the translators had worked faster, the theory still would not make sense. For if Stalin was a paranoiac he did not need Trotsky's book as psychological justification. During the 1930s the Russian émigré press, in particular the right-wing papers, were full of alleged revelations of anti-Stalin plots among the Soviet military leadership, and it is probably of some interest that these stories were usually peddled by agents of the Soviet secret police.

For similar reasons, a reference in the forged Nazi documents to plots in the Soviet high command transmitted to Stalin through President Benes of Czechoslovakia is unconvincing. There is no evidence that these forgeries had any significant impact on the decision to decapitate the Red Army, let alone on the other "purges."[41] The real mystery concerns not Stalin's motives but the readiness on the part of serious people to accept spurious explanations fifty years after the event.

Volkogonov concludes that, however disastrous Stalin's regime, there was no alternative at the time. This has been challenged, directly and indirectly, by other Soviet writers—indirectly in a great number of articles shedding new light on Stalin's real achievements as the builder of socialism and as the supreme warlord. From these revelations it would appear that economic progress even during the first five-year plan was much more modest than hitherto believed, and that Stalin's foreign policy and military mistakes were graver and costlier than generally assumed. At the same time Stalin's role as a philosopher, an authority on linguistics, and an economic theoretician has been derided. It has been argued that, far from being a Marxist and a disciple of Lenin, he discredited through his actions, speeches, and writings the theory and practice of socialism and caused it untold harm.[42]

However, even among Stalin's most severe critics only a few maintained that there had been political alternatives. Some critics, such as Igor Kliamkin, have argued that given the general backwardness of Russian society at the time, Stalinism was probably inescapable. One leading economic historian, Otto Latsis, insisted that there was an alternative, namely the policies advocated at the time by Bukharin and the other "right-wing deviationists." Even fewer have dared to suggest that for tracing the sources of Stalinism one has to go back to Lenin's policies such as having "black-

[41]Interview with D. A. Volkogonov in *Sovetskaia Molodezh*, May 4, 1988. From the secret police files which became accessible to a selected few after 1986 it appeared that "cases" were prepared against virtually every prominent figure in Soviet life, including Zhdanov and Voroshilov. It had been known even before that the wives of Molotov and Kalinin, the prime minister and head of state, were detained in a concentration camp and that Kaganovitch's brother was executed. No one dared to intervene, let alone to protest.
[42]On Stalin as a linguist, see Mikhail Gorbanevski in *Literaturnaia Gazeta*, May 25, 1988; on Stalin as a philosopher, Genrikh Volkov, *Sovetskaia Kultura*, June 7, 1988; on Stalin and the trials of the 1930s, the television film *Protsess* (The Trial) first shown in May 1988. Many accounts of meetings with Stalin were published, including Konstantin Simonov's "Glazami cheloveka moevo pokolenia" (Through the Eyes of a Man of My Generation), *Znamia*, 3–5, 1988, written more than a decade earlier. One Soviet periodical, *Argumenty i Fakty* (20, 1988), claimed that while Stalin had been a Communist, he had not been a Leninist, a not readily intelligible distinction.

marketers" (i.e., the only people trading at the time) shot on the spot, of "squeezing" the peasants and destroying Russian agriculture, of organizing large-scale labor camps within two months after the revolution. "The borders of coercion expanded immensely: first it was used for suppressing the enemies of the revolution; later it was applied to potential enemies (the "Red Terror") and eventually as an instrument to solve economic problems."[43]

Thus even under *glasnost* there were limits to the search for the true origins of Stalinism including some of the most obvious ones. It was not possible to state clearly that there was a connection between the dictatorship of the proletariat (that is to say, the leadership of the Communist Party) and the emergence of Stalin, or that in the absence of elementary democratic norms of behavior within the party and outside it and of legal guarantees, the rise of a dictator with unlimited power was, at the very least, a strong possibility. Nor was Stalinism (in contradiction to Stalin) discussed in any depth. While Stalin's paranoia and Russia's backwardness were undoubtedly factors of some importance, it is also true that the dictator could not possibly have run the country single-handedly; he had hundreds of thousands of eager assistants. How to explain Stalinism as a political system and as a state of mind, how to account for the fact that so many people were willing helpers in actions that were not only inhuman but manifestly absurd? These were the truly pertinent questions, but for the reasons indicated it was impossible to confront them squarely. With all the fascinating revelations about the Stalin era, it was still impossible to pursue the search for truth to the end.

In the meantime a great many articles were published in the Soviet media concerning Stalin's public and private life; his sons and wives; his eating and drinking habits; his taste in literature, painting, and music. Even a first analysis was given of the handwritten comments he had made in the margins of the books in his library. These publications were more often than not negative, but there were also recollections which made him appear in a sympathetic light, such as the notes of A. T. Rybin, one of his bodyguards, who described in considerable detail how Stalin had stopped his car on one occasion when he saw an old woman walking slowly, leaning on a cane; how he ordered his driver to take the old lady home though this meant a considerable detour. It ought

[43]Vasili Selyunin, *"Istoki"* (The Sources), *Novy Mir,* 5, 1988.

to be recalled that similar accounts were also published about Hitler after 1945 by those close to him: how he used to stop boys and girls on the road and invite them to have coffee and cake with him, how he made it a practice to prepare a snack for the driver of his car, and so on. The old saying that no man is a hero to his valet does not, apparently, apply to the great dictators of the twentieth century.[44]

This is not the time to examine in detail Stalin's place in history. All that can be said of his regime is that the price paid in human life, in degradation, in moral corruption was staggering, whereas the achievements—economic, political, and military— were far from unique; only a mendacious propaganda has made them appear this way.

The Soviet economy could have been built up in the 1920s and 1930s on the basis of a variety of approaches; killing millions of people, impoverishing them, and imposing iron discipline is not a precondition for speedy economic growth. Given Russia's enormous size, the patriotism of its citizens, and its huge resources, any civilian or military leader except a man of gross incompetence would have defeated the German army. Tsar Alexander I was not a ruler of genius nor was Kutuzov a military leader comparable to Alexander the Great or Napoleon. But it was under their leadership that the invincible French, by then dangerously overextended, were decisively beaten. The German defeats at Moscow and Stalingrad were no miracles but rather the inevitable outcome of Hitler's boundless ambitions.

The present party line regrets the excesses and brutality of Stalinism. But it is not yet willing to accept the fact that there were basic alternatives to Stalin's policies. Such reluctance may be politically expedient but it is dangerous in a wider perspective. For if other alternatives did not exist, then the roots of the evil will be looked for one day in Leninism.

"According to the present party line"—but was it still correct to invoke a party line in historiography in 1988? In a general way such a line still existed, but this no longer applied to details, and some-

[44]See the recollections of Stalin's bodyguard in *Sotsiologicheskie Issledovaniia*, 3, 1988; for Hitler's friendly gestures, see, for instance, the memoirs of his chief press officer, Otto Dietrich, in *The Hitler I Knew*, London, n.d., pp. 164–65, and the recollections of his driver Erich Kempka, *Ich habe Adolf Hitler verbrannt*, Munich, n.d., p. 15.

times these details were of importance. This was true with regard to the collectivization of agriculture as well as the five year plans; there were considerable discrepancies in the assessments.

The conservative historians of the Brezhnev period—as yet the majority—would argue, for instance, that while Stalin had over-done in his speeches (and *a fortiori,* so had Molotov) the expres-sions of friendship with Nazi Germany, basically there had been no alternative but to sign a nonaggression pact with Hitler in August 1939. They would also argue that this pact was of no consequence as far as the German attack against Poland was concerned, for Hitler would have attacked in any case. The same historians would argue that the West was entirely to blame for the outbreak of the Cold War in 1947–48, whereas others, more self-critically inclined, would concede that Soviet foreign policy bore a considerable part of the responsibility in 1939 as much as in 1947. Frequently, offi-cial party organs such as *Kommunist* would take a "centrist" line between the extremes. Sometimes these discrepancies were far-reaching and more than a little amusing: while the conservative historians claimed that one could not be certain that the secret protocol to the nonaggression pact of 1939 was not a forgery, the newspapers in the Baltic republics had already published the text of these documents concerning the division of Eastern Europe into spheres of influence.[45]

The writings of Dimitri Volkogonov have been mentioned. He is both an army general and a professor; his academic qualifica-tions are undisputed, and since his father was a victim of the great purge in 1937 there is no reason to suspect him of any innate pro-Stalin bias. He does not deny or belittle Stalin's crimes; in his portrait he goes so far as to suggest that Stalin suffered from a mental disease which was never diagnosed.[46] Yet in the end the author reaches the conclusion that after Lenin's death only Trotsky and Stalin had a real chance to lead the party. In his view the country would have suffered under Trotsky even more since he had no program for building socialism in the U.S.S.R. Bukharin did have such a program, but with all his sterling qualities he did

[45]A few examples will suffice. L. Bezymenski and V. Falin (*Pravda,* August 28, 1988) put all the blame for unleashing the Cold War on the West; Dashichev and others disagreed. Feliks Kovalev and Oleg Rzhezhevski (*Pravda,* September 1, 1988) claimed that Stalin's policy in August 1939 was fundamentally correct. But M. Semiyaga (*Literaturnaia Gazetta,* October 5, 1988) as well as Kulish (in *Komsomolskaia Pravda*) called it a blunder.

[46]*Triumf i tragediia.* The preface to the book was published in *Literaturnaia Gazetta,* December 9, 1987. The text of the first volume appeared in *Oktiber,* October and November 1988.

not understand for a long period that the economic power of the country had to be boosted in the shortest possible time. The other candidates for leadership are dismissed; Stalin was the most consistent and determined defender of the strategy of the party. According to Volkogonov, he was no great theoretician, and he was inferior morally to the others. But with all the "burden of his imperfections" he had more political will and firmness of purpose.

This interpretation rests on a number of tacit assumptions: First, that there was a clear party line on domestic and foreign affairs at the time of Lenin's death which Stalin represented better and more forcefully than the others. But such a line did not exist either in domestic or foreign affairs, except in a very vague way. Second, that the Bolshevik party needed a strong leader, and that collective leadership or the division of labor is an invitation for disaster. This was Stalin's firm belief but it is not a basic tenet of Marxism; the charismatic, omnipotent leader may be a precondition for a fascist movement but not for a socialist party, however radical in inspiration. The thesis that Stalin was not expendable rests on the assumption that only under him could the Soviet Union prepare for a war against Nazi Germany. Yet in actual fact Stalin systematically underrated the danger of a German invasion; if he would have been aware of the danger he would hardly have given orders to destroy the leadership of the Red Army in 1937–38, a decision which cost the country millions of victims and severe defeats in 1941–42.[47]

Finally, this interpretation is based on the assumption that in the final analysis Stalin's achievements outweigh his crimes because he did so much for building and strengthening socialism in the Soviet Union. This is perhaps the crucial question and it deserves close scrutiny. Does it mean that owing to Stalin a society was created which at the time of his death—or indeed thirty-five

[47]The case against Stalin's policy vis-à-vis Hitler was made in some detail by Evgeni Gnedin in Samizdat in the 1960s. Gnedin was a Soviet diplomat stationed in Berlin at the time. A more recent, shorter indictment is Ernest Genri's "Pismo istoricheskovo optimista" (*Druzhba Narodov*, March 1988). This essay is based on a letter written to Ilya Ehrenburg some thirty years earlier. Genri is the pseudonym of a Soviet author and political agent who worked in Western Europe in the 1930s. While Soviet heavy industry was quickly built up in the thirties, it is still true that owing to Stalin's strategy (or lack of it) half of the iron and steel production fell into German hands during the first three months of the war and was no longer at the disposal of the Soviet war effort. V. Dashichev, a professional historian, made the point that French and British appeasement of Hitler ("Munich") was not just dictated by anti-Sovietism; how could they see a reliable military ally in Stalin, who had just decapitated the Red Army? (*Sovetskaia Kultura*, May 18, 1988).

years afterward—was richer materially and spiritually than others, a society free of corruption, and democratic in character, more honest and truthful, deeply imbued with humanitarian ideals; a society in which citizens showed genuine concern for one another, in which children were better cared for and more respect shown to the elderly than in the exploitative societies of the West; a society rich in culture, of high ethical standards, in which the pursuit of money and material goods played no longer a central role?

To ask the question is to answer it. If it is argued that this is not the right yardstick, the question arises, What criteria have to be applied to assess the meaning of socialism? And it is on this count that the case for Stalin, or rather the case for mitigating circumstances for Stalin, finally breaks down.

But he retains considerable support in sections of the population. For as the strong reaction against de-Stalinization has shown, Stalin was genuinely popular, or at least respected, in wide circles of Soviet society. These sympathies have various motivations: the right wing admires him because, though a foreigner by birth, he made Russia a military superpower and stressed in his speeches the leading role of the Russian people. Others respect him because, as they remembered, under Stalin prices went down and criminals were punished. Yet others feel no particular concern about the "purges" because most of the victims were old Communists, or because they dislike present-day critics of Stalin—liberals, Jews, and such like. It is frequently said that every people gets the government it deserves. This is often unfair because "the people" may have no say in selecting their government. However, in Stalin's case the debate refers to a leader who has been dead for several decades. If there is still admiration for him it must be concluded that there was even more during his lifetime, and that Stalin's way of governing corresponded with the idea many of his subjects had about how their country should be run.[48]

So much then about the "historical compromise" on Stalin which prevailed under Gorbachev in 1987–88. Of course, it was a transitory measure; of course, it could not last. But while it lasted, it

[48]According to a poll published in *Vechernaia Moskva* (August 27, 1988) only 0.8 percent of those questioned regarded Stalin as a positive hero, in contrast to 16 percent the year before. Thirty percent thought that there were good sides as well as bad to his character.

had its undoubted uses: there was more freedom to express dissenting opinions, which in the past would have led the dissenters straight to a camp or a psychiatric hospital. Novelists and playwrights were permitted to publish works deviating up to a point from the party line—which, in any case, became quite blurred. A more sophisticated approach prevailed. Some Soviet historians noted that it was a mistake to run down systematically all opponents of Marx, Engels, and Lenin; many of them had been talented people, including socialist leaders such as Plekhanov and Martov. Describing them as fools and knaves neither conformed with historical truth nor did it add to the stature of the "classics of Marxism."

Critical historians quoted documents which could not possibly have been mentioned in the past, such as, for instance, Rosa Luxemburg's somber reflections on the future of Soviet rule written shortly before her death: "With the repression of political life in the land as a whole, life in the Soviets must also become more and more crippled. Without general elections, without unrestricted freedom of the press and assembly, without a free struggle of opinion life dies out in every public institution, becomes a mere semblance of life in which only the bureaucracy remains as the active element."[49]

Most of the early debate has dealt with the question of whether Stalin was good or bad for the Soviet Union and the cause of Communism. The discussion of the deeper issues, of Stalinism as a political system, of its popularity, of the many little Stalins and their style of work only slowly and hesitatingly came under way in 1988. The disappearance of millions of people under Stalin was a horrible thing, but as a Soviet critic wrote, the suppression of the feeling of dignity and assurance among those who survived was equally horrible and had a pernicious influence on society in general. But was it only fear which explains the strange affinity between Stalin and many millions of people, both semiliterate and highly educated? Stalin, as an historian has noted, remains a vital issue, perhaps the vital issue *par excellence* for the Soviet people: "Stalin beat out of us the capacity to think independently and to

[49]A debate between A. Yegova and V. Loginov in *Literaturnaia Gazetta,* October 28, 1987. Rosa Luxemburg wrote "unrestricted freedom of the press"; this became "freedom of the press" in the Russian translation. She had written earlier in the same essay: "Freedom only for the supporters of the government, only for the members of one party, however numerous they may be, is no freedom at all. Freedom is always and exclusively freedom for the one who thinks differently."

doubt, without which there is no search for truth."[50] But Stalin in this context is no more than an abbreviation for much wider issues: the source and consequences of Stalinism, the whole course of Soviet history, Russian social life, and the politics and culture of the Soviet people in the past and present.

Gorbachev told members of the CPSU Central Committee in June 1986 that a new style of work with the intelligentsia had to be adopted: it was harmful and inadmissible to order them about. Someone objected, claiming that it would be difficult to work in an environment where each individual was his own philosopher, his own foremost authority, and believed that he was right. Gorbachev replied that it was far worse to be dealing with a passive intelligentsia and with indifference and cynicism.

These were refreshing words and certainly a break with the spirit of the Brezhnev era. But they were based on the assumption that the "guidelines" for the intelligentsia (again according to Gorbachev) were not just based on a "new level of thinking and responsibility" but also "coincided with the political course of the CPSU."[51] What if the guidelines did not coincide, or if the intelligentsia engaged in controversies and quarrels, as usually happens when it is not strictly regimented? In such a situation, it must be assumed, the party would still have to intervene—not as crudely as in the past, but still strongly and decisively.

Paradoxically, the party faces fewer difficulties confronting its prerevolutionary and postrevolutionary bourgeois antagonists, the Tsars, their servants, and the bourgeois leaders. It is far easier to publish the writings of Karamzin, the advocate of Tsarist autocracy, or non-Marxist historians such as Solovyev and Kliuchevski[52] than some of the old Bolsheviks. It is easier to find mitigating circumstances for the political behavior of a leader of the White emigration—say, a General Denikin, who emerges as a patriot in some recent Soviet writings—than for the Mensheviks and Social

[50]The contribution of historians to this debate has been modest so far. An exception, apart from those already mentioned, is M. Hafter in *Vek 20 i mir*, 6, 1987. Other important essays have appeared in the literary journals—for instance, Igor Kliamkin in *Novy Mir*, 11, 1987; Yuri Burtin in *Oktyabr*, 12, 1987; A. Bocharov in a comment on Vasili Grossman's *Zhizn i Sudba*, in *Oktyabr*, 2, 1988; and the long essays by V. Selyunin and O. Latsis mentioned above. Many of these essays appeared in a collective volume *Inogo ne dano* (Moscow, 1988), which became the manifesto of the reform party.
[51]M. Gorbachev, *Perestroika*, pp. 81–83.
[52]In multivolume editions of 100,000–150,000 copies. Excerpts from Karamzin appeared in the literary journal *Moskva*, 1–3, 1988, an unprecedented accolade for a historian 160 years after his death.

Revolutionaries, who remain sworn enemies.

The liberals on the Soviet scene have tried to explore the parameters of the new freedom by trial and error, invoking the authority of Lenin as often as possible. An astute observer had noted as early as 1960 that "Leninism, in fact, has become an alibi for opponents of the regime."[53] He may have exaggerated but not by much. Lenin's works are an unending source of quotations concerning democracy and the evils of obscurantism. In the ideological shadow boxing which will no doubt continue, and in which a spade must every so often be called an agricultural implement, Lenin, the heir of the enlightenment, has become the apostle of freedom of thought in the Soviet Union.

One day, perhaps, the political leadership may reach the conclusion that truthful history books are no longer dangerous, and that it is, therefore, safe to publish the whole truth about Stalin and the past in general. But in the foreseeable future in all likelihood only the most blatant untruths will be eliminated to the extent that they concern party members unjustly "repressed" under Stalin. Unfettered historiography will remain potentially subversive and may have serious political consequences. It is a strange fact that the Soviet leadership can still afford more *glasnost* with regard to the present than the past, and this may not change soon.

[53]"They said Lenin, but what they really meant was liberty. An avowal of devotion to Lenin was the only way they could give their opposition the appearance of legality" (Klaus Mehnert, *Soviet Man and His World*, New York, 1962, p. 265).

CHAPTER 5

Artists Out of Uniform

HE MIRACULOUS YEARS of Soviet literature, 1987 and
1988, were a new "golden age," the richest harvest ever.
In the words of one critic it was more than a second thaw;
it was a true cultural blossoming, unfettered (or almost
unfettered) by the dead hand of censorship. These were years of
enormous spiritual ferment and creative openness such as a much-
suffering Soviet culture had not known for six decades. As the
German humanist of the Renaissance had written, *"Iuvat vivere"*—
"It is a joy to be alive." But not everyone shared this joy and some,
in fact, were firmly convinced that Satan and the forces of evil were
about to destroy all that was still good in Russia.

The fact that the literary magazines after years of almost unmitigated drought suddenly became very interesting would not
have been considered a matter of paramount importance in almost
any other country. But in Russia literature always had a function
and an impact more powerful than elsewhere. There had been
more freedom of expression in Russian literature under the Tsars
than in any other field. As Belinski had written in an often quoted
letter 150 years earlier, in literature alone, despite Tartar censorship, is there life and a forward movement. Something of interest,
however slight, could usually be found in one of the literary magazines.

The first thaw which had set in soon after Stalin's death had
been limited in duration, and even more restricted in extent. It was
all over by the late 1960s with the deposition of the editorial board
of *Novy Mir,* the last journal which had shown some inclination
toward cultural freedom. But even during the *zastoi,* the period of

stagnation, some mildly daring ideas were occasionally voiced in the pages of the literary journals—or on the stage of the more enterprising theaters—usually by way of hint and allusion, which would have been unthinkable in the professional journals, or in the general press.

True, the main benefactor of such latitude was the right-wing, conservative trend which had tried subtly, and sometimes not so subtly, to insinuate that there had been much to admire in prerevolutionary Russia. These circles tried to juxtapose, albeit in a roundabout way, Dostoyevski (the political publicist rather than the author of the *Brothers Karamazov*) to Marx; they praised Russian patriotism and denigrated foreigners—Jews and members of other minorities—even if they happened to speak and write in the Russian language. They took the side of the Slavophiles (or rather the more extreme among them) in their confrontation with the "Westerners": most of Russia's misfortunes, they argued, had come from the importation of European and Western ideas.

Such theories were not, of course, new. Novel was the implication that Marxism-Leninism was alien to the Russian heritage. From time to time when the journals of the right such as *Molodaia Guardia* or *Nash Sovremennik* had gone too far, they would be upbraided and compelled to retreat to ideologically more acceptable positions. Then, after an interval of a few years, one or a group of writers would make another Slavophile foray to find out how far the party line could be stretched, sometimes with partial success, sometimes to be called back, and given a warning by the ideological supervisors.

These semi-licensed deviations, more interesting from a political than a literary point of view, were not very risky. More revealing, and more rewarding, was the publication of novels and short stories during the seventies which conveyed a detailed and rather depressing picture of life in the Soviet countryside. "Socialist realism," the embellishment of reality, was invoked less and less frequently and gave way to truthful accounts, including, among others, the Siberian stories and novels of Valentin Rasputin, Vasili Shukshin, and Sergei Zalygin, and the stories from northern Russia by Fyodor Abramov and Vasili Belov. Moving works were in the tradition of the great Russian literature of the nineteenth century; they came like a breath of fresh air. Books which had a similar effect were the writings of Chingis Aitmatov, a Kirgiz who wrote Russian, and Vasili Bykov, who translated his works from his native White

Russian. From time to time they would be attacked by the official watchdogs for writing in a vein too pessimistic and depressing.

These authors were certainly more widely read and held in higher esteem than the official coterie, the organization men of the writers' association, the chief editors of the major literary magazines, and their friends and assistants. As in the movies there was a trend away from the public toward the private sphere of life and the nonpolitical; the case of Yuri Nagibin, who relatively late in life discovered an interest in classical music and composers, is an example. The works of some leading émigré writers were also published between the two thaws: Bunin's works had appeared in the 1960s, Igor Severianin's poems in 1979. Nor were the works of the victims of Stalin's purges all kept under lock and key. Some of Babel's stories appeared in the sixties, and a volume of Mandelstam's verse in 1979. Despite the ostracism of Pasternak, some of his poems were published in 1965 and his early prose in 1982. Works by Anna Akhmatova and Marina Tsvetaeva were also published. Andrei Platonov and Mikhail Bulgakov were rediscovered in the late 1960s: Bulgakov's *The Master and Margarita* was an enormous success when it was published posthumously in 1966. There was no *absolute* ban on these and other writers, but much of their most important work was still censored and they were brought out in small editions. The official histories of literature either bypassed these writers altogether or made some short, negative comments while growing ecstatic about hacks whom few took seriously or indeed read.

Thus even in the "age of stagnation" there had been some faint rays of hope. Nor was the Gorbachev era ushered in with a drum roll; it took about a year for *glasnost* to show its face in literature. But once it had come under way by the second half of 1986 it rapidly gathered momentum. The editorial chairs of some leading literary journals changed hands—Zalygin, a leading *derevenshik* and not a party member, became editor of *Novy Mir;* Serge Baruzdin improved the performance of *Druzhba Narodov;* and Georgi Baklanov was made editor of *Znamia;* none were known as extreme liberals. But they believed in greater freedom of expression and they were willing to publish writers dealing with subjects that were once tabu. *Literaturnaia Gazetta* and *Oktyabr* remained nominally, at least, in the hands of the stalwarts of the old literary order; but their orientation, too, changed considerably. *Sovetskaia Kultura,* previously one of the most tedious publications of all, began to feature interesting essays on a variety of subjects; *Ogonyok,* once one of the main bulwarks of the neo-Stalinists, featured political and literary revelations in almost every issue which drove neo-Stalinists and conservatives to a state of near apoplexy. Some of the journals outside the capital, such as *Neva* (in Leningrad) or *Don* (published in Rostov), also published novels and essays that were widely read and discussed.

The right still kept its positions; the monthlies *Molodaia Guardia, Nash Sovremennik,* and *Moskva* continued to belong to them, as well as the weekly *Literaturnaia Rossia, Pravda, Sovetskaia Rossia,* many of the regional literary journals, and above all the influential *Roman Gazetta,* which published recent novels in cheap mass editions. Not within living memory had anyone but a *bien pensant* writer been published under these auspices.

What annoyed above all the opponents of the new course was the "revaluation of values" which set in as the year 1986 drew to its close, and the fact that writers who had so far been barely tolerated found themselves in the center of the stage whereas yesterday's pillars of Soviet literature were ignored. They thought it a scandal that only a few writers and virtually no playwrights were writing any longer about the great achievements of the past—the transformation of a backward agrarian country to a great industrial power; the Second World War and the patriotism shown by the Soviet people. Why the negativism of the new writing with regard to yesterday's leaders? Why the disregard of tradition?[1]

As far as the opponents of the new course were concerned, Pasternak and Mandelstam were at best problematical characters, aliens happening to write in the Russian language. What did they know about the Russian people, its longings and suffering, its deepest feelings? The conservatives were willing to exonerate émigrés such as Bunin and Igor Severianin, misguided patriots to be sure, but Russian both according to their racial origin and their inspiration. The Ahkmatovas and Tsvetaevas had contributed little or nothing to praise the achievements of the Russian people in peace and war. They had been preoccupied with their personal little problems, their private mental anguish and various laments. The antiliberals had nothing against religious motives but not of

---

[1]The theme was belabored in countless speeches by officials throughout 1986 and 1987, and in articles in the right-wing and neo-Stalinist literary magazines—for example, Vyacheslav Gorbatov in *Molodaia Guardia,* 3, 1987, and 7, 1987, and V. Bondarenko in *Moskva,* 12, 1987.

the kind Pasternak had introduced; they were bitterly opposed to Western influences and literary innovation. The fact that Josef Brodski, yet another "cosmopolitan" writing in the Russian language, received the Nobel Prize for Literature in 1987 reinforced them in their belief in a giant Western conspiracy—a concern never far from the surface in these circles. *Novy Mir*'s publication of some of Brodski's poems in December 1987 provoked further indignation over the "cold cerebral verse" of this writer.[2]

While yesterday's outsiders were singled out for praise, the works of the former literary leaders dwindled into insignificance. There had been a time in Soviet literature, as Veniamin Kaverin wrote, back in the 1920s when literature and the history of literature—that is to say, the official standing of writers—had been the same. Subsequently an official literature had evolved which was widely published but frequently worthless and remained unread. As true literature regained its rightful place, schoolchildren would point with their fingers to the absent clothes of yesterday's princes of literature.

With some hesitation the opponents of *glasnost* would invoke their own literary pedigree. Alexander Blok, Mayakovski, and Yesenin were always mentioned, and Alexander Fadeyev and Tvardovski were usually added to show their tolerance. It was not a convincing list: Blok and Yesenin had not been Russian chauvinists or loyal Marxists-Leninists. Mayakovski had been a leading innovator and therefore did not fit. Fadeyev had committed suicide because of the state of Soviet literature, for which he felt responsibility. Tvardovski had been the protector of liberals and Jews under Khrushchev and Brezhnev, and had been hounded out of office by those who now claimed to be his heirs.

It was in the heat of these debates that the term *nekrofilstvo*—the morbid attraction to corpses—was first coined by the opponents of rehabilitation. Pasternak and Akhmatova were undeniably dead but their work was infinitely more alive than the writings of their detractors, and this, no doubt, annoyed the detractors no end. Had these patriots been more familiar with the history of their own

---

[2]For a typical attack against Chagall, Brodski, and other "alien elements," see *Sovetski Voin*, March 3, 1988. *Doctor Zhivago* was denigrated in *Pravda* by Dmitri Urnov, for political rather than literary reasons, and Brodski's verse was ridiculed in *Komsomolskaia Pravda* by a critic who adduced an émigré periodical of the extreme right as his star witness. However, these attacks did not pass without contradiction. Thus Urnov was taken to task by various other critics in *Pravda* (June 6, 1988), and Brodski's Nobel Prize lecture was printed in *Knizhnoe Obozrenie*, 24, 1988.

literature, they might have hesitated to use this term. "Nekropolis" had been the dateline of Cha'adayev's famous *Philosophical Letters* more than 150 years earlier, one of the most merciless, self-critical documents in Russian literature.

The publication of Anna Akhmatova's *Requiem* and Tvardovski's *By Right of Memory* were literary events of the highest order.[3] Many learned these long poems by heart. But it is also true that their public impact would have been infinitely greater if they had not been suppressed for twenty years or even longer. The same is true with regard to the Russian publication of *Dr. Zhivago* in 1988. As one critic noted, what if Gogol's *Dead Souls* had been published in 1862 rather than in 1842 (that is, *after* the liberation of the serfs)? What if Turgenev's *Fathers and Sons* had appeared in 1882 rather than in 1862?[4] They would still have been read as great works of world literature but their specific timely character would no longer have existed.

Those who complained about the "negativism" of the new literature were not altogether mistaken. But they were looking in the wrong direction. They should have worried about books like Rasputin's *Pozhar (Fire)*, Astafiev's *Sad Detective,* and Aitmatov's *Plakha,* as well as similar works by writers whom no one in his right mind could suspect of "cosmopolitanism" and "liberalism." *Pozhar* describes the moral decline in a small town in Siberia: the warehouses begin to burn, but instead of trying to put out the fire, the inhabitants engage in an orgy of looting and even killing. It is a new settlement; several villages had been merged artificially into one. The people have no loyalty and feeling of solidarity and belonging; they make money, drink, and steal. The story is told by Ivan Petrovich, a local militiaman; it ends when he decides to leave the little town, having lost his home. He has little hope of finding a new one where people still have moral standards and care about others, where the difference between good and evil is still clear.

Fire is a somber, pitiless description of life in the author's native Siberia. Ten or twenty years earlier, literary critics would have denounced the book for its "untypical" character and "depressing" message;[5] it was one of the signs of the times that Rasputin

---

[3]The former was published in *Oktiabr*, 3, 1987, and *Neva*, 6, 1987; the latter in *Znamia*, 2, 1987, and *Novy Mir*, 3, 1987. Such simultaneous publication was almost unheard of in Soviet literature.

[4]Y. Burtin, in *Oktiabr*, 8, 1987, p. 192.

[5]This was the fate of Rasputin's predecessor Fyodor Abramov in the 1960s and 1970s.

received for this novel the state prize for literature in 1987. Yet for an even more merciless description of life in a provincial town we have to turn to Rasputin's friend Victor Astafiev's *Sad Detective;*[6] Rasputin called it the "frankest book we have had, written with the blood of his heart."

This is the story of a suspended policeman turned author and is a wholesale condemnation of the values and the lifestyle of virtually all sections of society. Astafiev is particularly vitriolic about intellectuals; "tourists from Moscow"; modern Western civilization, with jeans as its symbol; emancipated and careerist women; and non-Russian minorities. But he is equally caustic about the lawless riffraff in town and countryside. Why does a policeman have to fear the crowd when he intends to make an arrest? Why are simple people indifferent vis-à-vis invalids and handicapped people? Why are they willing to share their last crumb of bread with an arrested criminal? Astafiev writes about parents who do not care about their children but starve them to death or even abandon them in a freezing street. He believes that the breakdown of the family and the decline of patriotism are the reasons for the general disintegration of Soviet society.

Like Astafiev, Vasili Belov believes that the fate of the contemporary family is perhaps the most painful problem for the writer as much as for the citizen. In an interview on the eve of the Twenty-seventh Party Congress (to which he was a delegate), Belov said that the destruction of the family "will cost dearly to our country, from an economic as much as from a demographic and moral point of view."[7] In the novel *Everything Is Still Ahead,* which was a *succès de scandale,* he describes the horrors of big-city life. Misha Brish, a cosmopolitan and "Zionist," breaks up a Russian family by enticing a woman to abandon her husband and to join him. The bait is a trip to Paris which he has arranged. The story opens with a group of Soviet tourists visiting the sinful French capital—symbolic of the destructive influence of the West on Russian life and character. Had they not been attracted by Paris, the ensuing tragedy might not have happened. But as in Astafiev, there is also much unfavorable comment on some of the Russian characters, especially the women, an attitude Belov shares with some other "village writers," which is in contrast to the classic Russian writers of the

---

[6]While Rasputin's novel was almost universally welcomed, Astafiev's encountered criticism. See, for instance, A. Kucherski in *Voprosy Literaturi,* 11, 1986.

[7]Vasili Belov, *Vse vperedi* (Everything Is Still Ahead), Moscow, 1987, p. 2.

last century; it will be recalled that in Tolstoi's and Turgenev's novels women often emerge as the stronger characters.

Lastly, Aitmatov's *Plakha (The Execution Block):* a Western commentator, referring to a previous Aitmatov novel which appeared in 1980, expressed astonishment at how it not only slipped by the Soviet censor but was highly praised as a Soviet novel with a positive hero and thus worthy of emulation.[8] Aitmatov is a great user of symbols, and it could be that the censors did not quite understand his message. But the content of *Plyakha,* complicated and multifaceted as it is, leaves little room for doubt. The hero is a religious believer (even though he was expelled from the seminary); and God, who is frequently invoked in the book, is always written in capital letters. To make the message even more explicit, the hero is crucified by the criminals whom he tried to convert. He had first tried his luck with drug runners, and later on with a gang of particularly nasty poachers. The message is quite simply that a return to the old values is needed, that religion or something akin to a religious faith is vitally needed.

Such "flirting with God," as the party critics used to call it, is less risky than it may appear at first sight; reverence for the Orthodox Church—not just for religion—had appeared as a motive in the published works of Russian writers such as Soloukhin for more than a decade without any lasting ill-effects for the authors. In any case, Aitmatov argued that he was not so much concerned with religion as with modern man: "I tried to forge a road across religion to man. . . . Jesus Christ gives me occasion to say something concealed to contemporary man. That is why I, an atheist, encountered him on my creative road."[9]

The party organs published a few articles in reply by specialists on atheism, but these were given short shrift by leading writers such as Yevtushenko and by critics who noted that the time for tired primitive argumentation ("God does not exist because the cosmonauts did not see him in the skies") had gone forever. They referred to the doubts and arguments as to whether God existed, and, if not, whether there was a psychological need to believe in a deity.

It had been said about young Russians in the 1960s that while they no longer believed in God they were still very much afraid of

[8]Katerina Clark, in her preface to *The Day Lasts More Than a Hundred Years,* Bloomington, 1983; originally published in *Novy Mir,* November 1980.
[9]*Literaturnaia Gazetta,* August 13, 1986.

the devil. By the 1980s some major Russian literary figures, albeit no longer in their first youth, showed unmistakable traces of super-stition and forms of paranoia commonly associated with the Mid-dle Ages. The literary critic Vladimir Lakshin, a survivor of the *Novy Mir* group of the 1960s noted, comparing Aitmatov's and Vasili Belov's recent books, that while Aitmatov's heroes debated the search for God, Belov's main figures talked with equal concern about the fateful role of the devil, whose corrupting influence was seemingly all-pervasive.[10]

By spring 1987 the conservative officials of the writers' organi-zations had become extremely worried by recent developments on the cultural scene. True, Rasputin's and Astafiev's books also made depressing reading, but these were Russian patriots, who had always preferred to keep out of the Moscow literary intrigues, living far away from the capital and not looking for offices and honors. The real danger, as the literary bureaucrats saw it, came from the liberal-democratic party firing their broadsides against neo-Stalinism and Russian nationalism. The ideological concern of the conservatives was genuine, and it was reinforced by fears concerning their own position in literature and society.

The appointments of new editors worried them. So did the fact that they lost ground at the eighth writers' congress in 1986 with the appointment of some liberals to the writers' union exec-utive, and that a near-revolution had taken place in the movie-makers' union. Their main ire was directed against the literary critics who were trouncing mercilessly those who until recently had been immune to criticism. For a long time there had been two camps in Soviet literature, and the liberals had had nothing but contempt for the court writers of the Brezhnev period. But they had not been able to say this openly and for this reason it did not greatly matter. Now they could speak out and the result was devastating: A young lady had dared to call Vasili Belov's attitude toward women "a manifestation of hatred for human be-ings." Others had ridiculed old stalwarts of the Stalinist period or accused them of denouncing their colleagues to the police. (One such case concerned the playwright Anatoli Sofronov.) Quite often the young critics treated their elders and betters as if they did not exist—Yuri Bondarev complained that his last novel,

[10]V. Lakshin, *Izvestiia,* December 3 and 4, 1986.

Igra, had not received for a long time a single lengthy review. He did not react gracefully: in a series of long articles and interviews he compared himself by implication to Tolstoi, arguing that *War and Peace* had also been lambasted by the critics at the time, and that the critics were quite incapable of deciding what books were good and would last.[11]

Squabbles between writers and critics have, of course, occurred at all times and places. (Goethe: "Kill him, he is a reviewer. . . .") But in Moscow, in the given circumstances, it was more than a matter of violated personal vanity; it was the struggle between two ideological camps. While the liberals, having been the aggrieved party for so long, were sometimes perhaps too sweeping in their attacks, the neo-Stalinists and the "Russian party" were far more extreme; they refused to find any merit in the writing of the "enemy." While the liberals would never doubt the literary significance of an Abramov, a Rasputin, or a Shukshin, the other camp would *a priori* reject the writings of all those who did not belong to their clique. The attitudes strikingly resembled those of right-wing writers in the Weimar Republic toward their liberal and Jewish colleagues: they were degenerates and traitors.

The accumulated frustration and anger of the leading figures of the Brezhnev era was voiced at the meeting of the secretariat of the writers' union of the R.S.F.S.R. in March 1987.[12] The meeting was opened by its president, Sergei Mikhalkov, who bitterly complained that behind the slogans *glasnost* and *perestroika,* "time-servers and speculators" were hiding, as well as people without talent and "sinister characters." What bothered Mikhalkov above all was that the critics were ignoring holders of the supreme awards and offices in the literary field, such as himself and the speakers which followed him. V. Dementyev also complained that the literary critics were not showing sufficient respect for the classics of Soviet literature; part of the young generation had become quite indifferent to the values cherished by their elders. He spoke with nostalgia about the good old days, meaning 1937, when (he claimed) so much had been done for the spiritual development of the Soviet

[11]Bondarev had been spoiled. His previous book had been compared by a Moscow professor of literature not only to the works of Tolstoi and Dostoyevski, but also to Kant, Leonardo, Shakespeare, Beethoven, Mozart, and Flaubert (Natalia Ilina, *Ogonyok,* 2, 1988).

[12]This organization had been founded in the late 1950s as a counterweight to the slightly less conservative all-Union writers' union.

people. He did, however, have some good words for Tvardovski's *Po pravu pamyati (By Right of Memory)*—no doubt to the annoyance of Nikolai Shundik and Mikhail Alexeev, the speakers who came after him and who, twenty years earlier, had been signatories of the denunciatory letter in which they appealed to the authorities to take sanctions against *Novy Mir*—this because of the dangerous ideological influences such as cosmopolitanism and liberalism of which the then-editor of *Novy Mir* had been guilty.[13] The response of the authorities did not fail to come.

Now the general mood had changed and erstwhile attackers were on the defensive. There was hysteria in the air. Shundik called the writers with whom he disagreed "our enemy"; as he saw it, de-Stalinization, like that after the Twentieth Congress, had gone much too far. For Mikhail Alexeev the protagonists of *glasnost* were demagogues who wanted to bury all the spiritual values of the Soviet people in a deep pit so that no trace would remain.

The most extreme and revealing speeches were those by Peter Proskurin and Yuri Bondarev. Proskurin lamented the fact that the young writers, by and large, were ashamed to use the word "Communist" in their novels. He also attacked the liberal journals who had turned into sectarian groups, and the critics who, "acting like hooligans," had dared to attack the great contemporary masters of Soviet literature. There was more than a little hypocrisy in these speeches, for the *groupovshina* (sectarianism) had originated precisely among the right-wingers. Nor was Proskurin's own attachment to Communism beyond suspicion, for his predilections were clearly for Russian nationalism. The early Leninist, "heroic" period (the spirit which Gorbachev wanted to revive) was anathema for people of his kind. Communism had become acceptable in these circles only after Stalin had killed off the old Bolsheviks and had incorporated a strong admixture of Russian nationalism.

Lastly, there was the case of Yuri Bondarev, a writer of talent. A officer in World War II, the author of moving novels in which there was no trace of paranoia, he had over the years become

[13]*Ogonyok*, 30, 1969. The surviving signatories of the letter came in for harsh attack in 1987–88. They tried to defend themselves but not very convincingly: they had dearly loved Tvardovski, they said; their criticism had been directed only against some of the doubtful characters, such as Siniavski, who had been published by *Novy Mir*. This was disingenuous, for Siniavski had not belonged to the *Novy Mir* inner circle and had not been frequently published. The infamous "letter" was written four years *after* Siniavski's arrest.

accustomed to delivering increasingly shrill apocalyptic warnings. The critics were out to destroy him. He was the first to use the term "civil war" to describe the state of affairs in Soviet literature. In fact, something worse had happened. Conditions were comparable to the situation in July 1941 following the invasion of the German armies, when the Russian forces had to retreat under the blows of the "civilized barbarians"—blows which were meant to destroy the great Russian culture. He continued, "If this retreat will continue and if there won't be a new Stalingrad, it will all end with the ruin of our national values and all that is spiritually dear to us."[14] Now the enemy was not Hitler but the "pseudo-democrats" trumpeting *glasnost.* In another speech he charged his enemies with cosmopolitanism; nervously they were paying attention to what was said in the West, thus humiliating themselves and losing their dignity and self-esteem.

The meeting in March 1987 was followed by another in May in which there were further clashes. But this time the framework was broader; the antiliberals were no longer among themselves and they had to be more cautious. Mikhail Alexeev demanded that *perestroika* be carried out with a minimum of victims. Kunaev, a neo-Stalinist, winner of the state prize for literature for 1987, complained that there was a hit list; some of his friends found it difficult to be published. Bondarev declared that Russians were the most talented of all people—but others were also talented. Baklanov, the new editor of *Znamia,* was criticized by an old Stalinist for not publishing in his journal enough material in praise of the Soviet armed forces. But on the whole the tenor was somewhat less shrill. Those who opposed *glasnost* constantly invoked Ligachev, who had earlier declared that literary criticism had always to be imbued with "social optimism." The problem facing the conservatives was, of course, that this prescription hardly fitted the works of the more gifted writers among them.

According to persistent rumors in Moscow, some of the leading writers of the right sent a collective letter to the Central Committee of the party drawing its attention to the seriousness of the

---

[14]*Literaturnaia Rossia,* March 27, 1987. By summer 1988 his excitement had somewhat abated; he regretted the "implacable enmity" among writers of various persuasions and thought that "in our profession one has to keep silent at times. . . ." But the hostility toward the liberals had not passed, a fact that emerged from his speech at the June 1988 all-Union party conference at which he was a delegate and in which he bitterly attacked the "princes of extremism," meaning the reformers. See *Literaturnaia Gazetta,* June 22, 1988.

situation in the literary field and suggesting its intervention. Various letter writers to leading newspapers announced that they had informed the KGB about poems, novels, and plays they thought dangerous and subversive. There is a hallowed tradition of "informing" in Russia, but in this case it seemed out of place. It could be taken for granted that the authorities were perfectly capable of reading and understanding what the literary journals were publishing.

The polemics continued. A typical example was a long attack by Vyacheslav Gorbachev, deputy editor of *Molodaia Guardia,* in which he suggested that Stalin might have been the victim of the bureaucracy and that it was wrong, therefore, to put all the blame on him. Perhaps it was the fault of Trotsky, who had proposed at the Ninth Party Congress that the peasants be "mobilized"; obviously Stalin had been influenced by Trotsky. Editor Gorbachev also suggested that *Ogonyok* be purged; perhaps another journal was needed, one lighter in vein, to be called *Broadway* or *Montparnasse;* if publicity had to be given to Marc Chagall and other such abominations, this would be the right place to do so.[15]

The liberals did not turn the other cheek; they published some very powerful essays against those responsible for suppressing for decades all that was good, healthy, and honest in Soviet literature. Yuri Karyakin's open letter to *Incognito* reminded one of Belinski's famous attack against Gogol, who toward the end of his life had embraced religious obscurantism.[16] There was moral pathos in his appeal to the apostles of stagnation and darkness for contrition at this late hour—for the sake of the young generation, on behalf of the future Russia of decent people, in the words of Dostoyevski.

It is doubtful whether Karyakin nursed any illusions with regard to the effects of his appeal. If the party had given instructions to repent, those he addressed would have repented with a vengeance. But there was no clear party line: *Oktyabr* announced it would not reply to the polemic initiated by *Molodaia Guardia,* while other organs were less reticent. The antiliberals found powerful defenders. Without mentioning names a writer in *Pravda* defended

[15]Vyacheslav Gorbachev's reputation as a leading critic of the materialist consumer society was slightly damaged when *Moskovski Literator* (the organ of the Moscow branch of the writers' union) published the text of a revealing letter he had written at about the same time to the executive of his union: As a man of high political principles he deserved a more spacious apartment. Unless he got one soon he might commit some act of despair. . . .
[16]*Znamia,* 9, 1987.

Astafiev, who had been a little too outspoken in a private letter[17] which had found its way (not through his fault) into the publication *Samizdat.* A Moscow Jewish professor of literature—thus threefold anathema to Astafiev—had entreated him not to make a habit of attacking minorities in his books such as the Jews in *Sad Detective* (the offending passage was later deleted). Astafiev, a war invalid with a short fuse, replied in a manner more befitting a Russian right-wing émigré ("Why did you Jews kill the Tsar and his family?") than a Soviet citizen. But *Pravda* knew that, all things considered, Astafiev was on the right side of the barricade and so he had to be defended against the *littérateur* who had provoked him.

Pravda represented the official line, but to make matters more confused, *Kommunist,* also an organ of the Central Committee, called for mutual tolerance: it defended the liberals who, the right alleged, had not shown sufficient respect to the authorities. The critical works of Rybakov and Tvardovski, of Bek and Dudintsev had been published (the *Kommunist* commentator wrote) and the skies had not fallen in. Some people were no doubt annoyed as a result, but the majority realized that "knowledge is our fate, there is no other road to the future."[18]

Tvardovski had written in *By Right of Memory* that he who was hiding the past jealously would not be on good terms with the future. Rybakov, Bek, and Dudintsev (the other authors mentioned in *Kommunist*) had all written books on the Stalin era which could not be published prior to the age of *glasnost.* Alexander Bek, who had died a few years earlier, dealt in "The New Assignment" with Tevosyan, for many years the minister in charge of heavy industry. Publication had been held up because the minister's widow had complained; the book had never been officially banned, but it had not been permitted either.

The late Vasili Grossman had fared worse; he had been told by Suslov, the chief party ideologist at the time, that his book would perhaps be published two hundred years hence. (It was published in *Oktiabr* in 1988.) Dudinstev had been a pioneer of *glasnost* in the

---

[17]*Pravda,* August 3, 1987. Astafiev had a misanthropic strain. He had previously offended the Georgians and also published an essay in which he bitterly attacked an army marshal of World War II fame, thus bringing upon himself the ire of the conservative circles: had he sold out to the liberals of *Literaturnaia Gazetta?*

[18]I. Dedkov, *Kommunist,* 12, 1987, p. 63.

early post-Stalin era and had burned his fingers as a result. *White Coats,* [19] the novel on which he had worked for many years, described the destruction of Soviet genetics in 1948–49 by the Lysenko school. Of all the scandals in the scientific field during the Stalin era this had been one of the most outrageous, and also one of the most costly to state and society: banning a poem or a play has no immediate untoward economic consequences, but agriculture is likely to suffer if it is based on mistaken theoretical assumptions. Dudintsev described in great, perhaps excessive, detail how the campaign against geneticism was staged, the intervention of the party leadership and the secret police, the reaction of individual scientists facing the attack. As usual, there had been some heroes and more scoundrels; the majority had collaborated with the authorities without inner conviction.

While Dudintsev's novel was a *roman à clef,* Granin's work *Zubr (The Aurochs)* is the story of a historical figure, Timofeev-Rezovski, also a geneticist. His case was in many respects unique: Delegated to work in Germany in the late 1920s, he refused to return when recalled in 1937; at that time his brother and most of his colleagues had already been arrested and some of them murdered. He was a Russian patriot, not a Nazi sympathizer; his son perished in a German concentration camp. When the war ended Timofeev remained in Berlin even though he knew that his compatriots would arrest him. He spent the next years in a Soviet camp and would almost certainly have died there of starvation had not someone suddenly recalled that he was the only Russian specialist in a field of great importance to national security. He was given a laboratory, first inside the Gulag, later in semi-freedom. *Zubr* triggered off many debates and there were, of course, some critics who claimed that it was Timofeev's moral duty to return in 1937 even if it was tantamount to suicide.[20] Most took a more lenient view.

---

[19]*Neva,* 1–4, 1987. The literary journals were far more enterprising and daring than the publishing houses, which took an unconscionably long time to bring out novels of this kind. Thus to give but one example, Rybakov's *Children of the Arbat* was brought out in an edition of 1,200,000, but could be obtained only in the special foreign currency shops. It could have easily sold millions of copies.

The publication of major novels previously banned in the literary magazines continued throughout 1988: *Druzhba Narodov* (3/4, 1988) featured Platonov's *Chevengur; Oktiabr* (1–4, 1988) published Grossman's *Zhizn i Sudba; Zamiatin's We* appeared in *Znamia* (4–5, 1988); *Dr. Zhivago* was printed in *Novy Mir* (1–4, 1988), to mention but a few. As a result, other important essays were crowded out or did not get sufficient attention; there simply was too much to read.

[20]A. Kazintsev, in *Sovetskaia Rossia,* June 17, 1987.

Anatoli Rybakov's *Children of the Arbat* is the story of a whole generation, the boys and girls of central Moscow, the graduates of the early 1930s. It has two heroes, one a student called Sasha Pankratov, handsome, a good son and friend, reasonably intelligent and above all an enthusiast, terribly naïve and a bit of a prig. An exemplary young Communist, he commits some minor ideological gaffe at his college. Normally this would be dismissed as a student's prank and he would get away with an admonition. But unknown to him the organs of state security are building up the case against an old Bolshevik, and Sasha is needed for completing the frame-up. Thus a student's prank becomes an act of treason; he is arrested and lucky to get away with a relatively mild sentence—three years of administrative exile in Siberia. (The story takes place just before the great purge.) Young Sasha does not, of course, understand what happens to him: he sincerely believes that it was all a horrible misunderstanding, that he would be immediately set free if only Stalin knew. Even his experience in Siberia cures him only in part.

The other hero in this book is Stalin. It is the story of a man who genuinely believes in the cause of Communism as he understands it (which is to say a dictatorship similar to Pharaonic Egypt), who thinks that he is irreplaceable and who, in the final analysis, happens to be a criminal. Stalin appears as a politician who came to power not because of his charisma, farsightedness, or oratorical gifts but because of his unlimited self-confidence, a first-class intriguer and more brutal than his colleagues. He totally lacks moral inhibitions, despises all those around him, and is firmly convinced that unless the Russian people fear their rulers, there will be chaos and a general breakdown. The novel describes how the downfall of Kirov, the second man in the Politburo and a far more popular leader, is planned by Stalin. But it stops short the day before Kirov's murder in December 1934, so that it is not made quite clear whether Stalin only gave general instructions to get rid of this potential rival (as he saw him) or whether he planned the murder in detail. This story of a lost generation of erstwhile enthusiasts is a very sad one; some get caught in the wheels of purges and trials, some turn informers and collaborators, and those who survive are also not unscathed morally.

Rybakov's book makes unprecedented revelations about an entire age but it cannot, or does not want to, tell the whole truth.[21] He exercises an objectivity which one feels he would have rejected had he written, for instance, about Hitler.

Rybakov believes that there is hope for Soviet society provided it squarely confronts the past, not only the question of what happened but also of why it happened. Vasili Grossman, the author of *Life and Fate,* had little such hope. Born in 1905, his career was always in strict conformity with the party and Stalin; during the Second World War as correspondent of the army newspaper *Red Star* he was one of the most widely read writers. In 1960 Grossman finished writing *Life and Fate,* a huge volume, the last part of an epopee, and submitted it to the editor of *Znamia,* who passed it straight on to the organs of state security. The manuscript was seized but the author was not arrested or exiled; these were the relatively free years of Khrushchev, and Grossman furthermore suffered from cancer, of which he died soon after. A copy of his work found its way to the West, where it was published.[22]

Life and Fate cannot be summarized in brief. It describes the battle of Stalingrad, but the action also takes place in the Soviet rear—in Nazi concentration camps in Germany, and in the Moscow Lyubianka, the central secret police prison. Some historical figures appear, such as generals Rodimtsev and Chuikov, and Stalin once intervenes when out of the blue a single telephone call changes the fate of Shtrom, a talented Soviet scientist who as a result of some political intrigues faces disaster. But this is almost the only ray of light in a story of unmitigated dark despair. True, Stalingrad is a decisive victory for the Soviet people, but it also means the further strengthening of the Stalinist regime and of servitude.

The basic theme of the book is the conflict between the individual and the all-powerful state. Grossman sees no basic difference between fascism and Communism (the "synthesis of unfreedom

---

[21]Critics of the right accused Rybakov of one-sidedness. One of them wrote that considering Rybakov's personal fate he was relatively objective (Idashkin, *Literaturnaia Rossia,* July 29, 1987). Rybakov had some difficulties with the regime as a young man in the 1930s, but he received the Stalin Prize in 1951 when a "cosmopolitan" like him was not *persona grata.* He had no personal reasons to feel more aggrieved than others. Rybakov's book is to a certain extent misleading inasmuch as he concentrates on Stalin as an individual, not showing sufficiently the importance and responsibility of Stalinism as a system. However, the book had an enormous educational importance and it was precisely for this reason that it was attacked—for instance, by K. Stepanian in *Literaturnaia Rossia,* December 25, 1987, and by Pompeyev and the right-winger Pikul in *Komsomolskoe Znamia,* December 6, 1987.

[22]In Lausanne in 1980. A German edition appeared in 1984, an American in 1986. Alexander Bek's book, of which mention has been made, also appeared in Germany before it was published in the Soviet Union.

and socialism"). True, those who carried out the revolution in 1917 were internationalists (unlike the Nazis); true again, they wanted the best for mankind. But the erstwhile internationalism has vanished, and the attempt to compel people to do what is best for them ended, like all previous such attempts, in slavery. In comparison to a work with such a message, *The Children of the Arbat,* let alone *Dr. Zhivago,* is politically harmless.

Many other interesting novels appeared in that memorable year, and many plays were staged which could not have been published or performed before. Some had been written many years earlier, such as Bulgakov's *Dog's Heart* (written in 1925) or Platonov's *Kotlovan* (on the collectivization of agriculture). Others had been written more recently but were devoted to a past which had so far been out of bounds, such as Pristavkin's *Nochevala Tuchka Zolotaia (A Little Golden Cloud Passed During the Night)* describing the deportation of nationalities in the Caucasus during the war. New names appeared dealing with contemporary subjects which no one would have been permitted to touch before. One striking example was Serge Kaledin's *Humble Graveyard,*[23] a story about gravediggers, the lower depths of Soviet society, semiliterate drunkards, the criminal underworld, the flotsam and jetsam of society looking for comfort in religion. These characters are very far from the handsome, ideologically motivated, and problem-free heroes of the age of socialist realism. One also finds the unconventional heroes in the stories of Vladimir Makanin, such as *Utrata (A Loss)* and *Odin i odna (A Lone Man and a Lone Woman),* or Boris Vasilev's *Zhila byla Klavochka*—all deeply tragical. As one critic put it, new writers appeared who were fully fledged masters without apparently having gone through any apprenticeship.

Of equal interest were the nonfictional comments on various aspects of social and cultural life published in the literary journals. The most outspoken essays on economic and social problems appeared not in the professional journals but in *Novy Mir* and *Oktiabr.*[24]

The journals of the right concentrated on the struggle against alcoholism and rock music and also on ecological problems—the

[23]*Smirnoe Kladbishe, Novy Mir,* 5, 1987. The title alludes to a Pushkin poem.
[24]This refers, for instance, to the article by N. Shmelyov, *"Payments on Account, and Debts," Novy Mir,* 6, 1987; V. Selyunin and G. Khanin in the same journal, 2, 1987; Mikhail Antonov, *"So What Is Happening to Us?" Oktiabr,* 9, 1987; and A. Nuykin, "Ideals or Interests?" *Novy Mir,* 1 & 2, 1988.

fate of the Siberian forests, of Urengai, the Baikal, the Aral Sea. The "liberal" publications also paid growing attention to this once neglected topic. On one issue they all agreed—the need for the struggle against the cultural bureaucracy. But this was easier said than done, for, as the Russian minister of culture revealed in an interview, according to hundreds of existing regulations the ministry of finance had far more power concerning things cultural than he did in his own office.

In the center of attention was the "human factor," which also figured prominently in speeches at party congresses and in the writings of economists and sociologists such as Tatyana Zaslavskaia. Daniil Granin wrote a widely discussed essay about *milosertse* (charity), relating an accident that had happened to him in the streets of Leningrad. Not one of hundreds of passersby had come to his help as he lay bleeding on the ground. This was the starting point for his reflections on what had happened to some of the wonderful qualities of the Russian people which once upon a time had been taken for granted. Some readers suggested the establishment of an organization to promote charity. But, as Granin rightly noted, it was doubtful whether this quality could be inculcated administratively. Another leading critic noted that "if you look at the masses, you think, my God, where does so much anger and alienation stem from?"[25] Essays were published on crime and punishment, on bad manners, on the behavior of Soviet tourists abroad. It was a time of *samobichevanie* (self-flagellation), of fouling one's own nest, as the opponents of *glasnost* saw it. It was the time of telling the truth after decades of enforced silence and of official mendacity. For some it was the best of times, for others it was the worst of times.

Glasnost and the Arts

The cultural ferment that took place under *glasnost* is most striking in the literary field. True, there were personal changes in the leadership of almost all the media,[26] but the results were curiously

[25]Lev Anninski, *Literaturnaia Gazetta,* April 22, 1987.
[26]Thus Vitali Korotich became editor of *Ogonyok* instead of Anatoli Sofronov, a prominent Stalinist; Ivan Frolov replaced Richard Kosolapov as editor of *Kommunist,* the official party fortnightly; Boris Pastukhov, who was made ambassador to Denmark, left as editor of the daily *Sovetskaia Rossia* and was replaced by Valentin Chikin, formerly of the state publishing house; Pavel Naumov was ousted as director of the *Novosti* news agency, and in his place came Valentin Falin, formerly ambassador to West Germany; Egor Yakovlev became editor

uneven. The number of subscriptions for *Novy Mir* more than doubled in 1987 and exceeded one million, an astonishing number for a "fat" literary journal. The figures for *Druzhba Naradov* and *Znamya* reached 750,000 and 520,000 respectively. (They had 155,000 and 250,000 subscribers in 1985.) As the literary critic V. Lakshin put it, these figures should be considered for entry into the *Guinness Book of Records*. Nor did they convey the full picture, for certain issues (for instance, those of *Druzhba Narodov* containing *Children of the Arbat*) were handed on and read by many people until they literally fell apart. The literary journals of the right did on the whole less well than those of the liberal left, but there were exceptions. *Moskva* added to its readership probably because of the publication in installments of Karamzin's *History of Russia*, a work of great patriotic fervor and considerable literary merit which had originally appeared in the early nineteenth century. *Izvestiia* added to its circulation (30 percent) whereas *Pravda* lost a little ground; this was no doubt connected with the fact that the former became the more interesting of the two.[27] The journals devoted to foreign affairs and foreign culture also declined in circulation, partly because events inside the Soviet Union were now so much more interesting, but also because readers had no longer to look for these specialized magazines to obtain information and knowl-

---

of *Moscow News,* one of the flagships of the new thaw, while his predecessor Genadi Gerassimov was made spokesman of the foreign ministry; Alexander Potapov, who had worked in the Central Committee, became editor of *Trud,* and Ivan Panov editor of *Krasnaia Zvesda,* the army newspaper; the state television and radio got a new director, Alexander Aksenov, who had been ambassador to Poland replacing Serge Lapin; Alexander Kamshalov was appointed head of Goskino instead of the veteran Filip Ermash; Albert Beliaev, also of the Central Committee, became editor of *Sovetskaia Kultura.* Even the chief censor, Pavel Romanov, lost his job. There were many other changes.

[27]The supply of newspapers and literary journals remained altogether insufficient during this period except by subscription, but there was a queue for subscriptions, too. The newsstands were quite empty; on occasion the present writer would find a copy of *Ashkhabad,* a literary magazine published in the capital of Turkmenia (and of no interest to anyone outside Ashkhabad), at the kiosk at the Kursk railway station, or with luck, and after much trying, a copy of *Sovetskaia Musika* or *Vestnik Statistiki* at a kiosk in a Moscow *kolkhoz* market where interest in these topics was limited. Even for the daily newspaper one frequently had to queue; they were usually sold out after one hour. One afternoon, on Kuznetski Most, the street of bookshops, I joined a queue following the sound principle that this was the only way to obtain a publication of interest. I returned with a copy of the first Soviet book on the subject of queues: V. L. Bogdanov and V. P. Kondakov, *Ochered, zlo ili neizbezhnost (The Queue, an Evil or an Inevitability?),* Moscow, 1987. Queuing is the second biggest industry in the Soviet Union, with sixty-five billion man-hours yearly; it employs more people than farming, the building trades, and science and technology taken together. See O. Latsis, *Znamya,* 2, 1988.

edge about political and cultural developments abroad. If a "provincial" magazine like *Neva* published Kafka, and if a Latvian publishing house announced the impending appearance of Orwell's *Animal Farm,* journals like *Za Rubezhom (Abroad)* or *Inostrannaia Literatura (Foreign Literature)* lost much of their attraction. Another significant development was the fact that television and radio, despite some interesting innovations, showed not remotely as much *glasnost* as the print media.

The differences in the degree of *glasnost* were so striking that one looks for specific causes and explanations. Did the ferment proceed on orders from above, or was it spontaneous, or perhaps a mixture of the two? The pattern was far from clear. In some fields there was a great deal of movement, in others hardly any at all. This is true, for instance, with regard to the "party sciences" such as philosophy, history, and economy; there was a reshuffle in the editorial board of *Questions of History* but it came late in the day (January 1988). How to explain that some institutions and their organs became more liberal whereas others hardly changed or even opposed change?

All appointments had to be approved by the party, and seen in this light the element of chance was minimal. The instruction given was: let the intellectuals and the artists have some more freedom. But some did not want more freedom and, on the other hand, in two specific cases something akin to a palace revolution took place and the old guard was unceremoniously ousted.

First there was the revolt of the Soviet moviemakers at the fifth congress of their union (May 1986). The situation in this field had been particularly bad, even though more movies were being produced than in Stalin's last years, when the industry had come to a virtual standstill. But the quality was low, and this expressed itself in steadily decreasing cinema attendance. Slightly unconventional films were either heavily censored or altogether shelved. Leading directors such as Tarkovski made their homes abroad; others were ostracized. A small clique decided what should be produced and by whom and how widely it should be distributed. When the elections to the secretariat of this organization—usually a formality— took place on the last day of the conference in 1986, Lev Kulizhanov, secretary general for the past twenty years, was replaced by Elem Klimov, a moviemaker of the avant-garde who had been in deep trouble for years with the censors. Two-thirds of the seats in the new executive also went to the rebels. In some ways it was a generational revolt—of those in their late forties and early fifties against those about ten years older who had dominated the scene during the Brezhnev era and even before. But the decisive issue was whether the moviemakers would have more creative freedom.

There had been rumblings even before the congress, such as bitter complaints in some leading newspapers about the dead hand of the censor (Goskino) which stifled all creative activity. The revolution in the union of moviemakers caused misgivings in the ranks of orthodox party leadership: What if the apparently spontaneous uprising would spread? Was it not a dangerous omen if a professional union slipped out of direct party control? But since at the time of the coup several leading representatives of the Central Committee, including Alexander Yakovlev, had been present, it must be taken that Klimov and his supporters had at least tacit approval from some party leaders. And when Gorbachev was approached in the weeks after, he explained to his apprehensive comrades that he regarded the upheaval among the filmmakers as a healthy development and that there was no room for fear and overreaction.

The revolution in the Soviet theater was equally sudden and in some respects even more far-reaching: At the time of the fifteenth congress of the all-Russian theater society (VTO) in October 1986, one of its members, Oleg Efremov, head of the Moscow Arts Theatre (Mkhat), got up and suggested the establishment of a new organization of Soviet theater workers. He received the support of a majority of those present and the new organization came into being soon after.

Such administrative reorganization may appear to Western observers of no particular significance, but in the Soviet context it was of very considerable importance. For according to established practice every Soviet theater had to have its repertory confirmed in Moscow. It was totally dependent on the decision of party officials with little or no competence in the field. It was defenseless against regional party secretaries who, for one reason or another, wanted to ban a certain play, even if it was performed elsewhere in the Soviet Union.[28]

The old generation had done nothing to defend theater work-

[28]The quality of party and government officials in the cultural field seems to have been particularly low. As the minister of culture said in an interview, "If a man has not been too good in party or economic work, he is sent to head a theater, a museum or a philharmonic orchestra." V. G. Zakharov in *Ogonyok,* 45, 1987.

ers against such intervention and censorship, whereas the new union was created specifically for the purpose of defending theatrical art against arbitrary administrative interference.[29] Even those who had been accused in previous years of being "modernists" or "subjectivists" were now given the opportunity to stage their plays in their own new theaters or within the framework of old established ones. At the same time plays on topics of Soviet history (Shatrov) which had hitherto been tabu or on controversial social issues (Gilman, Nisharin, and others) were shown.

The immediate results in the cinema were less spectacular than many had expected. The movie organization set up a committee to reexamine censorship decisions of past years; as a result some thirty feature films that had been shelved were shown for the first time in movie houses or on television, including those by Kira Muratova, Alexei German, Gleb Panfilov, and other talented and creative Soviet filmmakers. But most films tend to become dated after ten years, and furthermore they had been subject to self-censorship in the first place. Topics which had appeared daring in the late 1970s no longer seemed exciting a decade later. Abuladze's widely discussed *Pokayanie (Repentance)* was shown throughout the Soviet Union in January 1987. It is the story of the life and crimes of a local dictator who bears a strong physical resemblance to Beria, the head of the political police under Stalin. Its message was no more revolutionary than Khrushchev's famous speech at the Twentieth Party Congress in 1956; but Khrushchev's speech had never been published and it had lacked of necessity the emotional impact which could be achieved by focusing on specific people and situations.

Some notable television plays were produced in 1987 such as *Risk*, depicting the fate of Soviet pioneers of missile construction in the late Stalin period. But the new feature films shown were not essentially different from those produced five or ten years earlier.[30] Perhaps the hopes had been too high; perhaps it had been

---

[29]For the background of the reorganization, see Alexander Svobodin in *Nedelya*, November 10, 1986, and various articles and interviews in *Sovetskaia Kultura* and *Literaturnaia Gazetta* throughout November and December, 1986.

[30]Boris Berman, *Moscow News*, December 20, 1987. Berman was one of the first (another was Yevtushenko) to draw attention to Askoldov's film *The Commissar*, which had been banned for twenty-one years. Even the new leadership of the filmmakers' union was apparently reluctant to fight for this movie because of its pronounced Jewish angle. And so Askoldov's film received awards at Western festivals but was not shown in the Soviet Union. See Askoldov's press conference in San Francisco, *Russkaia Mysl*, June 3, 1988.

unrealistic to expect within a year or two a flood of works of genius. Removing the most repressive measures only created the precondictions for works of a new kind; it could not by itself provide the spark of genius. Artists needed time, even if the inspiration existed. While leading party officials would declare, more often abroad than at home, that "nothing was forbidden anymore," only foolhardy film producers would take such statements quite literally. But the question of artistic freedom quite apart, there was also the issue of popular taste. The most popular movies had always been thrillers (such as *The Pirates of the Twentieth Century*). Occasionally, a producer of the avant-garde such as Rolan Bykov or Klimov himself would produce a movie which was also a commercial success. But more often than not they would just be critical successes, as Tarkovski's films had been. Since Klimov and his supporters had announced more than once that the film studios were to become self-financing and that those that went broke would be disbanded,[31] the situation in the movie industry soon became critical, for the studios no more worked at a profit in 1987–88 than they had done in the past, albeit for different reasons. Soviet movies would get awards at international film festivals but the Soviet public, by and large, did not respond with similar enthusiasm. And those who had been against "too much freedom" in the cinema did not fail to exploit the difficulties facing the new leadership.

If the theater and the cinema were in the vanguard of *glasnost,* music and painting were in the rear. Both had suffered enormously under Stalin, and the general party line had not radically changed even after the death of the dictator. The famous Zhdanov decrees of 1948, which regimented art in the narrowest possible way, had been modified but they had not been openly and officially revoked until late 1988. The protagonists of "official art" who headed the professional organizations and journals, who decided on exhibitions and musical programs, were still in office or had passed their duties on to their pupils. This, too, had lasting consequences: the deterioration of standards even in fields in which Soviet art had been traditionally excellent (such as the ballet), and the emergence

[31]*Sovetski Ekran,* 4, 1987. For a good general survey on the changes in the Soviet cinema and literature, see John D. Dunlop, "Soviet Cultural Politics," *Problems of Communism,* November–December 1987. Victor Demin reviewed some of the main problems facing the Soviet film industry more than a year after its housecleaning, such as the difficulties in producing competent political films, finding a believable approach toward sex in the cinema, in dealing with social issues other than drugs, and in depicting the problems facing soldiers returning from Afghanistan. See *Sovetski Ekran,* 3, 1988.

of a second, unofficial culture, of composers, painters, and sculptors who were not members of the professional organizations and had their own exhibitions and concerts. Some cynics argued that it did not greatly matter whether Soviet fine arts were free or strictly regimented, because they did not boast of many geniuses in the first place. But there had been a time before and after the revolution when Russian art had flourished and attracted international attention; given a modicum of artistic freedom there might have been a revival. Cynicism was certainly out of place with regard to Soviet music. But precisely because in this very century there had been the likes of Stravinsky, Prokofiev, and Shostakovich, it was all the more difficult to understand the continued decline after 1953. When *glasnost* came, many observers seemed to agree that listeners were no longer interested in symphonic music and that music criticism was worthless.[32]

Some composers, such as Alfred Schnittke and Edison Denisov, made their living writing film music but found it exceedingly difficult to make a breakthrough to concert and stage. Millions listened to bards such as Vysotski, to variety music and jazz (which was semirespectable), and, increasingly from the late 1960s, to rock music, which for many years was altogether undesirable. When in 1987 the composers' union decided to transfer its plenary meeting from Moscow to Kemerovo, the coal-mining center in the Kuznetsk region, some observers interpreted it as a symbolic act for it meant getting as far away from the capital as possible.[33]

However, in the event even Kemerovo was not far enough to escape the repercussions of *glasnost*. In May 1988 Vera Gornostaeva, a professor at the Moscow conservatory, published an article which included long quotations from speeches made in 1947–48 by Tikhon Khrennikov, the then-head of the composers' union. They included attacks against Prokofiev, Shostakovich, and others, and generally speaking Khrennikov's full and servile acceptance of the Stalin-Zhdanov decrees. There was nothing extraordinary in

[32]Vladimir Dashkevich, *Moscow News*, 48, 1987.
[33]It is only fair to add that as the result of *glasnost* and *perestroika* there was some ferment in the publications of the union. *Sovetskaia Musika*, 3, 1988, appeared with a Chagall picture on its cover. *Isskustvo*, 2, 1988, the main organ of the artists' union, did not go this far but stressed editorially the need to reclaim as part of the national heritage the pre- and post-revolutionary modernist art which had been ignored or banned for many decades. But on the whole there was very little of the new spirit of self-criticism in the organs of the artists' and composers' unions. Progress was very slow and even *Pravda* complained that there had not been much *perestroika* among the artists (A. Kamenski, *Pravda*, September 9, 1988).

such behavior and there would have been no storm of indignation but for the fact that Khrennikov was still secretary of the union forty years after the event. He called a press conference but instead of expressing regret for his behavior he claimed that he had been a very young man at the time, that someone else had written his speeches, that his father and brothers had also been arrested in the purges. In short, it was not a very convincing performance; and though he had the support of most of his colleagues on the union excutive and was elected (or appointed) a delegate to the June 1988 party conference, many voices were very critical and it was clear that his incumbency was drawing to an end.[34]

The Soviet artistic scene had been dominated by mediocre, almost indistinguishable works but this began to change against much resistance under *glasnost.* True, the key positions in the Academy of Fine Arts stayed in the hands of the Gerasimov school; Gerasimov had been Stalin's court artist. But in January 1988, Andrei Vasnetsov became head of the artists' union. He was one of the "severe" artists (or naturalists) who had been in trouble with the authorities twenty-five years earlier. Not all former rebels had remained nonconformists. There was Ilya Glazunov, the patriotic-mystic-religious painter, once an outsider, whose exhibitions had drawn far bigger crowds than the official *vernissages* in the 1970s. He became a pillar of the establishment under *glasnost* and made it known that his ideal had always been a kind of "superior realism"; abstractionism was as alien to him as photographic naturalism. He was firmly convinced that all those who had not received formal training were mere dilettantes. Glazunov was deeply opposed to "extreme left-wing tendencies" in art—that is to say, to avant-gardism. What better teachers were there, he asked, than the great Russian masters of the past such as Repin and Surikov?[35] Thus another lost son had returned to the fold.

Outside the camp and lacking official recognition were the many nonofficial painters, abstract or nonconformist in other ways. They, too, had their public even though they were harassed from time to time by the police (for vagrancy) or by local party institutions who sent bulldozers to "bury" their exhibitions, as in a famous incident in 1974.

[34]The Gornostaeva article "Komu prinadlezhit isskustvo?" ("To Whom Does Art Belong?") was published in *Sovetskaia Kultura,* May 12, 1988. The discussion went on for many weeks; see, for instance, *Sovetskaia Kultura,* June 7 and 16, 1988.
[35]*Pravda,* September 27, 1987.

Glasnost manifested itself in a certain democratization: a few younger painters were coopted to the leadership of the professional organizations, and some of their work was shown in the big official exhibitions.[36] The younger painters continued to complain that the official exhibitions were of no interest to them; they ran their own showings at Kuznetski Most, in the Izmailovo Park, and elsewhere; the old Arbat for a while turned into a great market of alternative art which the custodians of the older schools considered "provincial" and "third class."[37]

The alternative exhibitions did not all consist of works of great mastery; there were reports about visitors demanding their entrance fee back, even if they had paid only twenty kopeks. But these were at least honest failures, which is more than can be said about the bankruptcy of the official art. As one reviewer put it, the leading painters of yesteryear were neither interested in art nor in the public but merely in their income from state orders. From time to time an ideological discussion would come under way; the journal *Khudozhnik (The Artist)*, the organ of the conservative artists' union of the Russian Federation, would attack *Isskustvo (Art)* for being insufficiently vigilant against the giant antirealistic conspiracy which was allegedly under way, against formalism and modernism.[38]

There were disputes as to what of contemporary art should be shown and where, and which of yesterday's "avant-gardists" and "cosmopolitans" should be rehabilitated. The publicity given to Marc Chagall on the occasion of his hundredth birthday provoked the ire of the conservatives. Their aversion, to be sure, extended almost equally to the avant-gardists of pure Russian stock of the early twentieth century. But after the minister of culture had made it known that while he personally preferred realistic art, the avant-garde was also a fact and painters like Kandinsky, Malevich, Tatlin, Larionov, or Filonov were "also part of our national achievements." All-out opposition had to cease and the old artistic establishment had to make some reluctant concessions. A similar trend took place in the musical field; Efim Golyshev, originator of a precursor of the twelve-tone technique and an émigré, was

[36]Alexander Yakimovich, *Dekorativnoe Isskustvo SSSR*, August 1987; on the situation in art history, see A. Chegodayev, *Sovetskaia Kultura*, October 24, 1987, and D. Sarabyamov in *Literaturnaia Gazetta*, December 2, 1987.
[37]*Sovetskaia Kultura*, September 19 and November 14, 1987. When I visited the Old Arbat last in April 1988 I found little alternative, or indeed any, art.
[38]B. Vishnyakov, *Khudozhnik*, 4, 1987; A. Kamenski's reply in *Ogonyok*, October 26, 1987.

rehabilitated; living modernists such as Schnittke, Gubaidulina, Denisov, and Hersovici were permitted to travel abroad. Soviet ensembles appearing abroad were permitted to perform hitherto banned works by the leading composers of the early, experimental postrevolutionary age.

A review of the cultural scene during the heyday of *glasnost* shows a contradictory picture: great changes in some fields and hardly any in others. These changes had not come as a present from above (as Yevtushenko once put it); they had been preceded by a long struggle on the part of some writers and artists. This struggle would not, however, have been crowned with success but for the emergence of a more tolerant leadership. In some respects it was a question of generational revolt, but since among the "rebels" were also men and women in their seventies and eighties, this was clearly only one aspect of the progress of liberalization. Resistance against the new freedom was very strong both for political reasons and because of the unwillingness of the old leadership to give up their dominant positions with all the social and financial privileges involved.

In many fields the hold of the enemies of *glasnost* was so strong that change was restricted to the very minimum. The price the conservatives had to pay was increasing isolation, the danger of being bypassed and becoming irrelevant. Such dangers were greater in journalism, music, and the arts than in party history or philosophy, where a monopoly of access to the sources and means of publications narrowly circumscribed the progress of opposition. Nor did future prospects appear entirely hopeless to those who resisted change. If the champions of *glasnost* invoked Gorbachev and Yakovlev, the conservatives could quote the authority of Ligachev, who had admonished the intellectuals on various occasions not to engage in destructive, purely negative criticism; truth, as he said, was not a single-minded concentration on what was bad in society.[39] As a protagonist representing the old order put it in one of Fyodor Burlatski's dialogues, "Well, we face a new wave; yesterday it was Ivan's style, now we face Vasili's. Such waves come and go, and this is what *perestroika* is all about."[40]

At times the conservatives must have felt misgivings about the future, but so did their antagonists. No one could be certain how far *glasnost* would go and how long it would last. Remembering

[39] *Teatr,* 8, 1986; *Sovetskaia Kultura,* July 7, 1987.
[40] *Literaturnaia Gazetta,* October 1, 1986.

past experiences, the reformers felt behind them the lengthening shadow of the gunman. Thus the situation in the arts, the sciences, and the media resembled the state of affairs in general. There was hope for more freedom but there was also great resistance to change, and there was no certainty that *glasnost* had come to stay. But there was greater courage than at any time in the past on the part of writers and artists, of composers and moviemakers, greater readiness to defend cultural freedom. And this was perhaps the most encouraging aspect of *glasnost* in the cultural field.

CHAPTER 6

The Reemergence of the Russian Right: Between Patriotism and Fascism

WITH THE RISE of *glasnost* it was widely believed in the West that Gorbachev's reforms would lead to a renaissance of left-wing, liberal democratic thought in the Soviet Union. The new Soviet ideology would seek its roots in the ideals of the Enlightenment, the French Revolution, and the democratic tradition of the Russian radical movement of the last century. Gorbachev and his supporters looked back with nostalgia to the early years after the revolution of 1917, the age of enthusiasm and relative freedom, a period of cultural experimentation when the skies of Russia had been bluer and the sun had been shining brighter than anywhere else, when Russian books, films, and educational ideas had attracted the attention and the support of men and women of goodwill all over the globe.

It should have been clear, however, that greater freedom would give rise to a variety of schools of thought. Neo-Stalinism still had its admirers. Other searchers for historical roots derived their inspiration from the Russian nationalist tradition, from the Slavophiles and their nineteenth-century rejection of Western ideas and modernism.

The reemergence of a "Russian party" as a serious contender should not have come as a surprise. The democratic experiment in Russian history had lasted for less than a year, from March to November 1917. Attitudes toward the West had always been ambivalent and there had been few true "Westerners" in Russian intellectual history. The victory of Marxism had been considered at one time the final triumph of Westernism in the long dispute with the East for Russian soul. But victories in history are seldom final, and over the next three generations Marxism with its progressive internationalist and modernist elements was tried and found wanting.

Thus the outlines of a new Russian ideology emerged in the search for a new equilibrium. If the old optimism had vanished; if there were universal complaints about the disappearance of goodness and compassion, of warmth and conscience; if materialism, naked egoism, and general moral anarchy were said to have prevailed, the cause seemed only too clear to many: it had been a fatal mistake to stamp out the prerevolutionary "accursed" past, to use Lenin's famous phrase.

According to post-Marxist Russian right-wing doctrine, the Russian people had not been shrouded in darkness as Westerners had claimed. On the contrary, even if they had been illiterate, they had developed over many generations values and beliefs, a humanity and a dignity of their own. There had been the warmth and security of the family and the village. These had been people of sterling character who cared about one another, who had been proud of their fatherland; gifted people, they had no need to copy foreigners. All this, or most of it, had been destroyed—the rural community, the family, religious belief, a positive attitude to work, respect for elders, a close link to nature. As the Russian people had been physically and morally uprooted, a general deterioration had ensued in the quality of life and in human relations. People were now better off as far as material goods were concerned. But they were unhappy, subject to the stress and strain and spiritual emptiness of big-city life. The inner wholeness which had once existed had vanished; what had been destroyed in Russia in the 1920s and 1930s had been replaced by a soulless, rootless materialist pseudo-culture on the one hand, and the all-conquering American way of life on the other, with Coca-Cola, rock music, and jeans as its most prominent symbols. This, in briefest outline, was the credo of the Russian party, but since they could not attack Marxism-Leninism *expressis verbis,* only by implication, "Westernism" became the main culprit.

Those searching for guidance and inspiration in the past were no longer looking to Belinski, Herzen, and Chernyshevski, the radical democrats of the last century, and certainly not to Plekhanov, who had no spiritual message to offer, but to Dostoyevski, to the *Pochveniki* of the 1860s, to the tradition of the Orthodox Church, to the feats of arms of Russian soldiers in bygone ages. In extreme cases it led the nationalists of the 1980s back to the chauvinism of the far right, the Black Hundred of the late Tsarist era. What Soloviev, one of the greatest of the late-nineteenth-century philosophers, had predicted was that chauvinism was the logical outcome of the Slavophile doctrine, that the worship of one's own people was bound to lead to the worship of "national anomalies" and obscurantism. It manifested itself in the denigration of foreign and modern influences, in the bitter attacks against the "hidden hand," the sinister forces allegedly plotting the downfall of all things sacred to Russians. It led to conjuring up again the specter of *Zhidomasonstvo* (the alleged Jewish-Masonic world conspiracy), sometimes in a mild, at others in a rabid, form.

All this sounded familiar to the student of ideas in modern Europe and prerevolutionary Russia. The glorification of the past, the attacks against the "putrid West," the idea that Russia would be blissfully happy if she could be cut off from Europe—these are not new. It is easy to detect in such moods the thoughts of the conservative German romantics of the nineteenth century and, on a different level of sophistication, the *Kulturkritiker* of the German right attacking the shallowness of rationalist Western civilization. There are striking parallels to the philosophy of the Russian village writers and the mystical figures created by Knut Hamsun, the great Norwegian author, admired by Gorki as well as by Thomas Mann and Gide, who subsequently became a prominent Nazi collaborator. Knut Hamsun's heroes were uncorrupted by civilization; they had escaped the soulless environment of the city and rejected materialism, modern industry, and the American way of life. They thought that progress was *a priori* bad, and believed in a new religion and communion with nature.

But with all these striking similarities there were certain differences, and the new doctrine of the "Russian party" was not simply a repeat performance of the Slavophile phenomenon. Furthermore, to make the picture even more complicated, the Russian party was by no means cut of one cloth. Some of its components were deeply political in inspiration, others were not; some were profoundly attracted to orthodox religion, others were antireligious or even preached a return to pagan, pre-Christian gods.

Some were unregenerated Stalinists, most were not. Some were deeply pessimistic with regard to the chances to reverse the trend toward modern civilization; others, on the contrary, firmly believed that, given the will and leadership, a spiritual renaissance would come to pass. Some were not only deeply critical of the sinful cities and "progress," but also painted a merciless picture of moral deterioration in the village. Others, to the contrary, believed that Russia had a world historical mission to redeem mankind, being the only people in whom spiritual values were still deeply engrained.

The nineteenth-century revolt against progress and modernity had been directed primarily against liberalism and the vulgarity of bourgeois culture. The new Russian nationalism was post-Marxist and emerged after seven decades of Soviet reality, and this made for essential differences between the two. The Slavophiles, as the German right-wing *Kulturkritiker,* living in a relatively liberal system, had been free, more or less, to preach what came to their mind. The political context in which the "Russian party" made its appearance was far more intricate. Ideological regimentation was still strong. They could, of course, attack Trotsky or Lunacharski, and they could ignore Marx, but it was still sacrilege to say anything bad about Lenin. There was an ideological vacuum and, up to a point, the authorities welcomed the fact that it was to be filled by patriotism, providing much needed internal cohesion. But there still was an official doctrine from which it was unwise to stray too far: It was safe to admire Dostoyevski, but it was ill-advised to condemn the heritage of the Enlightenment and the radical intelligentsia. One could praise, up to a point, certain positive aspects in the Orthodox Church as an aesthetic phenomenon, but one could not act as a missionary for the Church. One could quote Lenin in favor of Tsarist policies and Russian chauvinism, but this was not at all easy. Even the out-and-out anti-Semites were under constraints. Instead of simply resurrecting the old Black Hundred slogan of "Beat the Jews and save Russia," they had to stress that their attacks were directed only against the Zionists. Everyone understood, of course, what they meant, and yet the impact was not quite the same.

The emergence of a new Russian nationalism as part of the official ideology can be traced back to the early 1930s when the "anti-Russian," "nihilist" views of Pokrovski were denounced in

Soviet historiography. This was followed by the restoration of Alexander Nevski, Dimitri Donskoi, Minin, and Pozharski, as well as more recent traditional heroes of Russian history. During the Second World War the nationalist theme, not surprisingly, received a further major impetus. It reached its climax in the "anticosmopolitan campaign" in Stalin's last years.

However, it was only during the Brezhnev period in the late 1960s that something akin to a new Russian ideology made its appearance on the sidelines of official doctrine, in novels, movies, literary essays, and occasionally also outside the party within the confines of Samizdat. At about the same time there emerged the *derevenshiki,* the village writers of northern Russia and Siberia, novelists such as Abramov, Shukshin and Rasputin, who were among the most gifted contemporary Russian writers of their age. With great insight, compassion, and literary mastery their stories dealt with the fate of ordinary people, far away from the centers of political power and culture. There is a striking similarity in the ending of novels such as Astafiev's *Pastukh i Pastuzhka (Shepherd and Shepherdess),* Shukshin's *Kalina Krasnaia (Red Guelder Rose),* and Rasputin's *Farewell to Matyora* and *Pozhar (Fire),* to mention but some of the best known—the theme of the loneliness of human beings in life and death in the heart of Russia. This is not *Blut und Boden,* literature on the German model embellishing the past; there was some mystique of the soil, but none of blood. If nothing good ever emanated from the city, conditions in the village, past or present, are far from idyllic; Abramov's villagers are much of the time downright nasty to one another. There is no attempt to hide the moral deterioration in the countryside as the result of the breaking up of the old communities and the introduction of modern technology. Most of these works were written in a deeply pessimistic vein and there is no chauvinism and xenophobia, only some ridicule vis-à-vis the tourists from the city.

Concurrently with the *derevenshiki* and in part as the result of their writings, new societies with millions of members were founded, such as the All-Russian Society for the Preservation of Nature and the All-Russian Society for the Preservation of Historical and Cultural Monuments. The preservation of such monuments became part of Soviet law (paragraph 18 of the Basic Law) in the late 1970s. A public outcry prevented the rerouting of the major Siberian rivers in such a way that natural habitats would have been greatly affected. Similar public campaigns were launched against the pollution of Lake Baikal and other regions.

In all these initiatives there was nothing very offensive from an orthodox party line point of view; slightly more problematical were the well-attended exhibitions of Ilya Glazunov, the painter whose motives were in the patriotic-conservative tradition without even a nod to the Soviet period. But he, too, was gradually to return to the fold.

It was on the sidelines of this inchoate movement that a number of essayists of the radical right first made their appearance, mainly in the journal *Molodaia Guardia,* later also in *Nash Sovremennik, Moskva,* and other periodicals. Their message was that the fatherland was in grave danger mainly as the result of the moral corruption of the intellectuals who had cut themselves off from the soil of the people. Unless they returned to the Russian roots, the "miniskirt," the then-symbol of "spiritual Americanism," would triumph. These had been the views of the Slavophiles, except that in those days there were no miniskirts and America hardly figured yet; Europe was then considered as the great moral corrupter: "It is not in Europe therefore that salvation lies but in a return to the people and ancestral religion, in a reconstruction of former community life weakened by Europeanization." Thus Khomyakov, one of the pillars of Slavophilism. Then as now there were attacks against Russian "educated society" (the intellectuals, in our own age), which was in a state of deep spiritual malaise because it had cut itself off from the people, had become isolated and alienated. From Danilevski and Leontiev the new Slavophiles derived their contempt for bourgeois philistinism as well as their admiration for the Byzantine sources of Russian culture.

If the Slavophiles had been critical of the Petrine reforms because they had constituted a break with Old Russia, their successors were bound to regard the Bolshevik revolution as a similar calamity even though they could not say so openly. There were certain ways to circumvent this obstacle: one could argue, for instance, as some of them did, that Bolshevism had been a good thing *per se* and that it was the fault of the (non-Russian) early Bolsheviks who had been overeager to cut the ties with a past alien to them.

But this kind of argument was not very convincing. Lenin had always stressed that there were two Russian cultures, one reactionary, the other progressive, and that the former had to be rejected. The new Slavophiles, on the other hand, wanted to reverse the procedure. Furthermore, in Lenin's view socialism was the new fatherland *(sotsialism kak otechestvo)*, whereas for the Slavophiles Holy Russia and not some imported, alien, abstract concept was the fatherland. In a famous essay, Milyukov, the prerevolutionary Russian historian and politician, had drawn attention to the basic internal contradiction of Slavophilism which ultimately caused its disintegration and downfall: the struggle between chauvinism on the one hand and the Christian idea of a universal mission on the other. Chauvinism prevailed because for many (not all) Slavophiles the orthodox religion was not a supreme value by itself but of importance only because it had been a crucial feature of Russian life, because it was the religion of the Russian people. Many of the post-1960 Slavophiles (or national Bolsheviks, as some called them) were even less deeply tied to the Church. But they faced a similar dilemma vis-à-vis Bolshevism. They had at least to pay some lip service, and some went further in the search for a synthesis: if the Orthodox Church had been Russia's national religion before 1917, Bolshevism had fulfilled this function thereafter. Those advocating continuity in Russian history had to accept the one as well as the other.

One would have expected a sharp rebuke to these ideological deviations from the guardians of Communist Party orthodoxy: it is easy to imagine what would have happened had a novel, a play, or an essay been published advocating Trotskyite or Social Democratic views. But in the case of the nationalists official reaction was curiously mild and restrained. There was some criticism from above, and even Brezhnev is said to have complained on occasion that he heard church bells ringing whenever he switched on his television. The party philosophers said that the defense of Tsarist autocracy and the Orthodox Church were incompatible with Marxism-Leninism. As a result the writers and editors of the right wing became temporarily more cautious; a few of them were moved to other assignments. But those who had engaged in the attacks against the new nationalism on behalf of the party also lost their jobs. Alexander Yakovlev of the Central Committee department for agitation and propaganda, who had written a long article in 1972 attacking these views, became an ambassador to Canada, to reemerge in Moscow only under Gorbachev. The Russian right wing never forgave him this attack; it was regularly featured in Pamyat propaganda fifteen years later.

Molodaia Guardia slightly changed course. The "Russian party" writers moved on to other journals such as *Nash Sovremennik,* a literary journal founded by Gorki which became their main organ; its motto-imprint was not "Workers of the world, unite!" but "Russia, my fatherland!" The ups and downs continued for a number of years. There was new criticism against *Nash Sovremennik* in 1981–82, and some other journals such as *Sever (North)* also came under fire; editors had to apologize and one or two were again shifted. "Russia, my fatherland!" had to be dropped for a while.

How to explain such kid-glove treatment at a time when official attitudes toward other deviationists were harsh and uncompromising, when transgressions were punished by Gulag or forced psychiatric treatment?

The "Russian party" obviously had some patrons in high places who either shared their convictions or, in any case, believed that some "healthy patriotism" was needed at a time when Marxism-Leninism had lost much of its erstwhile attraction. Brezhnev probably did not greatly care one way or another; Suslov may have been a protector, and after him Chernenko, but all this belongs to the realm of speculation. It is not even certain that decisions of this kind were taken on the very top level of leadership, in the Politburo. But it is certain that the army, always concerned with the level of patriotic education and the motivation of recruits, helped the Russian party. On the other hand, Andropov and Gorbachev, preoccupied with the modernization of the country, did not have much use for them. The Russian right in turn regarded Andropov and Gorbachev as unpatriotic leaders, even though they had to pay outward respect to them.

There was no monolithic "Russian party" but many shades of opinion. On the other hand, the nationalists who had all been submitted to countless courses in Marxism-Leninism found it not too difficult to engage in ideological dissimulation, arguing that their aims were after all those of the Communist Party with perhaps slightly different emphasis. Nor would the right-wingers heap direct praise on the symbols of Tsarist autocracy, such as Nicholas II or the head of the Holy Synod. They would merely argue that among those who had served the Tsar—generals, diplomats, and others—there had been true patriots who had wanted to do the best for their country; this was a true and seemingly innocent proposition. Sometimes admittedly the Russian nationalists would come very close to blasphemy as they did when they expressed support for Stolypin, the most dangerous enemy of the left in late Tsarist Russia. On the whole, their attacks against Western influences in Russian history were in line with the official party line.[1]

The political lines in the right-wing camp were by no means clearly drawn. Thus the neo-Stalinists, frequently atheists of the old school, had no sympathy for the religious believers and "old women in old villages." The national Bolsheviks produced an all-embracing doctrine which made provisions for Tsarism as well as Stalinism and the religious prerevolutionary tradition. There was a tactical common front of neo-Stalinists and anti-Marxists against liberals and modernizers. They agreed that Russia needed strong leadership rather than a surfeit of democracy.

Some village writers expressed a patriotism that was not aggressively chauvinistic but carried a humanistic message. But in their later writings some of the same authors expressed contempt for the non-Russian nationalities. A pronounced feature of the Russian party was its inchoate character. It was a mood rather than a well-structured, rational, and logical doctrine. The village writers would sometimes argue that the destruction of the Russian village had been an irreparable disaster and at other times they would say that it had been inevitable.

During the last twenty years a fair number of Soviet intellectuals have undergone something akin to a spiritual crisis. This can be traced, for instance, in the writings of Vladimir Tendryakov, one of the leading figures of the post-Stalin era. His early short stories such as the "Miracle-Working Icon" were more or less atheistic, even though some critics did not think them sufficiently negative in their approach to religion. These stories were based on the assumption that a substantial number of people in Soviet society were religious because they were not highly educated or because they had suffered much in life. In his later stories, such as "On Apostolic Business" (1967) and "Darkness" (1977), the heroes were scientists, successful people, some even party members. But they needed the New Testament because they realized that science does not provide answers to the ultimate questions,

[1]There is an extensive literature on recent trends in the Soviet right. See above all John Dunlop's *The Faces of Contemporary Russian Nationalism*, Princeton, 1983, and *The New Russian Nationalism*, New York, 1985; see also Alexander Yanov, *The Russian Challenge and the Year 2000*, Oxford, 1987.

nor does it help to make people happier or better. True, most of these heroes were not churchgoers nor were they religious but they wanted to believe.

This theme occurs frequently in literary descriptions of Soviet life, and nowhere more clearly than in the essays of Vladimir Soloukhin, also a leading post-Stalin writer who became fascinated with icons and published a book about the subject. He wrote in 1981 that no sensible man in the twentieth century could possibly have any doubt that there existed a rational principle in the world, in the universe, in the variety of life.[2] But for the existence of such an element (meaning Providence) one would have to assume that complex organizations such as a flower, a bird, or a human being had appeared as the result of some happy coincidence, which seemed unlikely. The main question for Soloukhin was not whether a higher form of reason existed but "whether it knows about me and cared about me"—in other words, whether there existed a personal God or just a higher being. This kind of reasoning was, of course, unacceptable for the party. Soloukhin was submitted to scathing criticism and there were similar such attacks against other writers.

The retreat from the cult of science and the naïve erstwhile optimism took different forms: Among some it manifested itself simply in greater intellectual curiosity about religion, including sectarians such as the Old Believers. In others it expressed.itself in a collectors' mania for icons and other artifacts. Collecting seems to have been pronounced even among the early Slavophiles. Thus Cha'adayev, their first and perhaps most severe critic: "Our fanatical Slavs may be able from time to time to exhume objects of curiosity for museums and libraries through their researches, but I doubt whether they would ever succeed in drawing from our historic soil anything to fill the void in our souls, anything to give more body to the fogginess of our minds." In many it showed itself in greater tolerance of religion, which, it was believed, was compatible with science.

The orientation of the "God-seekers" varied from a pantheistic identification with nature to a fundamentalist credo dating back to the old prerevolutionary religious establishment. The religious renaissance by no means aimed at a confrontation with the party. It ignored Communist doctrine, which was somehow not consid-

[2]On religion in recent Soviet literature see Chapter Eight in Mary Seton Watson, *Scenes from Soviet Life,* London, 1986.

ered worthy of serious discussion. Some extreme Russophiles combined fervent religious belief with equally fervent anti-Westernism and belief in a giant Judaeo-Masonic conspiracy, the work of the Antichrist (Satan). They have suggested a common front between church and the (Bolshevik) state against this common enemy.

Even more extreme views were voiced by some neopaganists who consider the Bible (and Christianity) too much steeped in Judaism and who propagate a return to the pre-Christian pagan goddesses of old Russia, such as Perun and Dazh Bog. There are striking similarities to Alfred Rosenberg and certain pre-Nazi and Nazi sectarians such as Ludendorff, who were searching for a German religion. However, their chances for popular support were even smaller in the Soviet Union than in Germany.

How important is the religious renaissance in the context of the national revival? Much, perhaps too much, has been written about the subject; if there was a deeply rooted religious tradition in old Russia, the atheistic tradition was also more deeply rooted than in any other country. For a long time it was taken for granted that belonging to the Orthodox Church was a condition sine qua non for a Russian patriot. But at present the religious factor seems to be of less importance than nationalism. This has been put most succinctly by Osipov, one of the key figures in the religious revival: "I am myself a religious person. Christ and his doctrines are to me in the last resort preferable to nationalism. But I know the soul of the contemporary Russian: the national element in him is at the present time more vital and evident than the religious one."

The Pikulization of Russian History

A good example of a nationalism shorn of religion, indeed antireligious in inspiration, is the amazing career of a writer for whose name one would look in vain in the histories of literature, but whose writings are more widely known among Russian readers than the books of all other members of the Russian party.[3]

According to a recent report on Moscow black market book prices, the cost of Valentin Pikul's books is about one hundred

[3]There is an extensive literature on the Valentin Pikul phenomenon. See, for instance, *Moskva*, 7, 1985; E. V. Anissimov, "Fenomen Pikulia-glasami Istorika," *Voprosy Literaturi*, 10, 1987; *Sobesednik*, January 1986; *Sovetski Patriot*, June 5, 1988. See also interviews in *Krasnaia Zvezda*, December 8, 1987, and *Komsomolskoe Znamia*, December 6, 1987.

rubles, compared with fifty rubles for Pasternak; works by Anna Akhmatova, Tsvetaeva, and Vysotski can be obtained for about thirty rubles. And this despite the fact that Pikul's books have been printed in millions of copies. Only some thrillers (in the "contemporary detective" and "foreign detective" series) are traded at a higher price.[4]

Born in 1928 in the Ukraine, Valentin Pikul left school after five years and was trained in the Soviet navy; he was probably too young to see action. After some false starts he became a writer and has published a long series of historical novels over the years. Most of his writings deal with war, or with diplomacy. All his heroes are Russians; all villains are foreigners (or Jews or Masons). Observers not unsympathetic to the cause of Russian nationalism have accused Pikul of fascist sympathies. It would be more correct to see him a writer in the tradition of the pre-1917 extreme right. His books could easily have been published in the journals of right-wing émigrés in Berlin or Harbin. Writers of such political persuasion can be found in every country; some of them were (or are) of considerable talent, and the mere fact of their existence should not be a matter of surprise or indignation. The interesting fact is the response: Pikul's books are sold more widely than those of any other writer in the Soviet Union.[5] The fact that highbrow critics and professional historians administered a mild rebuke from time to time did not affect his appeal to the masses. His writings are deeply anti-Marxist, although a few Lenin quotations might be brought in from time to time for the sake of reassurance. For Pikul historical materialism never existed; his novels consist of anecdotes skillfully strung together, true, half-true, false; secrets of the alcove, the bedroom; court intrigues. His work is one great paean to the Russian navy and army and, on some occasions, to Russian diplomats.

His self-imposed task is to imbue the masses and especially the young generation with a spirit of patriotism, which, as he told an interviewer, cannot be learned in discothèques. While the village writers are preoccupied with the soil of Russia and with nature, Pikul stresses the "voice of blood" which reaches us from the past. Most of Pikul's novels take place before 1917, which prevents any head-on collision with the party line. But on the rare occasions

---

[4]*Izvestiia*, June 4, 1988.

[5]Or, at any case, were sold prior to *glasnost* when Pikul was overtaken by other best-selling authors. See *Ogonyok*, 12, 1988.

when the action is carried beyond the revolution, he has not hesitated to attack even the Cheka, the secret police, or at least the "cosmopolitan elements" in the Cheka. Thus an interrogation of an old naval officer in *Three Ages of Okini-San* by a Chekist: The admiral says that he served honorably not the monarchy but Mother Russia. The Bolshevik interrogator makes some snide remarks about the dark, illiterate masses, whereupon the admiral fervently reiterates his belief in eternal Russia which will eventually prevail. There can be no doubt with whom Pikul's sympathies lie.

Requiem for Convoy PQ 17, which sold more than three million copies, is the story of the British convoy which was to carry weapons and ammunition to Russia. Owing to a number of tragic misjudgments it was largely destroyed. According to Pikul, Churchill and his warlords were not just fools and cowards but criminals who deliberately sabotaged the Russian war effort. Foreign readers will not easily share his indignation; until the year before, Stalin had been Hitler's ally. Furthermore the story is factually untrue: the disaster was the result of wrong decisions. Churchill had no desire to lose so many ships and war matériel which Britain desperately needed at home. Pikul's story seems to have been derived from a book by David Irving, a British writer of the extreme right, which had appeared several years earlier.

A good illustration of Pikul's philosophy is his *Na Poslednei Chertei* (*On the Last Line*, 1981), describing the last years of the Romanov dynasty. The Tsar and his camarilla are weaklings, most of the politicians idle talkers. But the real culprits are the Jews, the eternal "ferment of decomposition" plotting Russia's downfall through their chosen tool, Rasputin. They give him unlimited amounts of money, a mistress, and even a set of artificial teeth to make him more presentable at court. There were indeed some Jews in Rasputin's surroundings, but they did not "manage" him. Generally speaking, power in Russia was in the hands of anti-Semites, such as Nicholas II, rather than the Jews, the objects of pogroms and bureaucratic mistreatment. On the other hand, there was a disproportionately high percentage of Jews in the revolutionary movement, a fact not mentioned even once in this book.

Following the appearance of this historical novel it was pointed out to Pikul that he had gone too far, whereupon in his next book *(Historical Miniatures)* he promptly brought in some minor Jewish figures which were described in a positive light; they were quite irrelevant as far as the story was concerned but they provided a useful political alibi. This points to a basic flaw in Pikul's books and also those of like-minded writers: they lack the courage of their convictions and go to great lengths to camouflage their xenophobic bias. Outrageous attacks against foreigners are introduced with an invocation of the writer's basic internationalist philosophy; bellicose statements are always accompanied with professions of undying attachment to the cause of world peace. Such lack of honesty does not go down well with the high moral pathos of this literature, nor is it in the tradition of the great Russian writers of the last century. If Pikul has lost some of his readers under *glasnost,* then it is partly because there has been much competition on the extreme right. He has remained the favorite writer of the Soviet army command, which has made reading his books almost mandatory and protected him against all attacks. However, it would be a mistake to consider Pikul the most extreme of present-day Russian writers. He was essentially a product of the Brezhnev period. By now he has become almost an Establishment writer, though he continues to shun official literary gatherings. Even his critics concede that his writings have at least stimulated interest in Russian history. Once the sluice gates of *glasnost* were opened, Pikul was overtaken on the extreme right by committed Black Hundred authors who made their spiritual home in and around Pamyat.[6]

From Left to Right

Pikul's views have not changed over the years, but this was certainly not the case for a number of erstwhile liberal writers who are now among the main spokesmen of the Russian party. Yuri Bondarev and Vasili Belov are the prime specimens in this category: both belong to the front ranks of Soviet literature. Bondarev, born in 1924, grew up mainly in Moscow, served as an artillery officer in the war, joined the party in 1944, and has been for twenty years a member of the presidium of Soviet writers. Belov was born in 1932 near Vologda in northern Russia, grew up in a small village, worked as a carpenter, joined the party in 1956, and (like Bondarev) studied literature at Moscow's Gorki Institute. He has also been for years a member of the presidium of the writers' union. Bondarev made his name with honest and moving war novels,

[6]For the full flavor of the true extremists on the literary scene see, for instance, Ivan Shevtsov in conversation with retired Soviet air marshal I. Pstygo in *Molodaia Guardia,* 7, 1988.

much in contrast with the official mendacious accounts of the Stalin period. Another novel, *Tishina (Silence)*, which also became a successful movie, gives an equally honest account of the oppressive climate of the late Stalin period. Yet another novel, *Bereg (The Shore)*, takes place in Germany: Nikitin, a well-known Soviet writer on a trip to West Germany, again sees the girl—now a woman—whom he had met in Berlin at the end of the war. He is still in love with her, but decides to return to his family in the Soviet Union. He dies of a heart attack on the plane during the flight home.

Bondarev is a "Hero of Socialist Labor" and the recipient of many high state prizes and decorations. In the 1970s he became increasingly preoccupied with *homo moralis* (the title of one of his essays), rejecting the "American-style society of universal prosperity," which he considered a spiritual vacuum and a rejection of morality. He wrote scathingly about the "mass worship of the Queen Vulgarity and her androgynous wizard Entertainment with all leisure hours devoted to *Kitsch*" and attacked women's liberation as "female fascism." In a long dialogue with a Russian-born Hollywood filmmaker in his most recent novel, *Igra (The Game)*, he gives vent to extreme views about rock music, technical progress, American illiteracy, and America as a big moral and intellectual concentration camp ("by the way, many want this"). America is the proponent of the corruption of the soul and the Big Lie.

Following his disillusionment with modernism abroad as well as at home, Bondarev became more and more alarmist: at the eighth congress of the writers' union he said that unless the destruction of architecture and nature came to an end, unless a moral explosion took place in science as well as in criticism, Russians would wake up one morning to find that everything had gone—the national culture of great Russia, its soul, its love of native soil, its great literature, philosophy, painting, and so on. He conjured an even more apocalyptic vision at a meeting in March 1987 of the secretariat of the writers' union of the R.S.F.S.R.

Vasili Belov is a writer of very different background. His great love had been village life in old Russia, which survived up to the time of the collectivization. He wrote with great feeling about the old craftsmen and the beggars of rural Russia, the close ties with nature and the (often charming) superstition of the peasants with their quaint customs and house spirits—uneducated people, perhaps, and poor, but essentially harmonious, living in peace with themselves and the cosmos. For Belov, as for most of the village writers, the town, and especially the big city, were always un-friendly and threatening, even dangerous.[7] The houses were too big and anonymous, the people cold and silent.[8] In the 1980s Belov moved away from his native ground to discover the root of the evil, first in a series of essays and subsequently in a novel, *Vse Vperedi (Everything Is Still Ahead)*. In an essay he wrote with great disgust about watching rock groups and striptease in the provincial town of Vologda: Onstage were some twenty almost-nude girls, clad only in bikinis. The Vologda girls tried desperately to be sultry, shaking their bellies and hips. "Where am I—in Vologda or on the Place Pigalle?" he wondered. Belov's novel opens on the Place Pigalle, where the heroine, a fickle Russian woman, watches a pornographic movie which, with iron logic, leads to her moral downfall.[9]

But if Paris is sinful, Moscow is not much better, a nightmare of metal, glass, rubber, the smell of gasoline and too many foreign-ers. Something devilish is going on, partly explained by the sys-tematic poisoning of the Russian soul and body by means of alco-hol and drugs, by rampant sexploitation, by the actions of Jews and other cosmopolitans as emissaries of Satan. Belov has both a diag-nosis and a cure: In order to destroy people one does not need hydrogen bombs. It is enough to make children quarrel with their parents, to put women against men: "It is not easy, but it can be done." And the cure: "The peasants' *izba* [hut] has always saved Russia. If we shall go under, it won't be at all because of the Pershings. The *izba* is like a submarine, it is capable of surviving for a long time, maintaining itself. And this is why they destroy with blind fury the *izba* all over the world."

Belov's novel was denounced by the liberal critics as obscuran-tist nonsense. Here was a sad case of a gifted writer who had moved out of his natural habitat into a world which he did not even try to understand, and the result was a grotesque caricature. It would be inaccurate, however, to explain anti-Westernism and antimodernism only with reference to a limited horizon and the resentment of provincials. Many of these writers make their home

[7] *Lad; ocherki po narodnoi Esthetike* (Essays in Popular Aesthetics), in *Nash Sovremennik,* 1979–81. *Lad* should be translated in this context as "harmony."

[8] See his long novel *Kanuny,* which he began to publish in 1972; the sequel was banned and could appear only in 1987.

[9] *Razdumia na rodine* (Thoughts in the Native Country), Moscow, 1986, p. 21. See also Luise Wangler, *Vasilij' Belov, Menschliche und gesellschaftliche Probleme,* Munich, 1985.

in Moscow and have visited foreign countries, but this has not prevented them from writing arrant nonsense. Thus we learn from Peter Proskurin, another card-carrying member of the right, that most Englishmen cannot afford to pay for a call from a public telephone box.

One recalls writers in many literary traditions who have moved from left to right, or from right to left; one can think of great writers who have written outrageous nonsense on politics, and even more who, at a certain stage in their life, decided that their main mission was to deliver pompous platitudes on topics of public interest. There is no reason why Russia should be an exception; in fact, the temptation in Russia must have been greater because Russian writers have traditionally possessed great prestige. Any well-known writer was half expected to deliver magisterial pronouncements on the moral state of the nation. The situation in the 1980s was further characterized by the general feeling of a spiritual void which somehow had to be filled. There were other features which played a role in the emergence of the right, such as antimodernism, anti-intellectualism, the specter of Russophobia, and a vague anti–big-city mood to which we shall turn next.

Moral Corruption in the City

The idea that modern city life is the source of corruption is not new and can be found on both extremes of the political spectrum. If Latin American revolutionaries (such as Guevara) claimed that city life was the grave of true revolutionaries, contemporary Green movements have argued the same. The animosity toward the city, as George Mosse has written, was an integral part of the rise of *völkisch* (and Nazi) thought in Germany. They would accept small-town life but the big city was an artificial, ominous colossus, rootless, international in character, the very opposite of rootedness in nature and therefore antithetical to the spirit of the *volk*. The city symbolized industrial progress and modernity, both abominated by the far right, whose slogans were "Cities are the tombs of Germanism" and "Berlin is the domain of the Jews." If Marx referred to the idiocy of rural life, Vadim Kozhinov, one of the ideologists of the Russian extreme right, has written that millions of people have felt the desire to break away from the artificial conditions of city life and live in an untouched corner of nature. According to Kozhinov, it is now more appropriate to speak of the idiocy of urban life with its air pollution, incessant noise, and the need for many commuters to waste hours every day.[10]

The exodus from the inner parts of big cities in the industrialized countries points to a real problem. The emergence of the concept of the garden city in Britain around the turn of the century and the "back-to-nature" movement in Germany at about the same time could be taken as early examples of this trend. The slogans of contemporary Russian right-wing critics sound similar to certain pre-Nazi spokesmen, but they should still be taken seriously. It is perfectly true that in the architectural enthusiasm of the 1930s (Moscow's "general plan" of 1935 and especially the work done in the late Stalin era), much sinning against good taste has been done in Moscow. Historical monuments have been needlessly destroyed, and most of the new or rapidly developing Russian cities are boring and ugly, lacking tradition and character. Moscow under Stalin became a city of high-rise buildings, monumental, eclectic, very much in line with the politics of the period. The mixture of styles in the new buildings, ranging from Greek temples to Renaissance, from neo-Gothic to the architecture of old Russian fortresses, has provoked much derision. However, at a closer look much of the Moscow of the turn of the century, of the *Jugendstil*, still exists, and the preservation of traditional architecture is *a fortiori* true with regard to Leningrad.

The social and aesthetic problems of big cities have nowhere been ideally solved. But neither was life in the countryside very healthy and convenient. "Where did the idea suddenly come from that the city corrupts?": Georgi Semyonov's explanation points not so much to what happened in the city as to the destruction of village life and the expropriation of the peasants in the 1930s and 1940s which led to a large-scale migration from the countryside.[11] But this does not explain the fanatical hatred against the big city on the one hand, and on the other the resistance to any and all architectural changes just because Dostoyevski stayed in a certain building for a few nights, even if the house is neither old nor beautiful and even if change has become imperative.

The less extreme among the anti-urbanists point with some justification to a general malaise: the anonymous character of big-

[10]V. Kozhinov, *Literaturnoe Obozrenie*, 3, 1977, p. 63 et seq.
[11]*Literaturnaia Rossia*, June 12, 1987. Semyonov is a native of Moscow, but much of his writing deals with the countryside. Nor can he be fairly accused of a lack of aesthetic sensibility: he began his career as a sculptor.

city life, alienation, the loss of a community spirit. This mood is shared by many and has to do with the dissatisfaction with Soviet life in general. The aesthetic sense of some Russians is genuinely offended by the town planning (or lack of it) of the last fifty years, and some care deeply about the disappearance of historical landmarks. Others regard this dissatisfaction as a useful platform for their political ambitions. And in the meantime, despite all the speeches and writings about the horror of big-city life, hundreds of thousands of illegal residents (the *limitchiki*) prefer to live in totally inadequate conditions in Moscow and Leningrad and other big cities rather than return to the warmth and the community spirit of the small town and the village.

The Specter of Russophobia

It is the profound belief of the Russian right that anti-Communism has been replaced by Russophobia, the fear and hate in the West of all things Russian. The idea that the whole world conspires against Russia, aided and abetted by the "internal enemy," is deeply rooted in the history of Russian thought; it can be traced back to the Slavophiles and even beyond. The tradition of deep distrust against foreigners has been amply documented as far back as the sixteenth century. The Slavophiles merely added a philosophical dimension. As Tyutchev wrote his sister in 1864, "There is not a single interest, not a single trend in the West which would not conspire against Russia, especially against its future, and would not try to harm us." On another occasion he mentioned a "conspiracy of all hell" aiming at the destruction of Russia. Or Ivan Aksakov: "We are not even the plebeians, we are the pariahs of humanity in the face of Europe, Russia is guilty by the very fact that it exists." Dostoyevski was another great paranoiac: he believed that the whole world conspired against him personally and against his country. Political use was made of such paranoia both by Tsarist governments and by Stalin, who exploited it for his state-of-siege propaganda. It is shared by some prominent thinkers in the Russian émigré community.

There was, of course, an anti-Russian party in nineteenth-century England, of which Karl Marx was one of the most extreme spokesmen, worried by Russia's constant expansion since the sixteenth century. But such views were considered a fringe phenomenon; in the Napoleonic wars, and in the two World Wars, Russia was Britain's ally. In Germany, the pro-Russian party was strong and neither in France nor the U.S. did the issue figure highly in public thought.

There were negative reports written by foreigners about Russia and Russians. But such accounts have been written about virtually every country—the United States, in fact, more often than Russia. Why should Russians have reacted so much more violently than others?

Britain and France have traditionally shrugged off the opinion of foreigners or merely noticed them with amusement. Germany and Russia on the other hand have been more self-conscious, which points to a lack of self-confidence. This has been noted by Russian observers such as Siniavski, who has drawn attention to the continuity between the perception of nineteenth-century Russophobia, Stalin's theory of encirclement, and present-day beliefs among the "Russian party."[12]

A corollary to the enormously exaggerated role of Russophobia is the anti-intellectualism of the Russian party. This motif appeared prominently as well in the writings of the Slavophiles. As they saw it, much of the evil had to be traced back to the Petrine reforms, but equally it was the fault of "society," which had turned its back on the people and traditional values in favor of imitating the West. The idea of the cleavage between the Europeanized intelligentsia and the Orthodox Russian people also appeared in Dostoyevski. In our age the hooligans from Moscow's suburbs have expressed their disdain for fashionable Moscow's "accelerating addiction to Western mocks and seesaws."[13]

Once again the parallels with the *völkisch* tradition in Germany are striking. In both cases "intellectual" became a term of contempt, a synonym for arid rationalism, estrangement from the *volk,* a corrupting influence lacking faith in the eternal values and the mission of the people.

In Stalin's Russia, too, there was deep antagonism against intellectuals, though it never went as far as it did in Germany. The intellectuals did figure as pillars of society, but only in third and last place, after the workers and the peasants. To make it clear that an intellectual was trustworthy an adjective such as *"narodni"* (people's) was added. He had a positive role to play in society but his

[12]*Sintaksis,* 14, 1985. Siniavski wrote that during many years of living abroad he never encountered the all-pervasive Russophobia frequently invoked by Russian nationalists.
[13]M. Walker, *The Listener,* April 7, 1988.

political instincts were not to be trusted, and he had to be subject to constant, close control.

Such anti-intellectualism became more pronounced after Stalin's death both among neo-Stalinists and the nationalists. For the neo-Stalinists, the (Moscow) intellectuals were the enemies *par excellence,* actual or potential traitors because they were in the forefront of de-Stalinization, forever trying to rehabilitate some convicted enemies of the people, forever open to the latest fashion from the West, be it human rights, yoga, or keeping a dog. For nationalists such as Astafiev and Belov the intellectuals were dishonest and ridiculous types. What to do about the intellectuals, one of the heroes of Astafiev's *Sad Detective* (1986) asks, providing an immediate answer: either kill them or cut them down to size.

But anti-intellectualism is almost dwarfed into insignificance by yet another ingredient of the neonationalist doctrine: the belief in sinister forces aiming to undermine and to bring about the downfall of the great Russian nation.

The Great Conspiracy

The belief in a worldwide conspiracy by the devil using Jews and Freemasons as his tools is deeply rooted in Russian history. Some of the original inspiration came from France and Germany, but the Russian contribution, including the *Protocols of the Elders of Zion,* the famous forgery concocted between 1903 and 1907, played a notable role in the history of modern anti-Semitism.[14] Such attitudes were to resurface in the 1980s.

The changing fortunes of Jews in the Soviet Union need not be retold in detail. While in the early days of Soviet rule there were a disproportionate number of Jews in the leadership of the Communist Party (as in the front ranks of other left-wing parties), their part steadily declined. For more than thirty years there has been no Jew in the Politburo, the highest echelons of the army, the security forces, and the ministry of foreign affairs. But while Jews have disappeared (or were squeezed out) from positions of influence and high visibility, there is still a fairly high concentration in the arts and sciences. Whether this fact has substantially contri-

[14]The classic account is Norman Cohn, *Warrant for Genocide,* London, 1967. On the history of the *Protocols* in Russia see also my *Russia and Germany,* New York, 1963. In recent decades there have been no Soviet publications on the *Protocols* or the Black Hundred. This tabu was broken only in 1988; see, for instance, *Ogonyok,* 23, 1988: "Attention, a Provocation."

buted to the growth of anti-Semitism is not certain; there was less anti-Semitism in Russia in the 1920s and the early 1930s despite the fact that there were so many Jews in positions of influence. But at that time anti-Semitism was frowned upon by the authorities and its open manifestations were punished.

While the gradual disappearance of Jews from positions of influence and their replacement by native elites was a natural phenomenon, and should not *per se* be regarded as a manifestation of racism, fairly strong anti-Jewish feeling developed after 1945 among the party leadership. Despite the official blessing it could not for ideological reasons be openly voiced: the target was the "cosmopolitan" and later the "Zionist," not the Jew *per se*. The Jew was suspect even if he denied any tie with other Jews; he was still considered a member of an international community. He was also suspect to Russian nationalists as a "ferment of decomposition," more open to alien (Western) influence than other citizens. Anti-Jewish discrimination led to Jewish emigration, which in turn fueled Russian suspicions, a vicious circle.

Individual Jews could still lead a comfortable and relatively sheltered life, especially among the intelligentsia. But they had to be doubly careful in their behavior for their loyalty was not taken for granted.[15] At a time when a general upsurge of nationalism took place, their position was anomalous: they could at best pass as *Soviet* patriots. But Soviet patriotism is an abstraction, not a living reality, like Russian nationalism. They could be ardent patriots, experts on Pushkin and Russian history, but in the eyes of their enemies they were aliens, using the Russian language but still not part of the Russian body politic.

All this may explain feelings of hostility against Jews; it does not, however, fully explain the belief in *Zhidomasonstvo,* the Judaeo-Masonic conspiracy, a term coined by the Russian far right in the early years of the century and subsequently embraced by the pro-fascist elements of the Russian emigration. Originally the alleged plot had also included groups such as the Illuminati and the Templars. But these were not well-known in Russia and were therefore dropped.

---

[15]In not a few cases they chose to hide their identity by changing their names. Thus the well-known playwright Shatrov was originally named Marshak, the editor of *Znamia,* Baklanov-Friedman. Such practices provoked poisonous comments on the part of the anti-Semites, who conveniently ignored the fact that Lenin, Stalin, and Gorki are also assumed names.

The idea that a giant conspiracy was afoot to bring about general economic disorder, subvert all traditional values, destroy religious faith, eventually unleash a world war, convert all mankind to Judaism, and bring about Jewish world domination found its way in the 1960s and 1970s into both Soviet *belles lettres* and Soviet historiography. In the most extreme way it appeared in fringe groups such as Pamyat. True, certain changes were made in packaging *Zhidomasonstvo.* In the original Black Hundred or Nazi version, the Jews had been the agents of all revolutionary movements from the days of the French Revolution and even before; Lenin and Stalin were for good measure counted as Jews, half Jews, quarter Jews or at least as agents of the Jews. The new Russian version dropped the concept of Jews as revolutionaries even though their alleged part in the murder of the Tsar's family, to give but one example, was occasionally mentioned. The Jews were now turned into agents of Nazi Germany and Wall Street, and Adolf Eichmann became one of the Elders of Zion.

It is not easy to find reasons and explanations. At a famous trial in Berne, Switzerland, in the 1930s, the *Protocols* were submitted to painstaking analysis to determine their authenticity. In his summary the presiding judge said, "I hope that there will come a time when nobody will any longer understand how in the year 1935 almost a dozen fully sane and reasonable men could for fourteen days torment their brains before a court at Berne over the authenticity of these so-called *Protocols,* which for all the harm they have caused, and may cause, are nothing but ridiculous nonsense."

Judge Meyer was overly optimistic. In the West the impact of the *Protocols* is now restricted to a small lunatic fringe, but there are countries with a greater proclivity for conspiracy theories. One such country was Germany in the 1930s, and there has been a similar tradition in the Soviet Union.

Why should men and women steeped in many decades of atheistic indoctrination live in mortal fear of Satan? Perhaps antireligious education has been less successful than commonly assumed; perhaps it never even began to eradicate the superstition deeply rooted in Russian history. Perhaps it was connected to the constant indoctrination under Stalin and after, and to the appeals for vigilance against various plots, conspiracies, and enemies of the people.

It is equally difficult to find a rational explanation for the fear of Masonic influences. The believers in *Zhidomasonstvo* are ardent admirers of Pushkin, and the Slavophiles are their great idols. But Pushkin and many Slavophiles did belong to Masonic lodges, which makes the whole phenomenon even less explicable. Leading Soviet historians, both academic and popular, have written books which purport to show that the March revolution of 1917 was carried out by the Masons. While it is true that some leading figures of the center and left-of-center parties belonged to Masonic lodges, the political implications of these links ranged from the insignificant to the nonexistent; it did not prevent conflicts between them on both issues of political substance and personal incompatibility. Above all, there was no coordinated plan: if Rasputin was alleged to be a member of a conspiracy, so was the Grand Duke who shot him. The very idea that Masonic influences were of paramount importance in the first revolution of 1917 denigrates the role of the Bolshevik party, which, according to the official version, was the decisive agent in the downfall of Tsarist Russia. But the paranoiac belief in conspiracy theories was palpably felt in books and articles published through the 1970s and 1980s. According to one recent source, both Nazi Germany and Fascist Italy were deeply penetrated by the Masons: Hitler took part in Masonic-spiritualist seances; Rudolf Hess was a Mason, as were Mussolini and the forty-five highest dignitaries of Fascist Italy.[16] The fact that Masonic lodges were banned in the Third Reich is considered mere eyewash. Even now, according to the same source, between ten and twelve million Masons are playing a crucial role in the political life of Western Europe and the United States.

A notable contribution to the revival of *Zhidomasonstvo* was made by the new "anti-Zionist" literature which developed in the 1970s. This literature had little to do with the specialized studies published by Soviet foreign affairs experts on the Middle East conflict, in which the Soviet Union for decades has supported the Arabs against Israel. The new anti-Zionist literature is not primarily interested in Zionism as commonly defined, or in the state of Israel—it is anti-Jewish *tout court*. While most of these writers will not publicly go so far as to rehabilitate Nazism or welcome genocide, whatever their private thoughts on the subject, they justify the anti-Jewish pogroms in Tsarist Russia and view the Nazis as mere puppets in the hands of the Zionists who drove them into

[16]Lolli Zamoiski, *Nedelia*, 20, 1987.

unleashing the Second World War. As far as this school of thought is concerned all Jews are villains and Jewish Communists are more dangerous than genuine Zionists. For tactical reasons such books may include on occasion minor "positive" Jewish characters so as to forestall charges of open anti-Semitism.[17]

Prior to the rise of *glasnost* such camouflage had been *de rigueur,* but with the coming of the new freedom there seemed to be no need to engage in dissimulation any longer. The Soviet media have reported speeches in meetings and "letters to the editor" in which it was claimed that Marxism was a Zionist doctrine which had to be discarded as quickly and radically as possible; that not only Trotsky but Lenin had been a Jew; that most party leaders were either Jews or Masons; and so on.[18] The cat was out of the bag and the party leadership found itself in the position of the sorcerer's apprentice: how to recapture the spirits it had helped to release? In reply there were some articles in specialized journals criticizing the open anti-Semites for deviating from the party line and "objectively" playing into the hands of the enemies of the Soviet state. For the most powerful enemy was alleged to be not the Jewish-Masonic conspiracy but world imperialism; to deny this was tantamount to spreading disinformation. Worse yet, the enemies of the Soviet Union were eagerly using every opportunity to point to Nazi and racist traces in Soviet publications; they were actually translating and reprinting such books and articles.

Several liberal Soviet writers took the initiative, pointing to the impact of Hitlerism on the writings of the anti-Semitic experts, whereupon those criticized sued for defamation.[19]

According to the official party line anti-Semitism and Zionism are equally reprehensible. In actual fact there has been a great deal of anti-Jewish writing, thinly camouflaged, whereas the publication of pro-Zionist books or articles is quite unthinkable. When a KGB spokesman suggested in June 1988 that Zionism and anti-Semitism should be defined as equally dangerous to socialism this was— strange as it may have appeared—a step toward liberalization.

[17]For example, Gari Nemenko, in *Nash Sovremennik,* 7, 1986, or I. Shamiakin, *Petrograd-Brest,* Moscow, 1986. The literary journal *Molodaia Guardia* has published the memoirs of the Jewish general Dragunski, an obvious case of ideological reinsurance.

[18]Lesoto, *Komsomolskaia Pravda,* December 19, 1987.

[19]This was the action against *Sovetskaia Kultura* brought by Romanenko, Begun, and others. They were criticized by the party press not so much because of their pro-Nazi views but because it was unbecoming for party members to go to court to decide an "ideological" dispute. The action was dismissed by a Moscow district court in early 1988.

Previously, only Zionism had been considered a danger of this kind; a great many "Zionists" but no anti-Semite had ever been arrested. Thus when Leningrad's Pamyat organized a series of mass meetings in Rumiantsev Square in the summer of 1988 ("in a hysterically charged atmosphere of hatred toward non-Russian nationalities," to quote a Soviet newspaper), protesters were arrested by the militia whereas the black-shirted members of the extremist movement were protected.[20] As V. Prilukov, the head of the Leningrad KGB, said in an interview: "We do not want these people [meaning Pamyat] to make political capital out of repressive measures taken against them." It was better to counter their arguments by ideological and political means rather than create martyrs. When he was asked why, in the circumstances repressive measures had been taken against the Democratic Union, a liberal "informal group," he replied that this was a different case in which repressive measures were fully justified.[21]

Toward a New Russian Ideology

In many respects the ideological crisis facing the Soviet Union is by no means unprecedented. An account of the views of the right-wing intellectuals in the Weimar Republic reads as follows:

The right reacted by advocating cultural remedies: a change in life style, a return to the old values, a more simple and natural life. Hence the call for the *völkische Kultur* as against cosmopolitan civilization. *Kultur*, as the right saw it, was rooted in the people, had a soul, whereas *Zivilisation* was soulless, external, artificial. Wherever a German patriot looked he found little to comfort him; the national values were openly undermined and turned into ridicule; pacifist novels abounded; the manly virtues were dragged into the dirt; on the stage incest, pederasty or at the very least marital infidelity was glorified. Berlin had taken over from Paris as the capital of lasciviousness and obscenity. Illustrated journals featured naked dancers and international gangsters, frequently shown in company

---

[20]*Moskovskie Novosti*, August 7, 1988; *Izvestiia*, August 13, 1988. Sixty Leningrad academics writing in *Izvestiia* suggested that Pamyat activities were in violation of Article 36 of the Soviet Constitution and Article 74 of the criminal code of the Russian Federation (incitement to racial hatred). But the legal authorities were in no hurry to prosecute. The reasons for the reluctance of the authorities to take action against the pro-fascist right are not entirely clear: whether they regard it as a political factor of no consequence, or whether, on the contrary, they are afraid of it; whether there is support for Pamyat in the party leadership; whether it has been penetrated by the organs of state security or whether the authorities believe that arrests would give the extremists more publicity.

[21]*Leningradskaia Pravda*, October 4, 1988.

with each other; the cinema corrupted the young generation by glamoriz-
ing sadism and rape, with prostitutes and their protectors as the main
heroes. It seemed as if only the criminal, the ugly, the blasphemous was
of any interest to modern art. The rest was low-, or at best middle-brow
culture, suitable for entertaining philistines. All over Germany the *literati*
were in command, enemies of order, profiteers of chaos. Like tubercular
bacilli they affected all weak cells in the body politic. Rootless themselves,
they were attacking any manifestation of healthy patriotism. They had no
shame or modesty; they were the apostles of sensationalism, forever in
search of new trends and fashions, however worthless. Their stranglehold
had to be broken to make cultural recovery possible.

Underlying the denunciation of Weimar culture was the assumption
that the process of cultural decay and moral disintegration was by no
means accidental. It was concerted and centrally planned: a deliberate
conspiracy by world Jewry to attack everything, to undermine everything
that was still healthy in Germany so that the country could never again
recover and rise to greatness.[22]

There is a strong resemblance between these attitudes and the
views of the Russian right. Even the fact that the one was pre-
Marxist, and the other post-Marxist seems not to be of much consequence. The components of the new Russian ideology are, in
fact, similar to those that have appeared over the last hundred
years as a reaction to modernity in many countries—the opposition
to a more permissive society and modern art.

While Soviet society has moved away for a very long time from
the permissive theories on sexual freedom of Alexandra Kollontai
(which in any case were never shared by more than a small part of
the upper crust of the urban population), the conservatives want
to see more births and fewer abortions and divorces, as well as
greater respect for their elders and betters on the part of the
young. They stand for more law and order and greater discipline
all round, which by necessity means a strengthening of authority
and not too much democracy. They may regret many of the mistakes (and even crimes) committed in the past. But they oppose too
much repentance and breast-beating because this will only spread
confusion among the people who need faith and certainty now
more than ever before.

They have no sympathy for avant-garde art (*Kulturbolschewismus*
in Nazi parlance), and they see an even greater danger in mass
culture imported from the West. There is a strong populist ele-

[22]W. Laqueur, *Weimar, a Cultural History, 1918–33*, New York, 1974, pp. 59–61.

ment in the ideology of the new right: attacks against Western plutocrats on the one hand, *meshanstvo* (philistinism) and the acquisitive lifestyle on the other. There have been constant complaints about the softness and lack of idealism among the young generation. Many of the critics have served as young men in the army during the "Great Fatherlandic War." They saw their best friends die, they were wounded and decorated for their courage. Why do the young people not show a similar sense of duty and self-sacrifice? They became doubly angry when they realized that the young showed little interest in the heroic deeds of their elders, took them for granted, or found them exaggerated and even slightly comical.

Needed, as they see it, is a profound cultural and moral revolution. But where could the impetus and the inspiration come from? Certainly not from the scientific-technological revolution (NTR) much vaunted in the 1960s and early 1970s. The ambivalence toward scientific progress is by no means the monopoly of the right wing; it was found even earlier among some of the science fiction writers; in Tendryakov's novels; in the essays of a leading literary critic such as Anninski, who wrote that for many years he had been living with a feeling of impending disaster. Yet the conservatives pursued this theme more relentlessly than others and their instinctive pessimism was darker.

If science does not offer an answer where could salvation come from? Obviously from the Russian past and the rich cultural heritage. But the inspiration is highly selective: Pushkin and Lermontov are, of course, admired, but the nationalists prefer the Pushkin who denounced the "denigrators of Russia" to Pushkin and Lermontov as the bards of freedom. They prefer Dostoyevski to Tolstoi, who seems more relevant for the present times. Gogol the great patriot and satirist of mores is "in," but not Turgenev and Chekhov, far too much exposed to Western influences. There is no room for the tradition of the radical Russian intelligentsia.

There is a readiness to rehabilitate some of the leading figures of the White camp in the Russian civil war and in the emigration. It is argued that many of those who had left their country after the revolution had done so as the result of a tragic misunderstanding. But they had been good Russian patriots like General Denikin, one of the leaders of the White armies who in World War II had advised his fellow émigrés not to collaborate with the Nazis. The cultural loss to Russia was immense and elementary justice demands the reintegration of these prodigal sons and daughters, for Russia in historical perspective is "one and indivisible"; this by accident also happened to be the slogan of the White armies.[23] This spirit of forgiveness covers writers like Bunin, ardent patriots, political leaders of the old right, even some of the extreme right. It does not extend to liberals, social democrats, and Jews.

The ideology of the Russian right has many facets, and what applies to one of its components is not necessarily true with regard to another. Some writers of the right have shown disdain for the non-Russian nationalities: There is widespread belief that the Central Asians as well as the Caucasians are deeply corrupt and ungrateful for the great blessings of Russian culture. The Balts are not corrupt, but are considered clannish, trying to keep the Russians out as much as possible. The Jews are the most visible antagonists, but in the final analysis only Russians can be trusted in an hour of crisis. The naïve belief of the old Slavophiles in Slavic solidarity vanished a long time ago. The Poles have been traitorous, the Czechs disobedient, the East Germans arrogant, and even the faithful Bulgarians are not what they used to be.

Views of this kind have been voiced openly from time to time; usually, it has been preferred not to air one's feelings in public about this sensitive issue. For it leads to a wider question that is crucial for Russia's future: Is ethnic purity the ideal, a state uncontaminated by outside corruption? Or are the Russians a people with a great historical mission, called by Providence to take smaller and less fortunate people under their protection?

There has been no clear answer to this question on the ideological level. But national pride as well as vested interest dictates a policy aiming at the survival of the Soviet empire, and the preachers of ethnic exclusiveness and purity will not be given much leeway.

Pamyat

Pamyat (Memory) is the most extreme, most visible, and in some respects most interesting group of the new Russian right to have

[23]For the rehabilitation of sections of the post-1917 emigration see A. P. Afanasiev, *Polyn v chuzhikh poliakh,* Moscow, 1984, and L. K. Shkarenkov, *Agoniia bieloi emigratsii,* Moscow, 1986.

emerged in recent years. There are conflicting accounts of its origins and history. According to one it was founded in the early 1980s as a small circle of enthusiasts in the ministry of aviation industry in Moscow. It consisted of people genuinely concerned about the destruction of historical monuments. They invited historians and other specialists for lectures and gave of their free time on weekends to voluntary help restoring neglected buildings and monuments, primarily churches and graveyards. They did not pursue openly any political aims.[24]

According to another version Pamyat was the name of a circle of friends of the late writer Vladimir Chivilikhin, who wrote a novel called *Pamyat* and was one of the first (in 1963) to call for urgent measures to save Lake Baikal from contamination. According to this version, too, it was not initially a group with pronounced political views. However, at some stage in 1985, coincidental with the arrival of *glasnost* and greater freedom of speech, radical members of Pamyat either broke away or reanimated the dormant group. Similar societies were founded in Sverdlovsk (Otechestvo), Leningrad (Spasenie), and other cities. But there does not seem to have been a countrywide leadership, and the differences in orientation between the various branches were marked.

Moscow's Pamyat became political with a vengeance. It established itself as a "patriotic" association, and its leaders were introduced at public meetings as "leading patriots." People began to appear in their ranks who had no interest in Russian cultural traditions: "More and more energy was devoted not to real problems but to the search for mythical enemies."[25] True, there were still cultural meetings on topics such as "How Much Moscow Means to Us" or "The Russian North." On one occasion a movie about the life of Lermontov was shown in which the responsibility for the death of the poet in a duel was put on Jews and Freemasons. But these "cultural" programs served as camouflage for different purposes. Professor Yanin, one of the leading Russian archaeologists who had been in charge of the Novgorod excavations, appeared as the invited speaker on one occasion, but his lecture was broken up by people who had not come to listen to speeches on such a distant

[24]The first detailed accounts of Pamyat activities appeared in the Russian émigré press such as *Kontinent*, 50, 1986, and the Paris *Russkaia Mysl*, November 21, 1986. The Soviet media began to report about them only later. *Sovetskaia Kultura*, March 31 and April 18, 1987; *Vechernaia Moskva*. May 18 and June 15, 1987; *Ogonyok*, 23, 1987; *Izvestiia*, June 2, 1987; etc.
[25]*Ogonyok*, 21, May 1987, p. 5.

and boring subject. When Pamyat speakers referred to the academician Likhachev, the leading Russian medievalist and the most respected writer on subjects such as the formation of the Russian national character and the preservation of the Russian national heritage, they dismissed him as "that servant of Zionism."[26]

Meetings of Pamyat have taken place in public places such as the Central House of Soviet Artists and the cultural centers of Dynamo and ZIL, Moscow's biggest factories. Elsewhere the party district bureau has been instrumental, knowingly or unknowingly, in providing meeting places. On one occasion (on May 6, 1987) several hundred members of Pamyat met for a demonstration in Oktiabr Square and then went on to the Moscow City Soviet asking for, and receiving, a meeting with Boris Yeltsin, then a deputy member of the Politburo and effectively the mayor of Moscow. The demonstrators carried banners with slogans such as "Pamyat must be recognized" and "Stop the construction work on Poklonaya Hill" (which had been stopped in any case) and "Long live *perestroika,* down with its enemies." All this seemed quite innocent but meanwhile the Soviet media also became aware of the fact that Pamyat "disseminated absurd fiction about a mysterious organization" allegedly operating in the world, but mainly in the Soviet Union with the task of annihilating the hallowed Russian culture, Americanizing Soviet society, and aggravating the socioeconomic problems of the U.S.S.R. by using bureaucracy, "that monster of world masonry, Zionism and imperialism."[27]

Branches of Pamyat were established in cities such as Leningrad and Sverdlovsk, sometimes as the result of visits by leading members of the Moscow branch, who brought tapes of the speeches that had been made in meetings in the capital. Attendance at these meetings was usually good, even though they were not officially advertised; the dates were spread by word of mouth. The official subjects of the meetings varied from time to time, and from place to place. Sometimes the fight against alcoholism was given pride of place. In Leningrad the planned destruction of the old Angleterre Hotel (where the poet Essenin had lived for a while)

[26]Likhachev is chairman of the Association for the Preservation of Cultural Monuments. In an interview with *Ogonyok* in 1985 he declared that monuments should be preserved not just to glorify the past. He opposed those who wanted to restore only Russian historical monuments and ignore those of the other peoples of the Soviet Union.
[27]*Moscow News,* May 17, 1987. The local Moscow paper *Moskovskaia Pravda* also reported the meeting but did not mention Pamyat by name, or its activities.

was the reason for street demonstrations; but the Leningrad members were less extremist in political orientation than their Moscow comrades. On other occasions movies with strong patriotic undertones were shown, and slides from trips to old cities in Russia to the accompaniment of military marches. Non-Russians were not permitted to attend.

Certain facts became gradually known about the leaders of Pamyat. One of the first to emerge from obscurity was "journalist and photographer" Dmitri Vasiliev, a buffoon and semi-educated demagogue of considerable oratorical talent. Another, Konstantin Andreev, was a party member, but most appeared as "nonparty Bolsheviks," deeply devoted to the party and its secretary general. Among them were Vinogradov, an architect, and several artists. Among the most extreme figures was a retired colonel regarded as an embarrassment by his more cautious colleagues afraid that unbridled talk could lead to the intervention of the state security organs. One of the leaders of Pamyat, Valeri Emelyanov, a former party member, had spent several years in a mental institution following the murder of his wife. By 1987 he was back in good standing, publishing articles in right-wing periodicals.[28]

Vasiliev's speeches often lasted three hours or more and ranged over a great many issues, usually without any apparent logical sequence. They were full of wild assertions based on an updated version of the *Protocols.*[29] His appearance was usually dramatic: he would announce that "sinister forces" were after him, that this could well be his last appearance ever, and that the public should therefore forgive him if he appeared with a mask or a false beard.

Ironically, even the Nazis had not been entirely convinced by the authenticity of the *Protocols;* even the Black Hundred used them with a certain reluctance. Stolypin, the great hero of Pamyat (according to *Izvestia,* his picture and Lenin's adorn Vasiliev's apartment), appointed a police commission for a secret inquiry into their authenticity, and it revealed their spuriousness. Tsar Nicholas II, who had hitherto fully believed in them, thereupon gave an order to no longer employ them: "Drop the *Protocols.* One cannot

[28]*Nash Sovremennik,* 8, 1987.

[29]Further detailed reports on Pamyat appeared in *Komsomolskaia Pravda,* May 22, 1987, and June 24, 1987; *Sovetskaia Rossia,* June 28, 1987, and July 17, 1987; *Nedelia,* June 22, 1987; and *Pravda,* July 18 and July 20, 1987. This publicity continued throughout 1988; Vasiliev was interviewed by Italian and Austrian television as well as the *Washington Post* and many other newspapers. In June 1988 he was given an official warning in connection with his antisocial activities, "which are liable to cause national discord" (*Argumenty i Fakty,* 23, 1988).

defend a pure cause by dirty methods." But what was inadmissible in 1908 became legitimate eighty years later. According to Vasiliev the official Soviet catalogue lists not less than three editions of the *Protocols* in Lenin's library: "If the leader of the international proletariat, the founder of our state, studied this question, I, a nonparty Bolshevik, am obliged to know with what our leader was preoccupied."

Some of the old ideas of the *Protocols* were given a new lease on life—for example, the Moscow metro has been mined so as to explode one day and destroy all the centers of government. But there are also some new ideas, such as the yogurt plot, introduced apparently by the academician Uglov, the leading antialcoholism ideologist. According to him, Russian children are systematically fed yogurt, which unbeknownst to most parents contains one and a half percent alcohol, thus preparing them for a life of debauchery and physical and mental deterioration. Another means of poisoning the minds of Soviet children is the picture of a moon (an old Masonic symbol) on toddlers' romper suits, and the printing of six-pointed stars which often appear in Soviet newspapers.

Leaders of Pamyat have made it known that Jewish architects are rebuilding Moscow in such a way that the main streets will resemble a Star of David. It was not a coincidence that the sculpture of Pushkin is turned with his back to the building behind him (the Rossia movie house), an obvious affront to the Russian people. Certain lines on a recent map of Moscow ought to be interpreted as an arrow, aiming directly at the Rossia hotel. On yet another poster the heart of a Russian peasant is pierced by a sword if one looks at it from a particular angle. On Chaska Street, on the site of a former church, a "grill bar" was about to be erected. The Pamyat speaker admitted that he was not certain what "grill" meant. But he had no doubt that their wives and daughters would be employed there as prostitutes.

According to Pamyat, it is exceedingly dangerous to reveal the truth about the sinister forces threatening Russia; those daring to speak out are likely to be killed or at least threatened over the telephone. The attitude of the respectable right toward Pamyat has been on the whole favorable.[30] Leading intellectuals in Leningrad

---

[30]Among the speakers in a Pamyat-like meeting in Leningrad (in which Marxism was rejected as a Zionist doctrine) there were V. Vykhodtsev, the author of the leading official textbook on Soviet literature, and Mikhail Antonov, one of the leading publicists of the *perestroika* period.

and Novosibirsk have participated in their meetings. Leading writers such as Rasputin and Proskurin have expressed qualified support; others have chosen to refrain from commenting when confronted with questions. The editor of *Nash Sovremennik* has published the writings of members of Pamyat and defended them against their detractors in public; Kozhinov, the noted literary critic, has called it a worthy group even though he dissociated himself from some of the extremist elements who had penetrated it and given it a bad name.[31] More interesting and less predictable was the reaction of party authorities and the noncommitted intelligentsia. Several articles about Pamyat and like-minded groups were published in leading Soviet newspapers, and its reactionary activities were denounced. However, there was an un-Bolshevik softness in these comments. Only on rare occasions was the impact of the Black Hundred and of Nazism mentioned, and usually in a hesitant way: many, perhaps most, members of Pamyat were described as well-meaning but misguided patriots who wanted to work for a good cause but had been misled by a small number of demagogues. Incitement to racial hatred is a crime under the Soviet constitution but there were no suggestions in the official media to take the inciters to task. Instead, it was suggested that there should be a dialogue, that members of Pamyat should be told how to invest their energies in constructive work for the good of the country. However, from the many readers' letters which were written in reply to the attacks against Pamyat it appeared that there was no readiness to enter a dialogue.[32]

There was similar reluctance to tackle Pamyat head-on on the part of those who could not be suspected of any sympathy for this movement. Various arguments were adduced. First, excessive publicity in the leading media would only draw attention to a marginal group. Second, Pamyat was taken to task not because

[31]Julia Vishnevsky, "The Emergence of Pamyat and Otechestvo," Radio Liberty, August 26, 1987; "A Second Pamyat Emerges," Radio Liberty, November 18 and *idem;* "A Russian Nationalist Gathering in Leningrad," Radio Liberty, December 2, 1987. Also, see *Sovetskaia Kultura,* November 24, 1987.
[32]Some of these letters were quoted by Y. Lesoto in *Komsomolskaia Pravda,* December 19, 1987. Her original article had been published in the same newspaper on May 22, and she had published a first selection of readers' letters on June 24. Further letters and comments were published in the same paper on December 19, 1987, when Lesoto first conceded that Pamyat was an embryonic neo-fascist party. She was attacked by *Nash Sovremennik,* 10, 1987; the same journal also came to the defense of Begun, a leading White Russian, anti-Semitic writer (*Nash Sovremennik,* 5, 1988).

its activities were inherently bad but because they made a bad impression abroad. One writer argued that if (according to Lenin) the growth of anarchism was the punishment for an opportunistic policy followed by the working-class movement, the emergence of Pamyat was the punishment for the bureaucratism of the Brezhnev era.[33] This explanation made sense if one assumed that the main aim of Pamyat was the preservation and restoration of monuments of Russian culture. But in fact their purpose was mainly political and, seen in this light, the recommendations appeared strange: should the Communist Party have taken over the anti-Marxist slogans of Pamyat so as to take the wind out of their sails? It is unlikely that Lenin would have approved, and even Stalin might have had misgivings.

The treatment of Pamyat by the authorities showed a lack of clarity and conviction. Who were the members of Pamyat, and what was their social origin? Why had their strange ideas been so readily absorbed? The traditional fascist and semi-fascist movements of the past, including the Black Hundred, had found their followers among the backward sections of society as well as the *déracinés* and *spostati,* the rootless, with a sprinkling of lawyers and clerks, a few physicians, relatively many semi-intellectuals, small shopkeepers, and a substantial portion of the *Lumpenproletariat*—street loungers, peasants recently arrived in the big city and not yet absorbed.

But it is not at all certain that class analysis will provide a key for the explanation of the Pamyat phenomenon. How to explain that a leading painter such as Ilya Glazunov and an even more prominent writer such as Valentin Rasputin should come on record arguing that there were many good people in Pamyat and that it was a shame that a group with such praiseworthy intentions should be persecuted by the authorities? A writer in *Izvestiia* noted that Pamyat was not simply a group of hysterical people but represented the views of a section of the population which found it difficult to reconsider certain truths that had been generally accepted only yesterday and which, as a result, were in a state of confusion and even panic. But an analysis of this kind did not make allowance for the fact (also conceded by the author) that the Soviet media had initially underrated the Pamyat phenomenon, that it

[33]G. Kh. Popov and N. Adzhubei, "Pamyat i 'Pamyat,' " *Znamia,* 1, 1988.

had the support of certain members of the intelligentsia, scientists and writers. In brief, the authorities were facing an attempt to introduce a very dangerous new ideology.[34]

The traditional character of conspiracy theories in Russia has certainly played a major role. The fantastic accusations in the Moscow trials in the 1930s have not been officially withdrawn to this day even though they were tacitly dropped. The charges against the killer-doctors of 1937 and 1953 are still remembered. Even under Gorbachev the U.S. was repeatedly accused of spreading AIDS as part of a worldwide plot. It has been argued in the Soviet media that the Jonestown mass suicide was a case of mass murder carried out by the CIA; that the young pilot who landed on Red Square had acted not on his own but was guided by sinister forces; that Rashid Karameh, Mahel, and other leaders were killed by the CIA and the Zionists who also instigated the conflict between Armenians and Azeris.

With so many demons in action any plot and conspiracy, however diabolical, becomes at least a possibility. Some theologians have explained the idea of a pact between the devil and human beings as a phenomenon particularly strong at a time of spiritual crisis, of impending doom, when despair over the injustice of this world replaces optimism. The resurgence of the belief in satanism in the Soviet Union could perhaps be explained in a similar light— the search for culprits at a time when the corruption of the outside world induces general pessimism.

But this is no more than a hypothesis; there are no obvious explanations for a phenomenon such as Pamyat from either history or psychopathology. How far are the ideas of Pamyat likely to spread? How influential could they become politically? When the influence of the Black Hundred was greatest, they attracted some 10 percent of the electorate; it seems unlikely that their successors will be much more successful. The spread of such ideas, it has been argued, would be suicidal as far as the cohesion of the Soviet empire is concerned. A Russian Pamyat is bound to lead to the

[34]Pavel Gutiontov, *Izvestiia,* February 27, 1988. See also Kazarin and Russovski in *Vechernaia Moskva,* February 25, 1988. Glazunov's article had appeared in *Pravda,* September 27, 1987. Several Soviet writers refused to give a clear answer when asked whether they were members of Pamyat or sympathizers, but there were frequent defenses of the cause of Pamyat in *Nash Sovremennik* and *Molodaia Guardia.* Rasputin said that he does not "fully identify" with Pamyat, but he denounced the "abusive articles" of which "there appeared so many in our press," and that he did not relate to them as fascists, Black Hundred, or nationalists (Moscow Central Television, June 26, 1988).

emergence of similar groups in the other Soviet republics and the political consequences can be easily foreseen. Some leaders of the Russian extreme right have said that this does not unduly bother them, but the politicians are showing less equanimity. For this reason, if for no other, stronger measures will probably be taken if the extremist fringe should ever become a real threat to the system.

More worrisome is the indirect impact of Pamyat, the influence exerted by some of their ideas on part of the political leaders, sections of the bureaucracy, and the people at large. While their more extreme thoughts are rejected as the eccentricities of well-meaning but confused activists, some of the obscurantism seems to have rubbed off. It is most unlikely that men and women who have grown up with the great Russian classics will give a chance to a group of this kind. But it would be rash to take the victory of reason and good sense for granted. Superstition and prejudice are deeply rooted in Russia; and if the humanism of Kant, Goethe, and Beethoven was no guarantee against a relapse into barbarism in Germany in the 1930s, Pushkin and Tolstoi may be no more effective in their native country.

Where to place Pamyat and its supporters in the European historical tradition? Vasiliev has publicly stated that he sees nothing wrong in either fascism or the Black Hundred. Pamyat's intellectual fellow travelers may feel uneasy about such plain speaking; they dislike Western mass culture, foreigners, and Jews, but they still resent being branded latter-day disciples of Adolf Hitler. Russians know that Hitler attacked the Soviet Union and that he was an evil man. But fascism in general is not a subject that had been widely investigated and discussed in the Soviet Union. Thus some Russians have embraced certain fascist ideas without even being fully aware of it. Ideologically the Pamyat fellow travelers are partly in the tradition of the French Action Française and the German thinkers of the far right. But there was also a specific Russian tradition of extreme right-wing thought, and this has been rediscovered and remembered in our own day. Such views would not have caused much scandal at the turn of the century. But they appeared in the 1980s, after seventy years of internationalist indoctrination which, as it emerged, had been neither deep nor lasting.

In late 1987 Pamyat split into various groups. The factions led by Valeri Emelyanov and Igor Sytchev dissociated themselves from the group headed by Vasiliev, which remained the strongest by far. These splits did not weaken the extreme right; on the contrary, Pamyat, the patriotic society, became a "front" in 1988, putting the emphasis on its political, fighting character.[35] At its meetings members appeared in classic fascist uniforms (black shirts) to be told by their leaders that Russians were turning into people like Red Indians who lived on reservations. Hence the need for immediate and radical de-Zionization, which encompassed banning mixed marriages, deporting Jews and other minorities to their original habitats, and cleansing Russian intellectual life of Marxist and liberal influences.[36] Pamyat was seldom, if ever, attacked by the more moderate wing of the Russian party, perhaps because they tended to belittle the importance of the extremists, perhaps because they felt that there were "no enemies on the right." In the alternative media (such as the journals *Glasnost* or *Vybor*), on the other hand, there were occasional articles written by orthodox or patriotic thinkers critical of Pamyat ideology.

Pamyat is not the "Russian party," just as as the Black Hundred was not identical with Russian conservativism; it is the extreme fringe of that party. Much of the critique of the Russian right is not specifically Russian in any case; it can be found elsewhere on the left as well as on the right. An aversion to certain manifestations of modernism and, *a fortiori,* mass culture is not necessarily "reactionary." The attacks against unbridled materialism in Soviet society, meaning the chase after material possessions, are not unjustified. These conservative moods become dangerous only when the sober analysis of present-day Soviet mores turns into hysterical and apocalyptic fantasies, when the justified anger with the present state of affairs begins to look for culprits where they are least to be found.

The basic weakness of the new Russian ideology is not so much its analysis of the current state of affairs, however extreme and eccentric, as its inability to provide reasonable prescriptions for the future. The inspiration for a moral and cultural regeneration cannot be found in Tsarist Russia, nor in villages which no longer

[35]S. Lesov, in *Strana i Mir*, 3, 1988.
[36]For an outspoken defense of Pamyat doctrine, see A. Kuzmin in *Nash Sovremennik*, 3, 1988, which went as far as possible in its denunciation of Marxism-Leninism, given the restrictions existing even under *glasnost*.

exist. The answers cannot be provided by harking back to the good old days of World War II patriotism and solidarity. It is toward the future that these critics, unhappy with the present state of affairs, should cast their eyes. But they are reluctant to do so because the future, unlike the past, is so full of the very uncertainties which they abhor.

Throughout history there have been liberal and conservative movements, parties of the left and the right, nationalist and internationalist. It would be a miracle if Russia alone were exempt from such diversity of political opinion. Seen in the context of seventy years of Soviet history, the right-wing reaction against the "left-wing excesses" of the twenties and thirties seems almost inevitable. Conservative policies have been advocated and conducted for decades in the Soviet Union under a left-wing veneer which has become progressively thinner. For having made Russia strong in military power and influence, the right is indebted to Stalin, and, within limits, also to his successors.[37] But the conservatives could not relish the Stalinist domestic system, nor could they accept Marxist-Leninist ideology even though most of the time all that was expected of them was routine lip service. They agreed with the neo-Stalinists on a wide range of issues. But they also had ideas and idols of their own which could not be accommodated in a Marxist-Leninist system, however leniently interpreted. They had common enemies, but their alliance still remained fragile.

For all one knows, the "Russian party" could make a contribution in a Russia liberated of old shackles and shibboleths. But as so often happened in Russia's past, the trend toward exaggeration, fanaticism, and extremism, the historical bane of the Russian left, has its counterpart on the right, and now, it would appear, more strongly than ever.

[37]There are fascinating similarities among the arguments used by neo-Stalinists and extreme Russian nationalists and those of the opponents of de-Nazification in Germany after 1945: Why accuse us? Everyone collaborated. . . . The corollary is, of course, that if everyone cooperated, no one is guilty. The German neo-Nazis have dredged up embarrassing quotations showing that even German internal émigrés published their verses and essays in Goebbels's newspapers, and these were written in conformity with the *Zeitgeist*. The Soviet writer Stanislav Kunyaev (*Nash Sovremennik*, September 1988) and some of his friends have done a similar service for the Stalin era. But there is a world of difference whether someone praised Stalin in 1935 because he genuinely thought him a genius (or because he was afraid for his life) or whether one justifies Stalinism fifty years after the event.

CHAPTER 7

"What Has Become of Us?": *Glasnost* and Soviet Society

S HUKSHIN'S *cri de coeur*, "What has become of us?", uttered many years before *glasnost*, could well have served as its slogan.[1] Most of the problems of Soviet society had been identified before; some were articulated on occasion, others such as drugs and prostitution were tabu. Everyone with his eyes and ears open was aware of the true state of affairs. What did change with the coming of *glasnost* was the perspective; previously these had been minor blemishes on an overall positive balance sheet; now they were recognized as major threats to society. Nor had the deeper reasons for the social evils ever been discussed fully and frankly; according to the official line they were remnants of Russia's unfortunate prerevolutionary past. But as the years passed, such explanations became less and less convincing; what if these evils were not rooted in the past but in the present? It is mainly owing to *glasnost*—that is to say, owing to greater honesty and the spirit of self-criticism—that we know now so much more about the true state of Soviet society. And it is to these extraordinary revelations that we ought to turn next, for they constitute the most important element of *glasnost*.

The 1960s and 1970s had been a period of virtually uninterrupted announcements of new victories in the battle for production. Little attention was paid to what later became known as the "human factor," to questions of morale and morality, to the quality

[1]Vasili Shukshin (1929–1974), born in Siberia; worker, teacher, and subsequently one of the leading writers, film producers, and actors of his time.

of life. True, people of various persuasion, "liberals" as well as Russophiles, and, of course, the dissidents, felt that something was seriously amiss. True again, there were occasional editorials and novels on corruption, embezzlement, and various other aspects of the darker side of Soviet society.[2] But these were considered marginal phenomena, atypical, describing situations to be rectified by administrative measures, more vigilance, and the imposition of stricter control. The fact that the issues went much deeper and that there were no easy solutions was admitted only with the age of *glasnost*.

Women and the Soviet Family

At one time women played a prominent role in radical Russian politics. Sofia Perovskaya, Vera Zasulich, and others featured prominently in the history of the Russian revolutionary movement. In Russian literature, from Pushkin and Turgenev to Maxim Gorki, women often appeared as more active and daring than men. If Rosa Luxemburg had migrated to the East rather than the West, she might have found a place as a leader of the revolutionary movement. But with the ascendancy of Stalin, women almost totally disappeared from the higher echelons of party and state, which no doubt saved the lives of many of them. This process continued after Stalin's death. In the late 1950s Mrs. Furtseva served for a while as minister of culture, but she was not a great success. Under Gorbachev, A. D. Biryukova became a secretary of the Central Committee (in charge of consumer industries—one out of twelve such secretaries) and another woman was appointed ambassador to Switzerland. But whereas in the twentieth century women attained high and highest positions in public affairs not only in Western countries but also in the Third World, the party apparatus remained virtually a male domain; there was, for instance, not a single woman among the all-important party district secretaries. And if from time to time a woman was appointed to a position of secondary importance, it was no doubt out of embarrassment or a feeling of duty as much as of conviction.

There was strong male prejudice against women in politics which manifested itself, for instance, in the aversion to Mrs. Gorba-

[2]For instance, Alexander Kron's *Bessonitsa* (Sleeplessness), *Novy Mir*, 4–6, 1977; Ilya Stemler's *Univermag*, *Novy Mir*, 8–10, 1982; Anatoli Pristavkin, *Vor Gorodok*, *Novy Mir*, 1–2, 1983.

chev's role in the travels undertaken by her husband. It had not been the custom for wives to accompany their husbands, or even be seen with them, in public on such occasions. On the other hand, there is no certainty that Soviet women were, in fact, consumed with a burning desire to take an active part in politics. Their main complaints concerned discrimination on a more elementary level: while women constituted some 75 percent of all teachers, 70 percent of the doctors, and 40 percent of those employed in scientific institutes, only a few of them made it to the top. They were also grossly underpaid: the salary of a teacher was little more than half that of a skilled worker, and the salary of a general practitioner (as distinct from a leading specialist) not much higher.

Furthermore, much of the least skilled work, including some involving heavy physical effort, was done by women. Soviet women certainly had been emancipated inasmuch as more of them worked in factories and offices than in any other developed country. But many of them felt that they still had no equal chance compared to their male colleagues, and that the price they had to pay was too high. Since Soviet men are less likely to help with domestic chores than males in most other developed countries, since Soviet households have fewer labor-saving devices than those in the West, and since, above all, the institution of the *babushka* [3] had gradually vanished, more and more Soviet women found the treble burden too heavy. How could they do an effective job at work, and at the same time take care of household and children, wait in the queues for hours, not to mention being wives and companions to their husbands—let alone have some time for themselves? How could they be tough and delicate, hard and feminine at the same time? They found themselves under increasing pressures from all sides, facing accusations that they failed at work as much as at home, or that success in one field was usually paid for by neglect of the others. What, for instance, was a working mother to do if one of her children fell ill, which was usually the case a few times a year? [4]

These pressures increased and were occasionally discussed during the 1970s but they became a subject of public debate only

[3] The grandmother who very often lived in and took care not only of cooking, cleaning and mending the clothes but also of the upbringing of children up to school age.
[4] The pressures on Soviet women were freely described in Soviet literature back in the 1960s. See, for instance, Natalia Baranskaia, "Nedelya Kak Nedelya" (A Week Like All Others), *Novy Mir*, 11, 1969.

under *glasnost.* There were growing voices that emancipation had gone too far and that the place of women was at home, at least while children were small. Men argued that working women had become coarse in their behavior as well as in speech, that they had lost their femininity. This, they claimed, had negative consequences both for conjugal life and even more for the children. In a typical letter to the editor a woman engineer from Omsk related how her little son requested her not to talk to him "with such a voice." She had talked to him as she was accustomed to talk at her place of work—that is to say, giving orders, shouting. What was she to do—to quit her job, as her neighbor had done?[5]

The women's case was that they had usually gone to work simply because their husbands' income was insufficient; that some of the difficulties arising could be attenuated if men were willing to help more at home and if the state would provide bigger apartments, more kindergartens, and other facilities. But the intrinsic difficulties remained. As one woman noted, the truly emancipated heroine of movies and novels, usually an actress or a journalist, free of all fetters and shackling obligations, needs at least two domestic servants if she wants to get married and still pursue creative work.[6]

But there were also voices which, following the more extreme slogans of Western women's liberation, suggested that a husband and children were not, after all, a precondition for happiness. Women should unite in "friendly associations of mutual help."

Mention has been made of the central role of the family in the thought of conservative Russian writers such as Vasili Belov and Yuri Bondarev. The same idea appears even more palpably in Astafiev's *Sad Detective,* the story of the police officer whose wife and children left him: "Dynasties, societies and empires have turned to dust when the family within them began to disintegrate. . . ."[7]

This kind of philosophy of history may not be quite convincing, but according to all evidence there is at present a great deal of

---

[5]*Ogonyok,* 23, 1987; see A. Yasnov's article in the same journal (46, 1986) and the subsequent exchanges, and for another example, *Pravda,* February 19, 1988. Melancholic thoughts on the occasion of International Woman's Day were expressed in *Rabotnitsa,* 3, 1988.

[6]Svetlana Kaidash, *Literaturnaia Rossia,* August 7, 1987.

[7]In a recent interview Astafiev again stressed the enormous importance of the family for the education of children (*Semia,* 11, 1988). He grew up in an orphanage, hence his specific sensitivity.

unhappiness in family life. Soviet statistics show not merely a scandalously high number of abortions[8] but a divorce rate which approached 90 percent in cities with a predominantly young population, such as Togliatti. (It was over 50 percent in Odessa, Kharkov, Moscow, Leningrad, Riga, Donetzk, and other places. It was considerably lower in the non-Russian republics.) At the same time there has been a steadily growing number of bachelors, both male and female, even though Soviet society has traditionally frowned on bachelorhood as an institution. Even under *glasnost* the negative attitude and the dire predictions have not changed: "Whatever consolation the bachelors may adduce to justify the fact that they are not married, their objective situation is unenviable from the beginning. It turns into great misfortune and ends in personal tragedy. For everything in this world there is a price, including the sweet years of nonmarital existence."[9]

Some of the advocates of the return of the woman to the family put much of the blame for the family's decline on the sexual revolution, meaning the greater permissiveness which has spread in the Soviet Union during the last decade. Underlying this there seems to be a feeling of nostalgia, sometimes articulated, for the patriarchal family of the old Russian village, which like so many other traditions has forever disappeared. Others believe that with improved living conditions and facilities for working mothers, and also with a decline in alcoholism, a prime factor in the breakdown of many marriages, the situation will ease.

They have pointed to the need for marriage counseling, virtually absent in the Soviet Union until recently; sexual education (frowned upon by the conservatives); and other educational measures. The roots of the crisis of the nuclear family may, however, be impervious to measures of this kind, and though the economic reforms may bring about a decline in the number of women gainfully employed and their return home, the pressures are bound to continue as long as the husband's salary is not sufficient, as long as the queues have not disappeared and the housing situation radically improved.

The war between the sexes is likely to remain as tangible a

[8]According to official, probably incomplete, figures, the rate was 272 per thousand pregnancies, ten times as much as, or even more than, in most other countries. According to *AFP*, June 18, 1988 (quoting *Meditsinskaia Gazetta*), condoms were available only on the black market in parts of the Soviet Union at a price higher than the official rate for abortion (five rubles).

[9]E. K. Tokareva, *Sotsiologicheskie Issledovaniia*, 2, 1987.

factor as class war once was, and the lot of many Soviet women continues to be a matter of much concern. "Our statistics [one woman commentator has written] give one the impression of Soviet women as happy, hard-working, well-educated professionals, good at sport, dancing and singing, and active in the trade unions and other public work. This is a highly inaccurate picture. . . ."[10] While the true facts had not been unknown, the depth of dissatisfaction and frustration emanating from fictional and nonfictional sources has come as a shock. Lenin once wrote that the success of the revolution depended in the long run on the degree of female participation. But Soviet women have been far too busy with a myriad of other, more urgent preoccupations, all connected with problems of survival rather than revolution.

A Lost Generation?

Of all the painful revelations of *glasnost,* the fate of the young generation shook the leadership and public opinion more than any other single problem. True, the concern tended sometimes to get lost in abstruse issues such as whether rock should be banned or integrated into the regime, whether rock produced not only moral but also biochemical changes in those affected, whether jeans were bad for the female body, and so on. But the basic questions were real enough: it is an old saying in politics that whoever has the youth has the future, and there was a great deal of evidence that Communism had lost the young generation.

It was all the more shocking since it was in such stark contrast to the enthusiasm of the young of the 1920s and early 1930s, which Communism had absorbed and channeled with great skill—the time of revolutionary romanticism and self-sacrifice which had found its expression not just in countless poems and novels but in mass movements of voluntary mobilization. This had been the heroic age when the Komsomol (the militant Communist youth league) had helped to build up Siberia, when work for the holy cause of Communism had been more important than any individual claim such as love, the family, or personal inclination and interests. These had been the young men and women who later fought bravely for their country, quite often as volunteers, from the early days of the war.

[10]Larissa Kuznetsova, *Novoye Vremia,* June 19, 1987.

The idealism of the twenties could not possibly have survived the horrors and cynicism of the Stalin age. Enthusiasm and identification with the regime did markedly decline, but the indoctrination of the young remained strong and quite effective in the early postwar period. By the time the critical faculties of the boys and girls had fully developed, by the time they realized that there was a world of difference between what they were taught in the Komsomol and what the world was really like, they had usually left school and the youth organizations.

While living conditions improved, the postwar decades were a period of steady disillusionment for the young generation. Activities in the Komsomol became more and more routine; there were few challenges left, and the elderly political leaders seemed not to need the young. The erstwhile idealism turned into open materialism, the realization that to have money was the key to happiness. True, when a youth magazine carried out a poll in 1987 asking a few hundred youngsters whether they believed in Communism, 51 percent still answered, "I believe even though there are doubts." But the negative voices were far more emphatic than the affirmative ones ("No, no, no—I think this is a bluff, a fairy tale"). Other correspondents answered that it was pointless even to ask questions of this kind ("Will there be Communism?") because the answers would not be truthful ("Don't you remember, five years ago we already had built Communism . . .").[11]

Some members of the older generation bitterly complained that the young were loud, destructive, lacked discipline and ideals, and showed no respect for their elders. They compared them unfavorably with themselves as children. Many suggested that to remedy the situation the young should be sent to do some hard work.

The difference between the generations manifested itself early on in literature. Typical products for the heroic period of the Komsomol had been Nikolai Ostrovski's *How the Steel Was Forged,* the story of the worker's son who became an exemplary leader in revolution and civil war—and eventually gave his life for the party; Nikolai Ognev's *Kostya Ryabzev;* and Alexander Bogdanov's *The*

[11] *Sobesednik,* 39, September 1987, p. 6 et seq. According to a poll among students of social science courses—that is, Marxist philosophy, history, and economy—considerably less than half had a positive attitude to these subjects. The majority thought of them as purely abstract and theoretical with no significance for real life (*Sotsiologicheskie Issledovaniia,* 4, 1987).

First Girl. These were primitive novels in many respects, but sincere and enthusiastic. There were light-years of difference between this spirit and Boris Vasilev's depressing *Velikolepnaya Shestorka (The Magnificent Six)*, the story of a youth camp in which the boys play cowboys and Indians, and through lack of elementary consideration or outright cruelty cause the death of several old and lame horses kept in the neighborhood. The police investigate, but since the camp leader does not want to ruin the careers of "the hope of the twenty-first century," as well as her own reputation, she decides to hush up the affair by means of some well-placed bribes.[12] It is difficult to decide whether to blame more the spoiled children or those in charge of their upbringing.

Vox populi complained about the children's ingratitude; those in search of deeper reasons came up with a more balanced assessment. Igor Kon, a philosopher and political sociologist, wrote in the party ideological organ *Kommunist* that decades of stagnation, when one thing was not allowed, another was dangerous, and yet another impossible, had corrupted most of the older generation. They grew used to such a life and fed this civic apathy to the young. The "discipline" of the older generation frequently amounted to little more than obsequious obedience and an inability to say "no." And they were shocked when the young were asking, "Who said that this is not allowed, who said it was impossible?"[13]

True, the Komsomol had more members than ever (forty million). Mironenko, its general secretary, was a young man, which had seldom been the case in the past. When its Twentieth congress took place in 1987, he admitted that the Komsomol had suffered an almost complete loss of authority, that today's youngsters regarded it as nothing but a ladder for those who wanted an establishment career. (Both Andropov and Gorbachev had started their careers in the Komsomol.) And, he went on, "For twenty years we lacked both courage and energy—we now hear the question, 'To be or not to be?' "[14]

Gorbachev appeared at the congress and added a few explana-

[12]*Yunost,* 6, 1980.

[13]*Soviet Weekly,* November 28, 1987. In another article the same author noted that little if anything was known in the Soviet Union about the psychology and sociology of youth—"the older the child, the less we know about it" ("Estafetta Pokolenii" [The Relay of Generations], *Kommunist,* March 1987, p. 103).

[14]*Komsomolskaia Pravda,* April 15–20, 1987. But there were also voices to the effect that the situation had not changed under Mironenko and that the leaders were still bearing the stamp of the ruling *nomenklatura (Yunost,* January 1987).

tions of his own. An elite, he said, had been formed inside the Komsomol which had many privileges, a fact which caused much dissatisfaction among the rank and file. Gorbachev also mentioned the fact that Komsomol leaders were given passing grades in institutions of higher learning irrespective of whether they attended lectures or not. But it was by no means all the fault of the young: the Komsomol had shown little initiative and independence, but then it had been, in fact, deprived of its independence by adult organizations such as the local party committees and the schools.[15]

The Komsomol leaders decided to "find their way back to the masses" by making concessions to the independent initiative groups which had sprung up outside their ranks. The Moscow Komsomol newspaper became a pioneer in commenting on homosexuality, prostitution, drug taking, and other tabu areas; as a result it was occasionally upbraided by the authorities, enough to acquire the reputation of a lively, daring, unorthodox journal while still remaining strictly within the fold. The paper even tried to start a "rock laboratory," but the rockers (the paper sadly noted) preferred to continue their own separate activities, such as their nightly escapades on their roaring motor bikes. The other informal groups also declined with thanks.

Independent youth activities took many different forms. At one time the Lyuberi figured prominently in the media. These were youngsters from a Moscow working class suburb who became known for their particular militancy; frequent clashes with punks, rockers, and other youth groups; and also for insubordination in the army.[16] Further investigation showed that while the Lyuberi had indeed frequented Moscow cafés, discothèques, and movie houses (of which there were but few in their own town), they were, on the whole, ordinary, aggressive teenagers with a special interest in bodybuilding who, on occasion, had attacked "heavy metalists." There were accusations against the militia that they turned a blind eye to the activities of the Lyuberi, whom they regarded as a welcome ally in the fight for law and order against dissidents. There seems to have been some truth in these charges. "Lyuberi" became a catchall term for various groups sometimes led and trained by Afghanistan veterans, of young people who were called upon to act as vigilantes against elements they did not like, such as

---

[15]*Pravda,* April 17, 1987.

[16]See, for instance, *Sovetskaia Rossia,* March 4, 1987; *Krasnaia Zvesda,* May 30, 1987. On the coverage of the Lyuberi story in the Soviet press, see *Zhurnalist,* 5, 1988.

long-haired students and other nonconformists. Such groups were by no means confined to Moscow.

Disturbing instances of neo-Nazi activities were reported from various parts of the country. In Leningrad there had existed for years groups of young people sporting brown shirts, swastikas, ranks such as *"Sturmbannführer,"* and other trappings of the Hitler movement who marched through the streets. Somehow no one had paid attention. In Kaliningrad (formerly Königsberg) many old German weapons had been discovered in underground bunkers and were appropriated by youngsters with swastikas on their sleeveless leather jackets who wore their hair cut short and dyed blond. According to the Soviet media these groups were socially heterogenous, but the overwhelming majority of their members came from well-to-do families willing to do everything for their offspring. Again, their activities had been ignored until the youngsters decided to hoist a swastika flag on one of the city's prominent buildings.

Usually their exploits were explained as the result of puerile high spirits, the wish to shock and attract public attention, the pursuit of perverse entertainment, and the lack of sufficient political indoctrination. But in Murmansk the young collectors of Nazi memorabilia, led by a veteran of the country's elite border guard, destroyed the local memorial erected to the fallen Soviet warriors in the Great Fatherland War. Similar vandalism was reported from Leningrad's famous Summer Garden.[17] Some Soviet commentators argued that the young generation simply had not been told enough about the last war; others believed the roots went deeper. Most agreed that not too much political importance should be attributed to exploits of this kind. It is easy to imagine to what extent such incidents would have been played up in the Soviet media had they taken place in a Western country.

Far more widespread and equally puzzling for the adults was the emergence of a counterculture, which, as in the West, manifested itself in many different ways, ranging from old-fashioned hippiedom and Hare Krishna to various forms of rock, in particular the "heavy metalists." These trends first appeared in Moscow and Leningrad in the late 1960s, and during the next decade spread

[17]On Murmansk-Moscow television, Channel One, November 25, 1987; on Kaliningrad, *Krasnaia Zvezda,* October 13, 1987. One member of the Irkutsk jazz family (the "seven Simons") who hijacked a Soviet plane in March 1988 had been involved in neo-Nazi activities (*Sobesednik,* 13, 1988).

even to remote provincial cities. The new trends proved to be immensely popular; eventually rock concerts would attract many thousands, often tens of thousands, of ecstatic boys and girls. They defied the authorities, who watched these concerts with dismay. "We do not care what you write in your despicable pamphlets," one youngster wrote to a newspaper. "There are many millions of us. . . ."

Official attitudes toward alternative music were at first similar to what they had been toward jazz in the 1920s and 1930s. It was mostly ignored, discouraged but not entirely banned. Even those who were in favor of banning it admitted that this had become virtually impossible since the invention of the tape recorder. Subsequently, the official line wavered between launching a major campaign against rock music and tacitly ignoring it in the hope that, like other fashions, it would sooner or later fade away. Yet rock music triggered off much deeper passions than jazz had ever done: For some it stood as the essence of all that had gone wrong in Soviet society in recent years, hence their indignation that little or nothing was done to combat it. For others, on the contrary, the extreme intolerance of rock was typical of the reactionary mentality still deeply rooted in wide and influential sections of the older generation.

Typical of the conservative attacks against rock was a letter published in *Pravda* by three of the best-known Soviet writers.[18] Taking an award-winning film, *Is It Easy to Be Young?*, [19] as a starting point, they expressed their deep pain and utmost indignation: Young people no longer want to work hard; their only interest is entertainment and the pursuit of material goods *(veshism)*. To the traditional educational factors, such as school and parents, powerful competitors had arisen, above all television, the radio, the cinema, but also specialized youth media, records, etc. They quoted a Soviet composer named Lobzov, of whom no one had heard, who said that variety rock had become a real social scourge and a poison. They put most of the blame on radio and television, which cater, they alleged, only for the taste of those within the Sadovaia Koltso (a Moscow circumference road), and are responsible not only for spreading this poison, but also for the furious propagation of pseudo-romanticism from abroad: French queens and countesses, British robbers (Robin Hoods), detectives, ban-

[18]Yuri Bondarev, Vasili Belov, and Valentin Rasputin, *Pravda*, November 9, 1987.
[19]It depicts a rock concert in Riga and the subsequent fate of some of the participants.

dits, and prostitutes making their appearance on Soviet television.

No wonder, their argument continued, that Soviet youth had lost all sense of true values. The psychic and moral damage caused by this counterculture had been documented by many doctors of medicine and students of art in foreign countries such as Japan, but "our competent doctors keep silent." The authors ended their appeal noting that while a total ban was probably not practical, the guardians of culture should not keep silent. The young needed lofty moral ideals and not pseudo-values: "They expect such heroes from us and we are obliged to supply them." This appeal was quite typical for a state of mind widespread among the older generation. The criticism was often not without reason, but it was voiced hysterically, with the stress on dark plots and sinister conspiracies on the part of the "inner enemy" and the foes of Russia abroad.

The three authors, after all, had done their civic duty; they had written many books, of which millions of copies had circulated. But it is unlikely that more books and more copies would have prevented the invasion of rock, even if every Soviet child had been compelled to read this patriotic literature for a few minutes every morning.

Spokesmen of the extreme right went even further: they quoted a Soviet professor of medicine who had claimed that "rockomania" was a true disease since it had a biochemical impact on the organism.[20] They saw in rock culture, with its negation of rational thought, the cult of the herd instinct, of power and cruelty. They stressed its neobarbarian character, its affinity to Hitler's SS and to Nazism. They maintained that it was a weapon used by Western imperialist *Kulturträger* as a deliberate attempt to erode the patriotism and the general value system of Soviet youth.[21] Since some of these characteristics, such as irrationality, were close to the world outlook of the Soviet right, one would have anticipated a more sympathetic attitude. But as the conservatives saw it, these influences (*Kulturbolschewismus*, as the Nazis would have called them) were Western and alien, undermining Russian culture, engineered by hidden forces. The terms "satanic" and "diabolical," favorite

---

[20]G. A. Aminov, *Sovetskaia Rossia*, June 4, 1987.

[21]A. Lysenkov and Y. Sergeev, in *Molodaia Guardia*, 10, 1987, pp. 256–70. Also, Tamara Khoroshilova in *Sobesednik*, 2, 1987, and Anatoli Doronin in *Molodaia Guardia*, 12, 1987. According to Doronin, rock culture was a clear case of American aggression. He mentioned a Sverdlovsk rock group which had pretended to open fire on the red flag with their guitars.

key words in these circles, were not missing in discussing "rocko-mania."

Official attitudes were, as noted, inconsistent. Alla Pugacheva, the best-known Soviet pop singer, was prevented for a long time from appearing following alleged misbehavior on her part in a Leningrad hotel. On the other hand, a record by one of the country's leading rock groups, Aquarium, headed by Boris Greben-shikov, was put out by Melodiia, the state record and tape producer, and 200,000 copies were sold in a few hours. State radio and television defended itself against the attacks by the conservatives. They argued that for almost twenty years rock music had become part of Soviet life and the fact that there were some who did not like it was hardly an objective yardstick. At one time Gypsy music had been far more popular than Tchaikovski or Rimsky-Korsakov, yet it caused no lasting damage.[22] A great deal of factual material was published to enable those in charge of political propaganda to explain the rock phenomenon—its origins, the various stages of its development, the difference between (relatively) inoffensive and bad rock, the difference between moderate rock (which mixed rock with blues and traditional folk motives) and the rock extremists who thought that only "heavy metal" was of any value.

For a time the rock theme acquired almost as much importance in the media as disarmament and the state of the economy.[23] The summer of 1987 was the high point of rock's emergence from the semi-underworld; large concerts were staged in which all the major trends were heard and Soviet television even introduced Michael Jackson.[24] By fall 1987, in anticipation of an official crackdown, television and radio began to limit their rock programs, even though a full, head-on collision and a total ban seemed unlikely in view of the enormous popularity of rock among Soviet youth. The position of the "centrists," while deeply hostile to "heavy metal" and other such manifestations of rock, was that the Western experience had shown that this specific fashion was bound to recede sooner or later. But there was no guarantee that it might not be replaced by something equally reprehensible. Hence the need for the psychological understanding of the background of the phe-

[22]O. Korovina in *Televidenie i Radioveshanie*, October 1987.
[23]The number of articles on this subject published in the Soviet press is truly enormous. See, for example, *Argumenty i Fakty*, 13, 1987, and many other issues of this journal. The debates continued well into 1988; see *Komsomolskaia Pravda*, April 2, 1988.
[24]*Washington Post*, November 27, 1987.

nomenon. Such understanding, the experts concluded, was as yet sadly lacking.[25] They warned that a total ban would be ineffective, the "sweet fruits" of what had been banned would be even more tempting, and Soviet youth would listen to Western radio stations more than they did in any case.

The emergence of rock music was the most prominent, certainly the most noisy, but by no means the only manifestation of cultural dissent on the part of Soviet youth. Even earlier, hippies had appeared, giving rise to a new term *(khipovat),* but they never attracted the masses of Soviet youth. Then, in the mid-1980s, informal youth societies sprouted and, according to *Pravda,* there were some 30,000 of them by the end of 1987.[26] Some of these gravitated to the extreme right, others to the left, some were apolitical, some were manipulated by the authorities. Some were groups of adolescents, whereas the average age of others was between twenty-five and thirty-five.[27]

In 1987 the word "Arbat" became the quintessence of the alternative youth culture for both its proponents and its detractors. Arbat, to the west of the Kremlin, is one of Moscow's oldest quarters; once Pushkin, Herzen, and Tolstoi had lived there. It was a mixture of upper-middle-class people, artists, and tradesmen, the Saint-Germain-des-Près of Moscow. Later yet, it became the site of Moscow's first skyscraper and cinema. It is also Moscow's first pedestrian zone. Bulat Okudzava dedicated a poem to the Arbat, and *Rybakov* his widely read novel. For reasons which are not entirely clear, the old Arbat became something akin to Hyde Park and Greenwich Village, a tribune for alternative youth culture, poets declaiming their verse, artists offering their pictures and sculpture, rockers and breakers and other music groups performing in front of the Vakhtangov Theater. The Arbat became the magnet, the Mecca of what was frowned upon by many: jeans, long hair, various cultural and religious sectarians. Masses of young people from all over Moscow, indeed from all over the Soviet Union, streamed to Arbat much to the disgust of the 2,500 people living there (usually elderly), the police, and the Komsomol. The Communist youth organization openly admitted that "we have lost this opportunity"; the militia announced that 3,000 arrests had been made at Arbat for various administrative offenses during

[25]See, for instance, Y. Tsagarelli in *Sovetskaia Kultura,* December 1, 1987.
[26]December 27, 1987.
[27]*Komsomolskaia Pravda,* December 11, 1987.

eight months in 1987.[28] The patience of the party authorities was thoroughly tried by the young bohemians, the provocative ugliness of their attire, the lyrics of the local bands. Yet once it had come into being, it was difficult to abolish it altogether; Arbat had become a symbol of freedom.

Special militia units equipped with walkie-talkies patrolled Arbat to weed out undesirable elements. A major was overheard saying to his men, "These kids are singing good songs, let them sing." But another young man, singing songs by Paul Simon, was taken away to the station; the controllers did not know English and his performance had raised suspicion. Thus of the spirit of *glasnost* and democracy, which in May and June of 1987 had permeated Arbat, only a censored version had survived by fall.[29] When spring came big crowds were still milling the pedestrian zone in search of "action" which no longer existed.

A Soviet newspaper asked: "Not long ago Arbat was a live, singing and dancing street, a place for debate during the week and at weekends. What has happened to all the singing, music making, debating and reciting verse? There has been no actual ban on such activity; very simply, the Moscow city Soviet executive has issued regulations concerning the activities of citizens in Arbat."[30]

Outside Arbat the militia showed less tolerance; proponents of alternative youth culture, or simply those who wore their hair long, stood a fair chance of being arrested or roughed up—usually for some technical violation such as not carrying their internal passport with them at all times, as every Soviet citizen is by law obliged to do.[31] Such incidents were not likely to improve relations between the young generation and the authorities.

There was another perturbing trend: the declining respect not only for the Komsomol but also for school and family. Soviet education had been far more effective, according to most observers, in the difficult fifties than in the eighties. Abel Aganbegyan, the

[28] *Izvestiia*, October 30, 1987; "Porazhenie na Arbate" (Defeat on the Arbat), *Komsomolskaia Pravda*, November 27, 1987.
[29] G. Krotchik of the informal group "Friendship and Dialogue," *Glasnost*, 7, 1987.
[30] *Moscow News*, 9, 1988. For reports on clashes between groups of young people at Arbat during the summer of 1988, see *Vechernaia Moskva*, July 9, 1988.
[31] *Sovetskaia Molodezh* (Riga), July 29, 1987. *Selskaia Zhizn*, December 16, 1987, carried a report about the torturing of schoolchildren by the militia in Insar (Mordovia) in an attempt to extract false confessions. *Komsomolskaia Pravda*, January 5, 1988, had a similar such report from Dnepropetrovsk and noted that there had been more such accounts of the violation of "socialist legality."

leading Soviet economist, deplored the fact that the allocation for education in the budget had declined from 12 percent to 7 percent, in contrast to most other countries, including America, where it had risen. Teachers were grossly underpaid and as a result the profession no longer attracted the best-qualified people. The level of the teaching of Russian language and literature seems to have declined; subjects such as drawing and singing were no longer taught in many Soviet schools for want of qualified teachers.

The heroine in a novel by Veniamin Kaverin, the veteran Soviet writer, admits that in the company of strangers—for example, at the beach—she would be ashamed to admit that she was a teacher. It was a profession that had not gained respect, in contrast, say, to managing a shoe shop. But it seemed doubtful whether Kaverin's suggestion to improve the teaching of Russian literature ("because it deals with conscience and moral duty . . .") would solve the crisis in education.

In the meantime a phenomenon reappeared which had been believed to be nonexistent for decades, that of the *bezprizorni* and of juvenile prostitutes: children whose parents had deserted them, who had no parents or who had run away from home. Most Russians knew this problem from books and films of the late 1920s and early 1930s such as *The Road Back,* or Makarenko's *Paedagogical Poem.* They were shocked when a conservative newspaper suddenly drew attention to its recurrence.[32] Elsewhere disturbing details were published about the treatment of children in an orphanage in Angarsk (Siberia) where the inmates were systematically beaten, starved, kept in isolation, and mistreated in various other ways. This article provoked thousands of readers' letters from which it appeared that the Angarsk case was by no means atypical, that similar or worse things had happened in many other places, that criticism had been voiced for a long time but had been ineffective.[33] "The educational work in many of our orphanages and *internats* is on the level of cavemen," another newspaper wrote.[34]

Even before these revelations had been made, the Politburo had discussed the establishment of a special children's fund named after Lenin. But it was doubtful whether administrative measures

[32]*Sotsialisticheskaia Industria,* October 27, 1987.
[33]"Diktat strakha" (Dictating Fear) and *Sovest protiv strakha* (Conscience Against Fear), *Sovetskaia Rossia,* September 4, 1987.
[34]"Liubim li my detei?" (Do We Love Children?), *Sovetskaia Kultura,* November 19, 1987. For a report of a similar case in Moscow, see *Sovetskaia Kultura,* March 10, 1988.

and the allocation of more money would constitute a cure. Such allocations could perhaps bring down the death rate of babies and infants (which was among the highest in Europe), but it was not at all certain whether it would help reduce juvenile criminality.

A change of heart was needed; it was conceded that there was a great distance between myth and reality in the attitude toward children in Soviet society. In theory, children were "the only privileged class in our society," to quote a famous slogan. In actual fact, children were all too often considered a nuisance—noisy, ill-behaved, materialistic, lazy, and in every respect inferior to the generation of the parents. Society was fighting with children in the clubs, in schools, in the doorways; it was no longer loving them, as one writer put it, and this in a country which once upon a time had been famous for the care and love for its offspring.

It was argued that this was to a large extent the outcome of the period of stagnation, that children had been among the main victims of the Brezhnev era.[35] But such explanations were unconvincing; neither Brezhnev nor his collaborators had hated children. If there was a change in the attitude of society, it had taken place over a longer period and it was unconnected with the composition of the Politburo.

The *veshism* (materialistic attitude) of the young generation reflected a similar attitude on the part of the adults; the unwillingness to work hard probably had similar reasons. True, the children of the 1980s did not suffer from the same deprivations their parents and grandparents had thirty and sixty years earlier; yet to expect gratitude from them was bad psychology as well as bad history. In Western societies there have been generational rebellions since time immemorial. In the Soviet Union, given the authoritarian character of the regime, such direct political confrontations were ruled out. But the system did not succeed any better in bequeathing to the young its beliefs, values, and way of life. The official propaganda was largely ignored, and dissent manifested itself in cultural revolt or simply in a retreat from politics. This greatly surprised some of the older people, but it should not have come as a shock, given the lack of attraction of Soviet ideology, the lack of excitement in Soviet society, and the enormous discrepancy

[35]But the reports about apathy among the young generation continued well into the *glasnost* era. Investigations showed that the younger the people, the less the desire to play an active role in society. Of those over sixty, 62 percent expressed such a desire; of those under twenty, only 32 percent (L. Ponomarev and V. Shinkarenko, *Izvestiia*, May 19, 1988).

between word and deed, to which young people are particularly sensitive. The advice offered to strengthen family ties, to intensify patriotic education, and to show more consideration and concern was not of much help. Such basic changes could not be effected as the result of a resolution of the Politburo, perhaps not even as the result of a moral crusade. It could come only following some profound change of heart, some basic change in the motivation and values of Soviet society.

Crime and Punishment

Glasnost was meant to achieve aims which, while not mutually exclusive, were not easily compatible: to restore law and order and, at the same time, to carry out legal reform, to enhance the rights of the individual and to prevent the miscarriage of justice. The existence of crime in Soviet society had never been a secret; from time to time it had been reported in the media that a group of thieves or embezzlers had been apprehended and had received their just punishment. *Belles lettres,* as usual, were a little more outspoken than the mass media, but attentive readers could deduce from studying the newspapers that corruption and embezzlement in certain sections of the economy, the retail and building trades for example, were widespread, and that an honest official might have a difficult time keeping his virtue.[36]

It was common knowledge in the Soviet Union that there was much more crime than officially admitted—hooliganism in the streets, robbery of public and private property, even murder, though official figures were never published. Nevertheless, the revelations about the extent of organized crime, and the existence of large-scale "mafias," must have come as a surprise; sometimes the facts were so shattering that they could not be published even under *glasnost.*

A well-researched study of Uzbekistan reported that the republic was divided among twenty clans ("families") who systematically extorted protection money, engaged in well-organized robberies, and provided contracts for murder, with fees ranging from 30,000 to 60,000 rubles.[37]

[36]Typical examples are Lazar Karelin's "The Snake Catcher," *Moskva* 4, 1982, and Alexander Astrakhantsev's "Raskaianie," *Nash Sovremennik,* 9, 1981.

[37]The article by Dmitri Likhanov should have appeared in *Ogonyok,* 27 and 28, 1987, but was suppressed and found its way to *Strana i Mir* (Munich), 4, 1987. There were many similar reports in the Central Asian Soviet press.

Usually party and state officials were involved in the rackets, and sometimes the militia and even the KGB. It appeared that even the highest officials in the Central Asian republics had known about crime and to a certain extent had benefited from it. The same seems to have been true with regard to Azerbaidzhan and Georgia, where recurrent purges became necessary. The lifestyle of the *nomenklatura* in these parts was such that their official income was not even remotely sufficient to sustain it. But this state of affairs was by no means limited to the non-Russian republics. It emerged that the party boss in Rostov was the chief protector of the local mafia; the situation in Moldavia was similar; and Grishin and Romanov, the Moscow and Leningrad party secretaries, seem to have, at the very least, closed their eyes to criminal activities. Corruption became an integral part of the system, and there was little contrition on the part of those who were apprehended. In fact, the authorities encountered defiance; the funeral of the Rostov party boss became the occasion for a demonstration on the part of the lesser mafiosi. They saw no reason to express contrition; it was, after all, an open secret that corruption had involved members of the Brezhnev family and the leadership of the MVD (the ministry of internal affairs).

If the incidence of crime was no great surprise, the participation of members, or former members, of the army and the organs of state security was a novel feature. Thus according to official sources a Soviet militia colonel named Soltanov had hired killers to murder a woman who had campaigned against corruption and had exposed bribe-taking by his wife. A secretary who gave evidence against Soltanov's wife was found hanged.[38]

A Wild West–style armed robbery of an armored car transporting money took place on the Mozhaisk Boulevard in Moscow. People were killed and wounded during this attack, helicopters took part in chasing the bandits, and when it was all over, it appeared that among the members of the gang who had undertaken the raid there were former employees of the KGB and the MVD, as well as the state attorney's office.[39]

Another unprecedented revelation concerned the hijacking of a plane at Ufa airport by members of an elite unit of the "internal forces" of the ministry of the interior. Those engaged in the attempt wanted to leave the Soviet Union at any price; in the course

[38]*Pravda*, December 28, 1987, quoted in *Guardian*, December 29, 1987.
[39]*Komsomolskaia Pravda*, November 18, 1987.

of the hijacking two men who resisted them were shot. Those involved in the plot had made no secret of their plan, yet no one had paid attention.[40] A great many heads rolled as a result, including those of the chief of the "internal forces," the chiefs of staff, and those of the political directorate. But there was still no satisfactory answer to the question, How could it have happened?

Crimes of violence by Afghanistan veterans became a frequent occurrence. Thus Andrei Bobunov, a former parachutist, an exemplary member of the Komsomol, a good son and fiancé, became head of an armed gang who, for the better part of a year, engaged in robberies and murder (including members of his own gang). Having been exposed to political propaganda for a long time, he had answers ready after his arrest: "What do you want of us—we acted only in the spirit of social justice; we were the avengers who expropriated goods and money acquired by black-marketers and other unproductive elements. We were fighters against double morality. . . ."[41] Subsequent investigations showed that the real motivation of these self-styled Robin Hoods had been anything but altruistic.

Another interesting case of murder with an ideological defense concerned Sergei Lopatin, a Leningrad Komsomol activist who had received a military medal in Afghanistan. Together with friends of a similar background, he had "bestially attacked two youngsters" (in the words of the official report), one of whom was killed, the other severely injured. Their defense was that the two boys they met in a cinema belonged to a group of "decadent, long-haired young people in strange clothes." After further investigation it appeared that one of the two victims was a social and psychological "case," the other fifteen years old and an exemplary student.

We do not know how much crime there is in the Soviet Union because few statistics have been published; some figures have been revealed but they are incomplete.[42] The minister of internal affairs has made it known that while there was too much of it, there was considerably less than in America. The colonel in charge of public relations at the Moscow police headquarters announced in September 1987 that "on the whole" the crime rate had gone down

[40]The case was first reported in detail in *Sovetskaia Rossia* in September 1987; for the follow-up, see *Sovetskaia Rossia,* October 28, 1987.
[41]*Molodaia Guardia,* 8, 1987, p. 222 et seq.
[42]For instance, in *Kommunist,* 5, 1988.

by 7 percent, especially murders, rapes, and muggings, but that the number of burglaries and car thefts had increased.

One of Russia's leading crime reporters sarcastically observed that while Soviet media published the most detailed figures about thefts not only in America, but also in Paraguay, Uruguay, and Madagascar, there were none at all about crimes committed in the Soviet Union.[43] From many reports it appears that such thefts had become a major plague and that professionals had been involved in hundreds of such crimes.

For this reason we do not know whether crime is on the increase or not. There has been a great outcry for tougher measures but not much progress in explaining the causes of crime. Traditionally, it has been argued that crime has been inherited by Soviet society from capitalism, that it is a very tenacious phenomenon, and that the propaganda of the bourgeois states and its impact on Soviet consciousness and behavior play a major role.[44] However, these explanations have satisfied Soviet experts less and less; they have suggested instead concrete studies of individual cases. This, in turn, has led the experts into studying other potential causes of criminal behavior and to the admission that antisocial manifestations must be somehow connected, not so much with capitalism but with the imperfections of Soviet society that engender their own problems.

Glasnost has also shed some light on the management of justice in the Soviet Union, on mistrials and the denials of justice in cases which were quite unpolitical in character. The writer Yuri Arakcheev described the Klimenko trial, the case of a young man accused of killing an elderly woman near the railway station of a small town in Turkmenistan in 1970.[45] Condemned to death, he was ultimately acquitted owing to the indefatigable efforts of his lawyer and a police officer, who risked his career. Errors of justice occur at all times and in all places; what was extraordinary about this particular case were the systematic efforts undertaken by various courts of law for about ten years to hush up the affair out of solidarity, or because of instructions from above, even though they were convinced that Klimenko was innocent. Not surprisingly, Arakcheev reached the conclusion that such cases could be prevented in the future only if

[43]Anatoli Rubinov, *Literaturnaia Gazetta,* March 26, 1987.
[44]See, for instance, G. A. Avanesian, "Osnovi Kriminologi," Moscow, 1981, *passim.*
[45]Yu. Arakcheev, *Pyramida, Znamia,* 7–8, 1987; also, *Moskovskie Novosti,* July 26, 1987.

there would be stronger guarantees for the rights of the individual.

Three other cases out of the many which came to light ought to be singled out. One concerns a doctor in Voroshilovgrad who ran afoul of the local party secretary, who wanted to build a case against a journalist who had made himself a nuisance. When Dr. Kreinin refused to collaborate, a search was made of his home and videocassettes of perfectly harmless foreign movies were found, whereupon the doctor was given a three-year sentence (for "organizing groups in order to watch foreign movies"). His brother got a two-and-one-half-year sentence, and their mother was excluded from the party for "lack of Bolshevik vigilance."[46] Again it took a long time; there were countless submissions and superhuman efforts until the brothers were released, not because there were any doubts about the merits of the case, but because among dozens of judges and other legal officers in the district not one could be found who had sufficient courage to opposes blatant intrigue such on the part of the local party leadership.

A major scandal occurred at Vitebsk. There, between 1971 and 1985, young women had been killed at the rate of one or two a year. There were many arrests; one of those accused was executed, another went blind in prison. All had confessed but the murders continued until the identity of the real murderer was discovered. He happened to be a part-time policeman. As a result, the affair brought the prosecutor general to Vitebsk to investigate the competence of the local police and, above all, the ways and means used by them to extract confessions.[47]

Lastly a case bordering on the ludicruous: A. M. Mirek, a leading musicologist and collector of instruments, sold part of his collection to a museum in Leningrad. Later on, the museum argued that it had been overcharged. Mirek was arrested and kept for months in prison until it was found that there was no case to answer. The affair was written up by the most widely known Soviet journalist specializing in legal affairs, who, in reply, received many letters justifying the illegal arrest of the musicologist or expressing satisfaction about it.[48]

There was a strong movement in favor of legal reform, but

[46]*Meditsinskaia Gazetta,* October 16, 1987. A spokesman for the supreme court mentioned "hundreds of legal mistakes" which had recently been committed (*Komsomolskaia Pravda,* December 4, 1987).
[47]The case was widely discussed. See, for instance, *Literaturnaia Gazetta,* March 30, 1988.
[48]Arkadi Waksberg, *Literaturnaia Gazetta,* October 14, 1987.

equally strong, or even stronger, opposition against it. A majority of Soviet citizens did not agree with Lenin, who in 1920, after the end of the civil war, had demanded the abolition of capital punishment. Arkadi Waksberg, the leading Soviet journalist, quoted letters by historians, writers, and artists written to the press in which they asked for the public execution not just of violent criminals but of thieves, impostors, and hooligans. Some asked for shooting, "and if possible quartering," in the case of the sadistic killing of a puppy by a group of adolescents. As one of them put it, "In these cruel times we do not need detached intellectuals but fighters without mercy, whose hands will not tremble when they destroy." Waksberg recalled that none of these fighters for the law had protested against blatant miscarriages of justice, including murder.[49]

A leading Soviet law expert, Professor A. Yakovlev, had a similar experience. He argued in an article that there was no evidence that the harsher the punishment, the less crime there would be. After the death penalty was introduced in 1962 for the theft of state property, the number of such cases had in fact increased, and those involved tended to steal more rather than less, for "hanged for a shilling, hanged for a pound." Hundreds of letter writers argued that he was wrong, that in a revolutionary period no mercy ought to be shown, that Stalin had been quite right for sending those to Siberia ("for a period of not less than ten years") who were a few minutes late at work or peasants who did not fulfill their work norms.[50] Other readers suggested the strictest possible punishment also for drunkards and homeless persons; they should be kept in dirt and given rotten potatoes.

Such opinions were based on pure hatred (as a commentator put it), not on revolutionary fervor, and on the belief that somehow, under Stalin, there had been less crime and that this was the only way to cope with it. In actual fact there had been more crime then, not including the number of crimes committed by the government. But the facts had not been published, and thus the impression of law and order had been created.

Capital punishment has had, and still has, strong popular support in many countries, especially at times of a crime wave. But it is interesting that the demand for the harshest punishment for both crimes of violence and nonviolence seems to be stronger in

[49]For instance, *Komsomolskaia Pravda*, November 11, 1987.
[50]A. M. Yakovlev, *Ogonyok*, 33, 1987; ibid., 50, 1987.

the Soviet Union than in most other developed countries. The deeper reasons for attitudes of this kind ought to be studied; they may well contain an important key to the political psychology of sections of society.

In the debate which took place under *glasnost* there was no unanimity with regard to the legal principle of presumption of innocence. Soviet legislation is inconsistent in this respect. While the constitution (paragraph 160) states that only those found guilty by a court of law should be punished, the very term does not appear in the Soviet penal code. According to a poll in 1987, it appeared that 40 percent of all Soviet judges assumed automatically that those brought to court were, in fact, guilty.

The number of acquittals in court was smaller in the Soviet Union than in virtually every other country. This caused much criticism, and in a decision published in December 1986 the supreme court of the U.S.S.R. upbraided the judges because they had ignored the principle of presumption of innocence. The judges did not fail to respond: an official spokesman made it known that during the first six months of 1987 there had been as many acquittals as in the whole year 1986, that the number of cases quashed by higher instances had grown by 50 percent, and that a considerably lower number of people had been given prison terms.[51] All this sounded encouraging but the basic questions remained: To what extent do Soviet judges simply follow orders from above? How much independence does the judiciary have, and what guarantees has the individual against arbitrary state organs?

[51]*Argumenty i Fakty,* 46, 1987; also, V. I. Terebilov, in *Chelovek i Zakon,* November 1987.

CHAPTER 8

"What Has Become of Us?": Alcoholism and Other Evils

Alcoholism

THE FIRST major social campaign launched under *glasnost* was directed against alcoholism (the Central Committee resolution of May 7, 1985), and the topic continued to figure prominently for a long time. It was one of the few subjects on which all the members of the Politburo, liberals as well as conservatives, were in full agreement. It was not the first such campaign in recent memory; the general problem of drunkenness goes back far into Russian history. Almost all foreign visitors, beginning in the sixteenth century, reported scenes of drunkenness, especially on holidays, even before the introduction of distilled alcoholic drinks, i.e., vodka. "Drink is their whole desire," George Turberville, a diplomat, wrote in 1568.

Hard liquor was allegedly imported first by Genoese merchants based on the Balearic Islands, by way of their Black Sea colonies; some alchemists also seem to have been involved.[1] However, it seems more likely that most of the hard drink arrived by way of the Baltic trade after the incorporation of Novgorod in 1477.[2] The first drink houses were established by Ivan IV. However, at first only the members of the Oprichnina, his private police, were permitted to drink there. Later on, toward the middle of the sixteenth century, the state-licensed drink house (Kabak) sold state-produced

[1] J. Billington, *The Icon and the Axe*, New York, 1966, pp. 660–61.
[2] R. F. Smith and David Christian, *Bread and Salt*, Cambridge, 1984, pp. 87–91.

drinks. Ever since then vodka has been an essential feature of the Russian way of life: "Vodka was the single most important item in the peasantry's festive diet. It was a basic ingredient of all celebrations, of church festivals, family celebrations and so on. It was also a sort of seal on ceremonials; vodka was drunk when a deal was made or a bargain struck."[3]

The social and medical consequences of alcoholism have been frequently described; there was a strong temperance movement in Russia supported by both the Church and most radicals, including Lenin. However, in view of the great financial stake of the government in alcohol, temperance had no lasting success until 1914, when, with the outbreak of the war, a total ban on the production of alcohol was announced. This did not, of course, prevent the distillation of illegal spirits at home *(samogon)*, but it lasted till 1925 and seems to have had a strong and immediate effect on crime, labor productivity, and the general state of health.[4] David Lloyd George, the British statesman, in his budget speech called it at the time the greatest act of national heroism known to him. (The imposition of a ban on hard liquor in Vichy France seems to have had similar consequences while it lasted.)

In the mid-1920s the production of spirits was resumed. At the Fourteenth Party Congress Stalin argued that the alternative to the profits accruing to the state from this source was to become financially enslaved to the capitalist powers. The vodka monopoly brought the state almost immediately half a billion rubles, a figure which continued to rise over the years. But there was an enormous price to be paid. One favorite comparison of the anti-alcoholics was between the rise in alcohol production and the increase in population between 1965 and 1980: the former increased thirty-seven times as much as the latter.[5] Such comparisons are doubtful, but it is true that the manufacture of spirits between 1950 and 1980 has increased tenfold in absolute terms.

Soviet experts believe that the measurable damage caused by alcoholism is at least twice as high, possibly three times or even

[3]Smith and Christian, p. 316.

[4]A. Mendelson, *Itogi prinuditelnoi trezvosti* (The Results of Forced Abstinence), St. Petersburg, 1916, *passim.*

[5]Academician F. Uglov in *Nash Sovremennik*, 7, 1987. Uglov's style and approach have been shrill, comparable to some of the excesses of the temperance movement in the West; for Uglov and his followers anti-alcoholism is a new religion with a strong admixture of extreme right-wing elements. *Ogonyok* (10, 1988) pointed out that among the "authorities" adduced by Uglov, there were the ideologists of the Black Hundred and other parafascist sources.

larger, than the income derived by the state. (Figures given for the United States reveal a similar ratio: revenues of $46 billion in 1983 as against losses of up to $100 billion.)[6]

Evidence on the extent of alcoholism in the Soviet Union diverges. According to the health authorities, there are no more than 4.5 million alcoholics in the U.S.S.R., which, if true, compares very favorably with the United States, which counts more than ten million alcoholics and another eight million problem drinkers.[7]

According to international comparisons, the per capita consumption of spirits in the Soviet Union was always less than in several Western countries. But the reliability of these figures is not certain. They do not take *samogon* into account, nor regional differences such as the fact that there is little drinking in (Muslim) Central Asia and correspondingly more in northern Russia.

A report in the media claimed that in 1983 there was a 36.7 percent incidence of "misuse of alcohol" among Soviet males. Soviet commentators explain the high infant-mortality rate over the last twenty years (four times as high as in Japan or Sweden) with reference to alcoholism. They have claimed that alcohol is the decisive factor in up to 80 percent of all divorces, that alcoholism had an enormous impact on labor productivity, that up to 40 percent of the allocations for the Soviet health service are somehow connected to alcoholism.[8] Equally, there is no doubt that alcoholism has a very substantial impact on the crime rate and that it is the decisive factor in many road accidents.

The Soviet media has been replete with horror stories about both the incidence and the consequences of alcoholism. Some appear grossly exaggerated. Such exaggeration may be considered inevitable: since alcoholism has become a major epidemic, and since it is so deeply rooted in Soviet society, those responsible for anti-alcoholic propaganda probably reached the conclusion that only shock therapy, including deliberate exaggeration, could be effective, and they may well be right. The measured, moderate approach of previous anti-alcoholism campaigns which permitted "cultural drinking," meaning a few glasses of wine, a drink or two

[6]W. R. Miller et al., *Understanding Alcoholism,* Davis, California, 1983, p. 15.
[7]*Argumenty i Fakty* 46, 1987.
[8]See, for instance, Igor Bestuzhev Lada, a well-known Soviet futurologist, in *Nedelia,* 33 and 34, 1987. A special journal, *Trezvost i Kultura,* is devoted to the struggle against alcoholism but it is not widely read. Politically, it is close to extreme right-wing circles. The most detailed Western account is Vladimir Treml, *Alcohol in the U.S.S.R.,* Rutgers University Press, 1982.

before or after a meal, had no effect; hence the need for harsher measures. But the shrill tenor of the anti-alcoholism campaign also has strong political undertones.

Such political exploitation of a legitimate cause takes various forms. There have been assertions to the effect that alcoholism is mainly the result of foreign intrigues, especially by Jews, Freemasons, and imperialists (including President Kennedy), aiming to poison the spirit and the body of the Russian people and thus bring about its moral and physical ruin. Thus it has been claimed that Samuel Alexeevich Greig, appointed chief supplier to the Russian army in the eighteenth century, decided to ruin the Russian soldiers by soaking them with alcohol. But Greig was a dour Scotsman; he merely supplied what was wanted. Drink, to be sure, had been in demand in Russia for a very long time. As the Chronicle of Nestor said, *"Veselie Rossii yest pitie"* ("Russia seeks its fun in drink"). According to the very first historical document on old Russia which has reached us, Vladimir, Prince of Kiev, rejected Islam as an alternative to paganism "because Rus loves to drink, because we cannot do without it."[9]

The lasting results of the campaign against alcoholism will be known only after many years. As for the short-term consequences, official spokesmen reported a noticeable decline in drink-related crime and an even greater fall (37 percent in 1986 compared with 1984) in road accidents caused by drunken drivers. Some reported equally startling immediate medical consequences, but this was contradicted by authoritative medical demographers.

But there were also reports of failure: The production of *samogon* in the Gomel region was up by about 25 percent; it was much in demand in Donetsk. There was a sharp increase in the sale of vodka in Poltava. Cognac output had increased in the Central Asian republics, Azerbaidjan, Georgia, and Latvia. In the Karelian republic 279 Communists had been detained in a state of inebriation.[10] Strict reprimands were given to leading officials, including the deputy chairman of Gosplan and secretaries of the Central Committee of various republics.

Least discussed in the heat of the campaign were causes of alcoholism. It had been the consensus in the 1920s that the growth

---

[9]*Povest vremenikh let*, Vol. 1, Moscow, 1950, p. 60.
[10]There were many such reports. See, for instance, *Selskaia Zhizn*, October 11, 1987; *Pravda*, October 31, 1987, ibid., October 19, ibid., September 13, 1987; *Sovetskaia Kultura*, December 8, 1987; etc.

of material well-being and spiritual culture of the toiling masses would destroy the ground on which drunkenness and alcoholism developed.[11] But in fact alcohol consumption has more than doubled in comparison with 1913, the last year before the ban was imposed. Standards of living as well as the cultural level have risen. If so, how is the steady growth of alcohol consumption explained?

Some right-wingers suggested that alcoholics should be treated as criminals and enemies of society. This corresponded with the traditional view, widespread in East and West, that alcoholics were not sick but sinful. But in recent decades the concept of alcoholism as a disease has gained ground in most countries. According to the definition in 1957 of the American Medical Association, "Alcoholism is an illness characterized by preoccupation with alcohol and loss of control over its consumption." Some of the physiological traits of alcoholics seem to be genetic in origin, and Soviet researchers, too, have drawn attention to the "factor of alarm" in the human psyche, grounded in biochemical processes.

However, these theories are by no means shared by all experts; many regard alcoholism as a behavioral rather than a clinical problem and believe that many drinkers could give up alcohol if they wanted to. Various socioeconomic reasons have been adduced in the Soviet Union to explain the causes of alcoholism. It has been explained with reference to the rapid urbanization in recent decades; but then it ought to be shown that there was less drinking in the villages than in the cities. The stresses of the new technological revolution have been mentioned but there have been also other, more disturbing hypotheses. What if alcoholism, like some other deviations which have grown of late, are connected with contradictions in the present society—the divergence between word and deed as one example?[12] The early optimism of the 1920s has certainly faded away. Academician Uglov thinks that general abstinence from drinking might be achieved in five years but few share his views.[13] In January 1988 two hundred new wine and beer shops were licensed in Moscow in view of the great unpopularity of the anti-alcoholism campaign. It was also meant to reduce the enormous queues which had become a new feature in the streets

[11]See entry, "Alcoholism," in the first volume of the *Bolshaia Sovietskaia Entsiklopedia (Great Soviet Encyclopedia),* Moscow, 1926.
[12]Interview with R. Muzalev, the mayor of Dnepropetrovsk, in *Sovetskaia Kultura,* December 8, 1987.
[13]*Sovetskaia Kultura,* July 25, 1987.

of Soviet cities. The opinion was gaining ground that the government was not winning the war against alcoholism, just as prohibition had not worked in the United States, and that new and different measures would be needed to reduce the damage caused by excessive alcohol consumption.[14]

Drugs and Prostitution

Narkomania, drug addiction, has been given almost as much publicity as alcoholism under *glasnost.* Until about 1985 the existence of a social problem of this kind was seldom if ever mentioned. Aitmatov's *Plakha* was one of the first, if not the first, admission that a major problem did exist,[15] and that it was homegrown, not imported by foreigners. There seems to have been some smuggling of drugs into the U.S.S.R., mainly by Third World students, but this was insignificant in comparison to the other sources, including Afghanistan. The magnitude of the Soviet drug problem is undoubtedly smaller than alcoholism; if in the U.S. alcohol takes twenty-five times as many lives as drug overdoses or infections, the ratio in the Soviet Union is probably even larger. But whereas everyone knew about alcoholism, there was no information about drugs and the admission came therefore as a major shock, all the more so because the new epidemic predominantly affected young people.

Plans to tackle the issue were adopted in the major cities, often to be rejected after a little while because they were found to be ineffective; senior police officers gave interviews, scientists were asked for explanations. The immediate reaction was to combat drug taking by way of bans, arrests, and punishment which, in the words of Moscow's district attorney, was quite insufficient: a great deal of prophylactic, educational work had to be done, and a strategy had to be developed to deal with underage drug takers. A detailed and apparently fairly realistic picture emerged from an interview with the senior police officer in charge of drug addiction in Leningrad. According to the information he provided, the problem went back to the early 1960s, but it was then limited in scope and had different social and psychological roots. The recent

[14]N. Shmelyov, *Novy Mir,* 4, 1988. *Izvestiia* (October 3, 1988) reported that 300 new beer and wine shops had been opened in the capital.
[15]Lazar Karelin's *Dayu Uroki* (I Give Lessons), published in 1987, described the chase after drug traffickers in the form of a thriller.

growth of drug addiction was connected with the general moral deterioration and the desire of "unstable elements to taste products of civilization" and to experience new and powerful sensations. In late 1987 some fifteen hundred men and women received medical help, but there were perhaps five thousand drug takers altogether in the city.[16] Leningrad addicts received most of the stuff from the Central Asian republics, but also from Transcaucasia, the Ukraine, and the Krasnodar region. Some was stolen from hospitals and pharmacies; more was produced locally by people with some knowledge of chemical engineering.

Not much knowledge seems to have been needed; according to a pupil in the ninth grade (about fifteen years of age), "In our class everyone knows how to extricate the narcotic essence from a given medicine." They had begun to talk about it even two years earlier.[17]

According to a senior Moscow police officer, about one quarter of all narcotics used in the capital was prepared from one specific drug used in medical practice. Following pressure on the part of the authorities, the use of this prescription was drastically reduced, but the number of drug addicts in the capital still continued to rise.[18] According to the same source the average drug addict needed about 170–200 rubles a day, which is nearly the average monthly income; according to a girl named Larissa, aged twenty, interviewed in the Moldavian republic, 140–150 rubles might be sufficient.[19] When the interviewer noted that no one earned five thousand rubles a month, Larissa replied that they found it not particularly difficult to steal in the streets and from apartments, to get it from "rich" visitors to town, and so forth. "And you have never been caught?" "Never. . . . "

From the many letters and interviews with drug addicts published in the Soviet media, a general picture emerged not dissimilar in some respects to the personality of drug addicts in the West. Most of the users are young or very young, and they were introduced to the habit by friends; parents and teachers were usually unaware and, if they learned about it, quite incapable of coping with it.[20] Many addicts believe that a cure is impossible; there is a

[16]*Leningradskaia Pravda,* July 29, 1987.

[17]"Tushinski pusheri," *Sovetskaia Rossia,* August 12, 1987. For a psychological profile of young addicts, see *Komsomolskoe Znamia,* Kiev, June 4, 1988.

[18]*Izvestiia,* September 4 and November 23, 1987.

[19]*Sovetskaia Moldavia,* September 20, 1987. More detailed figures are given in A. A. Gabiani, "Narkomania," *Sotsiologicheskie Issledovaniia,* 1, 1987.

[20]See, for instance, letters by drug addicts to *Komsomolskaia Pravda,* June 27, 1987.

great deal of despair and cynicism in their replies. A reporter was told by a sixteen-year-old youngster that "all of us got into drug taking out of boredom"; those affected do not read, and have few, if any, intellectual interests.

The question of whether more or less freedom should be given to young people has increasingly preoccupied the Soviet authorities. In the past Komsomol leaders were frequently charged with lack of independence, but when the young generation showed initiative there was no willingness on the part of the authorities to accept the fact that young people want to be among themselves. Such a sanctuary, away from the world of the adults, they thought to be dangerous. The only "cure" is work and the "integration of youth in the revolutionary process proceeding in the Soviet Union."

Suggestions of this kind and the demand for greater parental control and supervision in school did not prove very helpful. Overworked parents and teachers are not in a good position to exercise control, nor is the demand to make young people work (or work harder) realistic. A senior Moscow party official recently related that he tried to find part-time work for his son at the post office to finance the purchase of a new pair of skates. The boy was sent home, having been told that there was no work for people of his age.

If many of the complaints sound familiar to people in the West, the problem of the young generation seems to be aggravated by the inherent boredom in Soviet society and the exhaustion of the erstwhile ideological impulses. Generational conflict does not know borders and the idea of reimposing stricter adult control is unlikely to succeed, unless there are challenges and a message for the young. The German youth movement of the early twentieth century had an ethos of this kind; also, to a certain extent, did the Boy Scouts and the various religious youth movements. Fascism and Communism in their early phases had the capacity to generate great enthusiasm among their young followers; a few socialist parties, such as the Austrian between the two World Wars, were reasonably successful at educating their young cohorts. But in the contemporary world, responses which proved effective in the past are found wanting. Western societies, unlike the Communist systems, never claimed that they had a panacea; hence the greater depth of the shock in the Soviet Union.

Another problem which came to light with *glasnost* was the

spread of prostitution, female and male, venereal diseases, and, to a lesser degree, of AIDS, called Speed in the Soviet Union. According to Soviet law, prostitution is not a crime; like unemployment it was officially liquidated a long time ago. Unofficially it did exist, though, according to many reports, on a lesser scale than in most other societies. Since 1986 there have been innumerable reports about the growth of prostitution, mainly among young girls aged fifteen to nineteen, and of the rise of venereal diseases. In some cases foreign influences were adduced: the "bad girls" congregated in the bars and restaurants of the luxury hotels, aided and abetted by chief porters and receptionists. However, subsequently there were many reports about prostitution from regions all over the Soviet Union in which there are few, if any, foreigners.[21]

It appeared that prostitution in the higher classes of secondary schools was quite common; some of the girls apprehended by the militia were defiant—if they had sexual relations with strange men this was no one else's business. They were aware of the legal situation and insisted on their rights. (The situation of male prostitutes is more complicated since homosexual acts are punishable, according to the laws of most Soviet republics, by prison sentences of up to five years—in the case of minors up to eight years.) Most prostitutes were not professionals but worked in factories or offices, and were students or housewives. Only eleven hundred full-time prostitutes were registered in Moscow in 1987.[22] They considered part-time prostitution as an easy way to earn relatively large sums of money. This they saved for the purchase of goods otherwise outside their reach, such as private cars.

Even under *glasnost* it is difficult to assess the full extent of prostitution and related problems: it still belongs to the issues on which information is not volunteered. There are so far no novels or plays dealing with these subjects, and the Moscow Komsomol newspaper was sharply attacked by the authorities for reporting too plainly about it.[23]

---

[21]About Latvia, see *Sovetskaia Molodezh,* May 13, 1987; on Kiev, *Pravda Ukrainy,* July 23, 1987; on the Black Sea resorts, *Komsomolskaia Pravda,* September 19, 1987, and various articles in *Trud* and *Literaturnaia Gazetta* throughout July and August 1987; and about small-town prostitution, *Molod Ukraini,* November 18, 1987.

[22]*Moskovskaia Pravda,* October 16, 1987. According to a survey published in 1988, 70 percent of the prostitutes detained were under thirty years of age, three-quarters had medium or higher education, and half of them had children of their own (*Argumenty i Fakty,* 5, 1988).

[23]*Komsomolskaia Pravda,* March 27, 1987.

As for AIDS, by September 1987 one million people had been examined in the Soviet Union; only 102 carriers of the virus had been found, eighty of them foreign citizens, who had to leave the Soviet Union. (The first fatality was reported in October 1988.) Nevertheless, the problem was considered to be of sufficient importance to induce the authorities to establish a special section in the Ministry of Health. The Presidium of the Supreme Soviet announced these and other measures in a special resolution on measures of the prophylactic treatment of AIDS infection.[24] Despite the fact that AIDS has not so far spread widely, the issue became a major topic for Soviet public opinion. It created foreign political problems with Africans studying in the Soviet Union who were sometimes ostracized. There were the usual letters to editors suggesting the isolation of carriers of the virus in something akin to leper colonies or concentration camps. A group of graduates of a medical school expressed the hope that a cure for AIDS would not be found so that it would kill off within a short time all drug takers, homosexuals, and prostitutes.[25] Such demands for the improvement of racial health were not original; they have been voiced, as will be recalled, in other lands on previous occasions. It is only fair to add that there were many dissenting voices.

Soviet Medicine

The Soviet health service was for many years the pride of the authorities, to use Gorbachev's words in his book *Perestroika;* visiting foreigners were always shown some of the exemplary hospitals and crèches. The statistics were most impressive: there were 1.2 million doctors in the country and thirteen beds for every thousand people, figures unrivaled elsewhere. True, according to rumor the best Soviet physicians were very good, whereas the average physician was not; and though officially the health service was free, one's chances of being treated reasonably well in a hospital, or being seen by a leading doctor, were not good without additional payment. However, these were thought to be minor blemishes, or perhaps calumnies spread by Western propaganda.

Yet statistics published in the late 1970s pointed to an inexplicably high child-mortality rate, as well as to a fall in life expectancy; while it was seventy-seven for males in Japan and seventy-four in

[24]*Moskovskie Novosti,* September 6, 1987; *Literaturnaia Gazetta,* July 22, 1987.
[25]*Komsomolskaia Pravda,* August 1, 1987.

France and the U.S., it was only sixty-five in the Soviet Union. Male life expectancy for a Soviet citizen aged fifty was lower in 1986 than it had been in 1939. Furthermore, the life expectancy between men and women widened. While some of these negative trends could be explained with reference to alcoholism, bad nutrition, and a lack of exercise, the most important single factor was perhaps the inferior quality of medical care. In other countries, spending on health services had risen twofold during the last decade in terms of budgetary allocations (it was 11.3 percent in the U.S. in 1987). At the same time allocations in the Soviet Union had fallen from 4.1 percent to 3.9 percent.[26]

What this meant was spelled out in detail under *glasnost*. *Pravda* compared Soviet doctors with warriors fighting with bows and arrows; with such equipment Soviet medicine could obviously not begin to compete with the level of medicine in other countries. It appeared that the U.S. spent on medical technology alone a sum far in excess ($35 billion) of the whole Soviet health budget (16 billion rubles). The leading single cause of death in the Soviet Union was cardiac infarction, yet in the Soviet Union only a few open-heart operations were carried out each year as compared with hundreds of thousands in the Western countries.[27] It was revealed that the level of the Soviet pharmaceutical industry was abysmal; 40 percent of all drugs had to be imported from abroad; of the existing stock, much was stored in conditions in which the medicines would not keep, or were either misplaced or lost in transit.[28] Appliances such as syringes and needles were in short supply or altogether unobtainable.

As for the hospitals, it appeared that the horror stories which had been related about the subject in the 1960s and 1970s were correct. The picture that emerged from local reports was dismal: in Voronezh, for instance, hospital rooms had not been repaired for decades, and a patient had been killed by stucco which had fallen from the roof. Chazov, the new minister, visited Georgia and complained about the state of affairs in that republic. But elsewhere the situation was apparently not better: only 25–30 percent of the schoolchildren in Tadjikistan were found to be healthy.[29]

The Tadjik authorities were proud of having pioneered the

[26]*British Medical Journal,* September 12, 1987, p. 652.
[27]*Pravda,* September 28, 1987.
[28]*Izvestiia,* November 19, 1987.
[29]*Trud,* September 11, 1987; *Izvestia,* September 14, 1987.

construction of cheap hospitals; one unit was built for less than five thousand rubles, an all-Union record. However, further investigation showed that this was less than the money invested in building a cow shed on a cattle farm, with the quality accordingly.

Expectant mothers in Moscow were frantic to have their children almost anywhere but at a local maternity ward, and the minister did not blame them for their reluctance. According to him only twelve out of thirty-three were up to elementary sanitary standards.

As for the professional level of young doctors, it was found that 40 percent could interpret neither an X-ray nor an electrocardiogram, but then their monthly income was 135 rubles, 40 percent under the average monthly income in the U.S.S.R.

Chazov fought for bigger allocations for the health service and announced that according to promises he had received from the government, the share of the medical budget would amount to 8 percent of the total by the year 2000.[30]

But the year 2000 was far off, nor was it certain whether money alone would bring about a dramatic improvement in the level of medical care. It was difficult enough to admit that medical care was superior in Western countries; it was even more embarrassing to concede that the health service abroad was *de facto* and not just *de jure* free in most of them and also more comprehensive.

A letter writer to *Literaturnaia Gazetta* reported a young surgeon as saying, "What do you want? Our medicine is free, and therefore worth nothing" (*nitchevo ne stoit* in Russian means both being free of charge—and being worthless). Why had it taken so long for the public to wake up to the sad facts and to protest? Partly, no doubt, because the upper strata of society, the *nomenklatura*, had their own hospitals which were reportedly reasonably well-equipped.[31]

The revelations triggered off a public debate as to whether free health care should be discontinued.[32] The great majority came out

[30]*Literaturnaia Gazetta*, April 11, 1987; the new "basic guidelines" for restructuring the health service up to the year 2000 were published in *Pravda* on August 16, 1987.

[31]The detachedness of the *nomenklatura* from problems of daily life became legendary. In a scene in Alexander Bek's *Novoe Naznacheniia*, two government ministers have, for one reason or another, to go by metro to their place of destination, which they find exceedingly difficult since they never used the metro before.

[32]Some notable contributions to this debate were M. Tolz, *Sovetskaia Kultura*, July 21, 1987, and answers *ibid.*, September 22, 1987; also F. I. Chazov in *Moskovskie Novosti*, 26, 1987; N. Paroiatnikov, *ibid.*, 35, 1987, and readers' letters, *ibid.*, 44, 1987.

against any such proposals. True, a fee-charging clinic was opened in Moscow. The seven-story hospital had 120 beds in four departments and twenty-two physicians. There were also some twenty fee-charging polyclinics.[33] But it was clear that not many such institutions would be allowed to function. Nevertheless, the arguments adduced by both sides in the debate are of considerable interest. Those in favor argued that medical care had ceased to be free of charge in any case long ago. A journalist from Chita who had been a patient in five Moscow hospitals wrote: "No one is ashamed to take money; this is the norm in our medicine. Now we discuss in our press whether or not we should pay for medical care. But this is sheer hypocrisy—medical care has not been free of charge for a long time. In our hospitals, especially those in our capital, there is no room for people with empty pockets."

These impressionistic comments were fortified by figures. According to reliable estimates the sums changing hands between patients and medical staff amounted to about two to three billion rubles—that is to say, one-seventh of the whole health budget. According to the deputy head of Moscow's fraud squad, even doctors in Moscow's famous microsurgery eye clinic were taking 1,500–2,000 rubles for an operation. But Dr. Fyodorov, the head of the clinic, claimed that this was a plot on the part of his own enemies and those of *perestroika;* two of his doctors who had been arrested and interrogated continuously for six days had been released because there was no evidence of corruption. It is impossible for an outsider to comment on a case which has baffled even the Moscow police. Whether these surgeons had taken money or not, it would certainly have been unjust to single them out if the practice of accepting a fee was almost universal.

Those in favor of paid medicine further argued that Soviet citizens kept hundreds of billions of rubles in various saving schemes at the state bank. Why not use some of this money to get better health care?[34] Some letter writers expressed surprise that the great majority of patients were perfectly willing to pay five

[33]*Moscow News*, August 30, 1987. According to a later report, 18,000 were treated in this hospital during the first four months; the hospital, known by the acronym Lik, was recommended for the politeness and the attention shown to the patients as well as the high qualification of the physicians (*Moskovskaia Pravda*, March 31, 1988).

[34]The case in favor was made, for instance, by Professor V. M. Rutaisen in *Sovetskaia Kultura*, May 23, 1987. He did not argue that all doctors took money but claimed that the custom was widespread, and he provided the just-mentioned estimate.

rubles to the ward sister and ten to the doctor, the going rates for a regular, uncomplicated visit, but refused to accept a scheme which would have made the existing state of affairs legal.

A physician gave slightly different figures: For one ruble, "little auntie" seated at the entrance of the hospital would take food to patients, even if the parcel included food (or drink) which should not enter the building; one ruble would suffice to have bed linen changed or to get slippers; ten rubles would be necessary to gain the goodwill of the night sister to take care of an elderly relative. Some doctors would take brandy, some fifty, others five hundred rubles, all depending on their specialization and reputation. The nurse would take three rubles for an injection at home, the physiotherapist ten.

The physician concluded that he found it difficult to blame doctors and nurses, considering their workload and low payments. But he did take a dim view of the payments made for which no service at all was rendered, such as selling appointments for specialists, most of whom had a long waiting list. He agreed with the pregnant women of Moscow: "Why do the sick flee from our hospitals? Because even a doctor like himself who through his connections could obtain first-class medical help was horrified that he might fall ill and enter a hospital."[35]

Most doctors seem to be in favor of a radical change in the health care system, including the government minister who declared that "free medical care lets people stop thinking about their health."[36] However, this is unlikely to happen; many citizens have invoked socialist ideals and claim that paying for medical care would be a retreat from the socialist achievements in their country. Such worries about ideological purity should be taken with a pinch of salt. Decisive is the reluctance to pay for something they have received free in the past.

There are other arguments which cannot be easily dismissed: Given the low income of many Soviet citizens, particularly the young and elderly, these sections of the population would find it exceedingly difficult to pay, unless some means test were introduced. Nor is it certain that the quality of Soviet medicine, as distinct from the income of the doctors, would greatly benefit if health care were no longer free. For the main investments (in

[35] A. Rezhabek, *Literaturnaia Gazetta,* December 9, 1987.
[36] *Nedelia,* 34, 1987

buildings, medical technology, etc.) would still have to come from the state.

Neither the underfunding of the Soviet health service nor its dismal performance are a specific feature of the Brezhnev period. They go back several decades; the main difference is that it was not customary for the minister, leading health officials, and doctors to speak out and to insist on larger allocations. Nor could public dissatisfaction be aired openly. This is the main innovation brought about by *glasnost* in this field as in most others. Nevertheless, a radical improvement in public medicine seems unlikely; the means at the disposal of the government are limited, and health still figures well behind other priorities that have been set—above all, defense and industry.

The National Question—Not Quite Solved

The Soviet national anthem invokes the "unbreakable union of free republics joined together by Great Russia." Like the health service and the educational system, the way Soviet power had solved the national question was advertised as a model to mankind. While Tsarist Russia had been a prison house of peoples, consistent Marxist-Leninist policy had provided the key to the solution of national tensions and conflicts. Marx, to be sure, had never been very interested in these problems since he believed like most people of his age that national differences were bound to wither away in the not-too-distant future as the result of economic and technical progress. Nor had Lenin devoted much time or thought to national questions. Stalin, as a young man, had been interested in the subject, perhaps because he was not Russian by origin, and had provided a definition of nation and nationhood which was about as good as any of those in existence at the time.

The fact that various small nationalities were forcibly evacuated during the Second World War tended to show that non-Russians were not trusted despite the announcements about the great and lasting friendship among Soviet people. But by and large the few incidents of open national conflict that took place in the postwar period (such as in Georgia in 1956 and in Tashkent in 1969) were on a small scale. There was some soccer violence in the Ukraine and the Caucasus, but such clashes happened all over the world and did not give rise to much concern. True, many Jews left the Soviet Union in the late 1970s and even more expressed the desire to leave; the same was true with regard to Russian Germans. But these were thought to be the exceptions which confirmed the rule. Most Jews and Germans lived outside the Soviet Union; hence the strength of the centrifugal forces within these ethnic groups.

The outward picture was one of cooperation and harmony even though experts had long suspected that there was not much love lost between the nations of the Soviet Union, and in particular between them and the dominant nation, the Russians. The age of *glasnost* brought about a reexamination of these assumptions; there were manifestations of national unrest in Central Asia as well as the Baltic republics, among Tartars, Azeris, and Armenians. The ferment had existed before but for a variety of reasons did not manifest itself openly. There were other trends quite independent of *glasnost* which contributed toward conflict, such as the demographic upsurge of the Central Asian republics; a general rise of nationalist-religious trends in the Middle East and Asia which had repercussions in the Soviet Union; and, increasingly, an officially tolerated Russian nationalism which was bound to provoke similar trends in the non-Russian republics.

Prior to 1987 specific discussion of relations among the various Soviet nations had been more or less tabu. The way they had been depicted by social scientists (to quote Gorbachev) reminded one at times of self-congratulatory toasts rather than of serious discussions. But why put the blame on social scientists? The political leaders had not behaved any differently. True, Brezhnev had declared at the Twenty-sixth Party Congress (1981) that a large multinational state such as the Soviet Union was bound to generate certain problems. But he never found the time to specify what he had in mind, nor did anyone else. As one party expert wrote in retrospect, commonplaces and abstract ideas had been endlessly regurgitated; only with the Twenty-seventh Congress (1986) had the influence of dogmatism been broken and the thesis of the absence of national problems been given up.[37] It would be more correct to say that the Alma Ata riots in January 1987 were the real turning point when a definite change in perception took place.

Before *glasnost* it had been customary in Soviet publications (including the constitution of 1977) to invoke the existence of a Soviet nation and a Soviet people, unique in the history of mankind, which had been created under the leadership of the Commu-

---

[37]Eduard Bagramov, *Pravda*, August 14, 1987. The fullest recent discussion of the issue is Gerhard Simon, *Nationalismus und Nationalitätenpolitik in der Sowjetunion*, Baden-Baden, 1986.

nist Party some time during the late 1960s. This pure abstraction bore no relation to realities, but it did cause some apprehension among the non-Russians because the concept was based on the tacit assumption that the predominant role of the Russians in such a nation would lead to the denationalization of all others. Soviet experts seem to have been at least partly aware of the inconsistency in the doctrine and its provocative character.

Thus, with a very few exceptions (Andropov in December 1982), they ceased to talk about the merger *(slianiie)* of the various nations, a concept which at one time had been quite common. But at the same time the central leadership tried to bring about the cultural assimilation of the non-Russian peoples, mainly by intensifying Russian-language education from kindergarten to university. These measures encountered strong and partly successful resistance. There was further resentment as a result of the fact that most of the Russians living in the non-Russian republics, including the political leadership, made no effort to learn the local languages.

One could easily think of reasons why the study of Russian should have been promoted both as a matter of principle and for practical reasons; the training of Central Asian recruits in the Soviet army constituted a growing problem because they had an insufficient knowledge of Russian. But it should have been known in Moscow that administrative measures of this kind, unless applied with great tact, would provoke major protests and prove, in the final analysis, counterproductive.

Furthermore, it should have been known that cultural assimilation, even if successful, would not necessarily lead to political goodwill. The fact that most Irishmen have a better knowledge of English than their native language and that the Basque speak and understand Spanish better than Basque has not in any way reduced the separatist trends among these people.

Russian pressure for cultural assimilation collided with a trend toward national assertion among virtually all major non-Russian ethnic groups except the very small ones such as the Mordvin and the Mari. The young generation, far from being advocates of friendship among the peoples, and showing greater readiness to accept the culture and the way of life of the Russians, demonstrated greater national assertiveness. The number of mixed marriages declined. Russians emigrated from Central Asia and, to a lesser degree, from the Transcaucasian republics. Given the higher birth rate among the Central Asian peoples (three times that of the Russians), the political weight of the native population steadily grew. Even in Kazakhstan, the native population, which had been outnumbered by Russian settlers since about 1930, had achieved numerical equality by 1987.[38] Whereas as recently as the 1950s Soviet Central Asia had been a synonym for Bukhara and Samarkand—that is to say, exotic places rich in historical memory and medieval buildings—thirty years later one Soviet army recruit in four came from these republics, and according to demographic projections the ratio was likely to be soon one in three; there was increasing talk about the "yellowing of the Red army."

Glasnost showed that there had been no *slianiie* (merger) and not even much *sblizhenie* (rapprochment), and that the situation inside the non-Russian republics, especially those in Asia, was far from the idyllic picture that had been painted before. The extent of corruption must have been known to the leadership under Brezhnev but the Politburo at the time preferred to let sleeping dogs lie. This changed under Andropov; between late 1983 and 1987 all party heads in the five Central Asian republics were replaced, as well as most district and regional secretaries. Many were accused of corruption, embezzlement, and similar charges; some were deprived of their party membership, a few were sent to prison, and one district secretary was given a death sentence. According to the reports which came to light about the situation in Uzbekistan under Rashidow, and in Kazakhstan under Kunayev, the situation went well beyond the worst fears. Both men had been in office for many years and had belonged to the Moscow Politburo.

The economic situation was bad and did not improve, but a worse problem was the general political, social, and moral climate. It appeared that the impact of Communism had been far more superficial than even the skeptics had assumed, that religious customs and quasireligious traditions were unbroken.[39] The structure of society was still basically tribal; kinship, belonging to a clan, was of far greater political significance than membership in the party. Corruption was not the exception but the rule; the republics were

---

[38] Ann Sheehy, "Do Kazakhs Now Outnumber Russians?" Radio Liberty, February 19, 1987.
[39] According to one report 70 percent of the population observed Islamic religious customs, including half the teachers and many party members (*Pravda Vostoka*, August 25, 1987). Equality of women was a fiction and self-immolation by protesting young women was not rare (*Komsomolets Uzbekistana*, July 28, 1987).

divided among a number of mafias whose rule was unbreakable. They had taken over the party, local governments, institutes of higher learning. Two ideologies, value systems, ways of life coexisted. On official occasions the native leaders would repeat all the right formulas about Communism and friendship of the peoples just as in a mosque they would declaim the ritual prayers. Yet in actual fact there was no evidence that they believed in any of it. They were not separatists or pan-Islamists in inspiration; they preferred the *status quo,* provided only that they were left alone to rule and make money. But once their position was challenged, as happened in December 1986 when the Kazakh first secretary of the party was replaced by a Russian, there were demonstrations, clashes, and active and passive resistance, as shown by the events in Alma Ata.[40]

With their innate cronyism and nepotism the Central Asian republics resembled more a Middle Eastern state than a Soviet republic; there was also a fairly well-developed private sector of the economy.[41] To some extent these developments were the logical outcome of the traditional policy. If Ivan the Terrible had been reinstated as a positive hero in Russian history, it was illogical and unjustifiable to deny the Central Asian peoples the right to regard Timur or Babur as part of their historical heritage; nationalism could not be restricted to the Russian Federal Republic.

By and large the Russians had pursued a "correct" line. They had, for instance, followed a course of affirmative action, promoting the native intelligentsia even if it implied a lowering of standards. It was not so much that the policy was mistaken but that a clash of national aspirations prevented a satisfactory solution. Nor can one fairly blame the Russians for keeping certain local key positions for themselves (the second secretary, the head of the KGB, and a few others). But for their presence Moscow would have lost all control over the local scene. It was not the Russians' fault if the new intelligentsia which they had fostered turned eventually against them.

This had been the experience of all imperial powers in history, and the Soviet empire was no exception. Empires in history have

[40]Bess Brown, "How Many People Died in the Alma Ata Riots?," Radio Liberty, May 25, 1987.
[41]In the purge after Kunayev's dismissal, 1,800 police officers, 184 judges, and eighteen state prosecutors were dismissed in Kazakhstan because of allegations of corruption (*Kazakhstanskaia Pravda,* January 14, 1988).

frequently played a progressive role, and it is not readily obvious that full independence of the various components of the Soviet Union would contribute to peace, progress, and the pursuit of happiness; most of them would not be viable in any case. The problem was not that the Soviet Union had failed where others had also failed; it was that only the Soviet Union had claimed that it had solved the "national question." Perhaps this was even genuinely believed for a time in Moscow; the Marxist-Leninist heritage made the leaders ignore the importance of nationalism. Perhaps they were genuinely convinced that the "class factor" was in the long run far more important than national predilections and prejudices.

The "Muslim" republics constituted the most important and acute political problem simply because they were the most populous and had the highest birth rate. *Pravda* was so nervous about the subject of the birth rate that it objected to demographic projections.[42] In one form or another the same problems also occurred in other republics. Thus the anniversary of the signing of the German-Soviet pact in 1939 was the occasion of major demonstrations in the three Baltic republics in 1987. According to a secret protocol in this pact, the Baltic republics had become part of the Soviet sphere of influence and were occupied by the Red Army in 1940.

During the 1970s the three Baltic republics had drawn closer together; they were part of a single economic and administrative region and also one military ("Baltic") district. At the same time there was increasing cultural cooperation among them. They shared complaints against Moscow: the loss of their independence and the fact that many of their nationals had been deported to Siberia, as well as complaints about political and cultural Russification. Moscow's reaction was one of surprise and anger. It had been believed that the battle against (bourgeois) nationalism had been won in these republics; now it appeared that the struggle was far from over, and this despite the fact that the Soviet leadership had made many cultural concessions over the years to the Baltic republics.[43]

---

[42]*Pravda*, February 11, 1987.

[43]For examples of Russian reaction see *Pravda*, September 1, 1987, and *Sovetskaia Latvia*, August 29, 1987. The attacks went on for weeks in the local Baltic newspapers. However, in April 1988 the tide turned with Estonia in the forefront of the struggle for both more national sovereignty and *perestroika*. The movement sponsoring *glasnost* had a much stronger mass basis in the Baltic republics than elsewhere in the Soviet Union and it went much further; its story remains to be told. The charter of the Estonian National Front was

If in the case of Central Asia there was a readiness in the Kremlin to admit that some tactical mistakes had been committed, there was none in the case of the "far west," which, as seen from Moscow, not only enjoyed a higher living standard than the rest of the country but also considerable autonomy.

In between the Alma Ata riots in January 1987 and the Baltic protests in August of that year, the party leadership had to face three days of demonstrations by Tartars on Moscow's Red Square (July 21–23). Again the issue was not of recent date: for thirty years the Crimean Tartars, who had been deported to Central Asia during World War II, had campaigned for their return, and the reestablishment of their autonomous republic in the Crimea. Unlike the deported nationalities from the Caucasus they had never been rehabilitated and only a few thousand of them had been permitted to come back.

In this campaign the Tartars had shown remarkable solidarity and tenacity but the answer of the authorities had always been the same: other people had settled in the Crimea; it was overpopulated and there was no room for the Tartars. As a grudging concession they were told in July 1987 that a committee headed by Gromyko, the chief of state, had been set up to look into their complaint. But the anger of the authorities was unmistakable: in an official statement the Tartars were accused of having collaborated with the German invaders during the war,[44] and it was also claimed that the demonstrations had been organized by "hostile elements" and that most Tartars did not support the demonstrations in the first place.

The Caucasian republics have traditionally enjoyed a comparatively high living standard; like the Baltic republics they had also a certain degree of autonomy. Furthermore, the traditional tensions among them have been by and large greater than between them and the Russians. Nevertheless, there, too, *glasnost* released national tension which had accumulated; it was nourished by resentment about the attempts to relegate their native languages to a secondary place and also by the deteriorating economic situation

published in *Molodyozh Estonii,* September 6, 1988; the program of the Latvian National Front in *Sovetskaia Molodyozh,* September 8, 1988. For interim reports see also the *Ogonyok* interview (38, 1988) with Indrek Toome, the first secretary of the Estonian Communist party, and the article on developments in Estonia by Michael Dobbs, *Washington Post,* October 17, 1988.
[44]*Pravda,* July 24, 1987.

in these regions, even if the presence of a "second economy" mitigated the decline. There was a sudden and fairly substantial rise in the number of Armenians applying for exit visas. However, in contrast to Germans and Jews (whose applications were frequently turned down), the Armenians took great care to depoliticize their applications, not to engage in public protest, and to explain this exodus on compassionate grounds, such as family reunions.

Then in February and March 1988, with mass demonstrations in Erevan and the anti-Armenian pogrom in Sumgait, national conflict reached a new climax. The issue at stake was the fate of the Nagorno-Karabach autonomous region, an Armenian enclave inside Azerbaidjan that had overwhelmingly voted for merger with Armenia. The vote was ignored by the authorities in Moscow, no doubt on the assumption that any concession regarding change in status and borders would lead to other such demands elsewhere. Unlike those in Central Asia and the Baltic republics, the national outbursts were not directed against the Russians. Nevertheless, the uprisings confronted the party leadership with the difficult dilemma of having to choose between the national aspirations of Armenians and of Azeris, which was bound to antagonize one party in the conflict.

The immediate victim was *glasnost,* for those opposed to reform could now argue that in Stalin's day, and even in Brezhnev's, such clashes would have been unthinkable. The reports in the Soviet media were fragmentary and in part altogether untrue. As in other cases of national unrest in the Soviet Union the responsibility was put on small groups of extremists who had been instigated and manipulated by outside forces (American Sovietologists, in this specific case). They had conveyed their instructions to the mischief makers by means of radio stations in the United States, Britain, and West Germany. There were indications of a retreat from *glasnost* in theory as well as in practice. As one of those interviewed by *Pravda* put it, *"Glasnost* and democratization are very powerful weapons. But they have to be used with great caution."[45]

The Ukrainians and White Russians have been wooed by Mos-

---

[45]Academician Garibdianian, *Pravda,* April 2, 1988; Pamyat and the other organs of the extreme right put the blame as usual in such cases on Jews and Freemasons. See, for instance, Dimitri Vasiliev's interview in *Corriere della Sera,* March 12, 1988. Only after further strikes and protest demonstrations did the line take by *Pravda* and other media change concerning the roots of the conflict and the seriousness of the situation. See, for instance, *Pravda,* June 10, and *Komsomolskaia Pravda,* June 15, 1988.

cow more than any other ethnic group in the Soviet Union. As the percentage of Great Russians was falling to 50 percent or below, a common "Slavic front" became imperative. This had not always been the case and the suspicions in Moscow vis-à-vis manifestations of Ukrainian nationalism continued even during *glasnost.* The informal associations against which the central leadership's ire was directed professed to focus only on Ukrainian culture.[46] But it was argued in the Kremlin that a preoccupation with cultural affairs, however harmless *per se,* was bound to lead, sooner or later, to political activities. Ukrainian writers and sections of the intelligentsia pressed for the obligatory study of their native language in the schools. An action program adopted by the Ukrainian leadership in August 1987 went some way toward meeting these demands but left many others unfulfilled.

The official Soviet party line on the nationality question and the "friendship of the peoples" continues without much change. As Gorbachev stated on the seventieth anniversary of the October revolution, the national question was solved even though relations between the various Soviet nations were still a live issue. The party was to be exceedingly attentive and tactful in its policy: "If we encounter signs of legitimate discontent or protests we shall seriously get down to the primary causes of such phenomena." But who was to decide what were legitimate issues?

Given tact and the willingness to make concessions there is a reasonable chance to contain national conflict in the Baltic region, because the nations in question are small. But in Central Asia and also in the Caucasus the Soviet leadership faces a situation which may well be insoluble in the foreseeable future. Other empires such as the Austro-Hungarian had followed a liberal line, trying to give the native population a stake in the running of the country. Thus virtual independence was granted to Hungary by the Habsburgs, and many non-Germans served in key positions in the Vienna government (Badeni and Potocki as prime ministers, Bilinski as minister of finance, Dunajewski and Habitinek as ministers of justice, Madejski and Rittner as ministers of education, and so on). In the Soviet system it is quite unthinkable that natives of Central Asia will be given positions of similar importance. They are not sufficiently trusted, for as it appeared at the very latest under *glasnost*, Communism had not permeated very deeply in

[46]For instance, *Vecherni Kiiv,* November 19, 1987.

these regions, nor was there much sympathy for the descendants of the very people who had occupied and colonized Central Asia. But to some extent members of all minorities are now suspect; and the rise of another Stalin now seems impossible, if only because the Russians would not accept being ruled by someone not belonging to their nation.

The Moscow leadership followed a hard line in Central Asia not just by putting down riots and imposing stricter controls but also in economic development. While Siberia received 18 percent of Soviet internal investments, Central Asia obtained only 12 percent even though its population was considerably larger and growing faster. True, Siberia may be more promising as far as purely economic criteria are concerned, but this is not of much comfort to the Uzbek and the Kazakh. A good ecological case could be made for shelving the projects which aimed at redirecting some of the water of the Siberian rivers to the south. But the inhabitants of Central Asia certainly were the losers and the crumbs thrown to them after the Alma Ata riots, such as improving the supply situation, hardly affected the long-term economic prospects of the region.

There is no guarantee that a more liberal line in Central Asia will result in peace and goodwill on the part of the local population, just as the cooptation of some local leaders to the Politburo or the Secretariat of the Central Committee would not bring a fundamental change in attitudes. These leaders would be considered strangers, alienated from the communities they should represent. The coexistence of various nationalities within the framework of a single state is the cause of conflict everywhere; the idea that class solidarity is stronger than national solidarity has been disproved by reality all over the world. Thus a hard line taken by the Moscow leadership may well be the only feasible approach, but it is a strategy that leads to a dead end; it is based on the hope that nationalism will go away sooner or later. This may be true as a philosophical proposition over a period of several centuries. But the Soviet leaders, like politicians everywhere, are preoccupied with short-term perspectives; seen in this light, Central Asia is bound to remain a trouble zone. Whether the ferment will lead to active or merely passive resistance, whether there will be open insurrections or merely sullen compliance with instructions from above, will depend on the effectiveness of the organs of state security. Antinatal policies, along with the stick-and-carrot approach and the application of time-honored *divide et impera* principles, may reduce the acuteness of the problems and prevent an explosion.

But the sore is unlikely to heal; Communism has transformed human nature even less in Central Asia than in European Russia and the Caucasus. Neither tact nor appeals to reason and common interest will suffice to solve the problems. There are too many Central Asians for engaging in population transfer; even Stalin only touched the smaller nationalities. Thus, according to all past experience, the limits of *glasnost* and *perestroika,* let alone democratization, are bound to be far more narrow in Central Asia and the Caucasus than in other parts of the Union. The Soviet leaders will have to pursue a policy of strength, for if Central Asia has been so far relatively quiet, the main reason has been fear of the overwhelming power of the Russians and the assumption that they, unlike Western governments, would not hesitate to use it. In the Caucasus, on the other hand, even a display of strength proved not to be sufficient to prevent large-scale riots in 1988.

A Moral Revolution

Glasnost brought many revelations on the state of Soviet society and they have almost all been negative. This has created considerable anger among the conservatives who maintained that the revelations were one-sided and that their effect on morals has been bad. Giving excessive publicity (as they saw it) to the failures of past decades was bound to harm the legitimacy of the ruling party and to weaken the general resolve to work for a better future: if the overall balance sheet of seventy years included so much shade, what hope was there for a radical improvement at some future date?

A plausible case can be made for putting the shortcomings in a wider context. Drug taking, alcoholism, and prostitution are found in almost every society; the estrangement of the young generation is a common and recurrent phenomenon. If the Soviet health service was found wanting, was it not true that in the United States, many people had no medical coverage at all, and that they faced financial disaster in case of a major, protracted illness? National conflict, too, is a general phenomenon of our time; if the Soviet Union had not succeeded in finding ideal solutions, neither had anyone else. With all the failures and shortcomings was it not also true that most young people were neither alcoholics nor drug takers nor engaged in prostitution, that in most cases family life did not end in tragedy, that most Soviet citizens were not criminals and not all judges corrupt or incompetent?

In brief, there are a great many decent people in the Soviet Union. But such arguments do not go to the core of the debate, for the Soviet system alone has maintained for decades that in contrast to other societies it had solved all basic social problems. According to official propaganda, for both foreign and domestic consumption, the state of Soviet society had been excellent in every respect, its future prospects brilliant beyond one's imagination. And it was precisely in view of the enormous gap between propaganda and reality that the reaction was bound to be so violent.

It was maintained that the very admission of shortcomings and failures was a sign of strength. Gorbachev and his colleagues seldom failed to use this argument. But it also meant that the Soviet Union had to give up its claims of having succeeded where others had failed, and this cut away the ground from under the claim to have built the most progressive society in history. But it was not the only blow suffered, nor is it certain that the question initially asked—"What has become of us?"—referred primarily to the social evils that could be quantified: the declining life expectancy, alcoholism, and the insufficient allocations for the health service. Those who worried about the moral state of the nation were not primarily concerned with the economic growth rate but the developments that had affected the very character of the people.

Hence Rasputin's complaints about the low level of manners and morality, about indifference, about the general feeling of irritation, about imposture.[47] Hence the lamentation of another writer about *khamstvo*—that is to say, boorishness: people in Moscow were constantly pushing each other, without ever apologizing; the author claimed to have heard the expression "pardon" the last time in Leningrad in 1961. And it was clearly wrong to put the blame on foreign influences, on horror movies or doubtful video films, for these trends had developed on native grounds.[48] Hence Anninski's question: Where does all this spite and anger among the people come from?[49] Hence Granin's appeal for charity, once

[47]*Literaturnaia Gazetta,* January 1, 1988.
[48]*Literaturnaia Rossia,* December 4, 1987.
[49]*Literaturnaia Gazetta,* April 22, 1987.

a well-known characteristic of the Russian people. His essay, as has been mentioned, triggered a stream of letters and suggestions for how to set an example and effect a change. The crime rate seemed to bother many critics less than the vanishing kindness, generosity, and capacity for friendship.

What could have been the reason for making people hard and unfeeling? The harsh living conditions, perhaps, or the unending queuing, generating anger and envy, or a political system which breeds simulation and suspicion? But living conditions for most people had been even worse in the last century. There is no way of statistically measuring goodness; perhaps there was a tendency to glorify the good old days which, in fact, had not been so good after all. But the complaints came not just from a few village writers but from a great many quarters, and in the end it was the perception that counted. The perception was unanimous, common to "liberals" as much as to "conservatives." It was articulated on the extreme right as much as among people whose liberalism and tolerance were beyond suspicion, such as academician Likhachev.[50] The very fact that so many people were looking back to the past rather than casting their eyes to the future was evidence for dissatisfaction with the present state of affairs and lack of confidence about the future. There was the feeling that somehow, sometime, Russian history had taken a wrong turning and that as a result many of the old virtues had disappeared. There was the growing conviction that a higher standard of living was no alternative to kindness and that a cultural and moral revolution was needed for the Russian people to find its soul again. And there was also the growing conviction that the prevailing political doctrine could not serve as a compass for a revolution of this kind.

[50]Dm. Likhachev, *O russkom . . .*, Moscow, 1983.

CHAPTER 9

Glasnost and the Soviet Economy

G LASNOST has had a stronger impact on the economy than on any other aspect of society. It has not by itself brought about fundamental change, but by revealing the truth about the past performance and the present state of the Soviet economy it has made possible a realistic discussion of the need for and direction of change. There is an interesting parallel between these realistic economic discussions and the debate on Soviet history and Stalinism: the original impulse did not come from the leading academics in the field but from previously marginal figures. If the playwright Shatrov and the novelist Rybakov and some of their colleagues triggered off a national debate on Stalinism in Soviet politics, little-known economic journalists such as Selyunin and research workers such as Shmelyev fulfilled a similar function with regard to the Soviet economy. Their articles, published in the literary monthlies rather than the professional journals, were passed on from hand to hand, copied on typewriters, and discussed from one end of the Union to the other. True, once it had started there was greater support for this debate among academic figures in the economic field than among the historians in the academies and the universities. The need for open discussion and for new departures had been stressed, albeit more cautiously, by such figures as Aganbegyan, Abalkin, and Zaslavskaia for a long time, in part even before Gorbachev. But the true revelations were first made by the outsiders.

About the origins of the crisis we have Gorbachev's own evidence. Something happened in the late 1970s which at first sight seemed inexplicable. The country lost momentum, economic failures occurred more frequently, difficulties began to accumulate: "Elements of what we call stagnation and other phenomena alien to socialism began to appear in the life of society. A kind of 'braking mechanism' affecting social and economic development formed. . . . Something strange was taking place: The huge flywheel of a powerful machine was revolving, while either transmission from it to workplace was skidding or drive belts were too loose. . . . For all the 'gross output,' there was a shortage of goods. . . ."[1] The overall description seems accurate even if the metaphors are questionable; drive belts which are too loose can be fastened but this, quite obviously, was not the case with the economy. Nor was the stagnation sudden and inexplicable; it had been coming for a considerable time. Some Western and Soviet economists had, in fact, predicted it. The Soviet command economy had developed in certain historical conditions; it had always aimed at quantitative growth; it had functioned reasonably well in preparing for war. But it had not essentially changed since the days of Stalin, and with the approach of a new scientific-technological revolution it had become largely useless, a giant "braking mechanism."

The critical situation would have become manifest earlier but for the fact that the Soviet Union was not an open society. Quantitative output frequently continued to rise, and on paper there was no problem. Thus the shoe industry would report the annual manufacture of 788 million pairs of shoes, far in excess of any other country (three hundred million pairs are produced in the U.S.). It would not report that many of these shoes were either in sizes not needed or of such bad quality as to be of no use to anyone. The statistics were wrong or misleading, and since the elite in society did not have to queue up for shoes of reasonable quality, they may not even have been aware of the existence of the problem.

Yet after 1970 even the growth figures declined, showing that something was wrong with the Soviet economy: average annual growth between 1975 and 1985 was only 2 percent, and from 1979 to 1982 there was no growth at all. And since the population of the Soviet Union continued to increase—albeit more slowly than before—this meant that the standard of living of at least part of the population actually declined.

The managers reacted by increasing expenditures, by using more and more natural resources and manpower to counterbal-

[1]Gorbachev, *Perestroika*, p. 19.

ance the falling rates of growth. But the results were predictable: "It is the world's largest producer of energy but uses two to three times more energy per unit of economic output than the leading industrial countries. It is the world's largest producer of wheat but 20 percent of the crop is lost from field to mill because of inadequate transport and storage. It is one of the world's most populous nations but finds itself short of labor, partly because of low productivity."[2] Official spokesmen could have said in defense of the Soviet economic performance that growth in Switzerland and Sweden has not been very startling either during the last decade or two; that the stock market collapsed in 1987 in New York rather than in Moscow; that countries such as Britain, West Germany, and Spain had three million unemployed; and so on. It is to the credit of Soviet spokesmen that such specious arguments have but seldom been adduced. For citizens of the Soviet Union are not as well off as those of Switzerland or Sweden. Furthermore, neither capitalism nor a mixed economy has ever promised steady growth at all times; on the contrary, progress has been fitful, with many years of stagnation and decline. Even in Japan, there is no official ideology committed to constant substantial growth owing to the alleged superiority of her economic system. In the Soviet Union, on the other hand, such an ideological commitment to outproduce the rest of the world existed. Hence the embarrassment and sense of failure when the expected progress did not materialize.

One of the concomitants of *glasnost* was the attack on official statistics. In a remarkable article published in the literary monthly *Novy Mir* two authors gave examples for wrong and sometimes absurd figures that had been published without ever being questioned. Thus the overall rise in GNP from 1928 to 1965 had not been ninety times but only six or seven times, a respectable but not extraordinary performance.[3] This was disputed by the head of the U.S.S.R. Statistical Administration, who noted that in 1928 most of the country still lived without electricity, were only on the threshold of industrialization, and used the plow as the main implement in agriculture.[4] But he also admitted that his service worked far from irreproachably and that there were many omissions and

[2]*Gorbachev's Economic Plans*, Joint Economic Committee of the Congress of the United States, Vol. 1, November 1987, ix. After respectable growth in 1986, 1987 was another bad year, according to the CIA/DIA report to the Joint Committee (March 19, 1988).

[3]Vasili Selyunin and Grigori Khanin, "Lukavaia Tsifra," *Novy Mir*, 2, 1987. For a semiofficial answer, see *Vestnik Statistiki*, 3, 1988.

[4]M. A. Korolev, *Izvestiia*, June 23, 1987.

shortcomings: economic analysis was still replaced by a simple reiteration of figures without revealing the essence of the process taking place, without revealing shortcomings and problems.

According to leading Western experts, however, the manipulation of statistics for political reasons still continued even under *glasnost,* at least in certain fields—for instance, with regard to the unwelcome side effects of the anti-alcohol campaign.[5] No outsider can say for certain whether this was due in part to inaccurate figures being submitted to the Central Administration, or whether the chief statisticians knew the truth but tried to second-guess what they thought were the wishes of the leadership.

In August 1987 the Central Statistical Administration was subjected to *perestroika* and changed its name: it became the U.S.S.R. State Committee for Statistics.[6] It was also, to a certain extent, affected by *glasnost;* for the first time in many years figures on the grain harvest, infant mortality, and life expectancy were published. But other economic and social statistics such as crime and suicide rates remained tabu. Other published figures seemed highly doubtful; thus Selyunin openly disagreed with the official statistics according to which 75 percent of industrial production went to consumption and only 25 percent to investment. He claimed that the ratio was closer to sixty-forty.[7]

Overall statistics are abstractions for all but the experts; on the other hand every Soviet citizen has a vital interest in living conditions such as food supplies and housing. Everyone was aware of the true state of affairs, but until *glasnost* was inaugurated negative phenomena were discussed only rarely in public, and in literary journals more frequently than in the professional literature. Furthermore, the impression was created that these negative phenomena were the exception rather than the rule.

Even after 1986 some tabu zones continued to exist. But there is no denying that both experts and nonexperts began to talk and

[5] Jan Vannous, *Plan Econ Report,* February 13, 1987; Philip Hanson, *Sovset News,* March 23, 1987; *Wall Street Journal,* March 10, 1987.
[6] *Pravda,* August 7, 1987.
[7] *Sotsialisticheskaia Industria,* January 5, 1988. For some examples of the lack of statistical information still prevailing under *glasnost,* see Otto Latsis, "Tsena Ravnovesia," *Znamia,* 2, 1988. Complaints about the paucity of data in the Soviet census were voiced in the Soviet media. The census of 1926 had resulted in sixty volumes, the census of 1979 in one, "unsuitable for serious scientific work" (Arkadi Perevedentsev). But at least there had been consultations and conferences in preparation for previous censuses, whereas in 1988 there were none (*Moscow News,* 13, 1988).

to write with infinitely greater openness than before, and this was the crucial contribution made by *glasnost.* Not only the reformist periodicals but also the conservative newspapers and periodicals, as well as radio and television, offered long and depressing litanies about the true state of affairs and the need for change. We shall single out but one such account, highly authorative, because it came from academician Abel Aganbegyan, one of Gorbachev's close advisers. He noted that the country spent less on health than any other developed nation, that in the days of Sputnik Soviet education had been very good but that in the years since, American spending had tripled whereas Soviet expenditure had declined.[8] The Soviet Union had the lowest rents in the world but the quality of its dwellings was also about the lowest. Many people had a private car and color television but no running water, and one-third had no sewer system. Seventeen percent of all Soviet families had to be separated for want of their own apartment, and the plans to improve the situation were insufficient: if 10 million apartments were to be built during each five-year plan, the problem would be solved only in another fifty years. There was an enormous discrepancy between what people paid and the real cost of living space— about three rubles per square meter, or 180 rubles for a three-room apartment. But since 180 rubles was nearly the average monthly income in the Soviet Union, an apartment was clearly out of range for most citizens. Aganbegyan did not suggest that the full rent (in terms of real costs) be paid, but he dropped some broad hints that rentals should be increased: The Soviet people were keeping some 250 billion rubles in saving accounts in banks, for they could not buy or invest where they wanted. Why not use some of this money for improving housing conditions?

In the seventieth year of the Soviet Union, forty years after the end of the war, what was there to buy in the shops? The Soviet Union was a great power, yet it had to buy scissors for haircutting from abroad, and it could not produce a decent bicycle for children. The car produced in the 1950s (Pobeda) had been better in durability than the present Volga; the television sets of the 1950s had not been particularly elegant but they had lasted two decades, whereas those now sold were causing some two thousand fires yearly in Moscow alone. (Among these fires had been one of the

[8]*Ogonyok,* 29 and 30, 1987. More or less the same facts were quoted by Aganbegyan in a lecture to party speakers and editors in Moscow, followed by a question-and-answer period (*Nauka i Zhizn,* March, 1988).

most deadly—in the Rossia Hotel.) In short, the main problem was that of quality, the greatest misfortune—the dictatorship of the producer over the consumer. Food supplies were unsatisfactory, particularly vegetables and fruit: "Considering that we are a developed country, our diet is bad and unbalanced." The annual meat consumption should have been eighty kilograms per person, but it was only sixty-one kilograms, and most of it was sold frozen, that is to say having lost half of its nutritional value.

Aganbegyan saw basic flaws in the system of both wages and prices. It was unthinkable that the government should subsidize milk and meat to the tune of fifty billion rubles a year. On the other hand the wage structure was such that skilled mechanics worked as private chauffeurs for half the salary they would get in a factory (250–300 rubles a month). In this way they had far more time to do extra work and they could also use the boss's car *nalevo,* or for moonlighting. It was not even easy to blame these mechanics, considering the ugliness, the dirt, and the unsanitary working conditions prevailing in many factories.

The production of shoddy goods and the absence of services was at the root of the second, or shadow, economy, yet another issue that became a topic of general discussion under *glasnost.* [9] Everyone had known about it, almost everyone had used the shadow economy, permanently or sporadically, sometimes for altogether selfless reasons, such as a chief engineer buying a spare part outside regular channels because without this illegal purchase production would come to a halt. In the pre-*glasnost* period some of the most outrageous cases, like the Moscow and Rostov black caviar trade operations, had been reported in the media. But the size of the second economy had never been fully revealed: only now did it appear that if one considered all the people providing services which state industry and trade did not—those making records from X-ray photographs, making designer clothes, clipping poodles and lapdogs, engaging in clairvoyance or psychoanalysis in their homes, copying Western videos and making Xeroxes of *Lolita,* not to mention mechanics and building work-

[9]Some examples of the "third economy" appear in Igor Bestuzhev-Lada, "Tretaia Ekonomika," *Sotsiologicheskie Issledovaniia,* 1, 1988: A cook with an income of 120 rubles per month. Two school-age children, the wife works at home. His private residence is worth more than 100,000 rubles, his dacha (country house) about as much. He owns a Volga, expensive furniture and carpets, and buys only the best clothing for the family. He spends thousands each year on holidays. The amount of money in his bank account is a secret, because he has not yet been caught. And therefore he is not a thief.

ers—a figure of twenty million employed in the second economy seemed not unrealistic.[10] According to this and other sources, the first economy was frequently a producer of "mirages"; it made things that could be touched, but could not be used for the purpose they were intended: "the boots whose soles come off when you walk, the dresses you cannot look at without shuddering, the men's suits that were just right for scarecrows." When the state acceptance system began to operate in Moscow, it reportedly rejected a great part of the output of ministry light-industry enterprises.

Glasnost brought a great deal of plain speaking on the part of leading economists. Next to Aganbegyan, who published a great number of articles[11] and gave almost daily interviews in the Soviet Union and abroad, the voice of Tatyana Zaslavskaia was most frequently heard. She had argued in the famous Novosibirsk document of 1983[12] that a substantial section of the population (above all the manual workers) had become alienated from the system, that only about one-third of the labor force was working as well as it could. She continued to press home certain points: that in the 1970s and 1980s a situation had developed in which a corrupt section of administrative personnel and economic executives had become openly greedy and immoral and that this had become a norm of behavior. The material damage to society could be computed, but the damage to morality was even more harmful.[13] She was the first to emphasize the crucial importance of the "human factor."

Another leading economist who addressed himself to the state of the economy in the spirit of *glasnost* was L. I. Abalkin, a member of the Academy. He repeatedly made the point that there was no turning back to the old Stalinist command economy because it conformed neither to the development of Soviet society nor to the ideals of democracy and justice. It failed to take into account the level of the Soviet people's maturity, education, and skill, as well as the exigencies of the scientific-technological revolution.[14]

[10]G. Belikova and A. Shoklin, *Ogonyok,* 51, 1987. According to Western estimates, the shadow economy was between 15 percent and 30 percent of the GNP.
[11]For some of his more significant articles see *EKO,* November 1985; *EKO,* June 1986; *EKO,* November 1987.
[12]English translation in *Survey,* spring 1984.
[13]*Kommunist,* 13, 1986; *EKO,* March 1986; "Restructuring Begins with Everyone of Us," a brochure published by *Novosti,* 1987; also *Trud,* July 15, 1986; *Izvestiia,* June 1, 1986, etc.
[14]*Sovetskaia Rossia,* October 25, 1987; *Trud,* October 6 and 9, 1987.

However, some of the most unorthodox and most widely discussed contributions to the economy debate came from authors who had not been widely known before inside the profession, such as Nikolai Shmelyev, whose famous essay, "Advances and Debts," is a typical product of the age of *glasnost*. [15]

Shmelyev's thesis, very briefly, was that the revolution had not found the Bolsheviks armed with a well-thought-out, complete economic theory. "War Communism" decrees (1918–21) as the basic method of the socialist economy had been a temporary expedient. The NEP, on the other hand, was the first scientific, realistic approach; it had also been the victory of common sense. Unfortunately, the NEP was dismantled in the late 1920s, and this had the gravest effects on the Soviet economy. Unless this was admitted, "we will once again as in 1953 and in 1965 condemn ourselves to halfhearted measures." The command economy ("the administrative system of management") was by its very nature unable to deal with improving output quality or increasing production efficiency or ensuring that the greatest results were achieved for the smallest expenditure. The Gosplan (the supreme state planning authority) was so preoccupied with the everyday running of the economy ("watching with the utmost vigilance to ensure that shoemakers make shoes and pastry cooks bake pies") that it had no time for real, strategic planning.

There were far too many ministries and administrators hampering the works of the enterprises. Shmelyev quoted Lenin: "In our country everything is swamped in a foul bureaucratic morass of 'departments'—departments are shit, decrees are shit."

The command economy had devastating economic results, especially with regard to productivity and innovation. But echoing Zaslavskaia, Shmelyev argued that its social consequences were, if possible, even worse: "We now find on a mass scale apathy and indifference, thieving, lack of respect for honest labor and at the same time aggressive envy of those who earn a lot, even if they earn it honestly." Our concern in the present context is with Shmelyev's analysis of present conditions rather than his sugges-

[15]*Novy Mir,* June 1987. The author worked for one of the major Moscow research organizations. He had been married at one time to one of Khrushchev's daughters. One of the *Novy Mir* editors later revealed that Gorbachev had criticized him for publishing the article (*Arkhiv Samizdat,* AC 6017). But Gorbachev said in public that he agreed with some of Shmelyev's conclusions while disagreeing with others, especially those concerning the need for some unemployment. In later articles Shmelyev expressed regret about some of his formulations concerning unemployment.

tions for future reform, which included abolition of much of the administrative apparatus, giving more room to private initiative: "Let us lose our ideological virginity, which in any case exists only in newspaper editorials which are fairy tales." The individual cooperative sector in the cities had to be expanded, he said; there had to be choice and competition in the economy. And last (the most controversial part of his suggestions), he spoke of the harm done by "our parasitic confidence in guaranteed work . . . today it is, I believe, clear to everyone that we owe disorderliness, drunkenness and shoddy work largely to excessively full employment."

The criticism of Shmelyev and some other critics of the system went considerably further than the analysis of many Western experts who believed that job security as well as a high growth rate, a fixed price system, and a relatively flat income distribution were the main strengths of the Soviet system.[16] Or, as another Western scholar put it, the Soviet social contract rested on egalitarianism, stability, and security.[17] Not all Western social historians would have written in the 1970s as Shmelyev did in 1987 that "at one time the slogan was to eliminate the Kulaks as a class—but basically it was the peasant class that was abolished," with all the consequences that ensued. According to an article published in *Osteuropa Wirtschaft* as late as 1986, American experts had systematically denigrated the performance of the Soviet economy. In actual fact they had erred in overrating it.

It was amazing that Shmelyev's article could be published even under *glasnost*. It was more amazing that even those who disagreed with his recommendations did not fundamentally dispute his description of the current state of affairs.[18] Popkova argued in reply that the Soviet system could not hope to compete with the efficiency and output of the highly developed capitalist countries. But then it had other, higher, spiritual values to offer. The attempt to combine socialist and market mechanisms was doomed; such com-

[16]For instance, Ed. A. Hewett, *Reforming the Soviet Economy*, Washington, D.C., 1988, p. 39.
[17]Peter Hauslohner, "Gorbachev's Social Contract," *Soviet Economy*, January 1987, p. 54.
[18]This refers, for instance, to Popkova's "Gde pyshnee pirogi?" (Where Are the Pies Fluffier?), *Novy Mir*, 5, 1987; to Otto Latsis's articles in *Kommunist* in 1986 and 1987; to E. Gaidar, *Kommunist*, 2, 1988; and to Mikhail Antonov, "Tak chto zhe s nami proizkhodit?" (So What Is Happening with Us?), *Oktiabr*, 8, 1987; "Itti svoim putyom" (To Go One's Own Way), *Molodaia Guardia*, 1, 1988; "Na Perelome" (The Turning Point), *Moskva*, 3, 1988. Antonov's original article had contained elements of common sense; his subsequent essays became progressively crankier and he became the favorite expert of the extreme right.

promises were simply not realistic, just as a woman could not be "a little pregnant," a comparison which Latsis, a leading *glasnost* thinker and an editor of *Kommunist*, thought inappropriate.

Various slogans were introduced in the debate; Zaslavskaia differentiated between the "Prussian" and "American" approach to the economy, neither of which seemed appropriate to her. The most widely quoted was Strelyanni's "cavalrymen" and "merchants"—the former were the daredevils, believers in voluntarism who would solve all problems by order and decree.[19] The *kuptsi* (merchants), on the other hand, believed in careful accountability, in profit and loss.

Shmelyev clearly preferred the *kuptsi*, whereas Antonov, a conservative, maintained that both categories belonged to the past; if the cavalrymen had their way Russia would gradually turn into a third-rate underdeveloped country. But the merchants were even more insidious, for under their rule Soviet society would become a mercantile society like America or Israel, where everything was for sale, and in the end it would become the prey of capitalist entrepreneurs.[20] But there was a third way: the future belonged to a generation of "civilized cooperators." If Shmelyev based his ideas on enlightened self-interest and common sense, Antonov rejected such egoism out of which nothing good could ever come.

But his assessment of the present state of Soviet society and economy was not different from Shmelyev's; it was in some respects even more pessimistic. He argued that even if a growth rate of 3–5 percent could be attained in the next five-year plans, it would have only a minimal effect on the well-being of the people. One could increase, for instance, the lowest pensions by ten rubles. Altogether a few more billions would be at the disposal of the state—and this sum would not go far to remedy the pressing social needs.

Antonov expressed the view that the Russians were the most talented of all peoples. Yet at the same time he took a dim view of the moral state of both Soviet youth and the older generation, who are lacking moral restraint, tact, politeness, and many of the other virtues of the old Russia which had been destroyed. The only cure was a moral and cultural revolution—a return to old values, plenty

[19]In 1987 Strelyanni was a member of the editorial board of *Novy Mir*. His articles on agriculture and the economy were published in *Znamia*, 6, 1986; *Novy Mir*, 12, 1986; and *Literaturnaia Gazetta*, December 3, 1986. See also G. Popov in *Nauka i Zhizn*, 4, 1987.
[20]*Molodaia Guardia*, loc. cit., p. 200.

of patriotic education, antiliberalism, and anticapitalism, something akin to the right-wing *Kulturkritiker* of Germany and France toward the end of the nineteenth century.[21] Yet could it really be taken for granted that ardent patriotism would make Soviet citizens buy rubbish, work harder, and introduce more effectively new scientific-technological methods?

Antonov conceded that this was not very likely; the majority would not be motivated in the foreseeable future by *duknovnost* (spirituality), culture, and consciousness. Hence the task of an elite, an avant-garde to lead and to show the road ahead toward Communist unselfishness. These are counsels of despair which have more in common with the asceticism of some of the Saint-Simonians, or perhaps Dostoyevski, than with Marxism-Leninism. As in other lands the politics of cultural and social despair turns more easily to the right than to the left, with its engrained optimism and traditional belief in progress.[22]

A review of the economic debates which began in the early 1980s and gathered additional momentum under Gorbachev would have to cover a great many other topics ranging from the fate of Gosplan to the problem of the convertibility of the ruble. Our preoccupation is with the impact of *glasnost*—that is to say, relatively plain speaking. All the experts felt strongly about their field of specialization. But most were accustomed by training and convention to express their views in a cautious, measured way and often also in technical language. Thus the more interesting and challenging contributions to the debate came frequently from the sidelines of the profession.

"The Idiocy of Rural Life"

The story of Soviet agriculture has been a tale of woe for a long time. A resident of a village near Volgograd wrote at the end of a long and impassionate account of the miseries of life in the countryside that he had not "woken up just yesterday—all of us,

[21]There are interesting parallels with Julius Langbehn's best-selling *Rembrandt als Erzieher* (1890), one of the bibles of the German right.
[22]The "ascetism" of the advocates of extreme social justice (i.e., egalitarianism) was rooted in a deeply conservative approach opposed to innovation and progress, as G. Lisichkin pointed out in a widely discussed article ("Liudi i Veshi" (People and Things), *Oktiabr*, 2, 1988). The main spokesman of the "ascetist school" was the philosopher V. Z. Rogovin. His book *Obshestvo zrelovo sotsialisma* appeared in 1984 and he has published several articles since.

everyone in his own way, saw it, but we could not speak out. It shocked us, we wrote about it, but our attempts were stopped by the relevant authorities."[23]

This may be true as far as detailed facts and figures are concerned but a general picture had certainly emerged much earlier about the state of affairs in Soviet agriculture from hundreds of books and thousands of articles, beginning with Ovechkin's sketches in Stalin's last year and up to the writings of the village writers *(derevenshiki)*. More was written on life in the country than in the cities.

The Soviet leaders were not, of course, unaware of the problems and the need to take new initiatives. Under Brezhnev a big comprehensive "food plan" had been worked out, mainly by Gorbachev, who was responsible at the time for agriculture in the Politburo. About a quarter of all Soviet investments had gone for years into agriculture, a percentage unheard of in any other developed country. As a Soviet author put it, his country's industry produces six times as many tractors and sixteen times as many combine-harvesters as the United States. "But," he added wryly, "if U.S. industry wanted to produce as many combine-harvesters as stood around in our country in a state of disrepair, it would need seventy years."[24] Productivity in Soviet agriculture was estimated at 15–25 percent compared with the U.S. There had been countless reforms ever since Stalin's day, yet with all the enormous investments (six hundred billion rubles over twenty-five years) output grew only by 1 percent a year during the last decade and sometimes it did not grow at all. Wheat as well as other food had to be imported from abroad. A kilo of meat selling in the shops for 1.77 rubles carried a state subsidy of 3.68 rubles; a liter of milk selling for twenty-four kopeks had to be subsidized by twenty-nine kopeks. People lived badly in the Sovkhoz and Kolchoz; those who could left, especially from the non-Black Earth regions of northern and central Russia.

There were various explanations for the failure of Soviet agriculture. Some argued that the system was basically flawed, inasmuch as there was over-rigid central planning, no incentives, and a general orientation toward quantitative output.[25] True, 1986 was

[23]Boris Yekimov, *Literaturnaia Rossia,* August 14, 1987.
[24]E. Gaidar, *Kommunist,* 2, 1988, p. 48.
[25]K. Gray in *Gorbachev's Economic Plans,* Vol. 2, pp. 9 et seq.

a relatively good year, and according to Aganbegyan as much progress was made that year (5 percent) as in the whole preceding five-year plan. But it is not certain how far *glasnost* extended to agricultural statistics. Some Western experts suspected that the figures were manipulated, and Soviet writers also reported that it was too early to sound victory fanfares: "In 1986 in many places things went as they did in 1952 and in 1962 and in 1972 and in 1982. . . ."[26]

Gorbachev's reforms included the establishment of Gosagroprom, a supercommittee intended to supersede the many ministerial and party bureaucracies which made it next to impossible for the collective and state farms to function more or less rationally. But it was too early to say whether the new organizational setup would, in fact, make things easier for the farming communities or, on the contrary, more complicated. It seemed sensible not to increase investments in agriculture in view of the rapidly diminishing returns (20 percent by the early 1980s!), and not to plan for increased production but to concentrate on reducing wastage in storage as well as in transport. It seemed sensible to establish a closer link between wages and output, to give the farms greater freedom to dispense with their above-plan production, and, generally speaking, to give greater autonomy to brigades or subunits (*podryadi*) which might consist of members of a family. However, many of these innovations were not that new; there had been *podryadi* in Soviet agriculture since the earliest days of collectivization. Nor would there be any above-plan production to dispense with if the plan goals were set very high. And even if there was such excess production, there would be no additional income for the peasants unless they could transport their produce to town; transportation was and is a notoriously weak link in Soviet agriculture, even more so than in industry.

In short, most experts agreed that by rationalizing and tinkering, and with good fortune (such as a number of good harvests), it might be possible to reduce, and perhaps abolish altogether, imports of food from abroad within a few years. But no one expected a radical change in agriculture in the foreseeable future as the result of patchwork reform. In the meantime the main task facing the authorities was how to increase productivity. But it seemed unlikely that this could be achieved without substantially

[26]A. Strelyanni, *Novy Mir*, 12, 1986.

improving living conditions. Some argued that, given the inherent drawbacks of village life, it would be fair as well as necessary to pay people on the land more than those working in the cities.

The true extent of misery in large parts of the countryside emerged only under *glasnost:* the statistical office announced that while the average income in the cities was two hundred rubles, it was only 150 on the land. But this was only part of the story, and probably the less important part at that. Whereas the state was providing housing in the cities, the peasants had to pay for building a house. Food was considerably more expensive in the village than in the town; the price of meat and sausages, for example, was about twice as high. All industrial goods, including textiles, could be bought, if at all, only in the city; even to obtain bread the peasant frequently had to travel to the district center or to town.

Medical care was infinitely worse than in town. There were few if any hospitals, and one physician for twenty-five hundred people as compared with one for seven hundred in town. Working conditions for doctors were said to be abysmal. It was difficult, sometimes impossible, to find teachers, for there were no living quarters or food supplies for them. Children frequently had to walk a distance of ten or fifteen kilometers to school; in theory they were to be driven, but in practice, especially during the winter, the buses would not run for many months because there was no fuel. After a lifetime of hard work the peasant would be rewarded with the lowest pension in the country, about forty rubles a month, at a time when the living minimum was officially estimated to be at least twice as high. True, in the olden days the situation had been even worse, inasmuch as the peasant did not even possess an internal passport, which is to say that he was not entitled to leave his place of residence for another location. Now they could have a passport, and the result was that "frequently only those remained who were nowhere else needed."[27]

Ecological Concerns

Glasnost also had a major effect in the ecological field, and the victory of the "antidiversionists" (referring to the diversion of the Siberian rivers) is frequently adduced as the most obvious example for the impact of an emerging public opinion. The beginning of

[27]Yekimov, loc. cit.

the ecological movement goes back to well before the age of *glasnost.* If the planners of Soviet industrialization and the collectivization of agriculture had not much interest in the preservation of nature, such concerns began to develop even in Stalin's last days. Leonid Leonov's "Russian Forest" was perhaps its first major manifestation. Its message was clear even if its politics were a little primitive in accordance with the *Zeitgeist:* the main villain, the enemy of the forest (Gratsianov), had been in his younger years a Tsarist agent-provocateur. . . .

The cause was taken up again in the early 1960s by Vladimir Chivilikhin, a writer of the right, in a series of essays and articles focusing on the pollution of Lake Baikal.[28] By that time it was clear that the enemy was not Tsarism or Trotskyism but party leaders and industrial managers of impeccable credentials and great influence. The censorship tended to intervene, and as a critic later noted, courage was needed to press a cause which at the time was far from popular.[29] Yet a few years later the village writers, many of them Siberian by origin, adopted a cause movingly described in Rasputin's *Farewell to Matryona.* It is the story of a little settlement on an island which has to be evacuated to make room for a new industrial enterprise.

The most active fighter against the river diversion project and its ecological consequences was Sergei Zalygin, the veteran Siberian writer, a nonparty author who in 1986 was made editor-in-chief of *Novy Mir.* He virtually gave up writing for a number of years and his lobbying (which involved confronting not only the industrial establishment but also the president of the Academy of Science) was eventually successful: in a combined resolution the party Central Committee and the Council of Ministers decided in 1986 to stop the project. The good cause, represented by Zalygin and the conservationists, had triumphed.[30] But after a few months the counterattack started. Some experts claimed that Zalygin and his supporters had distorted the facts, and spokesmen for the Central Asian republics (who would have benefited from the diversion scheme) bitterly complained: the standard of living in their republics was already 30–40 percent lower than in other parts of the U.S.S.R. The Central Asian population was likely to increase

[28]V. Chivilikhin, the author of the novel *Pamyat,* was among the signatories of the notorious letter to the authorities in which intervention against the liberal *Novy Mir* was demanded.
[29]Viacheslav Gorbachev, *Sudby Narodnie,* Moscow, 1987, p. 30.
[30]"Povorot" (The Turning), *Novy Mir,* 1, 1987.

faster than elsewhere; and if the region was to be deprived of additional water supplies, it was bound to become even poorer.[31] The bitter debate continued; it was certainly the nearest thing to a public discussion that had taken place in the Soviet Union. It was also a case in which the supreme authorities were obviously swayed by public opinion.

With all their intrinsic importance and dramatic character, the Lake Baikal and Siberian river controversies were only part of a much wider problem—that of chronic water pollution in most major Soviet rivers, of severe regional water shortages (for instance, the shrinking of Lake Aral), of air pollution in many Soviet cities, and the negative ecological effects of new industrial projects such as the extraction of oil in western Siberia and the laying of pipelines.[32] The waste of natural resources was probably greater in the Soviet Union than in the West precisely because the resources seemed so abundant. The recognition that the resources were finite came only relatively late, and the means to combat waste and pollution were less sophisticated than in the West.

True, conservation laws had existed in all republics since 1963 but the legal enforcement was weak. The fines imposed were risible in relation to the damage caused, and until recently only a very few installations were actually closed down or transferred because they constituted a major danger to nature. Even in the case of Lake Baikal, after a quarter of a century of debates and the appointment of countless high-level committees, despite special sessions of the Central Committee (December 1986), the pollution problem has by no means been solved; only public awareness has increased.

Under *glasnost* and especially as a result of the Chernobyl disaster in April 1986, ecological concerns began to figure frequently and prominently in public debate. Soviet information policy after Chernobyl was not a page of glory in the annals of *glasnost*. For three days the event was not mentioned in the Soviet media, and even after this period some of the essential facts were not released. A play on Chernobyl by V. Gubaryov (*The Sarcophagus*) has been performed in London, Vienna, and other Western capitals but not in Moscow. Government policy was to provide only a minimum of

[31]*Izvestiia,* April 20, 1987; *Zvezda Vostoka,* June 1987.
[32]On the general problem see, among many others, the articles of Craig Zum Brunnen in the U.S. and of Ulrich Weissenburger in West Germany. Since the late 1970s, there have been fairly numerous Soviet publications on the subject, and many articles have appeared in *EKO, Voprosy Ekonomiki, Planovoe Khoziaiastvo,* and above all *Chelovek i Priroda.*

information, but far from reassuring the population this only gave rise to exaggerated rumors.[33] Y. Velikhov, one of the crisis managers at the time of Chernobyl, said in evidence before a U.S. Senate committee that the Soviet government had refrained from making some essential facts known during the first days of the disaster because of its concern about the domestic impact. Such self-criticism was encouraging and was welcomed as a manifestation of *glasnost* in the West. The fact that Velikhov's evidence and similar such declarations were not published in the Soviet media was less encouraging. Nor was the official Soviet report submitted to Western governments and the International Atomic Energy Commission (August 1986) made known at home in any detail. True, in the post-Chernobyl period Soviet coverage of subsequent disasters became more open, but none of these were even remotely of similar magnitude.

In July 1987 the supreme authorities passed a resolution to improve measures to preserve nature. About the same time a semi-official association called Green Peace was founded, chaired by Zalygin. President Gromyko welcomed in a speech the public discussion about ecological issues and the measures to be taken to remedy the situation.[34]

Following the passing of a resolution, "On the Radical Restructuring of the Protection of Nature in the Country," and the establishment of a State Committee for Environmental control, various master plans were prepared for the development and location of industry and agriculture. In late January 1988, in a special meeting of the Politburo, the progress of the plans for conserving raw materials was reviewed.[35]

Following all this official encouragement there have been in the Soviet media many reports and complaints about, even demonstrations against, flagrant cases of pollution. Thus it was reported that many lakes (Ladoga and Sevan, for instance) and rivers (including the Don, Ob, and Kama) had significantly deteriorated of late, that in 104 cities pollution exceeded the risk limits tenfold. Complaints were particularly frequent from cities in the Ukraine and Kazakhstan but also in Armenia, where thousands of people demonstrated

[33] *Trud,* January 13, 1987. The most detailed account of Chernobyl and its prehistory, including some strong criticism regarding the lack of *glasnost,* appeared in *Yunost,* 6, 1987. Its author was the Ukrainian physician and writer Yuri Sherbak, who also acted as special correspondent of *Literaturnaia Gazeta.*
[34] *Pravda,* July 15, 1987; *Izvestiia,* June 5, 1987.
[35] M. Lemeshev, *Moscow News,* 7, 1988.

against the toxic emissions of factories near Erevan and in the Ararat valley.[36]

The Ukrainian literary weekly *Literaturnaia Ukraina* published a letter by seven leading writers (including the secretary of the Poltava district party committee) in which they protested against the building of a nuclear construction site near Chigirin (once the capital of the Ukraine) on the Dnepr river. The signatories said that they were not in principle against nuclear installations but that it was undesirable to build them in a densely populated area and in the vicinity of a main river where irreversible damage could be inflicted.[37] In Kazan, to give yet another example, thousands of inhabitants signed a petition against the building of a biochemical installation, yet the authorities took no notice. As the *Izvestiia* correspondent concluded, "We are far from having mastered the science of democracy."[38]

The ecological debates constituted a step forward in the direction of *glasnost*. It was a modest step both because complaints were by no means always successful and because the discussions concerned a topic which was not politically controversial. Everyone, after all, wanted to preserve nature, no one had a vested interest in pollution, and the only question was how to achieve this aim without paying an unacceptable price. But in the final analysis, as Lemeshev wrote, "only the public is left to fight for the protection of nature. But the public lacks resources. Mighty business executives usually dismiss the public's demands for environmental protection as emotions that cannot be taken seriously. . . ."

Poverty and the "Underprovided"

Under *glasnost* a great deal of new light was shed on living conditions in the Soviet Union, on income distribution and social policy. Thus it was made known that per capita annual income in 1986 was 2,096 rubles and that the income in monetary terms of the 10 percent of the best-off families was 3.5 times higher than those least well-provided for.[39] According to another estimate, about 40

[36]Ecological concerns also played a role in the Erevan protest demonstrations of February 1988. Earlier ecological protest meetings had taken place in Erevan in October 1987 (*Bulletin Glasnost*, 10, 1988).
[37]*Literaturnaia Ukraina*, August 6, 1987.
[38]*Izvestia*, Feb. 1, 1988.
[39]N. Rimashevskaia in *Argumenty i Fakty*, 33, 1987.

percent of all families, that is to say about one hundred million people, had an income of less than one hundred rubles per person a month.[40] Since there are some sixty million pensioners in the Soviet Union and since the average old-age pension is sixty-seven rubles (lower for members of a *kolkhoz*), with the maximum pension fixed at 132 rubles, it is easy to see that the majority of retired people have an income below the poverty line.[41]

The situation of young families, especially those with children; of the chronically sick; and of families with only one breadwinner (unless he happens to be in a very high category) is similar. The poverty line varies considerably, of course, according to local conditions; in some regions it was reportedly fifty rubles, elsewhere ninety, and it was also noted that the pensions were always lagging behind creeping inflation.[42]

Such inflation expresses itself sometimes in mere kopeks—for instance, the entrance ticket to a Moscow swimming pool or an intercity telephone call, the monthly payment for heating or water. But these kopeks add up to considerable sums, as investigative journalists have shown.[43] While the general trend in the Brezhnev era was toward *uravnilovka* (egalitarianism) from which manual workers benefited most, it subsequently appeared that there were substantial sections of the population living in a state of poverty, or, to use the official language of circumlocution, were "underprovided." Accounts appeared in the media about an electrical engineer at the telegraph office who thought with fear about getting married because he could not afford it, about a cook with two children who made eighty-five rubles a month; a nurse who earned ninety rubles; a pensioner with seventy-six rubles. These were typical examples, and it was pointed out that on this level of income even elementary needs could not be satisfied.[44]

The Gorbachev Politburo came out sharply against *uravnilovka* as an impediment to higher productivity. At the same time the party leadership envisaged increases in the level of the lowest

[40]*Komsomolskaia Pravda*, August 13, 1986; *Literaturnaia Gazeta*, August 12, 1987.
[41]*Argumenty i Fakty*, 50, 1986; Mervin Matthews, *Poverty and Patterns of Deprivation in the Soviet Union*, Berkeley, 1986.
[42]*Sotsialisticheski Trud*, 10, 1986.
[43]A. Rubinov, *Literaturnaia Gazeta*, February 17, 1988; on creeping inflation see also N. Petrakov in *Argumenty i Fakty*, 6, 1988.
[44]These examples appeared in a *Pravda* survey of family budgets in Saratov ("Malenkaia Zarplata" ["A Small Wage"], February 4, 1988).

pensions which had declined in absolute terms. For how could prices be raised and subventions withdrawn as long as considerable sections of the population lived at, or below, the poverty line?

Under *glasnost* it became possible for the first time to discuss a phenomenon that had been previously denied: the homeless, or *bomzhi*, "people of no fixed address" in police language. They had apparently never been seen before and were now spotted not only in the big cities but almost everywhere, from run-down villages in Central Asia to the northern seaports, finding shelter in courtyards, cellars, and railway stations.[45]

It was officially conceded that whereas in 1960 the Soviet Union had been second in the world as far as per capita housing construction was concerned, it had fallen to eleventh place in 1980; at this rate it would take fifteen years to catch up with . . . East Germany.[46] Even more significant were the new public debates on topics such as wage policy, special benefits, nonlabor incomes, private-sector activity, and social justice in general.

It emerged from many articles and letters in the media as well as from some small-scale opinion polls that government plans to make the economy more efficient encountered great opposition on the part of large sections of the population. While many members of the intelligentsia favored wage and price reform, including the removal of a ceiling for salaries,[47] most workers and employees had great doubts about these changes. According to public opinion polls taken in 1987, only 21 percent of leading cadres and only 28 percent of the rank-and-file workers believed that their income would increase if they worked harder and produced more. Even more worrying from the authorities' point of view was the fact that in a similar poll taken a year earlier the number of the optimists among the rank and file had been twice as high.[48] They disliked the current system, but they feared that in the future they would have to work harder for a lower income. The argument that the subsidy burden for the state was becoming higher every year did not cut much ice among these sections. Frequently it was argued that prices had never risen under Stalin and why should they be increased under *perestroika?*

[45]*Literaturnaia Gazetta,* May 28, 1986; *Izvestiia,* February 10, 1988.
[46]P. Aven, *Kommunist,* 15, 1987.
[47]This had been suggested by, among others, Khasbulatov in *Pravda,* April 27, 1987.
[48]*Sotsialisticheskaia Industria,* February 9, 1988.

There was massive hostility against the modest concessions made to cooperatives in 1987. Some of this stemmed from feelings of envy: "If I cannot afford this, that, or another thing, why should the *chastnik* [private operator] enjoy it?" These feelings of jealousy were strong, but there was also real fear that private initiative would give rise to "legalized speculation" and that it was a step in the wrong direction away from Communist ideals.[49] A strong egalitarian bias of sections of the working class clashed with the demands of the technical personnel, scientists, teachers, and medical staff whose level of income had declined considerably in the Brezhnev era. There were similar fears among the population with regard to unemployment which, it was thought, would ensue from the campaign against overmanning which figured high on Gorbachev's agenda. What would happen to the workers and employees if inefficient enterprises would in future go bankrupt, if they would no longer be bailed out by the state? The government and its experts had to tread warily, the Polish example of the early 1980s clearly in mind, when similar reforms, including steep price rises, had triggered a movement of mass protest.

It is difficult to prove that the open debates on social and economic issues had an immediate positive effect on the speed and the extent of the envisaged reforms. *Glasnost* showed that there were open conflicts of interest among various social groups. Whether these were "antagonistic" or "nonantagonistic" in character (to hark back to the concepts of the Stalin era), whether these were social classes or simply professional groups, whether the social structure had become as complicated as academician Zaslavskaia maintained (she had counted more than seventy social groups), these were interesting theoretical questions that could be debated at great length. But there was no doubt that real social conflict had existed underneath the surface for a long time, and it was one of the consequences of *glasnost* that it came out into the open. This is not to say that these conflicts were insoluble. But it certainly meant that governing the country had become more complicated.

[49]For example, see readers' letters in *Sovetskaia Estonia,* October 29, 1987. For a defense of the *chastnik,* see, among many others, Vladimir Gubarev, *Literaturnaia Rossia,* December 25, 1987.

CHAPTER 10

Glasnost Abroad

New Thinking in Foreign Policy

THERE HAVE BEEN intriguing changes in Soviet foreign and defense policy since Gorbachev was chosen as *primus inter pares* by his colleagues in the Politburo. Various officials and commentators admitted that mistakes had been committed in the conduct of Soviet foreign policy in the past; Soviet troops were withdrawn from Afghanistan, and, generally speaking, there was a palpable improvement in the international climate. Shevardnadze, the new foreign minister, said that the old strategic concept of the Soviet Union being as strong as any possible coalition of states opposing it was not just wrong but contradicted the national interest.[1]

Nevertheless, the "new thinking" in foreign and defense policy has not been remotely as striking as *glasnost* on the domestic front. Foreign policy is based on some degree of secrecy even in democratic societies and the same is true, *a fortiori,* with regard to national security. If there were total openness between nations, there might be no need for diplomacy; if international relations were in accordance with the prescription of the prophet Isaiah and the Sermon on the Mount, there would be no need for defense budgets and standing armies, navies, and air forces.

Basic factors in Soviet foreign policy and defense are bound to remain constant, irrespective of developments on the domestic scene. There has been a priority of domestic over foreign policy in the history of the Soviet Union virtually since the revolution.

[1]*Pravda,* July 26, 1988.

Foreign policy will not be neglected in Moscow; opportunities will be used to enhance the influence and security of the Soviet Union whenever possible. But there is unanimity among the Soviet leaders that their major efforts have to be concentrated on the domestic front. This is based on the correct assumption that a weak or stagnant economy will have negative consequences not only at home but also with regard to the international standing of the Soviet Union. There have been many calls for more *glasnost* in the making of Soviet foreign policy, and yet it is pointless to speak about an "age of *glasnost*" in Soviet policy, as is frequently done in the West. The correct term for the new approach in Soviet foreign policy is *Novoe Myshlenie* (New Thinking) and its use goes back to well before the arrival of Gorbachev.[2]

This new thinking could be defined as the movement forward from the age of negativism, which characterized Soviet foreign policy in the early 1980s. There is a new emphasis on global concerns common to West and East, such as nuclear disarmament and certain ecological problems or epidemics—but without giving up the basic "class character" of Soviet foreign policy, a "peace strategy" which aims both at reducing the danger of world war and weakening the countries perceived as the main enemies of the Soviet Union. However, there are now certain differences in approach, in particular concerning the "class character" of Soviet foreign policy which, in practice in contrast to theory, was always subject to dilution. It is less easy now than ten or twenty years ago to define the party line, which has become more fuzzy and less monolithic. Relations between the Soviet Union and the West (in particular the United States) had deteriorated so much by the early 1980s that negotiations in almost all fields had come to a virtual standstill. It is not easy even in retrospect to establish with any certainty whether this was the result of a deliberate policy on the part of Soviet leaders, or whether, perhaps more likely, they had maneuvered themselves into the foreign policy equivalent of stagnation. By 1984 there was growing awareness that the militarization of Soviet foreign policy led to self-isolation and was not in the best interests of the country. Hence the gradual retreat from the "policy of boycott" which began under Andropov and continued under Gorbachev.

[2]For instance, Anatoli Gromyko and Vladimir Lomeiko, *Novoe Myshlenie v yaderny vek* (New Thinking in the Nuclear Age), Moscow, 1984. The term was allegedly coined by Gromyko and Lomeiko at a conference in Hamburg in 1984.

Gorbachev's first foreign policy statements were as cautious as his speeches on other topics. True, at the Twenty-seventh Party Congress, one year after his election, there was talk about tactical flexibility, about a preparedness to enter a dialogue and to reach mutually acceptable compromises.[3] But this was accompanied by the ritual invocation of the ever-growing crisis of parasitic, decaying imperialism, meaning not only the United States but also Western Europe and Japan, which had brought the "capitalist world" to the eve of revolution. The U.S. was characterized as "the locomotive of militarism, a system of monopolistic totalitarianism"(!). True, it was not denied that the capitalist world was still capable of increasing its productive capacities, but it was still doomed because of its inability to solve its social questions such as growing unemployment. There were some references to global interdependence and the possibility of cooperation in the mutual interest; was it not a waste to spend so many billions each year on arms budgets?

But these were only cautious feelers; if there was a desire to revive détente, there was no hint in these statements. There was even less of the spirit of détente in the interpretations of leading Soviet foreign policy spokesmen such as Zagladin or Dobrynin.[4] They emphasized the "world historical mission of the working class," the "revolutionary spirit of the New Thinking," and above all the thesis that the stress in the conduct of foreign policy was always to be laid on the class character, not the general human aspects. There was no letup in anti-Western and in particular anti-American propaganda: the Pentagon was responsible for the manufacture and the spread of the AIDS virus; the CIA had carried out the Jonestown massacre (in which almost a thousand members of an American religious sect had committed suicide); whenever a foreign leader was killed in circumstances that were not entirely clear, be it a plane accident or a terrorist attack, the Americans were behind it.[5] Muammar al-Qaddafi, the Libyan ruler, was intro-

[3] *Pravda*, March 7, 1986.
[4] V. V. Zagladin in *Voprosy Filosofii*, 2, 1986; A. Dobrynin in *Kommunist*, 16, 1986.
[5] The AIDS stories that caused particular anger in Washington were featured as allegations made by African sources, anonymous French-Algerian doctors, or obscure East German scientists; see, for instance, *Sobesednik*, 52, 1987. In the case of an official American complaint, it could always be argued that the Soviet media had picked up stories that had been circulated elsewhere. Valentin Pokrovski, president of the Soviet Academy of Medicine, said in July 1988 that the allegations about American development and spreading of AIDS were totally unfounded: "not a single Soviet scientist has ever shared this view" (*Sovetskaia Rossia*, July 20, 1988). But soon after, another horror story made the rounds about the use of Third World babies for human spare parts.

duced to the Soviet public as "Comrade," an epithet reserved in the past for members of Communist and allied parties.[6]

Soviet propaganda abroad did not make an overwhelming show of *glasnost* in 1985–86. Thus it was stated that the Soviet example had shown that the national question, "one of the most dramatic problems of mankind," could be solved within quite a short period of time. The right of housing in the Soviet Union was said to be guaranteed in the constitution and Soviet medicine was free; real income between 1986 and 1990 was going to increase by about one-third. Among the many Soviet achievements there were some not hitherto mentioned: "The Soviet people are very proud that our country has retained its title of the last bulwark of romantic love in the world."[7] Everyone expects a country to put its best foot forward in foreign propaganda, but assertions of this kind clearly went beyond accepted limits of good taste and plausibility.

If Soviet foreign policymakers had stuck closely to the doctrine articulated by these interpreters, there would not have been much progress in their relations with the West. But they did not. Beginning with Gorbachev's visit to London in 1984, even before he had become general secretary, Soviet diplomacy showed a willingness to establish closer relations with the West, and also with China and Japan. This manifested itself, above all, in the wish to attain agreements on arms control. There were also proposals to intensify trade relations by means of "joint ventures." There was the new readiness to put the stress on "matters of common human interest." The desire of the Soviet Union to pull out its military forces from Afghanistan was also frequently reiterated.

This new style made an excellent impression in the West. Mrs. Thatcher was the first to say that she liked Gorbachev and that one could do business with him; soon after, Mitterrand expressed similar views, and Prime Minister Kohl was equally taken by Gorbachev's "natural authority" and grasp of details. Eventually, President Reagan showed himself smitten by the Gorbachevs on the occasion of their visit to Washington in December 1987. The impact on public opinion and the Western media (on which more below) was even more striking.

However, many contradictions remained, above all the basic question of whether the new rapprochement constituted only a

[6]*Izvestiia,* March 3, 1987.
[7]V. S. Gurevich and V. T. Tretiakov, *Seventy Years of Soviet Government,* Moscow, 1987, pp. 65, 78, etc.

temporary adjustment, was tactical in character, and was scheduled to last merely a few years; or whether it constituted a real break in Soviet foreign policy, a long-term reorientation. Some Soviet commentators seem to have favored the latter course, arguing that it was unrealistic to expect real improvement in relations with the West unless the concept of a basic, irreconcilable antagonism, of an enemy to be defeated and destroyed sooner or later, was replaced.[8] Most Soviet spokesmen preferred to leave the question open.

There were further contradictions. According to the new political assessment, American power was declining and Western Europe and Japan were emerging as alternative seats of power. However, in actual fact the Soviet leaders found themselves negotiating most of the time with Washington, as yet the most important partner (and antagonist) by far. While favoring the "decoupling of Europe" from America, and advocating an independent European policy, the Russians were opposed to any move toward closer cooperation, political and military, inside Western Europe. In the field of arms control there was a similar contradiction between the wish to limit and reduce certain weapons systems because of their enormous (and growing) cost, and at the same time not to give up any of the advantages in the arms race which they had achieved in the 1970s.

Foreign trade was yet another field in which progress seemed difficult. There was genuine interest in expanding foreign trade relations with the West so as to enhance the modernization of the Soviet economy; this aim was repeatedly stated at the Twenty-seventh Party Congress and on subsequent occasions. However, in actual fact there was a substantial decline in 1985–87 in Soviet trade with its main foreign trade partners (more than 20 percent in the case of West Germany) as a result of the decline in the price of oil (the main Soviet export commodity), the fall in the value of the dollar, and for a number of other reasons. To compensate for the decline in foreign currency earnings the Soviet government decided on the establishment of joint ventures with Western and Japanese corporations. There had been similar schemes during the NEP in the early 1920s, but the attempts to revive this tradition were not clearly conceived; in view of bureaucratic complications and other difficulties, there was only minimal interest among potential foreign partners.

[8]E. Plimak in *Pravda,* November 14, 1986; various official philosophers expressed similar views throughout 1987 (*Voprosy Filosofii,* 10–12, 1987).

Arms control was the field with most of the action; the Soviet Union took the initiative with a number of suggestions which went well beyond the conditions that had been put by Gorbachev's predecessors,[9] including the reduction of strategic weapons by half (Geneva, October 1985) or at least by 30 percent (June 1986), the gradual dismantling of all nuclear weapons up to the year 2000, and the reduction of conventional forces in Europe (June 1986). These and other suggestions were rather vague and particularly weak on the important issue of verification. But they did help to restore the initiative to the Soviet negotiators inasmuch as the impression was created that Gorbachev was a man of peace whereas Reagan, obstinate and stonewalling, was not willing to make any significant concession for the cause of world peace.

This impression was to a certain point strengthened by the outcome of the Reykjavik conference (October 1986), at which the Soviets offered a reduction by 50 percent of all intercontinental strategic missiles over a period of five years and their total elimination up to the end of the century, as well as the "zero solution" for medium-range missiles. The Americans accepted these proposals in principle, and if the conference broke down, it was because the Russian side was unwilling to accept SDI ("Star Wars," in popular parlance). Many Western experts thought after Reykjavik that Gorbachev's far-reaching proposals had been made in the firm conviction that the package, all-or-nothing deal (i.e., the insistence on the discontinuation of SDI) would be unacceptable for the Americans. But Gorbachev subsequently relented and U.S. insistence on SDI (and equally determined Soviet opposition) did not prevent the successful negotiations on removing medium-range missiles which were crowned by success and led to the signing of an agreement at the Washington summit (December 1987). In December 1988 the unilateral reduction of the Soviet armed forces by 500,000 men was announced.

Neither the intricate arms talks nor Western fears and doubts ("decoupling," the greater vulnerability of Europe to conventional attack) are of immediate relevance in the present context; one of the issues which ought to be discussed, however briefly, is to what extent Soviet defense policy reflected the "New Thinking." Under

---

[9]In a speech in Tula in 1977 Brezhnev had rejected the idea of victory in a nuclear conflict and disavowed superiority as a goal. But this remained of little consequence since it encountered the opposition of the generals and never became the official Soviet line in negotiations.

Gorbachev's leadership the armed forces have not played a role as important as under Brezhnev, a political fact that has manifested itself in various ways.[10] As far as basic attitudes toward a strong defense were concerned, Gorbachev's commitment was second to none, but in contrast to Brezhnev he asked questions about the management of the armed forces and military spending. Being more acutely aware of the difficult economic situation of the country than his predecessors, Gorbachev was bound to reexamine the old consensus: Were the economic allocations for the armed forces put to the best use? Was the management of people and resources wasteful? If so, what changes and reforms could be made? This in turn led to a basic question concerning Soviet net strategic assessment: how strong was the Soviet Union in relation to her potential enemies? Similar questions had last been asked under Khrushchev and had resulted in cuts in military spending. Gorbachev seems to have taken a considerably less alarmist view of the world situation than enunciated by the military leaders, who throughout 1985 and 1986 tended to create the impression that the international tensions were explosive and that the world was hovering on the brink of a major global crisis.

The first reaction of the most senior officers toward *glasnost* and *perestroika* was one of polite neglect. Lip service was paid and the new slogans were mentioned on a few occasions, but the general impression was that the armed forces believed that the reforms concerned the civilian sector exclusively. Few if any changes in the structure and management of the armed forces were deemed necessary, and interference by civilians was certainly not welcomed. There was resentment in the army leadership over media accounts of the war in Afghanistan and the treatment of returning veterans which reflected badly on the performance of the army. No one dared to say this in so many words, but there was widespread public surprise that the mighty Soviet army, the strongest military force in the world, had been unable in seven years to inflict a decisive defeat on hordes of ill-trained and badly equipped Afghans. The army resented such insinuations, just as it complained about insufficient moral support on the part of the Soviet educational authorities and the media. Some filmmakers and writers (such as Alexander Prokhanov) had made a career out of glorifying

---

[10]Dale R. Herspring, "Gorbachev, Yazov and the Military," *Problems of Communism*, July 1987; H. H. Schröder, *Gorbachev und die Generäle*, Berichte des Bundesinstituts, 45, Cologne, 1987.

the exploits of the Soviet armed forces in Afghanistan and else-where, but most writers steered clear of the topic and the army commanders detected pacifist ("Remarquist") undertones in the writings of well-known authors such as Ales Adamovitch. The army command took a dim view of the suggestions made by leading scientists that it was counterproductive to enlist talented young science students, thus depriving the country (and, in the final anal-ysis, also national defense) of the contribution they could make during the best years of their scientific careers. There were com-plaints in the media that the sons of well-connected parents were given preferential treatment during their army service. Above all, there was widespread criticism that young recruits were mistreated during their initial basic training, not so much by the officers (who preferred to look the other way) but by the lower ranks, and, above all, by recruits during the last year of their service who had them-selves suffered the same indignities.[11]

In brief, the senior army command saw many complications emanating from *glasnost* and *perestroika;* hence the passive resist-ance which lasted by and large until the early months of 1987.

At the January 1988 plenum of the Central Committee, Gorba-chev threatened with demotion those unwilling to cooperate with the new reforms. Even earlier a reshuffle had come under way in the leadership in the Soviet high command and the Ministry of Defense. This did have a major impact on military attitudes, the more so because the new appointees were by no means always the next in rank, but senior officers known as supporters of reform. Marshal Sokolov, the defense minister, was replaced by General Dmitri Yazov, following the unscheduled landing of a Cessna 172 by a young German pilot on Red Square. In one of his speeches Yazov charged unnamed fellow officers with failing to stamp out negative tendencies in the armed forces: "We must look the truth in the eye: some of us have lost the sense of duty and responsibility for the fulfillment of our duties and tasks."[12]

Whatever the long-term results of admonitions of this kind, there certainly was a more outspoken commitment from spring

[11]There were countless articles and letters to this effect in the Soviet media during 1987 and also the publication of a widely discussed novel by Yuri Poliakov, *Sto Dnei do Prikaza,* dismissed as "untypical" by official army spokesmen but fully endorsed by others. The debate on bullying in the army continued throughout 1988.

[12]*Krasnaia Zvezda,* July 19, 1987. On *glasnost* Yazov said in one of his speeches that "plural-ism of opinions in no way runs counter to military order" (*Krasnaia Zvezda,* August 9, 1988). It may not be known for a long time to what extent these sentiments took root in army life.

1987 onward to the new reform policy in the speeches and articles by military leaders. They realized that they had been wrong belittling the resolve of the civilian leadership concerning the reform policy.

On questions of military doctrine some, though not all, Soviet military leaders moved toward a compromise with the civilian strategic thinkers, who clearly enjoyed the support of Gorbachev. Questions which had been previously unthinkable were asked in connection with the stationing of the SS-20 missiles in Eastern Europe. Alexander Bovin, a leading commentator, noted that constructing these missiles and getting them into place had obviously been quite expensive. "And if we agree to destroy them, the question arises why were they made in the first place? These questions are asked not by me alone, and one wishes there would be a competent answer."

Soviet military leaders found it more difficult to accept than the civilians that irrespective of what Clausewitz, Lenin, and others had said, thermonuclear war was no longer the continuation of policy by other means in the atomic age, that there would no longer be victors and vanquished. Some military writers continued to argue that while a great deal had changed since the nineteenth century, it was at the very least premature to give up the classical Marxist concept of just and unjust wars. Furthermore, there was always the danger of a surprise attack, a concept which had played a major role in Soviet military writing in the early 1980s.[13] The discussions seemingly proceeded on a level of abstraction but they led by necessity to eminently topical and practical questions— namely, how much to spend on defense, the character of a future war, the question of superiority in the arms race, and the need for a new Soviet military doctrine—questions not unfamiliar to West-

---

[13]Among the major contributions to the debate were A. Bovin's entry "war" in the *Filosoficheski Entsiklopedicheski Slovar,* Moscow, 1983; L. Floristov in *Kommunist,* 15, 1986; D. Proektor, *Moskovskie Novosti,* April 26, 1987; V. A. Zagladin, *Problemy Mira i Sotsialisma,* 5, 1987. These and other writers took the view that political aims could no longer be attained by nuclear war. The opposite view was taken by General Tabunov in *Kommunist Vooruzhonnikh Sil,* 13, 1987; General Serebryannikov in the same journal, 3, 1987; and General Gareev (the deputy chief of staff at the time) in a book on Frunze (1985). The civilian strategists maintained that a surprise attack in the nuclear age was most unlikely (V. Zhurkin et al. in *Kommunist,* 1, 1988) and that in a nuclear war even a successful defense was impossible (I. Velikhov, *Kommunist,* 1, 1988). For some well-known commentators, this realization was the starting point for speculations about the feasibility of a world government, with G. Shakhnazarov taking a more optimistic view than A. Bovin (*Pravda,* January 15 and February 1, 1988).

ern strategists and policymakers. There was the inclination to regard these debates as the mirror-imaging of similar discussion in the West, but this happened to be only half true.

There had been resistance to Gorbachev's apparent willingness to make concessions to Washington in the arms negotiations—for instance, with regard to the moratorium on nuclear tests.[14] Some was articulated, openly or in Aesopian language; more, it might be assumed, was never expressed in print but still deeply felt. This attitude went back to the ideas of Marshal Ogarkov, chief of staff up to 1984 (and virtually all his predecessors), that the international situation was critical, that there could be war at any moment, and that only Soviet superiority was a guarantee for successful defense and ultimate victory. However, as time went by, it appeared that war had not come, that the military consumed more and more resources, and that while superiority had been attained by the Soviet Union in some respects, it was not enough to give the country a decisive advantage.

These debates caused bitter conflicts, sharp discussions, and painful differences, as Dobrynin put it on one occasion.[15] The more radical new thinkers hinted at a new "global security system," even historical compromise (Burlatski). But these were speculations of outsiders. The mainstream strategists were preoccupied with a debate on *dostatochnost* (reasonable adequacy or sufficiency) which began in early 1987. The term was accepted by Akromeyev, the then Soviet chief of staff, and became part of official doctrine when it was included in the resolutions of the Warsaw Pact treaty organization.[16] But there was still the question of how to interpret sufficiency; the word "parity" was less frequently used. The army commanders still emphasized the growing danger of imperialist attack and "tended to exaggerate for political reasons Western advantages in certain respects."[17] Whether such civilian carping had any significant effect on those in charge of the political indoctrination of the army is doubtful. Thus A. I. Kirillov, head of the army newspaper *Za Rodinu:* "Imperialism is preparing for war. Nobody can deny it" (*Pravda,* March 16, 1987).

The more enlightened military leaders suggested that the So-

[14]See, for instance, General Chervov in *Sovetskaia Rossia,* August 23, 1986.
[15]A. Dobrynin, *Kommunist,* 9, 1986.
[16]*Sovetskaia Rossia,* February 21, 1987.
[17]L. Semeyko and others.

viet high command had every interest in the success of the reform policy, resulting in the modernization of the economy and thus, ultimately, the strengthening of the armed forces. It was therefore willing to accept sufficiency on a low level, but claimed that the Americans would probably not accept this. Some military thinkers and many civilian strategists argued that it was no longer necessary to match the Western buildup in every respect in order to ensure sufficiency, and that, on the contrary, such a response would be counterindicated ("because the Americans would like to wear us out").[18] Some civilian strategists even went so far as to claim that reasonable sufficiency should be interpreted as the ability to prevent a war and to defend the country successfully, a formula also used by Gorbachev: the ability to deter possible aggression. But it did not have to be sufficient for offensive warfare.[19]

All this was heady stuff compared to the strategic doctrine of the 1970s. Soviet foreign policy certainly became infinitely more dynamic under Gorbachev but this was in some ways a backhanded compliment, for as in *glasnost* the starting point had been so low. During the early 1980s the Soviet Union had maneuvered itself into an offside position, and the many diplomatic negotiations and state visits which accompanied *perestroika* at home were therefore bound to make a considerable impression abroad. The Soviet diplomats began to talk a different language; they were willing to discuss topics, following the lead given from above, that had been tabu before. They made jokes from time to time and they were smiling. Thus the impression was created that a breakthrough, a radical change in West-East relations, was bound to happen soon.

Were these hopes premature? Soviet diplomacy made an effort to improve relations with the United Kingdom and also with West Germany, which during the 1970s had been Moscow's favorite Western partner. But neither these activities nor the visits by Soviet leaders to Scandinavia, Spain, Latin America, and other parts of the world, nor the relative restraint shown by the Soviet media[20] brought about important immediate changes. But this, in all probability, was not even expected in the Kremlin. The purpose was to

[18]E. Primakov, "Novaia filosofia vnezhnei politiki" (The New Philosophy of Foreign Policy), *Pravda*, July 10, 1987.
[19]Gorbachev, *Izvestiia*, September 18, 1987.
[20]Side by side with the traditional anti-Western coverage in the Soviet media there was now some more objective information, and it was conceded that in some respects lessons could be learned from the West.

show the flag, demonstrating that the Soviet Union was a moderate, responsible force in world affairs, on top of being a superpower, and that it should be treated as such.

In Soviet Far Eastern policy, too, there was more continuity than change. The idea of an all-Asian forum was again mooted and in a speech in Vladivostok (July 1986), Gorbachev emphasized the Soviet Union's role as a Pacific power; but these ideas were not fundamentally different from Brezhnev's abortive scheme of a collective Far Eastern security system (June 1969). The Asian reaction in 1986 was not much more positive than it had been seventeen years earlier. There was a rapprochement with the newly independent Pacific countries and the Soviet foreign minister visited Tokyo, but there was no Soviet willingness to make concessions on territorial issues.

In talks with China the Russians made some concessions. They accepted the placement of the border between the two countries in the middle of the rivers Amur and Ussuri rather than on the Chinese side, and they promised to take certain steps concerning the three major bones of contention: Afghanistan, Cambodia, and the thinning out of troops along the 7,500-kilometer borders. Relations were normalized to a certain extent; the Chinese sent a delegation to the celebration of the seventieth anniversary of the October revolution, and trade between the two countries was increased. Gorbachev called China a "great Socialist power," and the Chinese toned down their hostile comments. But even if a satisfactory solution will be found in our time to all major outstanding questions, mutual suspicion between the two leading Communist powers was so deeply rooted that a return to the relatively close relationship which had prevailed under Stalin and Mao seemed illusory.

There was a considerable improvement in atmospherics in the Far East as well as in Europe, but no comparable substantive progress. Since the Soviet leaders had few illusions in the first place, the absence of dramatic breakthroughs should not be regarded as a failure. They knew from experience that there are conflicts as well as common interests in the relationship between the major foreign countries, and a sudden, radical *renversement des alliances* is therefore ruled out. Certain basic aims are pursued with persistence and flexibility by Soviet policymakers, such as the attempt to prevent the emergence of a coalition of potential enemies. Determined efforts were made to withdraw Soviet forces from Afghanistan. And yet the conduct of foreign affairs changed less, as far as substance was concerned, than policies in other fields. But this was only to be expected: even if Gorbachev and his colleagues were interested in a profound reorientation of Soviet policy, they would not have been able to pursue this aim while most of their attention and efforts had to be concentrated by necessity on domestic affairs. The priority of domestic over foreign policy was clear and undisputed: the last thing the secretary general wanted was to open a "second front" while the struggle on the home front was only just beginning.

The Soviet Foreign Ministry went through ritual motions invoking *glasnost* and *perestroika*. The publication of a house organ *(Vestnik)*, originally put out in 1918 but long discontinued, was renewed, and Shevardnadze made a speech in which he called for internal reforms. He gave an example of the kind of reforms he had in mind: It had come to his knowledge that for many years a great expert on some specific issue which was of great importance to the country (even under *glasnost* the minister would not be more specific) had worked in the ministry. Yet because this had been a very modest man who had never blown his own trumpet, no use had been made of his talents. And now the man was about to retire from the service. What a waste of talent![21]

It was a sad story, but then it could have happened almost anywhere in the world; it was a demonstration of humaneness and consideration on the part of the Soviet foreign minister. It was also a good illustration of how he interpreted *glasnost* and *perestroika*. Yet modest as Shevardnadze's reforms were, they encountered considerable resistance on the part of officials in the ministry. For in the same speech he made it known that many comrades, both former and present employees of the ministry, were offended by the policy of openness and *glasnost* and thought it detrimental to the authority of the foreign ministry. He, needless to say, did not share such views. As he saw it, the true party spirit in the new period demanded not only creative Marxism-Leninism and professional competence, but also the insistence on one's views against critics inside and outside the ministry—this rather than keeping a low profile, as had happened so often in the past.

True, there were certain indications of a more self-critical atti-

[21]The speech was originally published in *Vestnik Ministerstva Inostrannikh Del*, 1, 1987; it is quoted here from *Argumenty i Fakty*, 36, 1987.

tude in Soviet foreign political thought as time passed by. The last section (dealing with foreign policy) of the official working paper prepared for the extraordinary party conference in June 1988 exposed mistakes, at least in general terms, which had not been admitted in the past. Gromyko, for many years foreign minister; Arbatov, an influential figure under Brezhnev; and other "Mr. Nyets" came under attack, directly or by implication. Some errors were admitted by highly placed officials in a press conference in June 1988 and by a historian, Vladislav Dashichev, who pointed out on the basis of specific instances that it was ridiculous to argue that Soviet foreign policy had been infallible in the past.[22] Dashichev argued that the Munich policy of the Western powers on the eve of World War II was not only motivated by anti-Communism (as always argued by Moscow in the past) but also by the assumption that, having decapitated the Red Army command, Stalin was no longer a reliable ally. Nor was the West entirely to blame if it felt alarmed by Stalin's export of the Soviet system (in the "Blanquist-Trotskyite fashion") after the war and if the Western leaders failed to give credence to the slogans about the ardent attachment of the Soviet Union to the cause of peace. Dashichev noted that there had not been clear ideas in the 1960s and 1970s about the true national interests of the Soviet Union and that, as a result, wider interests were sacrificed in the pursuit of marginal, ephemeral gains in Third World countries.

However, admissions of this kind by individual authors or even by official spokesmen were still a long way from a fundamental change in Soviet foreign policy. Such rethinking was bound at best to be slow and unlikely to go beyond certain limits. Even Dashichev had made it clear that he by no means advocated "socialist isolationism." The most far-reaching authoritative statement of the New Thinking in foreign policy was made, as befitting protocol, by the foreign minister himself after the nineteenth party conference. Shevardnadze sharply condemned "traditional thinking," for which he gave more than one example and stated flatly that the doctrine which equated international relations with the class struggle could not be reconciled with the inevitability of peaceful coexistence. He stressed that the lessons of the Second World War had not been rethought with sufficient clarity in the light of recent experience: War could no longer be a rational means of policy and

[22]*Literaturnaia Gazetta,* May 18, 1988.

national security was not guaranteed by the quantity of the military arsenal. Shevardnadze mentioned that great damage had been done to Soviet reputation and the image of the nation as the result of building up a giant stockpile of (chemical) weapons "that can only be described as the most barbarian." He also criticized the fourteen lost years at the Vienna talks on reducing conventional weapons even though he put much on the blame for this failure on the West.[23] These and other expressions of self-criticism obviously constituted a new departure in Soviet foreign policy thought. But they did not necessarily lead immediately to momentous changes in Soviet foreign policy-making; progress was slow even on relatively minor issues such as on Berlin or Austrian cooperation with the European Community.

Glasnost in the West

Glasnost was welcomed with enthusiasm in the West. True, at first there was some reticence because the media had welcomed with excessive expectations the election of Andropov, and there had even been many good words for the good sense and the level-headedness of Chernenko. In view of the disappointment that followed, some caution seemed called for. But after one year of Gorbachev's rule there were first comments about a new style of Soviet leadership. Real enthusiasm was building up in 1987: a sea change had taken place; the cold war was finally over. One of the great turning points in the history of the Soviet Union had been reached with the coming of the Gorbachev revolution.

There were, as always, differences and nuances: enthusiasm was considerably greater in the United States and West Germany than in France or Italy, and even in America and West Germany there were discordant voices. Few economists shared the optimism of the mass media about Gorbachev's prospects. Liberal political observers such as Theodore Draper (writing in *Dissent*) warned against exaggerated hopes; Draper was seconded by Martin Walker, a British newspaper correspondent stationed in Moscow, who had been one of the most sanguine Western commentators at the scene. After a lecture tour in the United States, Walker ex-

[23]An abridged version was published in *Vestnik*, 15, 1988. The speech was made on July 25, 1988 but published only two months later. It was criticized by Ligachev, who emphasized that "our friends abroad" would be confused if Soviet foreign policy deviated from its traditional "class orientation." But then Ligachev suffered a setback in the struggle for power, Gromyko resigned, and the Shevardnadze speech became official policy.

pressed surprise about the readiness of the American Sovietologists to agree and even go beyond his guesses about the future course of the Gorbachev reforms. He was not entirely pleased: "The capacity of the American media to conjure up an instant myth, to glamorize the mundane and sanctify the profane, should never be underestimated." He expressed the fear that the American pendulum, at present in a state of euphoria, might swing back "from confidence to despair, from faith to rejection with great speed." A year later, upon leaving Moscow, Mr. Walker was even more emphatic: "I seem to have spent the first three [years in Moscow] grabbing the *Guardian*'s long-suffering readers by the lapels and insisting that things were really changing here in a dramatic and wondrous way. And I have spent the last year pleading to the pendulum swing of public opinion to hang on a bit, because they are not changing as much as all that. *Perestroika* chic in the West has got quite out of hand. This remains the Soviet Union, a place where *glasnost* gets suspended at the state's convenience."[24]

How to explain the cordial welcome extended to Gorbachev and his new course well beyond circles in the West normally sympathetic to Soviet policies? There were some obvious reasons. The style and the political program enunciated by Gorbachev were, of course, a tremendous step forward in comparison with the Brezhnev era, not to mention earlier chapters in Soviet history. A lasting turn for the better in Soviet policies had been expected and predicted many times: after the Soviet Union had entered the war in 1941, after the victory over the Axis powers, after Stalin's death in 1953, and on several subsequent occasions, for the last time following the election of Andropov. On all these occasions such hopes had been premature. But there was still a great reservoir of goodwill toward the Soviet Union; surely sooner or later the Soviet Union would turn into a European-style democracy.[25]

The implications of such a historical turning point were obvious: a safer world in which nuclear war would no longer be a possibility; enormous savings in arms spending; a world more prosperous and free of fear. The potential rewards of the democratization and liberalization of the Soviet Union were truly staggering, and it was therefore not surprising that the Western media with their innate tendency to exaggerate would fasten on hopes

[24]*Guardian*, September 30, 1987; *ibid.*, July 12, 1988.
[25]Edson W. Spencer, chairman of Honeywell, *International Herald Tribune*, February 2, 1988.

and possibilities and turn them into facts and certainties. Lastly, the trend toward personalization of political issues, always pronounced in the Western media, found in Gorbachev an excellent candidate, a "star," as *Der Spiegel* correctly noted as early as 1985, a "man of the year" in terms of the U.S. newsmagazines. Here, at long last, was a Soviet leader with whom Western reporters could identify: presentable, with an attractive wife, quick-witted, with a sense of humor, competent, a reasonable man and a man of peace, a leader with the common touch, an excellent communicator. It was not surprising that the popularity rating of such a new-style leader was very high in most Western countries, higher sometimes than that of their own leaders.

Ex-President Carter called Gorbachev the "most humanitarian of the world's leaders"; other media figures were similarly swept off their feet by so much charisma, as if they were confronting royalty. As one of them described the scene: ". . . there was a murmur of excitement and the Gorbachevs were entering the room, and it was as if royalty had appeared in our midst, or media celebrities whose actual faces—youthful, high-colored and smiling, assured—were considerably more attractive than their reproductions. In newspaper photographs, Gorbachev has looked jowly, heavy-set, and stolid; in person, he fairly radiates energy and vigor, the warmth of a naturally charismatic leader who knows his worth and delights in its reflection in other eyes."[26]

To a considerable extent such reactions were due to the real charm exuded by Mr. Gorbachev and his wife; neither Ligachev in Paris, nor Ryzhkov in Stockholm and Oslo, nor Shevardnadze in Latin America, nor any other Soviet leader, provoked similar ecstatic reactions.

The impression made by the leader by necessity affected the appraisal of his policy. Mr. Gorbachev was obviously a nice and decent man and had to be given credit. Why were some Western leaders so cool? Critics argued that Gorbachev had undertaken the most far-reaching revamping of the Soviet system in over half a century, that new opportunities existed because, on many issues, the Soviet Union was moving toward long-standing Western preferences.[27] But instead of coming to terms with these changes the

[26]Joyce Carol Oates, *New York Times*, January 3, 1988.
[27]Joseph Nye, Jr., and Edwin Mroz, *Washington Post*, October 4, 1987. The choice of "revamping" was unfortunate; it is defined by the dictionaries as "patching up from odds and ends."

West had generally adopted a wait-and-see attitude to the reform. Other commentators stressed the significance of the reforms in similar terms and warned against an unduly skeptical response which could retard the Soviet Union's further adaptation.[28] Such criticism seemed a little unfair, be it only because no Soviet leader had ever gotten such world acclaim; Gorbachev had become the symbol of Western hope for change in the Soviet Union. "If Henry Kissinger and a few senators warned that if Gorbachev succeeded, the democracies would become less secure," these were, as the *Washington Post* noted, "small voices amid the clamor."[29]

If, with all the goodwill and sympathy, there was a wait-and-see attitude in the West, the same was true, according to all accounts, with regard to the Soviet public;[30] Soviet citizens had heard too often the clarion call for reform. Western leaders from Mrs. Thatcher (who called him "a man of courage" in November 1987) to Dennis Healey, from German Social Democrats to Franz Joseph Strauss, the conservative leader, said all the right things about Gorbachev. If they had embraced him even more closely, this could well have been the kiss of death. Nor could Western economic leaders be fairly reproached for not showing goodwill. American bankers were willing to lend money at a lower rate to the Soviet Union than, for instance, to Brazil.

President Reagan had set the mood a few days before Gorbachev's arrival in December 1987, certifying on national television that Gorbachev (a) had given up the Communist idea of world domination, (b) was committed to total nuclear disarmament, and (c) was not responsible for the war in Afghanistan.[31] What more could be expected from the man who had coined the phrase "evil empire"?

Of the most prominent mouthpieces of Western capitalism, the *Financial Times,* gave Gorbachev's book, *Perestroika,* a rave review. George Kennan was also sanguine: "Gorbachev has mounted the most strenuous effort seen to date to change some of the conditions and the policies to which people here [in the U.S.] have so

[28]Robert Legvold, *Times* (London), November 18, 1987.
[29]*Washington Post,* November 30, 1987.
[30]According to an international Gallup poll carried out in December 1987, 22 percent of the Russians thought that 1988 would be better than 1987, 49 percent expected much the same, and 15 percent thought it would be worse. The respective figures for the U.S. were 56, 8, and 25 (*Daily Telegraph,* December 31, 1987).
[31]Charles Krauthammer, "The Week Washington Lost Its Head," *New Republic,* January 4, 1988.

negatively reacted. . . . The prospects on the Soviet side for a significant improvement of Soviet-American relations will continue to be greater, so long as Gorbachev's preeminence endures, than they have been at any time since the revolution."[32] The *New York Times* called it the "publishing event of the year"; only the *Wall Street Journal* was negative.[33] In West Germany, a country not known for excessive advances to authors, a publishing house paid an unprecedented DM 1.5 million for *Perestroika,* and within a few days it appeared that the publishers had not taken an unreasonable risk, for the magazine *Der Spiegel* paid DM 1.2 million for subsidiary rights for serialization, and the book remained for many months on the best-seller list.

Even among the Russian emigration in the West counsels were divided. In some émigré journals *glasnost* and *perestroika* were put in quotation marks, and Bukovski wrote that Gorbachev was a new Stalinist in power. Early on during the *glasnost* campaign, ten prominent Soviet émigrés had called on Gorbachev to give some tangible proof that basic changes had indeed taken place. They had emigrated not as the result of some tragic misunderstanding but because of profound differences with a regime unwilling to respect artistic freedom of expression. Would there be no such controls in the future?

Their letter, together with a long reply, was published in *Moscow News,* much to everyone's surprise. It was less surprising that the editor was upbraided for a decision considered politically mistaken by the authorities. But he was not deposed and this, too, was progress in the direction of *glasnost.*

Another émigré writer published an article entitled *"Glasnost: a Battle Half Won."* Boris Vail, who had been active in the human rights campaign, warned his fellow émigrés against "pure negativism": "In our maximalist demands of Gorbachev we bring to mind our opponents: Is it not pure Bolshevism to demand of Gorbachev that he should down the KGB tomorrow and introduce a multiparty system?"[34] Some recent arrivals from the Soviet Union such as Sharanski took a far more skeptical view, expressing fears that

[32]*New York Review of Books,* January 31, 1988.
[33]Archie Brown, *Financial Times,* November 26, 1987. See also Richard Pipes, *Wall Street Journal,* December 2, 1987: "a patchwork of clichés, half-truths and nontruths typical of vintage Soviet propaganda. The book aims at a very low level, one that Soviet experts must have decided represents the common Western denominator of ignorance and wishful thinking."
[34]*Times* (London), July 1, 1987.

the West would be seduced by *glasnost:* it was difficult for Western politicians and journalists to resist the charm of Gorbachev's Western-style politics. Gorbachev was a hope; he did present new opportunities, but only if he was seen as what he really was, and this was psychologically very difficult for Westerners. But other recent immigrants applied for a Soviet visa, and most have received permission to revisit their old homeland.

The Trotskyites, too, could not agree on the meaning of events in the Soviet Union. The "International Committee of the Fourth International" declared that Gorbachev was an inveterate foe of the working class, and accused him of lack of sympathy and support for the revolutionary movement outside Russia, as well as cowardice; how could he have signed the arms control agreement with Washington? But Ernest Mandel, the veteran Trotskyite ideologist, welcomed Gorbachev as the "representative of the most enlightened wing of the bureaucracy," and others, such as Healy and Banda (of the "Workers Revolutionary Party"), went even further and adopted a view hardly distinguishable from the Communists: this was no capitalist restoration in the U.S.S.R.; on the contrary it was a movement of great social and political significance.[35]

The non-Trotskyite extreme left also took a positive view of Gorbachev's reform movement. They were encouraged by reports written by Boris Kagarlitsky and a few other left-wing dissidents from Moscow and Leningrad, published in British journals such as *New Left Review* and the U.S.'s *In These Times.* According to these sources, all over the Soviet Union young people were streaming into socialist clubs, less interested in human rights than the dissidents of the 1970s and mainly preoccupied with a return to "positive Marxism." As one of them wrote, the big news out of the Soviet Union these days was of a grass-roots leftist revival taking place reminiscent of the sixties radicalization in the West. This, to put it mildly, was a case of gross exaggeration: a few young intellectuals had become interested in Marcuse and Gramsci, even in Bakunin, twenty years after the fashion had reached the West, and some of them had been arrested for a while in the early 1980s.

There is some reason to believe that the manifesto signed "Movement for Socialist Renewal" and dated Leningrad, 21 November 1985, which created a stir in some Western media, also

[35]See "Was geht in der Sowjet Union vor sich? Gorbachev und die Krise des Stalinismus," n.p., n.d., *Inprekorr,* April 1987, for Mandel's views.

emanated from these circles.[36] The manifesto called for systematic change and made a number of sensible suggestions. But it was not at all clear whom it represented—five, fifteen, or perhaps even fifty people—and whether they were, in fact, members of the party. By early 1988 Kagarlitsky conceded that there was not much interest in their ideas: on the one hand neo-Stalinism had become much more popular, and on the other the Soviet radical liberals were mainly "culture orientated" and left the economic spheres to the conservatives.[37]

Thus, by and large, most Western observers detected in the Soviet Union what they wanted to discover, not surprisingly perhaps, because in a confusing situation there was all kinds of contradictory evidence, something for almost everybody. It was not at all easy to choose among this welter of conflicting accounts the ones most close to Soviet realities rather than to Western wishes.

No mention has been made so far of the two groups most vitally interested in events in the Soviet Union, the Soviet experts in the West and the leaders of other Communist countries. Few Sovietologists could claim to have foreseen *perestroika* and even fewer *glasnost,* except perhaps the Panglosses who had always argued that the general situation in the Soviet Union was satisfactory and that a startling improvement was just around the corner. They made the old English proverb true: he that shooteth oft, at last shall hit the mark. Thus for more than a year after Gorbachev's election most observers of the Soviet scene, in Moscow and abroad, did not perceive dramatic changes, and it is difficult to blame them even in retrospect since there were no dramatic changes to report. True, it was not quite "Brezhnevism without Brezhnev," as some argued, but it certainly was not a mighty reform movement either: Gorbachev and his supporters were only slowly getting their act together; there was considerable resistance

[36]It was originally published in the *Guardian,* July 22, 1986, and was subsequently discussed as a document of great significance in other periodicals and books. See also Robert C. Tucker, *Political Culture and Leadership in Soviet Russia,* New York, 1987, pp. 199–202.

[37]Interview with Alexander Cockburn, *New Statesman,* January 29, 1988. In another review of the Soviet New Left in a Western newspaper (March 1988), it was said that the movement counted some 1,500 members. Kagarlitsky was again quoted: "The older people are fixed on the problem of Stalin, almost obsessed by it. The younger people feel it less. I'm also interested in things like the Third World."

in the Politburo, and it is not at all certain that Gorbachev himself knew at the time what his next steps would be.[38]

Thus during 1985 and much of 1986 the Sovietologists were cautious, and rightly so. But as *glasnost* became official policy and was pursued with much greater emphasis, growing excitement spread in their ranks. Some thought that events of momentous consequences were taking place in the Soviet Union, a true revolution, a return to an inner-party democracy that had not existed for six decades or more, the initiation of profound economic and social changes which could well lead beyond the system, a new spirit of honesty, a flowering of culture—in short, a dismantling, after many false starts, of the Stalinist system. They drew encouragement from the rehabilitation of Bukharin and other old Bolsheviks, from the airing of social ills which would have been utterly impossible even a few years earlier. True, there were differences about where it would all lead: to pristine Leninism and a political NEP, or perhaps even beyond, to democratic socialism. But there was the growing belief that democratization was irreversible, even if there might be temporary setbacks.

As Professor Moshe Lewin noted, the Soviet Union had profoundly changed in recent decades as the result of urbanization. Stalin had been the product of the Russian village, but most citizens now lived in towns and were well-educated. The new Soviet leadership had the political will, the courage, and the intellectual wherewithal to carry out the long-overdue reform; there was enormous pent-up social energy and creativity within the party which only had to be released. There were no insurmountable barriers to change and thus "one of the most remarkable stories of our time

[38]I wrote in late 1982 that if Andropov did not take the necessary steps (of economic reform), the generation of younger leaders succeeding him would: "These reforms will be palliatives, unlikely to affect the deeper sources of the evil. But they may suffice to get through yet another decade.... What Marx wrote in 1852 about the 'enormous French state bureaucracy' enmeshing the body of French society like a net 'choking all pores and stifling all innovation' is equally true of Soviet society today. The 'enormous French bureaucracy' counted half a million people at the time whereas in the Soviet Union their number is fifty times larger. ... They may tolerate a revolution from above but only if it does not harm its interests. And yet Soviet society simply cannot be streamlined without making many of these bureaucrats redundant. This is the dilemma facing Andropov and those who will come after him" ("What We Know About the Soviet Union," *Commentary*, February 1983; reprinted in *America, Europe and the Soviet Union*, New Brunswick, 1983). This was correct as far as it went, but I underrated the depth of the social crisis; and even if I stressed the need for reforms within the system, I did not anticipate *glasnost* within a period of three or four years.

is now unfolding."[39] The conservative forces had had their chance and failed. Reform would lead to a democratized one-party system—that is to say, a new authoritarianism *(à la Russe)*. But this was no reason to despair, for after all, "most regimes in history have been authoritarian."

Some Sovietologists counseled greater prudence so as not to oversell *glasnost* and *perestroika* as détente had been oversold in the 1970s, just to give way to bitter disappointment when the high hopes were not fulfilled.

There was a marked change in Soviet attitudes toward Western Soviet experts. In the past "Sovietology" had been a negative term second only to "fascism" and Trotskyism, and there had been a whole industry producing books and articles refuting the hostile and mendacious writings of all Western Sovietologists. In 1987 relatively objective accounts began to appear in the Soviet media about meetings of Soviet experts at Harvard and Berkeley, in London and Cologne, sometimes a trifle condescending and ironical, but not remotely as hostile as in the past. Some selected few were interviewed and published in the Soviet press.[40]

It ought to be recalled once again that our preoccupation is with *glasnost* rather than other aspects of the Soviet experience. It should also be remembered that according to some Western Sovietologists something akin to *glasnost* had existed even under Brezhnev, though the term had not yet gained currency. Thus, according to an influential textbook of the 1970s, it was perfectly possible to appeal for basic change in the political regime, vigorous debates were taking place in virtually every policy area, and the network of institutions to which a citizen could complain or appeal was extremely large ("larger than in Western countries"). There was no more secrecy in Russia than in Western democracies; "the principle of secrecy is that of cabinet secrecy typical

[39]M. Lewin, *The Gorbachev Phenomenon*, Berkeley, 1988, p. 153. Similar arguments had been propounded after Stalin's death by Isaac Deutscher. But if the predictions had been overoptimistic in 1953, the advocates of this theory could argue that it did not necessarily follow that this was still so in 1988. Meanwhile, Deutscher came under attack in the Soviet media with a delay of thirty-five years for having taken too sanguine a line in his well-known Stalin biography (*Pravda*, April 5, 1988). Lewin, in contrast to Deutscher, was preoccupied with the civil society concept, which had gained some currency in the United States: "Civil society is talking, gossipping, demanding, sulking, expressing its interests in many ways and thereby creating moods, ideologies and public opinion." A similar concept had been invoked in the essays of the Soviet publicist Fyodor Burlatski.

[40]G. Gerassimov, "Perestroika v. Sovietologii," *Sovetskaia Kultura*, October 13, 1987.

for a parliamentary system," though carried to an extreme.[41]

If this had been correct, there would have been no need for Gorbachev to introduce the age of *glasnost*. Quite a few Western Sovietologists had accepted both the official data and the assertions of the Brezhnev regime and consequently found themselves in the uncomfortable position of being disavowed by the new leadership in Moscow. They had taken too benign a view, whether their subject was the history of the Soviet Union (in particular collectivization and the purges, but also the war and the postwar period) or contemporary political and social problems. As Professor Severyn Bialer put it, "This [new data] goes beyond what even the most conservative critics have said about the Soviet system."[42] As another expert put it, *perestroika* was needed not only in the Soviet Union but also in the field of Soviet studies. To give a typical, by no means extreme example: some Western students of the Soviet legal system had argued that while the Stalinist terror had been a perversion of justice, it left a smaller mark on the administration of justice than commonly assumed. It sounded quite plausible but Soviet sources who should know revealed that, on the contrary, Vishinski's "legal" principles (such as the presumption of guilt rather than innocence) have had a lasting impact on the Soviet legal system to this very day.[43]

According to some Western studies the impact of the great purge of the 1930s had been greatly exaggerated: while it had affected the upper and middle echelons of the party, for much of the population life went on more or less as usual. Now under *glasnost* it became known that life did not go on as usual, that there was a climate of general fear, that, in fact, more people had disappeared, temporarily or forever, than had been commonly assumed. It would be pointless to single out individual Western studies for criticism for the simple reason that the phenomenon was quite widespread. In the light of *glasnost* a considerable part of the Western literature on Soviet society and politics in the 1960s and 1970s

[41]J. Hough, *How the Soviet Union Is Governed*, Cambridge, 1979, pp. 292, 316.

[42]*Insight*, December 28, 1987. Dunlop and Rowen voiced similar criticism with regard to the performance of Western students of the Soviet economy: The Soviet rate of growth was, it appeared, below the assessments of almost all Western scholars. "For years, many Western specialists discounted the émigré testimony, but the new evidence from Soviet authors supports it" (*The National Interest*, Spring 1988).

[43]Peter H. Salomon, Jr., "Soviet Criminal Justice and the Great Terror," *Slavic Studies*, Fall–Winter 1987; Arkadi Waksberg, *Literaturnaia Gazetta*, January 27, 1988.

(but also some of the historical work done during this period) appeared one-sided and misleading, having conveyed a picture more in line with Soviet official pronouncements than with Soviet reality. Some authors may have been genuinely misled, while others may have been too eager to accept sources which happened to confirm their predilections. Since it is not part of human nature to admit error and surrender positions gladly, there was no rush to analyze the mistakes of the past. The syndrome is known from other fields of learning and while it ought to be noted in passing, any further discussion would be outside the parameters of our investigation into *glasnost.*

It could be argued that the very emergence of *glasnost* was living proof that the Soviet regime was not totalitarian, that freedom was not dead in Russia (as some had claimed), that democracy had survived or was revived. But the record of Sovietology as far as predicting *glasnost* and *perestroika* was concerned was still not impressive. "Most of us were taken completely by surprise," according to Professor Stephen Cohen. "After Brezhnev we expected a muddling-through, conservative regime or a very narrow technocratic leadership. The field didn't do very well. . . ."[44] Since Sovietology is not a science, it is *a priori* unable to predict; such self-criticism is therefore a little too harsh. If there had been a failure, it was not one of prediction but of accepting without due critical analysis official announcements and figures which simply had been untrue. True, Gorbachev had figured before 1985 in some Kremlinological studies as one out of several possible successors; but the predictions were hedged with many "ifs" and "buts," and his policy views were said to be "largely unknown."[45]

In view of this unconvincing record some critics from outside the field called for the abolition of Kremlinology (if not the whole field of Soviet studies), arguing that the Soviet Union was an enigma wrapped inside a mystery, one of those countries about which no one could possibly know anything. Or, alternatively, they said that since everything in the age of *glasnost* was aired in the Soviet media, there was no need for arcane approaches which might (or might not) have had their uses in a previous period. Such criticism usually served as the introduction to the authors' own

[44]*Insight,* loc. cit.
[45]In an article on Soviet succession (*Problems of Communism,* September 1982) Professor Hough correctly applied the principle of *chefstvo* (patronage) to Gorbachev who, he said, "had a most striking range of connections."

views, often splenetic, about Soviet affairs; for if there were no true experts on the subject, it clearly followed that everyone had the right to serve as his (or her) own Sovietologist.

Not having spotted the advent of *glasnost* immediately, there was an inclination afterwards, particularly in the United States and West Germany, to draw premature conclusions. Some West German authors announced that *glasnost* had already won (which few Soviet commentators would have claimed), or they at least predicted that the struggle could not end in compromise but in the victory of one party or the other. They found fault with those of their colleagues who were a little more cautious in their assessment and accused them of overrating the power of the enemies of *glasnost*. [46]

French and Italian observers, on the other hand, including Italian Communists, noted developments in Moscow with great interest and sympathy but still were markedly more skeptical. Thus G. Chiesa, the Moscow correspondent of *Unità*, noted in a roundtable conference that he saw enormous obstacles facing Mr. Gorbachev and that, in any case, his perspectives and those of his colleagues in the Politburo were not quite identical.[47] Some British commentators, writing from both London and Moscow, shared the general enthusiasm about the progress of *glasnost* but also commented about the setbacks suffered and the limits still put to *glasnost*. Thus, to give but one example, upon attending the press conference in which it was announced that Bukharin had been rehabilitated, a British correspondent reflected:

I could not help feeling how tiny a beginning it is, this little sudden sparkle of truth peering through half a century of lies and how well-nigh impossible it is for Gorbachev to come clean about the entire past without mocking the entire system it has produced. . . . listening, as Gerassimov spoke, to the extraordinary phraseology we have come to expect from party officials, one felt something eerie. The terror may be gone but the

[46]For instance, Christian Schmidt-Haeuer, "Gorbatschews zweite Revolution," in Uwe Engelbrecht, *Glasnost—Neue Offenheit*, Cologne, 1987; Klaus von Beyme, in Margarete Mommsen and Hans-Henning Schröder, eds., *Gorbatschows Revolution von oben*, Berlin 1987, pp. 136 et seq. Boris Meissner (*Die Sowjetunion im Umbruch*, Stuttgart, 1988) takes a more skeptical view with regard to the prospects of *perestroika* but believes that the quest for more freedom in the Soviet Union will continue even if the reforms will not have the desired effect.

[47]*Literaturnaia Gazetta*, July 29, 1987. Simplifying somewhat the essence of Gorbachevism, Michel Tatu wrote of *glasnost* that "it was a new policy in the field of information and culture, but so far not much more than this" (M. Tatu, *Gorbachev*, Paris, 1987, p. 139).

dead language, the deeply ingrained custom of official circumlocution, the systematic omissions, selective truths and gaping half truths, the very existence of the same elaborate apparatus or party and party-controlled media to dispense the latest line, still parade themselves at press conferences. . . . This wondrous jargon moulds the consciousness of ordinary people. Hardly ever have I heard a Russian talk of Stalinist mass murder. They say "repressions." "Times were hard," they say, or, most common of all, "they were very complicated."[48]

One group who showed a large measure of consensus were the experts on the Soviet economy. Few denied that there might be some improvement in productivity growth (the "new-broom effect"), but virtually no one in the profession expected a breakthrough: "Gorbachev's modernization drive relies too much on pressure from above and over-taut plans to be conducive to a genuine transformation of the Soviet industrial scene."[49]

Lastly there were those who maintained that *glasnost* was a bluff, or, to put it more elegantly, mainly propaganda intended to make a favorable impression abroad and thus "disinformation." One of the pillars of this argument maintained that the discrepancy between words and deeds had never been as wide as in the age of *glasnost.* In reality it meant quicker rotation of cadres, informing on each other, and a breathing space for the intelligentsia, but stricter discipline for ordinary people.[50] Such extremely negative comment was hardly tenable in the light of factual evidence. Even if it should subsequently appear that *glasnost* was only a passing phenomenon and not irreversible, it was not a "fraud" and the revelations were not confined to *Moscow News.* It was still true that freer speech prevailed than at any time since 1927, and that open, or semi-open, debates were not the same as "informing on each other." Even if one regarded *glasnost* as a very unsatisfactory and incomplete step in the direction of greater freedom, it was certainly not a step backward.

And what of the reaction of other Communist regimes in Eastern Europe and elsewhere? Rumania and Cuba emphatically dissociated themselves from the reform movement from the beginning. Elsewhere, there was support for *perestroika* even though East Germany and Czechoslovakia were slow in giving due publicity to

[48]Xan Smiley, *Daily Telegraph,* February 8, 1988.
[49]See Philip Hanson, in *Gorbachev's Economic Plan,* Vol. 1, Joint Economic Committee, Congress of the United States, Washington, D.C., 1987, p. 366, and many other sources.
[50]For an exposition of this school, see A. Besancon in *National Interest,* summer 1987.

Gorbachev's more daring speeches. Poland and Hungary had carried out their own reforms well before 1986, the former out of necessity, the latter out of choice, and they welcomed the new initiatives emanating out of Moscow as a confirmation of the correct attitude they had taken. After some initial hesitation Bulgaria became an ardent champion of economic reform, so much so that in late 1987 Mr. Zhivkov had to be admonished by his Soviet friends to be less ambitious and more cautious; no one had suggested that the party should give up overall control over the economy.

Reform was clearly of no interest to North Korea; as for China it has gone through its own *glasnost* and *perestroika* different in many respects from the Soviet experience, on which more will have to be said later on. As time passed, and as a successor to Husak was appointed, the Czechs became somewhat more forthcoming. The East Germans on the other hand were unrepentant; they could claim that of all the East European economies theirs was in the best shape, and that this was the result of strict centralization—the concentration of all industrial enterprises in 150 large combines. Why change something that was functioning reasonably well, at least by East European standards? In actual fact the idea of East Germany as an economic powerhouse was largely a myth. Its growth was no more than modest, its trade with the West had steadily fallen, and in comparison with West Germany it was further behind than it had been twenty years ago.[51] But unlike Poland it had never faced bankruptcy.

As Kurt Hager, the Politburo member in charge of ideology, put it: if your neighbor is putting up new wallpaper in his apartment, does it mean that you have to do the same? This comparison must have irked the reform party in Moscow, but they had more urgent tasks to do than engaging in polemics with their East Berlin comrades.

All this concerned *perestroika;* for greater *glasnost* there was no enthusiasm in Eastern Europe outside Poland and Hungary. There was, on the contrary, widespread fear that its spread might destabilize the loyal regimes. The small, local dissident groups, in East Germany and elsewhere, drew encouragement from Gorbachev's new course and even invoked his authority. The East German leadership did not hesitate; if Gorbachev had released politi-

[51]*Economist,* February 20, 1988.

cal prisoners and permitted Sakharov to return from Gorky, Ho-
necker, on the contrary, ordered the carrying out of mass arrests,
and dozens of pacifists and church activists were deported to West
Germany. The Czech government, too, was embarrassed when
there was some soul-searching in Moscow, even if not in public,
as to whether the military invasion of 1968, which liquidated
the "Prague spring," had really been well-advised. It was immediately argued in Prague that the situation in Czechoslovakia had
been completely different at the time. The Czech reform movement ("Communism with a human face"), in contrast to the Soviet, had been engineered by the forces of reaction, domestic and
foreign . . .

Circumstances were indeed different. Historically, Russian
Communism had been homegrown whereas in Eastern Europe it
had been imported by the Red Army during and after the Second
World War. If there was some degree of national identification
with Communism in Russia, there was little or none in Eastern
Europe. There was latent nationalist resentment; the dissidents
were few perhaps in number but potentially they had great popular
support. Given a little finger they would take the whole hand—and
more. Even in a relatively stable Communist regime such as East
Germany, the pull of centrifugal forces remained strong. A reasonably high standard of living with lots of entertainment in the form
of Western television and achievements in athletics and swimming
had not made that much difference.

In the final analysis, domestic peace rested on the demobiliza-
tion of the masses, and *glasnost* and democratization would have
the opposite effect, infusing a great deal of uncertainty and in-
security. Hence, it was not surprising that a film like Abuladze's
Repentance should be bitterly condemned in the D.D.R. and ignored in most other East European countries. It was said to be
"historically incorrect," "nihilistic," "inhumane." It undermined
the unity of the party and the masses; it supplied grist to the mills
of the anti-Communist forces.[52]

Intellectuals in Eastern Europe were excited about the new
cultural freedom in the Soviet Union, but they were told that the
Soviet example, for once, was not to be emulated. Hungary and
Poland had about as much of *glasnost* as the party thought it could

[52]*Neues Deutschland,* October 30, 1987; *Junge Welt,* October 28, 1987. In November 1988 the
East German authorities banned the Soviet journal *Sputnik* and several anti-Stalin films of
Russian origin.

politically afford. In any case, they had practiced *glasnost* well before Gorbachev. As for the rest, it was considered an alien and disruptive element.

Thus the Eastern European political landscape showed some variety, with the majority opting for pragmatic changes in the economy but opposing political reform and *glasnost.* Such diversity could be interpreted as an encouraging sign; at least there was no longer the obligatory, monolithic "consensus" of Stalin's days. But the monolith had been breaking up ever since Tito's excommunication and the drifting away of Rumania and Albania.

Perestroika did cause discord in Eastern Europe: If the Soviet Union aimed at greater integration with her East European allies, how could this be achieved unless these countries accepted a reform policy, broadly speaking on Soviet lines? And was some common ideological basis beyond the old clichés not an imperative for the years ahead? There were no easy answers to these questions, but seen in a wider perspective economic reorganization seemed more acceptable in Eastern Europe than cultural freedom and political reform—that is to say, *glasnost* and democratization.

CHAPTER 11

The Limits of *Glasnost*

THE REVELATIONS of the *glasnost* era had a staggering
effect, but not because the truth about the Soviet past and
present had been totally unknown in Russia and abroad;
the great innovation was the fact that it was now possible
to talk and write openly about what had been tabu only yesterday.
Glasnost caused a state of euphoria, but more among people outside Russia, for Soviet citizens had learned from bitter experience
that what had been given by the state could be taken away at almost
any time. Few in the Soviet Union dared openly to oppose *glasnost;*
everyone paid lip service to it. But there was little enthusiasm for
glasnost among the political bosses and there is no denying that for
them it had been much easier to run the country under the old
system. Nor was *glasnost* as yet deeply rooted among wide sections
of the population.

At the same time the mistaken belief spread outside the Soviet
Union that *glasnost* was somehow a synonym for freedom and democracy. In America and Western Europe it became a catchall
phrase for radical change, which was believed to have already
taken place. But with all its positive elements *glasnost* was neither
freedom nor democracy, only one of their prerequisites. Nor was
it certain to what extent it had spread outside Moscow, and even
in the capital *glasnost* was not unlimited. The Soviet Union, and
Tsarist Russia before, had been secretive, unaccountable political
regimes. It was unrealistic to assume that the society would turn
overnight, or even over a few years, into an open democracy. Thus
the story of *glasnost* would be incomplete without mentioning its
limits and the obstacles facing it.

After Gorbachev's election on March 11, 1985, and following his keynote speech at the Mausoleum, *glasnost* was mentioned with increasing frequency in the Soviet media.[1] Yet for about a year it remained a mere slogan, and most of the tabus were still intact. The slogan was prominently reiterated at the Twenty-seventh Party Congress in February 1986. But the way the Chernobyl disaster in April 1986 was handled by the Soviet media threw doubts on whether the new openness was sincere.[2] True, Soviet media increasingly published news about earthquakes and other disasters, but this had happened, albeit on rare occasions, even earlier.

Gradually, during the second half of 1986, the media began to discuss issues such as prostitution and homosexuality, but there were some first warnings on the part of the authorities: *glasnost* was not a synonym for unlimited licence and sensationalism.[3] Academician Viktor Afanasiev, editor of *Pravda* (the newspaper least affected by *glasnost*), issued similar warnings at the sixth congress of the journalists' union (March 1987). Reactionary writers such as Yuri Bondarev, Peter Proskurin, and Feliks Chuyev claimed that *glasnost* had already gone much too far, that it had become mainly destructive, and that those who engaged in it were not sincere patriots but "pseudo-democrats."

By early 1987 *glasnost* had indeed gone well beyond articles about prostitution; there were editorials, articles, and readers' letters on many subjects which had hitherto been out of bounds. Novels, plays, and movies were published which had been banned for many years. Not all media took part in the *glasnost* campaign; newspapers outside of Moscow, Leningrad, and Kiev frequently read as if the new slogans had not reached them. Nor is it certain that there was that much spontaneous interest in *glasnost* outside the big cities. Abuladze's movie *Repentance* was watched by two million spectators in Moscow but only by eight more million in the whole of the Soviet Union. Truly popular Soviet films were watched by eighty million.[4] But the outreach of the central newspa-

[1]*Pravda* and *Izvestiia*, March 23, 1985.
[2]V. Tolz, "A Chronological Overview of Gorbachev's Campaign for *Glasnost*," *Radio Liberty*, January 21, 1987; Bernd Knabe, *Das neue Denken, Glasnost und Tschernobyl*, Bundesinstitut, 48, Cologne, 1987.
[3]*Komsomolskaia Pravda*, March 24, 1987, criticizing various articles in the Moscow youth paper *Moskovski Komsomolets*.
[4]Interview with Elem Klimov, *Ogonyok*, 2, 1988.

pers, the literary magazines, and the more provocative television programs, such as "Twelfth Floor," *Vzglyad* was such that issues which had been raised in Moscow were widely discussed all over the country within a day or two.

However, the more *glasnost* there was, the greater the resistance against it, and it did not come only from minor party secretaries in distant parts of the Union or from conservative writers who feared for their reputation and royalties. Opposition to *glasnost* came also from inside the Politburo. Enthusiasm for greater openness among Gorbachev's colleagues had never been overwhelming; they certainly used the term much less frequently than the general secretary. The most highly placed "braker" was Ligachev, the second man in the Soviet leadership in 1986–87. His first warnings were published in mid-1986 in a somewhat unlikely place—namely, the journal *Teatr.* [5] Criticism of negative phenomena was well and good, he wrote, but it had always to be matched with praise for the achievements of socialism in the Soviet Union. It had to be constructive and based on an optimistic approach. In the months that followed he returned many times to this theme. He was for *perestroika,* and *perestroika* without *glasnost* was unthinkable, he declared in an interview in Paris. But, as Ligachev saw it, there were obvious limits to *glasnost.* At the Twenty-seventh Party Congress he helped to put Yeltsin in his place. Yeltsin tended to overdo *glasnost* from the beginning and had argued that no party leader should be above criticism.

In March 1987 Ligachev said that the reexamination of history should emphasize above all the "period of the triumph of socialist construction." History should provide an "honest and open look back," and not a "portrait of our history as a series of continuous mistakes and disappointments." As Ligachev saw it, there was far too much emphasis on the negative sides of Soviet history—and also on negative reports on the current Soviet scene: "Of course, one must not ignore the failures and calamities." But if one focused only on them and ignored the great gains achieved by the Soviet people under the leadership of the party it would be impossible to educate strong-minded young patriots and Communists.[6] Such criticism was more than a little disingenuous since no one focused "only" on negative reports; even the vanguard of *glasnost,* such as *Moscow News* and *Ogonyok,* was careful not to overstep

[5] *Teatr,* August 1986.
[6] *Pravda,* January 7, 1988.

certain limits. What Ligachev and his supporters wanted was not a "golden mean" but a different mixture—say, one part *glasnost* and three or four positive reports on the great achievements of the Soviet people, past and present. Ligachev called in the editors of *Moscow News* and *Ogonyok* for a dressing down. He visited the offices of *Sovetskaia Kultura* and admonished the journalists to write responsibly and in a constructive way.

In July 1987 he turned to the writers and editors of literary magazines. *Glasnost* was throwing up too much froth and filth, he said; there was a danger that the classical writers of the Soviet period (meaning the likes of Sholokhov) would be neglected. The media should take a stronger ideological stand against immorality, vulgarity, and Western mass culture. There should be less clannishness *(groupovshina)* among the writers; the artistic unions had asked for more freedom, and now it appeared that they did not know what to do with it. He did not actually suggest that the freedom should be taken away but his views were usually quite close to the criticism of the right-wing writers. Ligachev no doubt supported their stand nor was it surprising that in the month that followed the conservatives far more often invoked his authority than the *glasnost* speeches of Gorbachev. Ligachev's warnings culminated in a speech in August 1987: "Abroad and in some places in our midst there are attempts to call into question the whole course of the construction of socialism in the Soviet Union, to represent it as a chain of never-ending mistakes, to disregard the historical feat of the people that created a mighty socialist power, and to do all this by referring to the facts of groundless repression. . . . After all, in the thirties the country reached second place in the world in industrial output, agriculture was collectivized and unprecedented heights were reached in the development of culture, education, literature and the arts."[7] This was in essence what the party line had been under Brezhnev. At the party conference in June 1988, Ligachev stressed his support for the anti-*glasnost* party among the intellectuals ("I support the speeches by Comrades Bondarev and Oleinik"); and he spoke with "deep bitterness" (his own words) about some editors who had "taken advantage of the respect and trust shown to them by the Central Committee and by Gorbachev to act willfully, to squirm out from under the party's control": "Comrades, how can we agree that under the banner of

[7]*Pravda,* August 27, 1987.

the restoration of historical truth very often the truth was, in fact, distorted? How can we agree that in our publications, the Soviet people are represented as slaves—and this is almost a quotation—who were fed only on lies and demagogy? . . ."

Yet Gorbachev was by no means for unconditional *glasnost* either. Yakolev, another member of the Politburo and a close Gorbachev supporter, had said that critical statements must be assessed by only one criterion: do they correspond to the actual state of affairs?[8] Gorbachev usually opened his definitions in a similar sweeping way but later on introduced some reservations. Thus in a meeting with leading media figures in January 1988, he said: "I stress once again: we are in favor of *glasnost* without reservations and limitations. But for *glasnost* in the interest of socialism. And we solemnly reply to the question whether *glasnost* criticism and democracy are in the interests of the people—they are limitless."[9] One year earlier in a similar meeting with key media figures he had taken exactly the same line. Openness, self-criticism were not a tactic but a matter of principle; they "have become the norms of our life," or, in Yakovlev's words, "our collective return to truth." But, again in Gorbachev's words, "Criticism must always be true to party ideology and based on the truth, and this depends on the party-mindedness of the editor."[10] Sorely tried Soviet editors with a longer memory would ask, like Pontius Pilate, "What is truth?" and a few might well remember that Joseph Stalin in his time had also admonished writers to write the truth and nothing but the truth.

Thus the limits of *glasnost* were clearly stated. It was to be not openness *per se* as a supreme value and a right of the people, but openness within a political framework, "socialism" as defined by the Politburo. Gorbachev, to be sure, interpreted *glasnost* far more liberally than Brezhnev, let alone Stalin. On more than one occasion he admonished overcautious comrades, high and low, that there was no reason for getting panicky because some critical remarks had appeared in the media or had been voiced at meetings. However, he warned (as Ligachev has done) against clannishness and "group prejudices," against the habit of putting a label on one's opponent, against excessive aggression in polemics, the attempts to "finish off one's opponents." A spirit of forgiveness

[8]*Moscow News,* Supplement, 31, 1987; speech in Kaluga.
[9]*Sovetskaia Kultura,* January 14, 1988.
[10]*Pravda,* February 15, 1987.

should be shown toward those who had been in the past protagonists of stagnation but were now genuinely ready to cooperate in
the process of *perestroika.* [11]

Gorbachev was a little vague by necessity or choice in his statements. In more concrete terms his attitude could be fairly summarized as follows: He agreed with the conservatives that *glasnost* was
not a value *per se* but a means of mass control. He also agreed that
in the final analysis the party leadership had to decide what was
correct. However, to be more effective the media had to be given
more leeway, and the same was true, *a fortiori,* with regard to the
intellectuals. This meant less hectoring, fewer exhortations; there
was no need to have a party line strictly adhered to for all subjects
under the sun, from the theory of relativity to modern ballet.

True, there was the possibility, indeed the likelihood, that mistakes would be committed by the media, that books would appear,
plays be performed, and news items published which would be
harmful and throw a shadow on certain aspects of Soviet life, or
even inspire pessimism with regard to the future. But this was the
price that had to be paid for overregimentation in the past: How
to correct mistakes that had been committed if it was forbidden to
identify them? Or should this knowledge be kept by the supreme
leadership? But this was impossible—news about shortcomings
and failures would reach the masses in any case by rumor and in
a distorted way. Furthermore, the public had to be mobilized for
various campaigns—to work more effectively, to drink less, to combat corruption—and this could not be achieved unless the public
was told that the present state of affairs was far from ideal. If the
media committed mistakes it was always possible to correct them;
the risk of *glasnost* was therefore not remotely as great as the
conservatives claimed. In many ways Gorbachev's approach was
based on an optimistic and self-confident attitude, which he seldom failed to articulate: "If we are critical of ourselves that the
feathers fly, as no one has even criticized us before, in West or
East, then it is because we are strong. . . ."[12]

But the conservatives also had a powerful case. Their approach
was rooted in the belief that the hold of the party was not that
strong, that too much *glasnost* had caused both polarization and
pessimism among the masses, and that change, if any, had to come,
as always, from above. Any other approach was against the tradi-

[11]*Sovetskaia Kultura,* January 11, 1988.
[12]Speech in Tselinograd, July 29, 1987.

tional style of running the country and would not work. The masses wanted a clear lead and certainties; to paint the past in dark colors and to admit too many shortcomings was bound to sow confusion and dispirit them. As Sartre had said four decades earlier, when some of his comrades wanted to reveal the truth about Stalinism: "The workers of Billancourt must not be deprived of their hopes. . . ."

Not all the conservatives went as far as Chebrikov, the head of the KGB up to October 1988, who expressed the deepest misgivings about the consequences of *glasnost* among the intelligentsia as well as the national minorities.[13] But even the more moderate leaders had grave doubts about the results of too much freedom of speech and excessive criticism. They wanted positive heroes in movies, plays, and novels, announcements of victories and achievements—and they saw not nearly enough of it. There were bitter complaints that Soviet writers and moviemakers had made hardly any effort to glorify the activities of the organs of state security and the armed forces. Instead there had been too many reports of illegal arrests, beating up of youngsters, corruption, and worse among highly placed MVD officers, and this was hardly the stuff to inspire popular confidence in the forces of law and order.

Glasnost was a dramatic step forward for two generations of newspaper readers, radio listeners, and television watchers who had been accustomed to a near-total denial of the freedom of information on the part of the official media. Only very old men and women whose memories reached back to the early 1920s would recall a measure of divergent views such as could again be voiced. Not a few old party members came on record saying that they shed tears of joy, having given up hope to see the day when greater honesty would again prevail.

The daily newspapers, the literary magazines, and certain television programs acquired many more readers and watchers than ever before. But while the step forward seemed enormous, this was so only because the previous situation had been so utterly dismal, and even in the age of *glasnost* some of the most important spheres of political life remained tabu zones. This referred to the delibera-

---

[13]*Pravda*, September 11, 1987. In an interview in September 1988, Chebrikov said that "we perceive glasnost as one of the forms of our contacts with working people." In evidence he mentioned that in 1987, 235 books had appeared about the KGB as well as 7,500 articles and many movies (*Pravda*, September 2, 1988). The figures are impressive, but how much *glasnost* was in these publications?

tions on high policy in the Politburo, the Central Committee, the Central Committee apparatus, and the various ministries. After the weekly meetings of the Politburo official communiques were published, a practice which had been introduced under Andropov. After Central Committee meetings the text of some of the official speeches was released but nothing about the debates. Thus, in the final analysis, Soviet citizens knew no more about decisions concerning their fate than they had known before; they did not know about differences of opinion in the leadership, except through rumors. And as long as there was no real *glasnost* on top, the local leaders saw no cogent reason to change their practices.

On any given day the Soviet media would publish outspoken reports about the slowness of the mail deliveries in Moscow and complaints that it was impossible to get a cup of tea at Sheremetovo Airport. There would be revelations on the behavior of Soviet tourists abroad, on hidden unemployment, on a slave farm in Uzbekistan, or on the fact that 60,000 villains had been sentenced for embezzlement in 1987. But there were no studies investigating the causes of Stalinism or why there had been stagnation under Brezhnev. Yet precisely for a Marxist these were the essential questions, not Stalin's dictatorial desires and tendency toward self-aggrandizement and adulation (the "cult of the individual") or Brezhnev's personal weaknesses, but the objective reasons, perhaps even the "historical laws," which had been at work shaping Soviet policy and society. All this remained within the "zone of silence."

No basic criticism, indeed no public debate, was permitted with regard to national security, except on issues which were common knowledge in any case, such as the fact that new recruits were frequently ill-treated, or that there were difficulties with the Afghanistan veterans. It was as unthinkable to voice fundamental objections to Leninism as to praise Trotsky. True, there were some instances when highly placed officials were criticized—certain ministers who had not performed well, including the first secretaries of the Moldavian and the Armenian republics, and the first secretary of the Leningrad town committee—but only after the lead had been given from higher up. Certain statistics which had been formerly highly classified were now released, but other figures were still kept secret even though they had nothing to do with national security. Otto Latsis, one of the chief spokesmen for *glasnost* in the economic field, noted that while the *Soviet Statistical Yearbook* for

1987 provided more information than during the previous year, many essential facts and figures remained secret. These included figures on family budgets, on the quantity of Soviet oil exported, on the effects of the fall in raw material prices on world markets, on the Soviet trade balance, and much more.[14]

Former Soviet citizens were permitted to visit their relations in Moscow and Leningrad, among them even a handful of journalists. Censorship in the media was replaced to a large degree by self-censorship, but the punishment for major "mistakes" was still dismissal. Postal interference with correspondence from abroad still continued; undesirable newspapers, books, or movies could still not be imported; and there were bitter complaints by Soviet scientists that pages were torn by the censors out of periodicals such as *Science* and *Nature* even though only a handful of them reached the Soviet Union in the first place. The number of restrictions concerning photography hardly changed; detailed maps of Soviet cities still did not exist. In brief, what actually happened was a far cry from the loud and frequent appeals for *glasnost*.

The Yeltsin affair was a good example of the limits of *glasnost*. Boris Yeltsin, a broad-shouldered Siberian, had been first party secretary at Sverdlovsk; in November 1985 he was transferred to Moscow to replace the deposed Grishin. He had the reputation of a bulldozer; tact was not among his main virtues and after it was all over Gorbachev called him "overzealous and impatient." His lack of tact was probably his undoing, for in view of the presence of all the central state and party institutions in the capital, a great deal of patience and diplomacy was needed to get one's way.

There was a far-reaching shake-up in the Moscow party organization following Yeltsin's appointment; he visited unannounced shops, clinics, and housing estates, and never hesitated to speak his mind. While he mercilessly criticized his subordinates, he did not spare his own failures. He became the scourge of the local party officials, and even the cynical Muscovites, who had given up hope that there would ever be a real clean-up in their city, gave him their grudging admiration.

[14]Otto Latsis, "Tsena Ravnovesia" ("The price of equilibrium"), *Znamia*, 2, 1988, p. 197. Some, but no full, items about grain imports were published for the first time in 1987. The statistical authorities declared 1987 the "year of the figures that were made accessible"; according to official reports this referred to 90,000 units of figures. But many still remained closed (*Vestnik Statistiki*, 3, 1988).

Yeltsin made enemies in the party leadership with what most of his colleagues considered excessive fervor in promoting *glasnost* and democratization. He told a group of foreign diplomats on October 6, 1987, that "we do not subdivide information into that for home consumption and for foreign use. In accordance with *glasnost* and democratization we tell all the truth, and not half-truths to readers at home and abroad."[15] This greatly incensed the KGB as it appeared after a few weeks. He annoyed the *nomenklatura* with his suggestions that they should give up some of their privileges such as the special shops, and also the special consideration given to the careers of their children. He irritated the Politburo by making speeches on the eve of the celebrations of the seventieth anniversary of the revolution, claiming that there was so much interference on the part of the central institutions that he could not possibly succeed in his job. After a stormy Central Committee session on October 21, 1987, in which everyone, including Gorbachev, his erstwhile protector, turned against him, he offered to resign. After a very short interval his resignation was accepted.

It could well be that Yeltsin's approach was sometimes inappropriate; the final showdown which he provoked was certainly ill-timed, as he admitted in his speech to the party conference in 1988. But he was not a novice; seven years in Sverdlovsk were as good a preparation as any. Perhaps someone with greater diplomatic experience was needed in Moscow; perhaps he was bound to be replaced sooner or later. In view of the absence of facts it is impossible to judge: the public was not told what had really happened and demands for information were brushed aside without much ado; this was said to be an internal party leadership affair.

What made this a test case for *glasnost* was not so much the fact that Yeltsin was forced to resign but how it was done. Just as he had been unanimously elected eighteen months earlier, everyone at the session of the Moscow city council turned against him: he was accused of being a demagogue, a dictator, and altogether incompetent.[16] Even Yeltsin's own speech to the Central Committee stating his case was not published; the whole affair reminded observers of pre-*glasnost,* even of Stalinist practices. There was

---

[15] *Washington Post,* November 12, 1987.

[16] *Pravda,* November 13, 1987; *Moskovskaia Pravda,* November 13, 1987. But Yeltsin was given a chance to speak at the nineteenth party conference even if the reception was unfriendly, and he gave interviews to Western and Soviet media in 1988.

considerable agitation in the capital, mainly among young Communists; meetings were arranged in the university, resolutions passed. If a high-ranking party official such as Yeltsin, an alternate member of the Politburo, could not talk openly, what was *glasnost* all about? Several months later Gorbachev spoke with regret about the Yeltsin affair: "We shall not conceal the fact that the party's rebuff . . . was viewed by many intellectuals, especially young people, as a blow to *perestroika.* That is the greatest delusion. . . ."[17] He could not very well have said anything else. But he must have also known that the people who were aggrieved were precisely those who cared about *glasnost* and *perestroika,* whereas those who welcomed Yeltsin's downfall had been against democratization and the reform policy in the first place.

Thus the limits of the *glasnost* policy gradually became obvious, and in politics and the mass media more clearly than in the literary field. Most of the applications for marches and demonstrations were turned down by the authorities; those which went ahead irrespective of permission were broken up by the police and some of the participants arrested. Such was the case, for instance, with the anti-Stalin protest demonstration in Moscow on March 5, 1988, the anniversary of the death of the dictator. It was promised that a "speaker's corner" along the lines of London's Hyde Park would be established somewhere in the Soviet capital. Such extraterritorialization of freedom of speech was a step forward but not a big one. As the media announced, the organs of public rule would not stand for wild outbursts of this kind of "democracy."[18] When it appeared that expectations about *glasnost* had been excessive, disappointment set in. As a leading Western newspaper wrote: "When as with ethnic disputes and living political critics (as distinct from dead émigré writers) the happy ending is not apparent and the aftermath unpredictable and possibly uncontainable, the shutters remain closed."[19] Perhaps it had been unrealistic to expect more, and one should have counted one's blessings while *Moscow News, Ogonyok, Znamia* and *Novy Mir* were more or less free to publish what they saw fit. Outside Moscow the situation was more complicated. A Soviet teacher suggested in one of the weeklies that there were various categories of *glasnost:*

[17] *Sovetskaia Kultura,* January 14, 1988.
[18] *Vechernaia Moskva,* March 5, 1988.
[19] *Times* (London), March 24, 1988.

Category one, the maximum, was somewhere far away, in Moscow. In Kiev a different kind of *glasnost* prevailed. In Cherkassy [the writer's place of residence] there was less than in Kiev, and in Mirgorod, Smeta, and Konotop just a trace was left. If such a thing as first-class *glasnost* and second- and fourth-class *glasnost* exist, this means that there is no *glasnost* but only a semblance of it. . . . Of course, people in the provinces also read the central publications and thus avail themselves of the opportunities provided by Moscow *glasnost* (*glasnost* one), but as we can see, even *glasnost* one is limited in scope. Republican *glasnost* (*glasnost* two) is even more limited. As a rule it goes over ground that has already been covered by the central newspapers—drug taking, prostitution, the repression of the Stalin era. When it comes to the Brezhnev period the motto is: Let us wait until this has been raised in Moscow.[20]

Mr. Lubenski, the teacher from Cherkassy, concluded that the general tendency outside Moscow was to look over one's shoulder at *glasnost* one so as not to move beyond it. But how could one fairly blame those looking over their shoulders if political freedom was not yet anchored in law and even less in practice? According to a law promulgated in 1987, Soviet citizens had the right to sue government officials but with one notable exception—the KGB; there was no legal redress against their actions. According to another law passed in 1986 (the Individual Labor Law), the authorities kept their monopoly even on the organization of entertainment. According to a law of 1984 the interpretation of official secrets remained as arbitrary as before. In brief, resolutions on *glasnost* taken by party conferences were most welcome, but they amounted to little as long as they were not implemented country-wide and anchored in the law of the land.

Unofficial *Glasnost*

The sprouting of the "informal groups" was one of the characteristic features of the era of *glasnost;* a few people would gather from time to time to discuss current events or to engage in activities of common interest. Sometimes these were friends or neighbors; at other times their place of work provided the outward framework. Some were interested in public affairs; others set themselves more

[20]*Ogonyok*, 28, 1988. One of the means of restricting the impact of *glasnost* one outside Moscow was the administrative restriction of individual subscriptions to reformist periodicals and the rationing of paper for books.

narrow aims. This was in stark contrast to previous decades when the Communist Party and its various branches had a monopoly on organization and no spontaneous activity was possible.

The existence of such a monopoly was one of the essential features of the Communist regime; it was also the reason for the mushrooming of the informal groups once the reins were loosened. As a close observer noted, this new and startling phenomenon was the direct result of the bureaucratization of public life, of the absence of all and any initiatives, except those which had been imposed from above.[21]

By August 1987 more than a thousand such circles were said to exist in Moscow alone. But no one knew for certain and it could have been ten times as many; in any case, their number continued to grow. In January 1988 some 30,000 were counted throughout the Soviet Union. Most consisted of a handful of members; a few had hundreds of members or sympathizers. A first meeting of representatives of some forty-seven of the more important groups took place in August 1987 in a hall that had been put at their disposal by the Brezhnev regional committee of the party in Moscow. The meeting was vaguely reported in some official Soviet media and more explicitly in the nonofficial organs.[22] Subsequently, these groups continued to sprout, to unite, and to split; the bulletins reporting their activities grew in size with each number.

The emergence of these groups came as a surprise to the Soviet authorities and to Western observers alike, but there is much evidence that, in one form or another, some of them had existed even before 1985. This refers to the various dissident groups of the 1960s and 1970s but also to the Moscow *Trust* groups of scientists which had been founded in 1982 to generate greater confidence between West and East. The dissident groups set themselves in deliberate opposition to the authorities; they were infiltrated by the state organs of security, persecuted, and sooner or later destroyed—except the patriotic groups, which had a considerable reservoir of support both from below and above. However, such opposition quite apart, there was also a substantial gray zone of activities neither officially banned nor permitted; public life was, after all, not totally atomized or paralyzed in the post-Stalin era. There were, for example, various unofficial religious and youth

[21]E. E. Levanov, *Komsomolskaia Pravda*, December 11, 1987.
[22]*Ogonyok*, 36, 1987; *Bulletin Glasnost*, 7, 1987.

groups. The organs of state security no doubt knew about their existence but did not, on the whole, bother them.

The emergence of unofficial groups, "like mushrooms after the rain,"[23] is by no means unprecedented in history; it is the rule rather than the exception in times of social and political ferment. In democratic systems this ferment manifests itself in the rise of political parties or committees; where such freedom does not exist it finds other forms of expression. Two examples should suffice: the banquet campaign in France during 1847–48, which contributed to a considerable extent to the February revolution, and the banquet campaign in Russia in 1904–1905, initiated by groups of the center and the left. From Arkhangelsk in the north to Pyatigorsk in the south, it brought together on such occasions up to a thousand people. There were speeches, toasts, resolutions—each event taken in isolation of no great consequence, but together having a certain public impact. They pointed to a mood prevailing in the country, to a nascent public opinion which had not existed before and was gradually becoming a factor which could not easily be disregarded. True, it is impossible, even in retrospect, to measure with any certainty the importance of these groups; perhaps they were just a manifestation of inchoate political and social energies which had not found an outlet before.

The groups which had existed in the Brezhnev era had been strictly unpolitical in character.[24] The new groups, on the other hand, were unabashedly political. As far as can be ascertained the politicization had come gradually. In later years there were complaints that greater attention should have been paid to the informal groups, but this was wisdom after the event.[25] There had been thousands of choirs, male, female, and mixed, all over the Soviet Union. There had been, as in the West, organized soccer rowdyism, the so-called *fanaty* which had originated at the Moscow club Spartak. It went through an upsurge in 1979–82, and yet another in 1986. Such activities seemed hardly reason enough for studies in depth and elaborate investigations: there had always been lovers of music in Russia and, on the other hand, soccer rowdyism is a global phenomenon, which should be controlled by the police without much difficulty.

[23]*Komsomolskaia Pravda*, October 10, 1986.
[24]*Pravda*, March 30, 1987; I. Yu. Sundiev, in *Sotsiologicheskie Issledovaniia*, 5, 1987. Sundiev is both a sociologist and a police major and therefore, no doubt, well-informed.
[25]Levanov, loc. cit.

Toward the middle 1970s, small pacifist groups appeared and also a wider and more inchoate movement called Sistema, or the "people of the system." These were young people between the ages of sixteen and thirty, most of them pro-hippy in a vague way; they were on the whole considered harmless by the authorities. If the activities of the Komsomol had become routine, and uninteresting, Sistema provided discussion groups, not primarily political, but often devoted to subjects such as art appreciation. True, at the margins of Sistema a new interest emerged in religion and mysticism, particularly in its Far Eastern forms, but all this seemed a far cry from any organized (or potential) political opposition.

There was yet another trend called the "Optimists," consisting mainly of students and members of the upper forms of the schools who discussed politics, both domestic and foreign, more openly than this could be done within the party. But these were purely educational groups that never expressed any wish to engage in political action; neither were they thought to be dangerous. The same attitude was shown toward the various karate, Kung fu, and other martial arts groups which appeared all over Moscow and other big cities.[26] Their aim was self-defense. To the extent that there was the desire in these circles to engage in political and social action, it was in support of the police.

Various vigilante groups came into being with names such as Law and Order, combating corruption and hooliganism. Afghanistan veterans took a prominent part in these initiatives. Lastly, certain ecological groups appeared, called Eco, Flora, and Zelenie (the Greens), with the declared aim of preserving nature. In addition, there were, of course, the rock groups which have already been mentioned.

All these existed on a local basis and, to repeat once again, did not constitute an opposition. But the authorities clearly underrated the rapidity with which they would spread once the reins were a little loosened and thus, by early 1987, one out of three Moscow teenagers belonged to an informal group. The authorities also underrated the possibility that unpolitical groups would turn political or, at any rate, start discussing problems, which, in the view of their elders and betters, were none of their business. Just as Pamyat had turned from the preservation of historical monuments to the *Protocols of the Elders of Zion,* other groups would

---

[26]At a later stage karate was banned because it contributed to the spread of rowdyism, but the ban seems to have been ineffective (*Sovetski Sport,* December 19, 1987).

debate democratization, the history of the CPSU, or even engage in demonstrations. It is one of the basic tenets of totalitarianism, as defined first by Mussolini, that there ought to be no social activity outside the state; once this golden rule is broken, there is no obvious limit where it will stop. There is the danger of losing control, for with the mushrooming of thousands of groups it must have become virtually impossible for the KGB to penetrate all of them and to know which were harmless, which could be used by the regime, and which were dangerous and had to be harassed and eventually suppressed.

The work of the organs of state security was not made any easier by the fact that they were frequently dealing with young people of political sophistication, which is more than can be said about the rank and file of the police and even the KGB. Thus the young pacifists would refrain from criticizing outright Soviet military policy, let alone specific weapon systems. Instead, they concentrated on constructive and "confidence-building activities," invoking peace slogans and speeches made by the party leadership.[27] Such tactics were not, of course, foolproof. During 1984–86 their members were beaten up and put into psychiatric clinics, prisons, and camps; some were exiled from the Soviet Union. But by 1987 the authorities found it difficult to apply, at least temporarily, strong-arm measures, and the emphasis shifted to propagandistic campaigns against undesirable informal groups.

In December 1986 Dr. Sakharov was permitted to return to Moscow from his exile in Gorky; he gave a few interviews, expressing critical support for Gorbachev's policies after his return, but on the whole abstained from political activity. In January 1987 the first issue of *Den za Den* by the *Trust* (Doverie) group was published; in March the Democracy and Humanism group (consisting mainly of former political prisoners) published a manifesto. Five cultural groups in Leningrad merged in April as Epicenter to publish a literary journal called *Merkuri*. An amnesty in June brought about the release of about one-quarter of the political prisoners. In July 1987 the first issue of a journal sponsored by a Christian group appeared, edited by Alexander Ogorodnikov. Also in July the first issue of *Glasnost,* the most widely read of the informal bulletins, was published; it was edited by Serge Grigoriants, who also initiated an international press club. On August 1 the first issue of

[27] *From Below* (Helsinki Watch report), New York, October 1987, pp. 111–12.

Express Khronika was put out, edited by Alexander Podrabinek. It provided an annotated calendar of ongoing activities of informal groups. In September 1987 yet another group, Grazhdanskoe Dostoinstvo (Civic Dignity), was founded and, upon the private initiative of an ex-army officer, a Jewish library was established in Moscow. In December the first issue of *Referendum,* yet another informal magazine, was put out, edited by Lev Timofeev.

There were various demonstrations in front of the Pushkin monument and elsewhere in the streets of Moscow. Thus, to give but one example, ninety-six demonstrators were arrested at a Democratic Union rally in Moscow on August 22, 1988. Special police units injured on this occasion both journalists and innocent bystanders, and after a few days the militia command conceded that mistakes had been made. The Democratic Union was accused of shouting provocative slogans, carrying placards offending the dignity of Soviet citizens, handing out libelous leaflets, and obstructing traffic. The organization had asked the Moscow municipality in advance for authorization to hold this meeting but the application was turned down under a new decree passed by the Supreme Soviet on July 29, 1988. Since the Democratic Union had been declared anti-Soviet for opposing a one-party system, the authorities were, of course, within their rights. Pamyat, on the other hand, did not bother to ask for permission and even though members tore up the placards of counterdemonstrators with slogans such as "Workers of the world, unite!," they were not dispersed nor were they accused of broadcasting antistate slogans or violating the public order.[28]

Yet despite continuing harassment by the police, the sponsors of informal activities had more freedom of maneuver than in former years.[29] In addition there were various activities outside Moscow and Leningrad; the Helsinki Watch group was blamed for the demonstrations in Riga and other Baltic countries by the authorities; an Armenian-language version of the publication *Glasnost*

[28]On the Moscow demonstrations, see *Trud,* August 23, 1988, *Pravda,* August 24, and *Vechernaia Moskva,* August 22. The Pamyat demonstrations in Leningrad were reported in *Guardian,* August 15, 1988, and also in Soviet publications such as *Moscow News, Leningradskaia Pravda,* and *Literaturnaia Gazetta.*

[29]Details appeared regularly in the Paris weekly *Russkaia Mysl,* which was the best-informed of the Russian-language publications outside Russia. Thus, for instance, on the Novosibirsk demonstration, see *Express Khronika,* February 28, 1988, and *Russkaia Mysl,* March 11, 1988. For a general survey, see Wolfgang Eichwede, "Buergerrechtsbewegung und neue Oeffentlichkeit in der UdSSR," *Osteuropa,* 1, 1988.

began to appear; and a small pacifist demonstration was dispersed in Lvov.

What was the specific character of these groups? How strong were they, and what was the response of the authorities? The coordinating meeting in August gave a general idea of the aims and activities of the various political clubs. It appeared that all groups except Pamyat were quite small; their number of militants was perhaps fifteen to thirty in most cases, though a greater number of sympathizers would from time to time attend their lectures and discussions. A few groups would keep in close contact with foreign journalists and publish articles or manifestos abroad (including the London *Guardian,* the *New Left Review,* or *The Times Literary Supplement*); others would not. As a result some groups would figure prominently in the Western media whereas others, more numerous and influential, would hardly be known in the West. A few groups advocated left-wing socialist or Marxist ideas such as Obshina and the radio club Alie Parus; Obshina opposed the presence of Democracy and Humanism at the coordination meeting. Obshina announced that it accepted the leading role of the Communist party in society and would not break the law. But if they accepted the leading role of the party, why not work for *perestroika* from within? There was no clear answer. There was a small New Left in Moscow and Leningrad following with passionate interest ideas and political developments among the West European Communist parties and also in Hungary. They argued that it was premature to jettison socialism since it had never been given a real chance in Russia. Support for this New Left seems to have been greater in the United States and among Western European sympathizers than inside the Soviet Union.[30]

"Breaking the law" in the Soviet Union has always been a matter of interpretation; the Soviet constitution, even under Stalin, has provided freedom of speech and assembly, but only if it was "in the interest of the people and in order to strengthen and develop the socialist system" (Paragraph 50 of the constitution). Thus the party, through the KGB and the MVD, decided when freedom was to be granted and when it was denied. For this reason the deideologization of the Soviet constitution became the main demand of the more radical political clubs. They stressed that

[30]On Kagarlitsky, the "Club of Social Initiatives," and kindred groups, see p. 238, "*Glasnost* Abroad." See also Boris Kagarlitsky, *The Thinking Reed,* New York, 1988, a New Left Books publication.

unless freedom meant freedom for the political opponent it was meaningless. Ecological concerns—in the widest sense—played an important role in the discussions of the political clubs. Lastly, there were some groups which did not attempt to agree on a common program but merely acted as a forum for educational purposes; they invited well-known personalities for a lecture and discussions, sometimes on Russian history, sometimes on current cultural concerns.[31]

The multitude of opinions as well as their limited outreach were all too apparent at a meeting of editors of informal publications which took place in Leningrad in October 1987.[32] Most of the journals represented were of recent date but others, such as *Chasy*, had appeared for sixteen years, and the Jewish magazine *Leah* for six. Most of the journals were literary in character; some ran up to five hundred typewritten pages. But their circulation was extremely restricted (twenty to fifty copies) and even if it is assumed that each copy was read by several individuals, they could reach only a small circle.

The literary journals were by no means all in deliberate political opposition; some claimed to be apolitical, arguing that the official magazines could not possibly publish all the individual voices in Russian literature. Young writers submitting novels or essays to the leading magazines often had to wait several years in view of the great backlog of manuscripts. They argued that if, in 1914, 438 journals had been published in Petersburg alone, the appearance of a few dozen in 1987 surely was no reason for surprise or dismay.

The authorities watched the rise of the informal groups with misgivings. They preferred, for obvious reasons, the nonpolitical groups to the political clubs, and within the political sphere they preferred the patriotic, right-wing factions to the radical democratic groups. The decisive yardstick for the authorities was not abstract-ideological; it was obedience, not Marxism-Leninism. Seen in this light, the tamer informal groups which accepted without protest the party line on *glasnost* and the leading role of the Communist Party were, of course, more acceptable than those who, like Democracy and Humanism (later the *Democratic*

[31]For a description of a lecture sponsored by the *perestroika* club in Moscow by a foreign correspondent, see *The Independent*, London, October 23, 1987.
[32]*Express Khronika*, 13, 1987.

Union), wanted to broaden the parameters of democracy, preached pluralism, and even suggested free elections and a real parliament.[33]

In earlier years these groups would have been accused of being tools of the CIA and/or consisting of common criminals. Under *glasnost,* in accordance with the softer line, it was argued that though the rogue groups might not actually be paid by the CIA, their aims were similar if not identical. Strictly speaking, it was further argued, the activities of the political clubs were illegal because their real aim was to found new political parties and unions. At the same time the authorities tried to take the wind out of the sails of the informal groups by establishing semi-official ecological human rights and peace groups headed by liberal, universally respected establishment representatives such as the official Soviet Committee for the Defense of Peace or the official Human Rights group headed by Fyodor Burlatski. The informal groups were then given to understand that their activities were unnecessary and that they should look for cooperation with the already existing legal and official associations which were following the same aims under the control of the party.

In the literary field, too, attempts were made to coopt the unofficials in journals or almanacs which were neither quite legal nor illegal, but obviously under the supervision of the security organs.[34] Revelations and complaints which had previously been the domain of the dissident publications were now published in journals such as *Ogonyok* with a circulation of more than a million. This was regarded as a safety valve by the more enlightened party leaders and security officials, and it detracted from the interest exuded by the informal groups.

The official attitude toward the informal groups was by no means consistent and became a bone of contention between the more liberal media and the conservative newspapers. Thus the Leningrad evening paper sharply attacked the demonstration against the demolition of the Hotel Angleterre, a historical monument for lovers of Russian literature, reflecting the point of view

[33]Hence the bitter attacks against Democracy and Humanism in *Sobesednik,* 44, October 1987; *Vechernaia Moskva,* October 6 and October 28, 1987; and the *Pravda* editorial of December 27, 1987, in which it was said that some informal groups were led by rogues, that democratization in the Soviet Union did not mean liberalization, and that there would be no political pluralism in the U.S.S.R.
[34]Sally Laird, *Index on Censorship,* July–August 1987.

of the party town committee, whereas *Izvestiia* in Moscow blamed the local Leningrad leaders for showing lack of sensitivity on an issue not to be decided by bureaucratic fiat.[35]

Attempts were made throughout 1988 to bring about more coordination if not united action among the informals. In January a meeting took place at the Yunost hotel in Moscow sponsored by informal groups of socialist persuasion (the New Left) and also the Komsomol. The policy of the party officials was to help to deepen the splits among the informals, to attract back to the fold the loyalists among them and to isolate the rest. The divisions among the left wing were deep: some identified themselves with the more radical reformers inside the party, some even collaborated in official or semi-official publications edited by the party (such as *20th Century and Peace*), whereas others, such as Valeria Novodvorskaia, who came under heavy fire on the part of the authorities, opposed such collaboration.[36]

More radical and more representative was the founding meeting in April 1988 of a group called the Democratic Union, which intended to provide a platform for new political parties to be established in the Soviet Union. The authorities arrested some of the leaders of the new group, albeit only for a week, showing that there was no intention to make concessions to the demands of the "Union" such as the abolition of the KGB, changes in the constitution, or indeed political pluralism.[37]

Lastly, suggestions were made by spokesmen for the reform wing inside the party to establish a "Popular Front" or "Union" to promote *perestroika,* in which party members and those belonging to some informal groups could work side by side.[38] However,

[35]The affair came up again several months later at a meeting of the Soviet journalists' union, when the editor of *Izvestiia* was attacked by a representative of the Leningrad papers for "undemocratic instigation." The editor replied that popular initiatives should be observed with due attention and that imposing a ban would only cause harm (*Sovetskaia Kultura,* December 8, 1987). For an official but sympathetic account of the Angleterre affair, see *Ogonyok,* 20, 1987. For a detailed description by a participant, see T. Likhanova, *Glasnost,* 10, 1988. For a detailed, factual survey of the various informal groups, see Olga Alexandrova, *Informelle Gruppen und Perestrojka in der Sowjetunion, Berichte des Bundesinstituts,* 18, Cologne, 1988.

[36]For a discussion of the internal divisions among the socialist informals, see *Strana i Mir,* 2, 1988, pp. 24–26, and *Dagens Nyheter,* May 17, 1988.

[37]For the program of the "Democratic Union," see *Materiali Samizdata,* Radio Liberty, 24, 1988.

[38]Among the sponsors were academician Zaslavskaia and the lawyer Boris Kurashvili (*Moscow News,* May 6, 1988, and *Sovetskaia Molodezh,* April 27, 1988).

these proposals encountered suspicion and resistance among the party leadership and no progress was made.[39]

The informal groups were of considerable interest as a symptom of ferment among sections of Soviet society, particularly the young. Even if short-lived, these groups expressed certain moods of both hope and dissatisfaction. Their cultural impact was limited as long as some of the official media afforded greater freedom of expression. Their political influence was even more restricted, for unlike the nationalist movements among both Russians and other ethnic groups, they lacked cohesion and a reservoir of popular support.[40]

[39]The freedom-of-assembly law adopted by the Supreme Soviet in summer 1988 was a compromise between the proponents of *glasnost* and the forces of law and order (*Sovetskaia Rossia,* July 29, 1988; *Izvestiia,* July 30, 1988). The attempts to prepare a new press law ran into major difficulties; the internal pass laws which had existed in Tsarist Russia were abolished in 1917 but reintroduced in 1932, and continued to be in force even though they were in contradiction to the Soviet constitution, as readers of newspapers pointed out (*Izvestiia,* August 24, 1988). It would be easy to cite many more such examples; the columns of readers' letters in the Soviet press were full of complaints.

[40]No mention has been made in this review of the popular fronts that emerged in the Baltic republics, attracted hundreds of thousands of members, and became a factor of political importance. Their story is part of the political revival in the non-Russian areas of the U.S.S.R.

CHAPTER 12

Glasnost and Russia's Future

LIBERATION has been proclaimed. The ruler has acknowledged it. This is a great achievement, but it is not all: The word has to become reality, the liberation [of serfs] has to become truth. It is *glasnost*'s turn now."[1] The year was 1861 and the words those of Alexander Herzen in a manifesto which started as follows: "The first step has been taken. . . ."

The preceding chapters have related how the first steps toward freedom were taken in the late 1980s and how this affected Soviet society, economy, and culture. It has been a great achievement but no more than a beginning. Various opinion polls reflect Gorbachev's enormous popularity in the West; unfortunately this is not matched by equal enthusiasm for the new policies inside the Soviet Union. There is considerable resistance and even more apathy and *priterpelost* (submissive patience). In any case, *glasnost*, with its courageous revelations about the true state of affairs in the Soviet Union, is a far cry from real, radical change.

Western *glasnost* chic has produced some strange flowers. Mr. Gorbachev has been called not only a democrat but also a humanitarian and a cosmopolitan,[2] which he may well be in comparison with his predecessors. Yet even if Gorbachev were a paragon of democracy it is still true that democracy has never developed by order from above; it has to be learned, and the learning process is likely to be a long one with many reversals.

[1]*Kolokol*, April 1, 1861.
[2]*Guardian* (London), August 9, 1988.

But with all his enthusiasm for *glasnost,* Gorbachev's mentor and idol is still Lenin and he does not want to change the one-party system. Whether democracy is compatible with such a system is doubtful, at the very least. Furthermore, there are various degrees of *glasnost* in contemporary Russia and, as has been shown, it is not yet deeply rooted outside the capital. The Soviet Union today is a halfway house between tyranny and freedom. We may witness further progress toward democracy in the not-too-distant future, but retreat is also possible, as is the likelihood that the present uneasy equilibrium will prevail for some considerable time. All options are open and this adds much fascination to the present state of affairs. It would be churlish to belittle the advances made so far in the age of *glasnost,* nor is there any good reason for ecstatic joy, ignoring the present limits of *glasnost.* It has been a good beginning, no less and no more.

The most recent edition of the *Soviet Political Dictionary* says of *glasnost:* "One of the most important democratic principles guaranteeing the openness of the work of the organs of government; access, so that society can inform itself about its activities. *Glasnost* is the most developed form of control by the masses of the population over the organs of government, especially the local ones, and of the struggle against bureaucratism. The most important channels of *glasnost* are the means of mass information, oral propaganda and visual aids such as displays. Information which concerns state and military secrets, scientific-technological information as well as secrets in (industrial) production, crime investigation and medicine, are not subject to *glasnost.* (See also *Revolutionary vigilance.*)"

This is a fairly accurate definition; it could be argued that "oral propaganda" or visual displays are incongruent in this context, or that nobody ever assumed that the doctor-patient relationship should be subject to *glasnost.* The reference to revolutionary vigilance (with its special connotations dating back to Stalin's days) points to the limits of *glasnost.*

Why is a lengthy explanation needed? Why is it so difficult to find synonyms or a translation for *glasnost* in other languages? It is neither freedom of speech nor cultural or political freedom as known in the West, but a specific Russian phenomenon. It is the attempt to combine a nondemocratic mode of government with a certain degree of cultural freedom, accountability (especially on the lower levels), and "transparency." It could be interpreted as a step toward democracy, but it isn't democracy, because in the presence of democratic freedoms there is no need for *glasnost,* which is an inherent part of the system.

The decisive questions concerning *glasnost* go, of course, beyond mere definition. They are threefold: What do we know about the Soviet Union as the result of *glasnost* that we did not know before? What difference has *glasnost* made in Soviet society and politics? And what is its future likely to be? Will it last? Is it irreversible?

A New Era?

Glasnost has opened one of the most fascinating chapters in Russian cultural history. The choice of words is deliberate, both the emphasis on history and the stress on "cultural" (albeit in a wide sense). Whether *glasnost* will have a lasting impact on the political future of the country is uncertain and, in any case, cannot be answered today. Under *glasnost* complaints about many aspects of Soviet society have been voiced in a way that was unthinkable even a few years ago; cultural controls and restrictions have been either lifted or loosened; books have been published, plays and movies performed, pictures and sculptures exhibited, that were banned for many years. Informal societies have sprung up outside the party and the officially sponsored organizations, freely (or almost freely) discussing topics that were formerly tabu.

It was as if a wave of pent-up energy suddenly found release; it has been compared to the exhilarating effect of inhaling oxygen on one hand and on the other to a thaw of seemingly unmeltable ice.

There had been vaguely similar developments in Russian history. The emancipation of the serfs under Alexander II comes to mind; it provoked for a while great acclaim among the opposition of the day, but it did not take long until the limits of the reform were realized.

The impact of the October manifesto of 1905 probably provides a better parallel. Following the defeats in the war against Japan and the growing unrest at home, the Tsar reluctantly published a constitution. This, contemporaries report, came like a bolt from the blue. There was singing and dancing in the streets and similar manifestations of joy; as an eyewitness in Riga reported, "for a few days 'West European conditions' prevailed here."[3] When the first jubilation was over the radical left issued an appeal:

Thus we have a constitution: There is freedom of assembly, but the meetings are cordoned off by the troops. There is freedom of speech, but the censorship had remained inviolable. There is freedom of research, but the universities are occupied by the army. There is the inviolability of the personality, but the prisons are full with those arrested. Witte [the liberal prime minister] has come, but Trepov [the reactionary minister of internal affairs] has remained. A constitution has been given, but the autocracy has remained. Everything has been granted—and nothing has been granted.[4]

The skepticism was, as it subsequently appeared, justified; Max Weber, for one, also commented on Russia's way into "pseudo-constitutionalism" *(Scheinkonstitutionalismus)*.

Such comments make fascinating reading eighty years and several revolutions later. It is interesting to read now about the confusion prevailing among the bureaucracy, about the jubilation among the intelligentsia and the indifference or even hostile attitude among sections of the middle class and particularly the *meshanstvo:* "All the old things to which they got accustomed and with which they had lived, had been destroyed, and something new had been created, alien, unintelligible and even annoying. . . ."

With all the striking parallels, there are enormous differences. The constitution of 1905 was given under duress by a reluctant autocrat, advised by his ministers that but for such concessions his rule would not last. *Glasnost* was given voluntarily by a new leader who thought it would help the modernization of Soviet society. It was not a new constitution, only a new interpretation of a constitution which already existed, at least on paper. The constitution of 1905 went much further than *glasnost* inasmuch as it envisaged free elections contested by political parties (including the Bolsheviks). The Soviet constitution was not at all pluralist, and even the reforms envisaged by Gorbachev provided only for contests between different candidates of the one legal party. The most striking aspect of *glasnost* was not political reform, in contrast to 1905, but greater cultural freedom. The cultural policy of the Tsarist authorities had been relatively liberal even

---

[3]I. Martov, et al. *Obshestvennoe dvizhenie v Rossii,* Vol. 2, part 1, St. Petersburg, 1910, p. 97.
[4]Ibid.

before 1905; works by Gorki and other bitter opponents of the regime had been printed or performed well before. There were opposition newspapers and 1905 was thus not a hiatus comparable to 1987.

The emergence of "public opinion" is of absorbing interest. It had developed throughout the nineteenth century independent of and usually in opposition to the government. But it had coexisted with the autocracy, and in 1905 it became for a while a factor of political importance. Even after many of the political concessions made that year had been withdrawn, a certain amount of cultural freedom continued to exist.

The party and state bureaucracy was as little prepared for *glasnost* in 1987 as the Tsarist bureaucracy had been in 1905. Some party secretaries were more liberal than others, but the whole style of the administration was authoritarian, accustomed to rule by order and decree. They were prepared for criticism from above but they had not been trained, and were not psychologically ready, to cope with criticism from below. There was a group of party officials, men and women of Gorbachev's generation, communicators such as Yakovlev, Burlatski, or Bovin, who strongly believed that political and psychological de-Stalinization had not gone far enough under Khrushchev. They were repelled by the persistence of make-believe and mendacity. They sincerely believed in Communism with a human face and without too many unnecessary lies. But these were people active in the center in Moscow, and it was easier to be a liberal there than in Verkhne Udinsk. They certainly did not carry the majority with them, not in the higher party institutions, not in the lower ranks, not in the country at large, not apparently among the largely apolitical youth. Their main support came from the intelligentsia, an important social group, to be sure, numbering millions of people with considerable influence in view of their access to the media.[5] But even the intelligentsia was split, as had been the case in Tsarist Russia.

Something akin to a "great schism" *(veliki raskol)* in the nineteenth-century tradition had taken place over the years. The opposition to reform among the intelligentsia reflected deep-seated attitudes in the party and the country at large. The main opposi-

[5]Whereas in Tsarist Russia, and in other similar circumstances, students had played a key role in revolutionary movements, this was not the case in the drive for *glasnost.* On some occasions, such as the protest against Yeltsin's removal, students played a certain part, but these cases were the exception rather than the rule.

tion came, as a highly placed official put it, not so much from individuals but from a way of thought, the "old petrified thinking."[6] The largest group of "resisters," according to this analysis, consisted of passive people who had seen words and deeds differ in the past, who were unhappy about the fact that standards of living stagnated or even declined: "We have survived *zastoi* [stagnation], we shall also survive *glasnost* and *perestroika*," they said.[7] Others argued that many promises had been made in the past and had not been fulfilled. Why should they believe the new promises? Still others, to quote Soviet sources, consisted of the privileged who had led a good life, had helped their friends and relations to get good positions and were afraid to lose their privileges. They opposed reform almost as a matter of principle, believing in what is known in secret-service parlance as the "need-to-know principle": "They think that people should know only what is necessary for them, and that they (i.e., the bosses) have the right to judge what is necessary" (Bestuzhev-Lada).

Glasnost, according to one leading advocate of reform, was above all information, both about the Soviet Union and the outside world, and there were still many scholars and journalists who did not like this. They continued to judge the Western world "in terms of unemployment and inferiority to the Communist world in all fields; they extolled the Soviet system without comparing it with reality."[8] As a foreign editor of *Izvestiia* put it, of course, their coverage had been even-handed: for a hundred stories about the down-and-out in New York there had been one about cows in Holland. But the reader of the Soviet press would never learn that pensions in Sweden were higher, that the health service in Britain was really free, and that the American Senate was not just a millionaire's club but could really brake the President. As for Soviet military secrets, everyone knew them except Soviet citizens: "We even used their names for our weapons which officially did not exist. . . ."[9]

Some Soviet observers tried to explain the antireform opposi-

---

[6]V. Falin, director of Novosti, in *Stern,* April 2, 1987.

[7]Andrei Nuikin, *Novy Mir,* 1 and 2, 1988.

[8]F. Burlatski, interview in *La Repubblica,* March 27, 1987. Burlatski's essays have since appeared under the title *Novoe Myshlenie* (New Thinking), Moscow, 1988.

[9]St. Kondrashov, *Kommunist,* 14, 1987. A. Bovin argued a year later that there had not been as yet basic changes in the foreign news coverage and analysis of the Soviet media (*Moscow News,* April 24, 1988). The same case was made by Boris Tumanov in *Ogonyok* (21, 1988): "We were nourished by surrogates of reality. . . ."

tion with reference to psycho-social factors. The constantly grow-ing administrative apparatus had given birth to a "conservative syndrome" based on a pseudo-scientific dogmatism and ideologi-cal hysteria which stifled all true creative activity except that done for show or on paper *(pokazukha)*. The Soviet system of all-embrac-ing rule and management rested on a technocratic approach based in turn on three *a priori* assumptions: that all measures taken by the leadership benefited all members of society, that the welfare of society was constantly improving, and that the leadership was infal-lible.

These assumptions were all profoundly optimistic and they collided increasingly with realities. Therefore the leadership had to adopt an authoritarian-command style: rational explanation had to be replaced by the invocation of slogans and symbols ("social-ism," "the people," etc.) and other sacral elements. Hence the transition to totalitarian control over the masses, to a conservative revolution—that is to say, changes imposed from above. But this was impossible without repressive measures. At the same time the delusion grew among the rulers that all changes could be carried out whereas in actual fact the chasm between the objective situa-tion and the perception of the conservative leadership steadily grew.[10]

A Soviet sociologist trying to explain the resistance to reform claimed that it was predominantly limited to members of the older generation such as veterans and old-age pensioners. To those who lived through or fought in the war, the Soviet Union and Stalin appear in retrospect as synonyms; to dissociate themselves from Stalin's heritage would have meant that their work, their courage, and all their sacrifices had been in vain—clearly an intolerable idea. There are at present in the Soviet Union some fifty million "veterans of war and labor," to give them their official title. These are the survivors, and in some cases the benefactors, of the Stalin-ist regime. If they made sometimes startling careers it was mainly

---

[10]L. G. Yunin, "Konservativni Sindrom," in *Sotsiologicheskie Issledovaniia*, 6, 1987. The author freely uses terms such as "sacral" and "magic," derived from Max Weber and Simmel. He also notes yet another source of conservatism, the irrational "Umom Rossii ne poniat," nineteenth-century Russian autocratic-étatist tradition with its "organic" growth and "disci-plined enthusiasm" (Danilevski) which, in a secularized form, made a comeback with the rise of Stalin. See also I. Kon, "Psikhologia sotsialnoi inertsii," *Kommunist*, 1, 1988. For an interesting example of the Stalinist mentality, see M. I. Malakhov, "Smysl nashei Zhizni. Pismo veterana KPSS" (The Sense of Our Life. The Letter of a CPSU Veteran), *Molodaia Guardia*, 4, 1988, defending the idealism and the achievements of the "good old days."

because those whom they succeeded were purged, sent to Siberia or executed. This is the generation whose moral backbone was broken under Stalin and those who followed him in the Kremlin. But they still want to enter history as the heroic defenders of the fatherland and those who rebuilt the Soviet Union after the war. Not all of them defend the old order but most of them probably do.

However, the opposition to *glasnost* and *perestroika* is not, in fact, limited to the older generation; resistance could be found also among the young. Some believed that "the fashion of *glasnost* is bound to pass."[11] They accepted the substance of the relevations but thought their impact harmful for the population at large, whose belief in the rulers and the system should not be undermined. How could the young generation be educated in a positive spirit if so much of the past experience had been negative? As a mother of three wrote *Pravda:* I am all in favor of truth, but . . . "How to educate my children if as a result of *glasnost* everything is blackened? Are we not bound to lose all faith?"[12] This strong resentment against revealing the truth about the past found even more clear expression in a document which provoked a major row on the highest level, the letter of Nina Andreieva, a Leningrad chemistry teacher, to the *Sovetskaia Rossia.* It took up more than an entire page and was attacked in an equally long article in *Pravda.* [13] Andreieva's argument was, in brief, that the repressions of the past had been blown up out of all proportion in some young people's imagination and overshadowed an objective interpretation of the past. As a result of all the talk of "terrorism," "the peoples' political servility," "spiritual slavery," "universal fear," and so on, nihilistic sentiments had become strong among some students and there were instances of ideological confusion; some even went as

[11]Igor Bestuzhev-Lada, "Pravda i tolko pravda," *Nedelia,* 5, 1988.
[12]*Pravda,* November 18, 1987.
[13]*Sovetskaia Rossia,* March 13, 1988. The reply appeared in *Pravda* on April 5, 1988. The Andreieva article was reprinted in provincial newspapers such as *Uralski Rabochi* and *Vecherni Donetsk* (*Zhurnalist,* 5, 1988); only one newspaper, *Tambovskaia Pravda,* dared to criticize Andreieva before *Pravda* had made it clear that this "open letter" did not express the new party line. The antireform regime in East Germany had reprinted almost immediately the Andreieva article; they subsequently carried the *Pravda* reply. It is only fair to add that even the Soviet military spokesmen, with all their concern to provide an evenhanded assessment of Stalin, poked fun at the uncritical adulation of certain foreigners who had written (like Henri Barbusse) that "Stalin was a man with the head of a scientist and the face of a worker, dressed as an ordinary soldier" (*Krasnaia Zvezda,* March 12, 1988). For further details on the background of the Andreieva affair, see pp. 304–05.

far as suggesting that the Communists had dehumanized the political life of the country after 1917.

These were intolerable practices, and they made it difficult to educate the young generation in an objective—that is to say constructive—party line spirit. The argument is familiar to students of extreme nationalist movements all over the world and has become known as the "syndrome of the holy lie." From the point of view of educational efficiency, it is of course infinitely better if there is no break in continuity, if past crimes, lies, and mistakes are not admitted so as not to undermine the authority of the powers that be. Some opponents of *glasnost* had been deeply antagonized by the unlawfulness, the social injustice, the corruption, the black market, and the rule of the mafiosi during the era of stagnation. But instead of joining the campaign for social change and democratization, they believed in a strong leader, an "iron hand." They persuaded themselves that under Stalin all these abominations had not existed. Hence the Stalin pictures in the windows of cars and trucks, but also the display of crosses and even swastikas and all kinds of other shocking symbols and slogans.

The Bureaucracy

On one essential point reformers and conservatives were in full agreement: the baneful role of the bureaucracy and its responsibility for much that had gone wrong in Soviet society. There is a hallowed tradition of antibureaucratism both on the Russian right and the left. It has been a central theme of Russian literature from Gogol to Saltykov-Shedrin and Andrei Byeli. On the right it reaches from Karamzin to the Slavophiles and the Black Hundred, all of whom saw in the bureaucrat one of the main villains (second only to the "sinister foreign elements") for the shortcomings of Russian society. On the left the ideal was the Paris Commune (as Marx had seen it), that is to say the destruction of state power and a minimum of administration by the working class acting through an assembly of delegates. As Lenin wrote in *State and Revolution:* "We shall reduce the role of the state officials to that of simply carrying out our instructions as responsible, revocable and modestly paid foremen and accountants. . . ." He genuinely believed that the bureaucracy would be overcome through proletarian consciousness: "All may become bureaucrats for a time and therefore nobody will be able to become a bureaucrat."

If Lenin and the Soviet leaders who followed him had ever heard of the bureaucratization of the world, a concept developed by successive generations of Western sociologists, they seem to have believed that Soviet society would somehow be exempt. Yet there was every reason to fear that precisely in Soviet conditions the bureaucracy would become a crucial problem. Officialdom has always been more important in Russia than in other countries: bureaucracy had been highly centralized, all-powerful and often corrupt. It should have been clear from the beginning that there would be a great demand for administrators and supervisors in a Communist system based on planning and controls.

True, toward the end of his life Lenin began to recognize that he had vastly underrated the importance of the bureaucracy. But his ideas as to how to combat it (by organization and discipline through the initiative of the Communist Party) were quite utopian. He admitted defeat: "We have become a bureaucratic utopia." His warning that the revolution might be "drowned in a sea of paper" was not unfounded; the cost of paper used by the state apparatus was three times higher in 1926 than it had been in 1914, and it has been rising ever since. Whereas in 1897 the whole Tsarist bureaucracy employed 432,000 officials (including medical and educational personel), the Soviet bureaucracy in 1920 consisted of 416,000 officials in Moscow and Petrograd alone. By the time of Lenin's death, the Council of National Economy had one controller per productive employee; the Commissariat of Communication had one for every two.[14] In Tsarist Russia the government consisted of about two dozen ministers; when Gorbachev came to power there were 615.[15] Today, Soviet sources estimate that there are some eighteen million "bosses" of one form or another in their country. They are revocable but not by the people; and whether, considering their social utility, they are modestly paid (as Lenin suggested) is uncertain.

And yet the indiscriminate attacks against bureaucracy, whether emanating from the left or the right, are often a deliberate attempt to sidestep the real issue and to divert criticism from where it belongs—i.e., the supreme leadership and its policies—to

[14]See W. M. Pintner and D. K. Rowney, *Russian Officialdom*, Chapel Hill, 1980, p. 321, for sources.
[15]All Union and Republic ministers; see *Argumenty i Fakty*, 7, 1988. According to *Argumenty i Fakty*, 11, 1988, there were eight hundred ministries and government committees with the rank of ministry.

those who merely carry out orders. Thus some neo-Stalinists now argue that most of the blame for Stalinism should go to the bureaucracy, and that Stalin was to a large extent a prisoner of the bureaucracy. (The same argument is used by some German revisionists with regard to Hitler.) The more complex modern society has become, the more administration is needed even in ideal conditions.

The true problem with Soviet bureaucracy is not gross overstaffing nor its centralized or hierarchical character but its negative impact on society—corruption, inertia, formalism, routine thinking, the stifling of innovation and initiative, and similar *deformations professionelles.*

Glasnost produced a wave of complaints over the specific impact of bureaucracy on Soviet science. Thus Vitali Ginsburg, head of the department of theoretical physics in the Academy of Science, noted that bureaucracy was the main cause if Soviet science was lagging behind: Foreign scientific periodicals arrived more slowly than in the days of horse and buggy. On the other hand, the Academy was swamped with millions of papers and memos, most of them quite unnecessary. Asked by an interviewer about the basic reason for such bureaucratism he answered, "It is rooted in the desire to 'reinsure oneself' (politically), in incompetence, in the fact that people are no longer accustomed to take a decision and to answer for what has been done. He who gives a permission is taking a risk, whereas he who forbids—never. Moreover, the boss who says 'no,' whether it refers to an official trip or the publication of an article, is always correct; he is a hero, he defends state interests. . . ."[16]

These tendencies exist in every bureaucracy; they have been particularly pronounced in the Soviet Union. Even if Soviet state and party officials had not felt threatened by a reform which aimed at curtailing its numbers (sometimes by a third or even more) and powers, it would not have any sympathy for *glasnost.* Its monopoly on information happens to be one of its crucial pillars of strength, and accountability to the public must therefore seem incompatible with effective administration.

What has been said about bureaucratic secrecy applies, *a forti-*

---

[16]*Ogonyok,* 7, 1988. A great number of articles expressing fervent antibureaucratic zeal were published throughout 1987–88; thus, to give but one example, L. Ponomarev and V. Shinkarenko announced in *Izvestiia* (May 19, 1988) that 40–50 percent of the bureaucratic apparatus in the Russian Federative Republic would be eliminated in the near future.

ori, to police secrecy. Russia was always the country of secrecy *par excellence,* and it has been a police state for more than a hundred years; a political police existed even before 1881 when the Okhrana was established. Since the statute of emergency in 1881 Russia has been ruled by extraordinary measures which were renewed every year under the Tsars. It is useful to recall that the original name of the Cheka, the forerunner of the KGB, was Extraordinary (Chrezvychainaya) Commission. The following lines written in 1905 are as true now as they were then: "Under this state of emergency the activity of the gendarmery is performed under the protection of an impenetrable secrecy according to the instructions of the highest governmental levels which reach only the police; and no Russian is able, no matter how much he tries, to draw any conclusions about the rights and duties of the gendarmes from the published laws open to scrutiny of all."[17]

A secret police force, even under the control of the party leadership, cannot possibly favor *glasnost.* For the special powers of the organs of state security rest on the assumption that the Soviet Union is in a stage of siege, under constant, relentless attack by powerful enemies who want to steal its secrets and to undermine the confidence of the citizens in the system of government. In these circumstances, real *glasnost* is a luxury the system can ill afford.

During the heyday of *glasnost,* Chebrikov, the then head of the KGB, made only one programmatic speech but his message was clear enough: The KGB was all in favor of the restructuring process; in fact, it was improving the methods of its work. But it should never be forgotten that the CPSU policy of broadening democracy and *glasnost* had provoked a negative reaction from militant anti-Communists. And since, unfortunately, there were still people holding views alien and even hostile to socialism, "speculating on the subjects of human rights," state security was needed as much as before to supervise *glasnost* and democratization, to make sure that it was not abused. This applied particularly to certain sections of the Soviet population "infected by the virus of nationalism." It applied to the various "informal" associations and also the Soviet creative intelligentsia. The works of writers, moviemakers, artists, musicians, theater figures—in a word, all "creative workers"— have a tremendous power of emotional influence on people.

[17]Moskwitsch, "Die Polizei," in J. Melnik, ed., *Russen über Russland,* Frankfurt, 1906, p. 430.

"Realizing this, our opponents are trying to push individual representatives of the artistic intelligentsia into positions of carping, demagoguery, nihilism, the blackening of certain stages of our society's historical development, and the abandonment of the main purpose of socialist culture—the spiritual elevation of the working person."[18]

Hence the conclusion that it was quite natural that there should be debates and perhaps even a clash of opinions. But there must be someone to supervise this process, to take care that it did not go too far, that there was an "organic combination of socialist democracy and discipline, of autonomy and responsibility. . . ." Someone was needed to "protect the revolutionary process against subversive intrigues" and it was obvious that this important assignment could only be fulfilled by the organs of state security.

This approach was, of course, not new. It rested on the assumption that the Soviet people were far too kind, good-hearted, and gullible, and that but for the presence of a stern shepherd the socialist sheep would be devoured by the imperialist wolves. The Tsarist Okhrana, indeed every political police force through history, has used similar arguments, and there had, of course, always been some grain of truth in them. Revolutionary agitators were active in Tsarist Russia, and it was equally true that under *glasnost* and democratization all kinds of liberal or nationalist trends came to the fore which tended to go much further than the rulers wanted. As a Soviet author noted, capitalism (and the foreign enemy) was for these people what God had been for Voltaire: "If it did not exist, it had to be invented."[19]

There are, in brief, substantial sections of the population which have vested interests opposed to democratization and *glasnost* not just because their style of work and their whole philosophy are endangered; their livelihood depends on the existing system of administration. True, work would be found for them if they became unemployed. But the old power and privileges of the whole bureaucracy would be adversely affected.

These fears may be misplaced at least in part because Gorbachev never intended to carry out such radical reforms. Further-

[18]*Pravda*, September 11, 1987. Speech on the occasion of the one hundred tenth anniversary of the death of F. Dzerzhinski.

[19]Andrei Nuikin in *Novy Mir*, 1–2, 1988. But Nuikin believes that *glasnost* is by no means deadly for the bureaucracy, which is well-organized and not stupid: "There are many ways to get possession of *glasnost*, to choke and to disavow it." See also Alexander Egorunin, *Literaturnaia Rossia*, February 19, 1988.

more, generalizations about the bureaucracy are no more correct than about any other class or caste. At all times there have been people inspired by ideals of freedom and social justice who have acted against their own material interests. In Tsarist Russia there were not a few landowners who gave their serfs freedom without waiting for a government decree. The author of a panoramic, highly critical survey of Tsarist Russia in 1914 noted that "it would be quite wrong to say that the Russian Civil Service is wholly composed of bureaucrats, pure and simple. There are bureaucrats, a great many of them, and there are also a number of government employees who today are more or less tinged with the bureaucratic spirit, but tomorrow would do their duty as well or even better if a constitutional regime were in full swing."[20] Likewise, it could be argued that Gorbachev and those who supported him (like Dubcek before) were, after all, also products of the apparatus.[21] At times such people constituted significant minorities, in particular when it became obvious that the system functioned badly. But the majority of those involved, and especially the lower echelons, the most likely victims, cannot be expected to show great enthusiasm for *glasnost* and to cooperate with those proclaiming it.

Vested Interests

Certain social groups have been identified which are bound to oppose the reform policy. In addition there is the innate conservatism present in every society, the fear of change and innovation. This is not to say that inertia and vested interests cannot be overcome, for if this proposition were true, there would be no change at all in history. Vested interests are not all-powerful: Keynes, writing at the time of the Great Depression, noted that if the ideas of the economists are correct, they are likely to prevail sooner or later over the vested interests of civil servants and politicians: "I

[20]Harold Williams, *Russia of the Russians*, London, 1914, p. 54.
[21]Some Western Sovietologists have argued that the bureaucracy is among the strongest supporters of the reform movement, except perhaps the very oldest among them (J. Hough, *Russia and the West*, New York, 1988, p. 180). While it is true that the bureaucracy is not a monolithic bloc and while senior officials have less to fear about their jobs, the evidence points in the other direction. It is not just the fact that a serious reform endangers the livelihood of hundreds of thousands of them; it involves deep psychological changes— toward their work and toward their clients. In any case such views about the benign character are not shared by Soviet experts: "Either people will come . . . who break the bureaucratic apparatus or the apparatus will return everything to the *status quo ante*" (Professor Y. Volkov, *Moskovskie Novosti*, February 14, 1988).

am sure that the power of vested interests is vastly exaggerated compared with the gradual encroachment of ideas."[22] This is certainly true in the long run (and it is more true in Britain than in Russia); but in the long run, as Keynes sagely noted, we are all dead. He furthermore inserted a stipulation: "if the ideas [of the reformers] are correct." While there has been growing awareness in the Soviet Union that the present state of affairs is intolerable, there is no certainty that the ideas of the reformers are correct, or indeed applicable to the Soviet system.

There is a certain fatalism in the Soviet Union that with all its shortcomings the present socioeconomic system may be the only viable one. More important yet, Keynes thought of economic ideas whereas reform in the Soviet Union implies today social and political change and thus goes substantially deeper. If consistently applied it would amount in the long run to a new social revolution. The reformers such as Gorbachev stand for far-reaching economic changes with a minimum of social and political upheaval. But there is widespread feeling that this may just not be possible, and hence the fear of change and the resistance to it.

The Great Schism

It has been one of the great merits of *glasnost* that we know now much more about public opinion, about views and moods, about the people at large, and above all the intelligentsia. There has always been a public opinion in Russia—or, to be precise, public *opinions;* even during the most repressive years the official media were not given universal credence, especially if their message too blatantly contradicted reality. Public opinion, needless to say, is no synonym for political dissidence or protest; it refers to a great many beliefs and attitudes on a great variety of subjects, often contradictory, sometimes in stark contrast to the official ideology. It refers, for instance, to the strong national antagonisms and prejudices which existed, were known to all and sundry, but whose existence was ignored or denied in official speeches and articles. Even when public opinion polls were carried out in the late sixties and seventies and learned sociological journals began to appear, these explosive subjects could not be explored. When Gorbachev himself said in a speech that the party recognized public opinion,

[22]J. F. Keynes, *The General Theory of Employment,* New York, 1936, p. 383.

he meant, of course, the positive, or at least neutral, elements in public opinion rather than the others, which had to be left to the observation and treatment of the organs of state security.

There have been no free elections and no one can say for certain, for instance, how many supporters the "Russian party" has among the intelligentsia. But there are approximations. The circulation of the various literary magazines is no secret, and though paper allocation is arbitrary to a certain extent, one does know what papers and periodicals sell out within ten minutes after their appearance in the kiosks of Soyuzpechat, and which remain unsold.[23]

Glasnost has brought to light, among other things, the great schism which occurred among the intelligentsia. The debates and attacks between the two camps, "ours" and "theirs," are now an essential part of public opinion. They are far more bitter than in the last century and one almost tends to forget, because of the heat generated, that, as in Tsarist Russia, there is also an official ideology to which, certainly for the time being, both sides have to pay certain lip service.

The official ideology has been canonized and can be consulted in countless textbooks and catechisms. It is unlikely that a significant number of people still believes *in toto* in this ideology; the distance between theory and practice has become too great. Even among the truest of believers there must be doubts, precisely because Marxism-Leninism was not just another attempt to interpret the world, but an effort to change it. It was a key to action and a vision of the future. This future is now more than seventy years old and while it somehow works, it certainly differs greatly from the original vision.

What happens when prophecy fails? The problem has preoccupied sociologists and philosophers for a long time and is now a topical issue in the Soviet Union. The erstwhile, almost boundless optimism gave way to a pessimistic mood, and a spiritual void came into being that had to be filled somehow by another set of beliefs, be it a traditional or secular religion, or patriotism.

There is a spiritual crisis but it does not affect all sections of the population to an equal degree. Those in leading positions who benefit from the present regime may feel uneasy about the state of

[23]*Moscow News*, February 1, 1988. The upsurge in the readership of newspapers and magazines between 1986 and 1988 recalls a similar rise in the first decade of this century: in 1900 there were 125 daily newspapers in Tsarist Russia; in 1913, 1,158.

affairs, but they will think of a hundred different ways in which it can and will improve without painful surgery. Nor does the fact that the old ideology is no longer believed *tout court* mean that all its parts are discarded; some may have become deeply rooted in the population.

Old-style Marxism has certainly gone out of fashion; it can be shown without difficulty that Marx and Engels are less and less quoted in the manifestos and speeches of the leaders, and not just because both were Germans and one was also a Jew. In all his years in power Brezhnev, I believe, never once quoted Marx, and in Gorbachev's three volumes of articles and speeches there are countless references to Vladimir Ilich Lenin but none to Karl Marx.[24] This is only natural: a political theory belonging to the nineteenth century, conceived in the Victorian age, even if a work of genius, cannot possibly be a guide to action for the year 2000 and beyond. History did not stand still and Soviet leaders have even said that much on occasion. True, the need to apply Marxism "creatively" has been mentioned thousands of times over many years. But sooner or later the point is reached where the creative element becomes far more important than the original ideology, and this stage was reached in the Soviet Union a long time ago. True, one can always fall back on Lenin and Leninism, but the founder of the party became incapacitated a few years after the revolution and while one can find in his writings suitable quotations for almost any purpose, the Soviet leadership needs not only quotations but a political compass. This can no longer be found in the volumes of his collected works.

Lenin has been quoted more than ever before in the Gorbachev era—for instance, in connection with the NEP which figured so prominently in Gorbachev's reforms. This hearkens back to the situation in the Soviet Union in 1920 when the civil war ended, when there was peasant unrest and a catastrophic decline in industrial output. Facing economic disaster, Lenin argued that the Soviet state could still learn much from the capitalists. Accordingly, the reins were loosened, some limited room was given to private initiative, a new economic policy (NEP) inaugurated. As one observer, Victor Serge, described it: "Within a few months there were marvelous results. One could tell the difference from week to

[24]He did quote Marx in his report at the Twenty-seventh Party Congress, but this was an exception.

week. Food was easier to get, the restaurants were reopening their doors, more incredible still, they were selling pastries." It was a miracle, like the one after the German currency reform following World War II.

It was more than tactical; it was a strategic retreat, and there is no reason to disbelieve Lenin's words that it was adopted in 1921 "seriously and for a long time." But it is still true that, in the words of the historian E. H. Carr, it was a "temporary withdrawal from positions impossible to hold at the moment but which would have to be regained sooner or later."[25]

Economic freedom under the NEP was always very restricted but it still made a contribution to Russia's economic recovery, and the premature liquidation of the experiment after 1926 was, seen in retrospect, undoubtedly a mistake. But there is no reviving the NEP in the last decade of the twentieth century, a fact pointed out even by those who refer to the new economic policy as an example of the general direction they have in mind to find solutions to the present economic problems. What they really want (but cannot openly state) is not a temporary retreat but a movement forward in a different direction, away from *uravnilovka* (excessive egalitarianism), away from an overplanned command economy toward a more rational system which leaves greater room for creativity, initiative, and enterprise.

There have been similar such experiments not only in smaller East European countries such as Hungary but also in the most populous of the Communist states, China, with sometimes startling results. Under Den Xiaoping one-quarter of the central bureaucracy was dismissed, accountability was introduced, there were price and wage reforms (with prices going up by 30–50 percent), and many cities were opened up to foreign capital. By 1987 twenty-five million Chinese worked in the private sector, twenty-two million in state enterprises.

Reference will again be made to the Chinese model, but experience gained in a country with a different tradition is not readily applicable to the Soviet Union. There has been a tradition of private enterprise, a commercial sense, and a strong work ethic throughout Chinese history which did not exist in Russia. Generations of Chinese were not educated in the belief that the state

[25]*History of Soviet Russia: The Bolshevik Revolution,* Vol. 2, London, 1952, p. 275.

would plan everything, supervise everything, provide everything. There was no traditional disdain or stigma attached to economic success in China and less envy, whereas "Nepman" has entered the Russian language as an expression of utter contempt. For this reason "something like the NEP" could at best provide a temporary palliative; it does not open new, long-term perspectives. Quotations from Lenin in praise of the NEP are only of limited help sixty-seven years after the event.

If official ideology was at a loss to overcome the difficulties, could salvation come from giving freer rein to the social sciences? These sciences (sociology, politology, social psychology) had been given a very modest freedom of maneuver in the 1960s and 1970s. Earlier, their very *raison d'être* was denied because it was believed that Marxism-Leninism contained all the answers that were needed. Once upon a time it had been said that Marxism was based upon, and partly the synthesis of, classical German philosophy, British economic thought, and French sociology. But since then a lot of water has flown down the Seine and the other rivers. Soviet sociologists, though few in number, are probably not less talented than their professional colleagues in the West, and they have provided some interesting data in their journals. Owing to their work we now know that 61 percent of male children in Turkmenistan are circumcised at birth.[26] Also, we have clearer ideas about the views and preoccupations of Soviet youth, about the fluctuation of the labor force, about religion and other subjects which are no longer tabu.

Given greater freedom, the social sciences could no doubt help to identify problem areas in social life and suggest ways to remove certain bottlenecks, even though they have no monopoly in this direction. But the idea of the sociologist as a visionary and a prophet, mobilizing the masses and succeeding where the ideologist has failed, is more than a little fanciful. He can be, given the right circumstances, a useful handyman, keeping the car in good order; he can even act as a chauffeur; but he cannot and should not decide in what direction the journey should go. He (or she) can write about the need of generating social energy and creativity among the masses, as Dr. Zaslavskaia has done. But he cannot generate this energy. As a Western observer has written, these are good, creative, ambitious dreams about the scien-

[26]See, for instance, the articles by I. M. Ilinski in *Sotsiologicheskie Issledovania*, 2, 1987; F. N. Iliasov, ibid., 5, 1987; etc.

tific community becoming a "third" or "fourth" estate.[27] Alas, there is much reason to believe that they will remain dreams forever. And though Gorbachev, unlike his predecessors, has surrounded himself with a number of talented economists, these cannot help him with the truly difficult decisions for the simple reason that these are not technical but political in character.

A political system such as the Soviet can exist, if necessary, without extensive sociological research; if needed, the KGB will produce the information. It can perhaps exist without economic theory; the Japanese after all have not been doing badly even though their country has not yet produced an economist of world renown. It cannot exist without a vision of and a belief in the future, something for the heart as well as for the mind. This cannot possibly come from the sociologists or economists using sophisticated mathematical models.

Like the Psalmist, the Soviet leaders lift up their eyes unto the hills whence may cometh their help, but there is no spiritual help in sight; they will have to do for years to come with their old ideology. Leninism will have to provide quotations for speeches at least for another decade or two, and no one can look beyond this with any assurance. The leaders have to muddle through as before, casting furtive glances in all kinds of directions. But they are shackled to the doctrines of the past and they will not be able to move very far.

The Conservatives

A strong patriotic, right-wing, conservative trend has emerged over the years in Soviet public opinion. It is a minority group among the intelligentsia but seems to be more influential in the country at large. At the root of this mood is deep disappointment with the way Soviet society has developed. It is a movement of cultural, perhaps even more than political, despair. In Russian intellectual history pessimism has a long and honorable tradition; it reaches from Pushkin ("What a sad country, our Russia," he said, upon reading Gogol's *Dead Souls*) to Chekhov and beyond.

[27]M. Lewin, *The Gorbachev Phenomenon,* loc. cit., p. 100. A more realistic view concerning the tasks and the efficacy of Soviet sociology is taken by Professor René Ahlberg, who argues that the solution of the main problems facing Soviet society, such as overcoming social apathy, are well beyond the competence of this discipline ("Die Aufgaben der Soziologie," *Osteuropa,* 3, 1988).

Its basic philosophy can be summarized briefly as follows: The destruction of so many Russian traditions in the 1920s and early 1930s was a disaster; Marxism-Leninism is bankrupt, hence the need to return to the roots, to patriotism, to religion, the community spirit, and the values of old rural Russia. One would expect that conservatives would turn first and foremost against those who destroyed the old Russia, namely Lenin and Stalin, but this is not so. Lenin cannot be openly attacked, and as for Stalin, it is (in their eyes) to his credit that he made Russia strong again and restored Russian patriotism. In any case, he fought against cosmopolitanism, and all kinds of nihilistic and destructive trends. Lenin and Stalin in any case have been dead for a long time; the enemy today is liberalism, cosmopolitanism, an excess of freedom which manifests itself in the general moral breakdown and the absence of patriotism and discipline. The impact of Western mass culture is seen in the atomization of society, the alienation of the young generation—in brief, in modernization, which is alien to the Russian spirit. Those who today attack Stalin happen to be also the enemies of the conservatives—the Jews, the liberals, the true believers in socialism. For this reason the conservatives are willing to forgive Stalin his sins against the Russian peasantry, even collectivization. They have no clear economic or social program but they are opposed to a market economy.

Many conservatives seem to believe that Stalinism is not specifically Russian but a global phenomenon, "from Madrid to Shanghai." According to these sources much of the inspiration of Stalinism came from aliens such as Trotsky (the bureaucratic approach), Yakovlev (people's commissar of agriculture in the late 1920s), Kaganovitch (one of the chief destroyers of old Russian monuments), and Mekhlis (one of Stalin's hatchetmen during the purges and the war). Again, according to these thinkers of the far right, not only Soviet citizens were singing Stalin's praise during the "cult of the individual"; they could not but join the chorus. Many Western intellectuals such as Romain Rolland and Henri Barbusse, Lion Feuchtwanger and Albert Einstein, who were under no compulsion or pressure, took part in the genuflections whenever Stalin's name was invoked. There is a fascinating coincidence with the views of some German right-wing thinkers of the 1980s who argued in a similar vein that fascism had not been a German (or Italian) phenomenon but a universal European one and that, in any case, the inspiration for the terror had come from abroad—that is to say, from the Soviet Union.[28]

Their weakness is the same under which the antiliberal, anticapitalist right all over Europe labored in the twentieth century. On the one hand they stand for a strong, central government and a powerful army; on the other they lament the evils of industrialization and big-city life, and praise the village of the past. They would like to restore women to the home and the family, but they have no answer as to how families would exist on the basis of only one salary. They have no answers either to home economics questions or to the economic problems facing the nation, for how to combine political romanticism with modernization?

This philosophy of cultural despair and resentment, the belief that the Russian people are the most gifted in the world yet at the same time the most degraded, is neither new nor unique; it could be found in pre-fascist intellectual thought in various European countries, most pronounced perhaps in Germany. It was perhaps no accident that the most prominent spokesman of the "conservative revolution" in Germany, Moeller van den Bruck, was also the editor of Dostoyevski's collected works. For in Dostoyevski, the political thinker, the Germans found the ideological ammunition they needed, the contempt for the putrid West, the antiliberalism, anti-Semitism, anti-industrialism, anticapitalism, the unconditional belief in a leader (or Tsar), the aggressive nationalism, the enmity toward *meshanstvo* and bureaucracy. (One element was missing, "scientific racialism," but this came later on from other sources.)

All this refers not to the author of *Crime and Punishment* but to the pamphleteer of *Diary of a Writer,* not the preacher of all-embracing love, humility, suffering, and compassion, but the purveyor of chauvinism and strident prejudice. The second Dostoyevski more than the Slavophiles is today the spiritual mentor of the Russian conservatives, a fact which has not escaped the official Soviet ideologists.[29]

[28]This is *mutatis mutandis,* what the German *Historikerstreit* in 1986–87 was all about. The argument was picked up by a dissident of the right, Igor Shafarevich (*Moskovskie Novosti,* June 12, 1988).

[29]The political report of the Twenty-seventh Party Congress warned against the idealization of the past. The official commentary specifically referred to the dangerous activities of those invoking the revolutionary program of Dostoyevski and expressed dislike for the struggle of the revolutionary Russian intelligentsia against the *Oblomovshina.* See *XXVII seizd KPSS i zadachi Kafedr obshestvennikh nauk* (The twenty-seventh Party Congress and the Problems of the Chairs of Social Science), Moscow, 1987, passim.

Yet with all the reactionary and absurd elements in Dostoyevski's writings it is difficult to see him as a precursor of Adolf Hitler, whereas the present-day extreme right has lifted whole chunks out of the Nazi *Weltanschauung,* a fact that has been freely admitted by Soviet media.[30] That this has happened is probably less remarkable than the official, almost Hamlet-like attitude: True, what these eccentrics are doing is bad, and above all embarrassing in view of the publicity in the West. But the Communist Party members among them have not been excluded and the prominent writers supporting them have escaped with the mildest of rebukes.[31] The Jews who want to defend themselves against this rehash from *Mein Kampf* have been treated far less ceremoniously.

The emergence of a strong conservative strand in Russian political thought does not come as a surprise in view of the disenchantment with the social and moral state of the nation. Nor are the prevalent antiliberal and anti-Western views, and the fear of freedom, particularly startling in the light of Russian intellectual history and the attempts to impose a Western ideology on a reluctant and hostile people. As a writer in the Soviet philosophical journal *Voprosy Filosofii* put it, subjectively the village writers were crystal clear and pure, "but their pain is transformed into a new quality—hate" (6, 1988). Therefore, it was dangerous to play down the danger of anti-Semitism and fascism in the Soviet Union.

The conservative ideology collides with most fundamental tenets of Leninism but above all its internationalist character. Lenin quoted Chernyshevski, who wrote in one of his novels, "A wretched nation, a nation of slaves, from top to bottom all slaves," adding that the "overt and covert Great Russian slaves" do not like to recall these words. But there were two Russian political and cultural traditions, "one rooted in the struggle for freedom and socialism, the other characterized by great pogroms, rows of gallows, dungeons, great famines, and great servility to priests, Tsars, landowners, and capitalists."[32] Such references to "our slavish past" are anathema to the "Russian party," which sees Russia's past in a brilliant light. True, official Soviet ideology has retreated for a long time from what Marx and Lenin wrote about Russia under Tsarism; such a retreat was inevitable after it came to pass that socialism was to be built in only one country. But official

---

[30]Pavel Gutiontov, *Izvestiia,* February 27, 1988.
[31]For instance, V. Rasputin in *Nash Sovremennik,* January 1988.
[32]"On the National Pride of the Great Russians," *Sotsial Demokrat,* 36, 1914.

Soviet doctrine has merely "modified" Lenin's internationalism; it has not openly dissociated itself, nor could it do so without fundamentally changing its character.

The emergence of a Russian right was natural in the light of Soviet history, but the synthesis of Stalin and Dostoyevski was probably not inevitable. The outcome so far has been a curious, incongruous mixture of views and attitudes which express resentment and are, at best, irrelevant with regard to the present and future of Russia.

These sentiments hark back to a past which, in good part, never existed. But even if it had existed it could no more be restored than Atlantis, the Lost Continent. Even if the peasant *izba* was indeed (as some conservative writers claim) the subterranean base on which all Russia's values, its harmony, and its wholesomeness rested, it cannot be revived in the age of computers and television. In nineteenth-century Russian literature and political thought there had been a tendency to glorify peasant life. As Maksim Gorki wrote: "The populist painted the peasants as attractively as a cake. Our peasant was good, there was no comparison to the European peasants. They were all Platon Karataevs. . . ."[33] Even some outside observers like Mackenzie Wallace wrote with admiration about the self-reliant, independent spirit among peasants in northern Russia.[34] The British journalist grew enthusiastic about the fact that he found a copy of Buckle's *History of Civilization* in a peasant hut.

But Gorki and others who also knew the Russian countryside wrote with unmitigated bitterness about the cruelty and the low instincts, the apathy and emptiness ("a lot of superstition and no ideas") of the Russian peasantry, the fanaticism of the religious sectarians, the result, no doubt, of centuries of servitude.[35] If Gorki's judgment was perhaps exaggerated, peasant life does not appear in a rosy light in the novels of Gleb Uspenski or Ivan Bunin, and least of all in the accounts of prerevolutionary peasant writers such as Ivan Volny or Semyon Podyachev.

The attitude of the conservatives toward the Russian peasantry reminds one of the approach of Western European Romantics to

---

[33]*Novaia Zhizn,* 53, 1918. This refers to the peasant hero in *War and Peace.*
[34]*Russia,* London, 1881.
[35]Gorki's wholly negative attitude prevented the publication of his essay "O russkom Krestianstve" (About the Russian Peasantry) inside the Soviet Union. It appeared in Berlin in 1922, and was reprinted in 1987 in a Paris émigré journal, *Sintaksis.*

the Middle Ages: They singled out some attractive features and chose to ignore the rest, the social evils and the inhuman behavior. They saw the beautiful cult of the Virgin Mary but refused to see the dirt, the diseases, and the torture rack.

This modified version of the blood-and-soil doctrine of other lands is the antithetical to the views of the Russian radical intelligentsia, the total negation of Lenin's views about "two nations and two cultures" in prerevolutionary Russia. In the 1920s it would have been suppressed without mercy for its reactionary and counterrevolutionary character. Sixty years later it encounters no more than reluctant, half-hearted criticism. It is quite popular but it has no message to offer to the modern world except patriotic indoctrination, recalling historical victories (such as Kulikovo) over Tatar, German, and French invaders—proud memories, no doubt, but not of much help as a compass in the atomic age.

The Russian conservatives charge their ideological foes with *zapadomania,* that is, the uncritical acceptance of Western fashions. But it is not at all certain whether a "Western party" does in fact exist in the Soviet Union except perhaps among the adepts of rock culture; even they have assiduously adapted foreign fashions to Russian tastes. Like the "Westerners" of the nineteenth century, today's Russian intellectuals are attracted by the Western idea of freedom. But they are far from enthusiastic about Western realities after what they have heard and seen on the subject. Like Herzen they feel that the West has been incapable of living up to its own ideals. Nor is there a Russian groundswell in favor of the introduction of Western institutions such as parliamentary democracy; they believe that this could not work in present circumstances. They demand more freedom and education toward democracy, but they are aware that a long road still has to be traveled. The spirit moving them found expression almost 150 years ago in Belinsky's famous letter to Gogol, the recognition that what Russia needs is the success of civilization, enlightenment, and humanity, the awakening in the people of a sense of human dignity that has been lost during centuries of dirt and refuse. They reject the messages of the advocates of obedience, of the "proponents of the whip" and apostles of ignorance. Nor do they want to hear that the guilty and the innocent alike should be flogged.[36]

Yet they are even less united than their foes: a few believe in

[36]R. Mathew, ed., "Belinsky, Chernyshevsky and Dobrolyubov," *Selected Criticism,* New York, 1962, pp. 83 et seq.

a possible revival of pristine Leninism, which, they think, was a combination of freedom and democracy, of Marxism adapted to late-twentieth-century conditions and a revolutionary spirit. Like the old village of the Russophiles this kind of humanistic Communism never existed, but it still seems exceedingly attractive in the light of developments since Lenin's death. Such a vision would also have the great advantage of preserving some ideological continuity.

Lastly, there are those who believe neither in a revival of Leninism nor of Dostoyevski's political ideas; they advocate common sense, justice, and tolerance rather than the preaching of doctrines. Common sense and tolerance have not traditionally been in great demand in Russia; they seem too obvious, not inspired enough, almost philistine, which takes us back to the disdain for *meshanstvo* common to radicals of the left and right. The absence of common sense and tolerance has cost Russia dearly in the past and it is not certain that there is overwhelming support for these messages now.

Others in this camp belonged to liberal groups in the 1960s, such as the literary journal *Novy Mir* under Alexander Tvardovski. There are even quite a few former Brezhnevites who may not be proud of their record. They did not stand up to be counted when Pasternak and *Novy Mir* were attacked, when Brodski and other writers were arrested. But at least they did not join the attack against the liberals at the time. It is easy to deride some of the establishment liberals of the Gorbachev era in the light of their past record; the courage to fight for a good cause came to them when the risks had been much reduced. It is easy to disparage them from a safe distance but it is useful to recall that many burned their bridges behind them in 1987. And since it was not at all certain whether the liberal wave would be lasting or was merely a short interval in the sad, long history of cultural repression, some courage was after all needed to join the liberal camp even when the going seemed good.

These are the mainstreams of political and cultural thought at the present time. No mention has been made of the majority, far more interested in decent housing and a better supply of consumer goods than either Bolshevism or national Bolshevism, neo-Stalinism or anti-Stalinism. Its interest in both *glasnost* and *perestroika* is limited to one criterion: Will it help to improve living conditions? It is by this yardstick that the reform movement will be judged.

Freedom and Censorship

An interim balance of *glasnost* ought to start with stating the obvious, that it is predominantly a cultural phenomenon, and that there has been a great deal of it in some fields and very little in others. It has been most palpably felt in literature and the cinema as well as in some other media, at least in the capital and some major cities. But there has also been considerable resistance, and if the moviemakers and theater unions passed into liberal hands, the journalists' association has remained a bastion of the conservatives. There has been limited change in the leadership of the writers', composers', and artists' unions, but much of the activity of the younger artists and composers has proceeded outside the official organizations anyway. In some of the party sciences such as economy and sociology, those inclined toward reform have made much use of the new freedom, even though this is hardly reflected in leading journals such as *Voprosy Ekonomiki* or *Planovoe Khoziaistvo*. The historians and philosophers, with a few exceptions, did not move far from their former positions and some did not move at all. Thus an interesting dichotomy developed in which the organs of the Central Committee (such as *Kommunist*) took a more liberal line than many philosophers and historians. The reasons were not difficult to divine; it must have been next to impossible for those who spent many years of their working life in the party sciences, closely following the official line, suddenly to show independent thought, and to revoke most of what they had said and written in the past. It was not just a matter of "retooling," but of changing their basic approach; such adaptability can be found perhaps among young people but only seldom among their seniors, who had been accustomed to adjust their work to changing instructions from above but not to show independent initiative. A long time may have to pass until the impact of *glasnost* on political life, on party and state activity, and on the administration of justice can be judged.

The ouster of Yeltsin, or, to be more precise, the official silence imposed, was not a shining example of increased "transparency." Or, to give another example, the public discussion of the "law of enterprises" was not very impressive either. The draft of this law was made public in the summer of 1987, and the public was asked to participate in the debate, which it did. But when the law went into force on January 1, 1988, it appeared that there had been virtually no changes. The debate had no effect on the eventual outcome.

Glasnost did not imply by any means that non–Marxist-Leninist viewpoints could be voiced, except in the literary field under the banner of patriotism. The interpretation of the party line was far more liberal than in the past, but it was still unthinkable that nonsocialist ideas could be brought into the discussion on how to solve the economic crisis. Indeed, "socialism" in this context did not mean what it meant in other parts of the world, but as interpreted by the CPSU. Old Bolsheviks who had fallen victims to Stalin's terror were rehabilitated, but by no means all of them. Nor could justice be done to democratic socialists such as the Social Revolutionaries or the Mensheviks, who had played an equal or more important part in the struggle against Tsarism.

How much freedom did *glasnost* bring? Compared with Stalinism or the Brezhnev era a great deal. The balance sheet is less impressive if prerevolutionary Russia is taken as a yardstick. Capital punishment was abolished (in theory) in the criminal courts in 1754, and (in practice) in the middle of the nineteenth century. It could still be imposed by military courts, but throughout the whole nineteenth century no more than one hundred people were in fact executed—probably less than in other European countries.[37] As Leroy-Beaulieu wrote, "Hard labor was the worst that could befall the assassins of provincial governors or chiefs of police."[38]

It is instructive to compare Tsarist censorship with Soviet censorship before and under *glasnost*. Tsarist censorship was hypocritical and arbitrary; "it induced nausea, but not quite enough to cause vomiting." The words are those of Fyodor Tyutchev, the poet, himself a chief censor for many years. Yet according to the press law of 1865 books of more than ten printed sheets (160 pages) were exempted from censorship.

Russia had a relatively free press after 1905, and the opposition could publish many of their journals and pamphlets. Thus sixty Bolshevik publications appeared in 1906, and eighty-seven the year after. If *Pravda* was banned, it could appear the next day under a different name. Even before 1905 Marx's works were passed because they were considered serious contributions to political economy; Nietzsche's works, on the other hand, could not

[37]S. S. Oldenbourg, *Tsarstvovanie Imperatora Nikolaia II*, Vol. 1, Belgrade, 1939, p. 24.
[38]A. Leroy-Beaulieu, *The Empire of the Tsars*, Vol. 2, New York, 1902, p. 324.

be published before 1906.[39] As a historian of Tsarist censorship wrote: "Some censors considered themselves silent partners with writers and journalists in the task of enlightening the Russian public. For these reasons the censors imposed limits on their own activity. They hesitated before they closed a periodical or even issued a warning. . . ."[40] Perhaps there were similar liberally minded censors operating under *glasnost* but they still had to move cautiously.

An interesting account of *glasnost* in the 1860s has been provided by a leading historian of the Russian revolutionary movement. It concerns a young revolutionary from the city of Kazan who served a prison sentence in the local fortress:

The university library provided him with books and so he was able to read Holbach's *System of Nature,* Cabet's *Voyage to Icaria* and also Fourier, Proudhon, Louis Blanc and Boerne. He read Engels' *Conditions of the Working Class in England,* and translated it for his friends. But he was unable to obtain two books which he specially wanted—Louis Blanc's *History of Ten Years* and the works of Lassalle. One day, after he had saved up his pay for three or four months, he got permission to come out of prison accompanied by a guard. He went to the only foreign bookshop in town and found the books he was looking for. He paid for them and took them back to his cell, incidentally giving the German bookseller a bad fright at the sight of the policeman.[41]

One day perhaps Gulag and Lefortovo will provide similar services, but not yet.

While *Brockhaus,* the well-known German encyclopaedic dictionary, was freely available in nineteenth-century Russia, a reader's letter published in Moscow in November 1987 reported that three of the volumes of the most recent edition could be consulted in the Soviet Union only with special permission. The writer asked: "Why are the books kept in the special collection? They constitute about one-quarter of all foreign books. Do they deal with sex or do they contain instructions on how to build nuclear bombs in one's own department? Nothing of the sort. A typical example is 'Theo Elm, *The contemporary parable. The theory and history of parables,* Munich, 1982.' "[42]

[39]Marianna T. Choldin, *A Fence Around the Empire,* Chapel Hill, 1985, p. 108; Daniel Balmuth, *Censorship in Russia, 1865–1905,* Washington, D.C., 1979, p. 136.
[40]Balmuth, p. 142.
[41]F. Venturi, *Roots of Revolution,* New York, 1960, p. 306.
[42]*Ogonyok,* 48, 1987.

Comparisons between the system of controls in Tsarist Russia and the Soviet Union are not flattering for the latter. It has been pointed out that censorship in Imperial Russia fell within a European cultural framework; there was censorship in Imperial Germany until 1874. Whereas Tsarist censorship gradually gave the press more freedom, the Soviet system was based on the rejection of press freedom and steadily became more severe.[43]

There was no radio and television in 1910, and the newspapers of the day reached only a small part of the population. Soviet television programs showing the impact of *glasnost* such as the immensely popular (and provocative) "Telebridges," or "Prozhektor Perestroiki" were watched by a hundred million viewers or more. On the other hand, the Soviet mass media did not remotely go as far in their openness and self-criticism as some literary journals or *Ogonyok.* "Prozhektor" focused on shortcomings in Soviet industry and consumer services, and directed its criticism toward individual bureaucrats rather than toward the system. But feature films and outspoken documentaries were also shown (for instance, on the Soviet space program), something which would have been unthinkable even a year or two earlier.

The "Telebridges" episodes, bringing together a selected number of people from a Soviet city and a town abroad, were tame, even boring affairs for blasé Westerners accustomed to free travel and a free press. But for Soviet citizens who could not travel these were a revolutionary innovation. The fact that foreigners were openly questioning institutions and views which had never been thought a fit subject for debate in the Soviet Union, indeed the very practice of relatively free speech, fascinated many Soviet citizens and disturbed some of them.[44]

Glasnost in Public Life

It has emerged from the many examples given that a genuine and sincere effort has been made by members of the Soviet leadership to introduce more freedom in Soviet public life. But an equal number of examples could have been given to the effect that in

[43]C. Ruud, *Fighting Words,* Toronto, 1982, p. 7. There is, however, a remarkable continuity in the arguments of the censors. Thus the Moscow censorship board in 1903 about *Novosti Dnya:* "Jewish cosmopolitanism and false liberalism" (Balmuth, p. 118).

[44]On the impact of "telebridges," see Victor Yasman in *Soviet and East European Survey,* Boulder, 1988, pp. 72–77.

some respects little progress has been made, and in others none. *Glasnost* was the new element in the situation; the absence of freedom was not novel, and it was often difficult to decide whether to emphasize one or the other.

A few illustrations should suffice. Anonymous denunciations have been for a long time one of the great plagues of Soviet life. A law introduced in 1986 and, more specifically, in February 1988, ordered that all anonymous complaints be ignored in the future. Yet there is no evidence that these laws had any significant effect; the anonymous letters continued to arrive in government offices, the newspapers, and, of course, the police.[45] Hatred, envy, and lack of courage are deeply rooted in a people exposed for so long to tyrannical regimes. And it is impossible to say whether the assumptions shared by the writers of the anonymous letters were entirely wrong: Perhaps the new laws did not apply to the security organs who would read them, as in the past, with interest. Perhaps civic courage would have unpleasant consequences. At a time when many jobs were cut in the bureaucracy, the temptation would be great for the bosses to get rid of inconvenient, critical subordinates. (Under paragraph 29 of the civil code of the Russian Federation, no reason need be given in case of dismissal.)

Another example concerns the banning of books and periodicals in the Soviet Union, the existence of the so-called special collections, made accessible only with special permission by the security authorities. In 1987 a special committee was appointed by the Politburo to reexamine the list of books kept in those sections not open to the public. The report published after one year of its activities is less than impressive.[46] True, the committee released thirty-five hundred books out of four thousand it investigated. But a closer look at the list of books released shows that it mainly consists of books by Lenin (in which Trotsky was favorably mentioned), his wife, other old Bolsheviks, poems by Essenin, and books on Russian grammar which had entered the special collections because of a bureaucratic mistake or because the author had many years ago become an "enemy of the people." On the other hand, the list apparently excluded books by authors of the "left-wing opposition," the Mensheviks, the Social Revolutionaries, and other critics of the Bolsheviks, as well as books published outside the Soviet Union. It is not even clear whether it contained books

[45]"Otstavka Anonimke," *Moskovskaia Pravda*, April 3, 1988.
[46]Interview with V. A. Solodin, *Sovetskaia Kultura*, March 26, 1988.

published in Russia before 1917. Since the number of such books is not four thousand but hundreds of thousands, it may take decades at the present rate to open the Soviet libraries.

The situation with regard to Soviet films seems to have been better; some one hundred movies which had been shelved were released in 1987–88.[47] Some of these had been banned two or three years earlier; others had been removed by the censors fifteen or even twenty years ago. Some of the newly released movies, such as Askoldov's *Commissar,* were even regarded now with some disfavor; they had been shown earlier and more widely outside the Soviet Union than inside the country. But at least the ban had been removed.

The new law on secrecy and the practice of censorship was drafted without consulting public and professional bodies directly concerned.[48] There has been no public debate, and the demand by some research workers to introduce in the Soviet Union something akin to a fifty- (or forty-) year rule will certainly not be considered.

A law was prepared in 1988 covering access to archives which left, according to a leading authority, the decision whether to declassify a document or not entirely to the head of the institution concerned. In any case, documents in the archives of the ministries of foreign affairs, foreign trade, the Communist Party, the army, and the KGB were exempt—that is to say, they remained inaccessible to outsiders. Hence the estimate that about half of all the documents on Soviet history (and probably the great majority of the more important ones) have remained classified so far even under *glasnost.* Yuri Baturin, the secretary of the *glasnost* law committee, noted in passing that while under the Tsarist autocracy all censorship laws since 1804 had been openly published, it was now "virtually impossible even to mention *Glavlit* [the main administration for safeguarding state secrets] in the press."[49]

There is a strange dichotomy between, on the one hand, the chorus of voices proclaiming that *glasnost* is a wonderful thing and should be the norm of Soviet politics and public life, and, on the other, the real state of affairs.[50] Thus Soviet journalists com-

[47]*Argumenty i Fakty,* 22, 1988.
[48]*Literaturnaia Gazetta,* March 16, 1988. For a critique of the modest achievements of *glasnost* in this field, see I. Ilizarov, *Sovetskaia Kultura,* June 1, 1988.
[49]*Izvestiia,* June 9, 1988.
[50]For an example of the literature maintaining that *glasnost* was as much needed as fresh air, see A. A. Bezuglov and V. A. Kryashkov, *Glasnost raboty sovetov* (Glasnost in the Work

plained, to give but a few examples, that the ministries for nuclear power and radio were not listed in any directory and that inquiries resulted in the standard answer: "There is no such thing in Moscow." Yet at the same time foreign maps of Moscow were not only showing the location of these institutions but even the flower beds at the entrance to the Kurchatov Atomic Energy Institute, another of these phantom buildings. Another Soviet journalist complained that while the U.S. secretary of defense had been invited to inspect the Soviet "Blackjack" bomber, requests by Soviet newspapers for photographs of the bomber had been refused. A professor of genetics from Novosibirsk made it known that he had been asked to sign a paper concerning access to secret work, adding that it seemed to him that this was done merely to deprive people of the opportunity to travel abroad and to engage in research there. Elsewhere it was mentioned that photocopying scientific papers on open topics was still banned, and that the publication of discoveries was delayed by many months at considerable cost to science and the economy. On the other hand there were those who benefited from the secrecy still prevailing. When a young researcher whose work was less than satisfactory was asked why he had made his dissertation secret, he explained that for a "closed dissertation" he was free to choose his own opponents, and he could of course find people who would not mess up things for him.

As for the issue of *glasnost* in party life, throughout 1987 and the early months of 1988 there were constant complaints that little had changed. Reports about party executive meetings on all levels have usually been short and unrevealing. Appointments and demotions were not explained and only a minimum of biographical detail was given about new appointees.[51] Critics put the blame on the leadership and, above all, the bureaucracy, and it is certainly true that the elections for the 1988 party conference were manipulated as in the past by party officials. But it was also true that, as one participant in this debate put it, the antidemocratic tendencies had entered the bloodstream of many people who were opposed to any change in current practices.[52]

---

of the Soviets), Moscow, 1988. The examples of the lack of *glasnost* are taken from *Argumenty i Fakty,* August 13, 1988.
[51] *Sovetskaia Kultura,* March 15, 1988.
[52] Yu. Borisov, *Komsomolskaia Pravda,* April 2, 1988. For a comparison of Stalinism and Hitlerism as two different species of totalitarian ideology, see Jan Kaplinski, *Raduga,* 7, 1988.

During the weeks preceding the party conference of June 1988, *glasnost* received a new fillip; almost every day brought new revelations about the past and suggestions for the democratization of public life. Some foreign observers in Moscow reported the outbreak of the "Russian revolution of 1988" comparable only to the overthrow of the old order which had taken place seventy-one years earlier.[53] The party conference, unlike previous such occasions, was ill-structured and badly prepared, which is to say that it was infinitely freer and its participants more outspoken. Gorbachev did not exaggerate when he said in his concluding speech that the palace of congresses had not known such discussions, that nothing of the kind had occurred for nearly six decades. But the conference also showed that there were not many delegates willing to stand up for more *glasnost* in public life, and this was boding ill for the future.

Was true *glasnost* really compatible with a one-party system and total control of internal security and propaganda? Even under *glasnost* the head of the KGB was telling the media not only what not to publish but also on what to concentrate.[54] True, it could be argued that there was a great difference in comparison with the past. Whereas in bygone days any such speech would have produced fear, trembling, and immediate compliance, in the age of *glasnost* there would be less fear and only partial compliance. Chebrikov, the head of state security in 1988, was certainly not a Yezhov or a Beria, only a servant of the party and the state. But he obviously must have felt that his position entitled him to make pronouncements of this kind, and this raised wider issues. As one Soviet citizen put it, would de-Nazification have been possible with the Gestapo still in place? True, it was a much more enlightened Gestapo under new management and different personnel, among some of whom there was apparently sympathy for *glasnost*—within limits.

Those who argued that it was unrealistic to expect the Communist Party of the Soviet Union to share power with other political groups or the KGB to go into voluntary liquidation were, of course, correct. But this also meant that there could not be full *glasnost*, let alone true democratization as long as there was no radical political change. No one in his right mind had expected that Gorbachev would say, to paraphrase the Bible, "Let there be *glas-*

[53] *The Independent* (London), June 14, 1988; *Der Spiegel*, July 4, 1988.
[54] Tass, April 13, 1988.

nost" and there *would* be *glasnost,* full, pure, and unalloyed. It was obvious from the beginning that *glasnost* would be an uphill struggle, that the results would be partial and imperfect, and that it would be unjust to regard it as a total failure just because it was not a full success. But even the well-wishers of *glasnost* seem to have underrated the difficulties on the road ahead and the limits that could not be overstepped.

Glasnost: Politics, Laws, and the Reality

The meeting of the Central Committee in January 1987 had decided that the country needed a law on *glasnost.* Why it needed such a law was not absolutely clear, for there were sufficient provisions in the Soviet constitution (paragraphs 5, 9, 94, 157) for safeguarding *glasnost.* That these provisions had not had much effect in the past was a different story. As Yuri Baturin, the secretary of the committee that was appointed to prepare the new law, noted, either there was a political culture which made *glasnost* a norm of public life, or there was no such political culture, in which case no amount of laws would help.[55] Those who were not persuaded by the case for a new law on *glasnost* suggested instead a law defining state secrecy, but this was turned down by the authorities. During two years various drafts of the new *glasnost* law were discussed and discarded, and eventually the experts of the Law Institute of the Academy of Sciences were commissioned to prepare a final draft.[56]

An interesting test for the extent of democratization that had taken place came in March 1988 with the publication of the article "I Cannot Sacrifice Principles" by Nina Andreieva of Leningrad in *Sovetskaia Rossiia.* Whether this manifesto of the anti-*perestroika* forces (as *Pravda* later put it) had indeed been composed by an obscure Leningrad teacher is not clear; there is evidence that other hands were involved. The letter was an interesting mixture of orthodox Communist and racialist views, and there is no reason why it should have been suppressed under *glasnost:* Mrs. Andreieva's views were clearly shared by many others. What disturbed the proponents was the fact that no one dared to contradict this widely reprinted article. It was generally believed that Mrs.

[55]Interview with Baturin, Moscow Central Television, March 26, 1988; Baturin's article in *Kommunist,* Erevan, April 23, 1988; interview in *Pravda,* June 19, 1988.
[56]An early draft was published in *Glasnost,* 12, November 1987; reprinted in *Arkhiv Samizdata,* Radio Liberty, May 13, 1988.

Andreieva had been chosen to express the new party line and if this was the case, *glasnost* or no *glasnost,* it was not to be criticized. There were a very few exceptions. The playwright Aleksander Gelman launched an attack at a meeting of the cinema workers' union, but this appeared in the press only after the *Pravda* rebuttal. Only then did the sluice gates open. There was a veritable flood of indignant articles and letters in the Soviet press. Poor Mrs. Andreieva claimed that she had to leave her apartment temporarily because of the unwelcome publicity; she also related that she received many messages of support.[57] The Andreieva affair was not very important *per se* but as a sign of the times it was depressing: after two years of breast-beating about the need to be brave and to speak out, even if some risk is involved, public behavior showed that civic courage had not yet become the norm in Soviet public life.

The three weeks between the publication of the Andreieva article and the *Pravda* rebuttal became known as the "short *zastoi*" (the small stagnation period). This was followed by a new surge of *glasnost* publications in May and June 1988. According to some Western observers, the nineteenth party conference was a victory for *glasnost,*[58] which was certainly true inasmuch as there were more open exchanges than on previous such occasions. Many Soviet advocates of *glasnost* did not share this optimism. To begin with, the election of the five thousand delegates was manipulated in such a way as to give a great majority to party officials and others who could be trusted to express the orthodox, antiliberal line. This, in any case, was how the reformers saw it; in fact the composition of the delegates may well have reflected the prevailing mood among the party bureaucracy and perhaps even the rank and file, who believed that *glasnost* had gone too far.

As on past occasions Gorbachev in his long speech came out both in favor of *glasnost* and against the excesses of *glasnost* so that everyone could draw some comfort. When he said that it was no longer necessary to argue that there could be no *perestroika* without *glasnost* there was silence, nor did his following words produce any storm of enthusiasm:

---

[57]For the authorship of the Andreieva letter, see G. Baklanov in *Sovetskaia Kultura,* May 26, 1988, and Gioletto Chiesa in *Unita,* May 23, 1988. Gorbachev announced at the nineteenth party conference that a letter from Mrs. Andreieva had been received in the Central Committee according to which she had not changed her mind.

[58]"Gorbachev Steers the Conference to Victory for *Glasnost,*" *The Independent,* July 2, 1988.

"Without it [*glasnost*] we would have been unable to do the great amount of work analyzing the reasons for the negative phenomena and the ways of overcoming them. We would have been unable to create a new moral and political atmosphere in society to bring the ideas of *perestroika* to the forefront. *Glasnost* means pluralism of opinion on all issues of domestic and foreign policy, free collation of different points of views, debates."[59]

But when he went on warning against the abuses of *glasnost,* Gorbachev was interrupted by frequent applause. *Glasnost,* he said, bears great responsibility; it cannot be combined with claims to a monopoly of views, with the imposition of different dogmas to replace the old ones which had been rejected. *Glasnost* should not serve group interests, distortion, settling personal scores, wrangling, hurling insults, or labeling. These code words were well understood and warmly welcomed by those present. They meant that the proponents of *glasnost* should be careful not to overstep certain unwritten boundaries and that the conservatives in the party were not to be offended because they constituted a majority and their cooperation was needed by Gorbachev.

Ligachev launched an attack against the media who had abused the trust of the party, as did the writer Yuri Bondarev and the secretary of the writers' union, Karpov, who complained that instead of producing works in the tradition, on the scale, and of the quality of *War and Peace* and *Crime and Punishment,* some of his colleagues had engaged in negative and destructive criticism.[60]

Considering the mood prevailing at the conference, the resolution on *glasnost* passed at the end was mild.[61] The further development of *glasnost* was defined as one of the most important political tasks. Its expansion was essential for the expression of the democratic essence of the socialist system. It was equally important in foreign affairs so as to facilitate the solution of complex international problems. Attempts to curb *glasnost* were denounced and it was noted that much information had not yet been made accessible. This referred to statistics and the ecological situation. It was also said that every citizen had the inalienable right to obtain full and authentic information on any social issue to the extent that it did not represent a state and military secret. Legal guarantees had to be created for *glasnost* to define the rights and obligations of the

[59]*Pravda,* June 29, 1988.
[60]*Pravda,* June 30, 1988.
[61]*Pravda,* July 5, 1988.

state, officials, and citizens in the implementing of the principles of *glasnost*. *Glasnost* was not to be used to harm the interests of the Soviet state or society, the rights of the individual, to preach war or violence, racism, national and religious intolerance, to propagate cruelty, or to spread pornography.

The mass media were admonished to maintain high ideological standards, competence, and absolute reliability of information, and to observe the right of each citizen who had been criticized to publish a valid response in the same press organ. Openness was not to serve the growth of cliquishness, manifestations of demagoguery, and national, regional, or corporate egoism. No one had a monopoly on truth, and there must be no monopoly on *glasnost* either. These were fine sentiments; only the future would tell how the call for absolute objectivity could be combined with high ideological standards.

Toward the Future

Glasnost obviously means more than the showing of movies that have been on the shelf for many years and the publication of banned novels after a delay of ten or twenty years. The Soviet media have discussed the state of the nation much more freely than before. But as the experience before 1917 has shown, even a comparatively large degree of cultural freedom can coexist with an autocratic system. What will happen once the banned novels and movies have appeared and all the revelations about the state of agriculture and the shortcomings of the health service are common knowledge? Major tabu zones remain, and they concern not only the present leadership but also the history of the Communist Party and the role of the organs of security; indeed, cynics may argue, they cover most truly important issues which have a bearing on the character of the regime. Seen in this light the publication of *Dr. Zhivago*, in 1988, and even of Platonov, Zamyatin, and Orwell; the showing of abstract paintings; or the performance of contemporary musical compositions is a great achievement but of interest only to a small part of the population. It is permitted because the new rulers realize that it does not constitute a political threat to the regime.

If this were all there is to *glasnost* it would still be a very interesting development, because it has widened so much our knowledge about things Soviet. But what hope does it offer for the future?

Glasnost is not irreversible, as long as there are no democratic guarantees; what has been given can be taken away. It seems likely that the farther limits of *glasnost* have been reached and that in the years to come there will be no major progress beyond them. There could well be a partial retreat, a more narrow redefinition of these limits.

Glasnost has meant plain speaking about shortcomings of Soviet politics, society, and other aspects of life. But what if the revelations and the debates do not lead to an improvement? *Glasnost* was based on hope; it was felt by many like a breath of fresh air, after the suffocating years of stagnation. But if the changes do not materialize, the hopes are bound to fade and the air will again get stale.

It is unlikely that the reforms of Soviet society will be a full success within the next five or ten years. The economic and social problems are structural; the political shortcomings are rooted deeply in the past. Something akin to a cultural revolution would be needed to effect real change. Such revolutions have occurred but rarely in history, and there are no signs that anything of this kind will take place in the Soviet Union in the near future. The situation may have been precritical (in Gorbachev's words), but it is not critical enough for truly radical change. There will no doubt be minor improvements, as the result of what some economists call the "new broom" effect, of greater energy and new initiatives emerging from the top leadership. But the newness of the broom passes with every year, and what then?

Glasnost will increasingly be in danger because it makes governing the country more difficult than in the past. All kinds of tensions, national and social, which were suppressed before are coming to the fore. There are bound to be clashes and disorder, and this will play into the hands of those who were arguing all along that the Soviet people are not ready now, and will perhaps not be ready for generations to come, for political freedom. The authoritarian style, which has prevailed through virtually all its history it will be said, is the only one befitting it, an enlightened authoritarianism to be sure, but not a system based on freedom and broad, voluntary popular participation. The greater the problems that will face the Soviet leadership in the years to come, the greater the temptation to return to the past style.

Radical changes may take place in the leadership but they are not a foregone conclusion. If the economic and social reforms do not show the desired results, it will always be possible to argue that the Western countries, not to mention the Third World, also face serious difficulties, as no doubt they will in the years to come, and that the Soviet system with all its shortcomings is no worse off than they are. If economic progress will be slow, if social problems abound, the same may well be true with regard to most other countries. Whether a sociopolitical system is bankrupt or not is a comparative statement. If the rest of the world were to face a long period of steady growth and prosperity, of diminishing national antagonisms and social tensions, the Soviet system, by comparison, would reach the end of its rope in no more than a few years. But since the prospects for the Western world are not that rosy, the outlook for the Soviet system is less gloomy, at least for the rest of the century. As neoisolationist trends grow stronger in the United States, as China is increasingly preoccupied with domestic affairs and Western Europe fails to make significant progress toward greater political unity, the standing of the Soviet Union as a superpower will not be in danger.

Some progress will probably be made in the Soviet Union in the years to come and some degree of *glasnost* will no doubt remain in force, come what may. The atmosphere in the country will be less stifling than it was in the 1960s and 1970s; the intelligentsia will probe the outer limits of *glasnost* from time to time, trying to push them a little further; as the high hopes of 1986–88 do not materialize, some of its members will perhaps withdraw from public life to the private or professional sphere as they have done in the past.

This seems to be the most likely scenario, but it is, of course, not the only possible one. The imposition of far stricter dictatorial rule cannot be ruled out if things threaten to go out of control. Rebellious nationalities, striking workers, a further decline of discipline among the youth, unruly intellectuals undermining general morale—all this could bring about the feeling of general crisis, and with it the introduction of the harsh measures used in the past. This would mean the end of *glasnost,* which would then be denounced as a bourgeois-liberal aberration from Leninism. Such a development seems possible but not very likely, and the emergence of a "Russian party" military dictatorship seems even more unlikely. The influence of the Russian party is not to be belittled, but it acts more as a brake than an alternative government. It expresses a mood but it has no program; it divides the country to such an extent that it could stay in power only by applying extreme measures. The return of a fully fledged Stalinist regime also seems unlikely because those in power still seem to have all the instruments to impose control at any time, if needed. True, the tensions inside the Soviet Union may be more explosive than the outsider can know, the hold of the leadership more precarious. If so, these developments are beyond the powers of perception of outside observers.

This leaves the last, equally unlikely, possibility: What if the reform should be a full, or nearly a full, success? This would no doubt be the best outcome for Russia and the world; the arguments that a substantial strengthening of the Soviet Union would by necessity mean the weakening of the West are unconvincing. But is it a possibility that should be discussed seriously at the present time? Most informed observers inside the Soviet Union and abroad agree that the reforms are long overdue, and that they are a step in the right direction. But no one expects overwhelming success in the near future.

This is not to belittle the goodwill, even the idealism, of those in the Soviet Union, in high places and low, who, feeling acute unhappiness about the state of their country, would like to effect a genuine break with the past. One wishes them well, but the odds against them are heavy. It is necessary to hope, Dr. Johnson said, "though hope should always be deluded; for hope itself is happiness and its frustrations, however frequent, are yet less dreadful than its extinction." Faith, it is said, can move mountains and miracles do happen. There is a striking scene in a recent Soviet novel in which the author, near despair as the result of the corruption, apathy, lawlessness, and drunkenness she has witnessed, has a dream—a few days before Brezhnev's death—in which she sees a bright comet in the sky which gives her fresh hope.[62]

I am more impressed by Mrs. Ganina's comet than by the writings of some Western scholars that the political and economic reform movement is bound to succeed for "objective" reasons such as urbanization or the growing educational level of the Soviet people. One should never give up hope but hope is not a synonym for wishful thinking, for ignoring the enormous obstacles on the road to change and improvement.

[62]Maia Ganina, *Poka zhivu-nadeius* (I Hope as Long as I Am Alive), Part I, *Oktiabr*, 10, 1986; Part II, *Oktiabr*, 11, 1987. The original title of the novel was *Ten Days Before Brezhnev's Death* (*Moscow News*, 7, 1988). See also Mary Seton Watson, "Soviet Literature," *Washington Quarterly*, Spring 1988.

The Soviet Union is not exempt from the laws of change, and time no more stands still in Communist regimes than in other countries. For years it has been argued in China that certain tenets of the official doctrine are obsolete and should be repudiated, that there should be an independent press, greater academic freedom, and perhaps even a multiparty system. Against this many party leaders have claimed that the relaxation of controls has gone too far, and that "bourgeois liberalism" should be fought as in the past.[63] Even Chinese intellectuals seem to fear that pluralism might lead to chaos. They do not want an institutionalized opposition but more regularized and enlightened, less arbitrary party rule which consults them more frequently.

The Communist system in China is less deeply rooted than in the Soviet Union; less time passed from Mao's victory to the beginning of the age of reform. There is a pragmatic streak in Chinese political life which is less developed in the Soviet Union, and the Sinification of Marxism-Leninism began much earlier (and went further) than the Russification of the official ideology in the Soviet Union. But even in China the transition toward a new political system does not proceed by leaps and bounds but very cautiously. Progress in the Soviet Union for a great variety of reasons goes even more slowly.

Thus, to reiterate, there is reason to believe that the *glasnost* era has now reached its climax and that no great further advances should be expected for years to come. With luck, the achievements that have been made will be safeguarded and the country will be spared a major retreat and the loss of the positions that have been gained. With luck, another major attempt will be made at some future date to push forward the parameters of freedom. This is about as far as any realistic assessment can take us. More dramatic and far-reaching progress would be a near miracle, for cultural revolutions involve not just the replacement of one political elite by another but lasting and radical change in the mentality of a nation. This may happen one day as the result of a major shock, or the culmination of many small steps, or in consequence of the appearance on the scene of a new generation. Such a revolution in the Soviet Union seems not to be at this time part of the historical agenda.

[63]Harry Harding, *China's Second Revolution,* Washington, 1987, passim; Uli Franz, *Den Xiaoping,* Stuttgart, 1987.

A Note on the Historical Origins of the Term *"Glasnost"*

Following Alexander Herzen, *glasnost* was frequently invoked by his ideological opponents, the Slavophiles, above all by Ivan Aksakov, one of the leading journalists of the time and a prominent advocate of freedom of the press. ("Freedom of speech is not a political but a natural right of every human being."[1]) The Tsar himself was not in principle against *glasnost;* in his instruction to the censors he said that the press should have *glasnost* in discussing legal reforms. *Glasnost* was mentioned countless times in commentary on the so-called Pskov affair. This refers to the arbitrary arrest for six days of P. Iakushkin, a writer and specialist on peasant culture, near Pskov, in 1859. Iakushin walked about in peasant clothes, and his strange behavior, unbecoming a gentleman in the eyes of the local authorities, had made him suspect.

Iakushkin reported his adventures in a long, well-written letter published in the journal *Russkaia Beseda,* of which Aksakov was the editor:

His long letter was a masterpiece of its kind, fully bringing out the arbitrary behavior to which he had been subjected, his own bewildered innocence, and neglecting no small detail that might bring him sympathy; the stench of the cellar where he had spent his first night, the pitiable plight of the peasant boy (with whom he had shared the cell), the profanity of

[1] *Sochineniia I. S. Aksakova,* Vol. 4, Moscow, 1887, pp. 361–445.

the police, and the way they had called him by the familiar form, rather than the more respectful *Vy.* Iakushkin's account, in other words, had the wit, controlled indignation, and mastery of detail that the best liberal outrage always has.[2]

The liberal press of the day hailed this exposure as an excellent demonstration of *glasnost.* Thus *Russki Vestnik:* "At long last we have real, not algebraic *glasnost.*"

But *glasnost* at this time also became a favorite subject for the satirists. Vasili Kurochkin, a leading populist poet, wrote in the poem "Glasnost 1859 and 1862":

> O *glasnost, glasnost,* in the fullness of thy years
> you began to mumble like an old woman.[3]

Panin, another satirist of the day, in an essay full of allusions, compared *glasnost* to a small child: "it was born only recently, its steps are small and uncertain, its voice is hardly heard, it hobbles and staggers along, it loses its head and shouts about small things, imagining that it does something of importance—all this is, of course, amusing for the adults."[4] Other radical writers of the period, such as Dobroliubov and Chernychevsky, not known for their sense of humor, were not amused but opposed *glasnost* and the euphoria it had created among the liberal intelligentsia. "Shouldn't we call a halt to our *glasnost?*" Dobroliubov asked. "Why bother? Our publicity will lead to nothing. . . ." Chernychevsky was even more negative about *glasnost.* It was, he said, a "bureaucratic expression scheduled to replace the term 'freedom of speech.' It had been invented on the surmise that 'freedom of speech' might be considered unpleasant or too sharp by someone. . . ."[5] Writing to a British editor in 1895 about the sad fate of the Dukhobors, the religious sect, Tolstoi pointed out that *glasnost* was of value for both persecuted and persecutors. The former would receive in the court of public opinion sympathy and encouragement in their suffering. But the persecutors would also benefit because their cruelty was often committed out of darkness and

[2]Abbot Gleason, *Young Russia,* New York, 1980, passim.
[3]*Sobranie Stikhotvorenia Vasilia Kuruchkina,* Vol. 2, St. Petersburg, 1869, p. 119.
[4]Panayev in *Svistok.* This was a satirical supplement to *Sovremennik.* Newly edited by A. A. Zhek and A. A. Demchenko, Moscow, 1981, p. 200.
[5]N. Chernyshevski, *Pisma bez adressa,* Moscow, 1983 (reprint), p. 495.

ignorance; they did not know what they were doing, and the disapproval of public opinion might restrain them.[6]

It ought to be added that *glasnost* was used frequently in the 1960s and 1970s by the dissidents Chalidze, Bukovski, and others in their demands for official disclosures as far as the proceedings against them were concerned.[7]

As for *perestroika,* my original assumption that it was first used in the 1920s was mistaken. I found the term used in Ivanov-Razumnik's *History of Russian Social Thought,* written well before World War I, in connection with the need of the late-nineteenth-century Populists to modify their *Weltanschauung;* in all probability it had been used even before.[8] The word *perestroika* appeared widely, as has been mentioned, in the early 1930s and 1940s, less frequently thereafter. But it again figured in the discussions of economic experts, sociologists, and psychologists well before Gorbachev's rise to power, and there were even discussions about the psychological resistance against *perestroika* well before Gorbachev.[9]

[6]L. N. Tolstoi, *Sobrannie Sochineniia,* Moscow, 1965, Vol. 18, p. 155.
[7]See, for instance, Peter Reddaway, *Uncensored Russia,* New York, 1974, pp. 86–88; Frederick Barghoorn, *Détente and the Democratic Movement in the U.S.S.R.,* New York, 1976, pp. 26, 91, 95.
[8]Ivanov-Razumnik, *Istoriia russkoi obshestvennoi mysli,* 3rd ed., Vol. II, St. Petersburg, 1911, p. xiii.
[9]S. A. I. Kitov, *Psikhologia Khoziaistvennogo upravleniia,* Moscow, 1984.

INDEX

Walter Laqueur is Chairman of the International Research Council of the Center for Strategic and International Studies, Washington, D.C.; University Professor at Georgetown University; and Director of the Institute of Contemporary History (the Wiener Library) in London. He was the founder and first editor of *Survey* (1955–63), a leading journal in the field of Soviet studies. His books, which have appeared in many editions and translations, include *Russia and Germany* and *The Fate of the Revolution: Interpretations of Soviet History from 1917 to the Present* (first published in 1967, updated and revised edition published in 1987).